POLITICAL
TERRORISM
AND
BUSINESS

Foreword by **Ray S. Cline**

Published in cooperation with Georgetown University Center for Strategic and International Studies and State University of New York Institute for Studies in International Terrorism.

POLITICAL TERRORISM AND BUSINESS

The Threat and Response

Edited by
Yonah Alexander
Robert A. Kilmarx

PRAEGER

PRAEGER SPECIAL STUDIES • PRAEGER SCIENTIFIC

Library of Congress Cataloging in Publication Data

Main entry under title:

Political terrorism and business.

"Published in cooperation with Georgetown University
Center for Strategic and International Studies, and
State University of New York Institute for Studies in
International Terrorism."
  Bibliography: p.
  Includes index.
  1. Terrorism--Addresses, essays, lectures.
2. Business enterprises--Security measures--Ad-
dresses, essays, lectures. I. Alexander, Yonah.
II. Kilmarx, Robert A.
HV6431.P62   658.4'7   79-16374
ISBN 0-03-046686-5

Published in 1979 by Praeger Publishers
A Division of Holt, Rinehart and Winston/CBS, Inc.
383 Madison Avenue, New York, New York 10017 U.S.A.

© 1979 by Praeger Publishers

0 038 098765432

Printed in the United States of America

FOREWORD

The facilities, personnel, and operations of the business community at home and abroad are becoming increasingly vulnerable to threats and acts of terrorism, including bombing, kidnapping, hijacking, maiming and assassination. During 1970-1978, this form of violence was directed against business targets in 2,427 cases out of a total of 5,529 terrorist incidents during the period. It caused losses of over $500 million in material damage, ransom paid in abductions, and funds taken in robberies. Moreover, thousands of business executives and personnel were held hostage, wounded, or killed.

This challenge to business operations and economic development is presented by many revolutionary movements ideologically committed to the total destruction of the free enterprise system as well as by parochial groups seeking more limited political objectives. More assessments forecast that the level of terrorist activity aimed at human and nonhuman targets of corporations will persist in the foreseeable future and perhaps even escalate.

Clearly, the stability of our economic system requires a serious consideration of the following questions: First, what types and forms of threats and acts of terrorism will pose the greatest danger during the last quarter of this century? Second, what should corporations do to assess their respective vulnerabilities and to design appropriate strategies of risk reduction? And third, what should governments do on national, regional, and global levels to improve counter-terrorist capabilities?

A commendable attempt to deal with these questions is made in this book. It is hoped that this multinational scholarly and professional effort will assist corporations in their security planning and will also contribute to the development of realistic public policies and comprehensive crisis management systems.

Ray S. Cline
Executive Director
World Power Studies
The Center for Strategic and International Studies

CONTENTS

Page

LIST OF TABLES AND FIGURES

INTRODUCTION

Yonah Alexander
Robert A. Kilmarx

On August 8, 1968, an underwater explosion from a bomb placed by El Ponder Cubano damaged a British vessel in Miami. Two Tupamaro terrorists dressed in police uniforms attacked a facility of General Motors Corporation in Montevideo on June 20 of the following year, causing damage estimated at $1 million. In a well-coordinated operation on September 6, 1970, the Popular Front for the Liberation of Palestine hijacked four planes owned by TWA, BOAC, Swissair, and Pan Am, which were bound for New York from Europe, and directed them to the Middle East. All the passengers were released; however, the four jets were blown up.

On October 14 of the following year, members of the United Front for Guerrilla Action bombed a Sinclair pipeline in Colombia. In April 1972, Argentinian terrorists kidnapped the president of Fiat and demanded $1 million in ransom. The Argentine government refused to negotiate with the terrorists. Shortly thereafter, the executive was found dead. A powerful bomb blast damaged a branch of the Spanish Banco Popular in Paris on January 28, 1973. A letter-bomb exploded at the *Daily Express* in London in February 1974, injuring a guard.

Seven European and African tourists, who were taken hostage by Palestinian guerrillas at a Tel Aviv hotel on March 5, 1975, were killed during a shootout with the Israeli rescue team. Three U.S. civilian employees of Rockwell International were assassinated in Tehran on August 28, 1976, by Islamic-Marxist terrorists. Left-wing extremists attacked West German businesses and property in Italian and French cities on October 19, 1977, to avenge the deaths of three terrorist leaders in German jails. Finally, on February 2, 1978, it was reported that Israeli citrus fruit contaminated with liquid mercury was found in West Germany and Holland. The Arab Revolutionary Army Palestinian Commando indicated that the poisonings were designed to sabotage the Israeli economy. Subsequently, Israel had to cut back its exports by 40 percent.

The foregoing incidents, selected at random from over 5,000 cases recorded during the past decade, clearly illustrate that we have entered an "age of terrorism," with all its unique and formidable problems. To be sure, ideological and political violence is not a new form of conflict. Rather, there are only new aspects of terrorism in terms of motivation, technology, tactics, victimization, and security. Our complex modern society is extremely vulnerable to serious threats and intimidation, as well as to direct attacks, including arson and bombing, sabotage and hijacking, and kidnapping and murder. The very process of modernization can carry in its wake the virus of social, economic, and political upheaval, with the attendant vulnerability of nations to terrorist activity. The convulsion of Iran bears contemporary witness to this fact. Airports, harbors, and railroads; oil fields and refineries; natural gas pipelines; electric power grids; nuclear facilities; computer and data centers; factories; and banks and businesses cannot always be protected from the will of groups seeking to obtain realistic or imaginary, often revolutionary, goals.

Moreover, as soft targets, business executives are extremely vulnerable. For example, since 1970, out of the 370 attempted or accomplished kidnapping operations, 199 (54 percent) have involved the corporate sector. Indeed, the trend is up: 49 percent of these kidnappings were recorded only in the past three years. Corporations have already paid millions of dollars in ransom money for the release of their executives. Business enterprises in some countries, such as Argentina and Italy, have contributed substantial payoffs to terrorist movements in order to secure relative peace. As commerce, industry, transportation, and communications have become more complex, they have also become more susceptible to more unpredictable demonic schemes by bands of dedicated and determined terrorists. Since more ideological and political violence can be anticipated, terrorism will continue to challenge business, property, and profit.

Even the United States, the most powerful free enterprise system in the world, is becoming more vulnerable. This is primarily because European and other terrorists are looking to the United States as a new target area for their havoc, as security measures from foreign governments increasingly are applying pressure against terrorist operations. Not unexpectedly, European terrorists reportedly have begun to enter the United States through the Canadian border. Growing U.S. vulnerability is due to the fact that the U.S. public is disillusioned about the effectiveness and responsiveness of the system insofar as it meets public needs, is more burdened by economic and social strains, is more distrustful of authority and leadership, and is less committed to civic responsibility and public duty.

There are many symptoms of the increasing fragility of the social fabric of the United States. Repeatedly, polls show a lack of public confidence in the effectiveness of the president and the Congress and a sense of helplessness or even despair about the manifest inability of the government to deal with high inflation and unemployment. There are many signs of erosion in the coalitions of groups and interests that have contributed to compromise, stability, and tranquility: the disappointments of black leadership with progress on civil rights, the growth of public sentiment opposing public welfare programs, the polarization of political interests along more ideological lines, and the strengthening of disparate regional interests at the expense of the national interest. There is now powerful grass roots opposition to high taxes, which are appropriated to meet the need of the less advantaged. The requirements of larger defense budgets, justified by the burgeoning Soviet military threat and resurgent Soviet expansionism, come at a time when anti-inflation policy dictates fiscal constraint. Thus, other programs must face larger cutbacks. Work stoppages and strikes by increasingly organized and more militant public workers, groups, including police and firemen, farmers, and other workers, are already on the rise. Growing prospects of insolvency of urban centers are countered by the growing unwillingness of Congress to assume the added burden. In brief, conditions are emerging and taking root that could lead to many explosive forms of illegal and terrorist activity by individuals or groups, in response to a future crisis, such as uncontrolled inflation, a deep recession, or a serious military challenge abroad. If rampant inflation or a deep recession occurs, tears in the social fabric could provide perhaps unprecedented challenges to the stability of our society and our political system. Our economy and society therefore face unparalleled challenges from unsatisfied economic and social demands at home, as well as mounting military threats from a more expansionist Soviet Union abroad. It is especially difficult for a free society to cope with such threats without violating its fundamental principles and values. In addition, Americans have become less tolerant of extralegal intrusions and constraints since the Vietnam War and the Watergate crisis.

Businessmen in the United States are increasingly sensing the changing environment of risks, but are uncertain how to assess it and how to respond. The inexorable advancement of technology is adding to the concerns of business. New technologies present business with both new points of vulnerability, through ever more complex business organizations, management controls, and production systems, and, at the same time, add to the lethality and effectiveness of weapons and devices at the disposal of terrorists and their criminal confederates or emulators.

In spite of improvements made in law enforcement, public authorities cannot offer any guarantee of protection against terrorists' threats and attacks in their many forms. Thus, it is increasingly important that the private business sector better understand the threat before it becomes more serious and better prepare itself to handle threats and acts of terrorism. How to reduce this vulnerability is a major problem of improving the security system of U.S. and foreign corporations at home and abroad.

Recognizing the seriousness and complexity of this problem, we have decided to focus in this book on a number of significant aspects of terrorism and business:

1. The levels and kinds of terroristic victimization involving the facilities, personnel, and operations of U.S. and foreign corporations

2. The direct, indirect, and intangible costs of terrorism and the implications for both the business community and government

3. Corporate, government, and intergovernmental attitudes, policies, and procedures on prevention and response

4. Corporate and government efforts undertaken by private and public security personnel in specific cases of terrorism

5. Relations between corporate security and law enforcement agencies

6. The need and prospects for developing a comprehensive national management system dealing with terrorism and corporate targets.

Essays on these and related matters were originally prepared in connection with a conference on "Terrorism and U.S. Business," held on December 14, 1977, in Washington, D.C., and sponsored by the Georgetown University Center for Strategic and International Studies, with the cooperation of the Institute for Studies in International Terrorism of the State University of New York. This meeting dealt with the terrorist threat and discussed what corporations could do to minimize risks to their employees and facilities. The editors wish to thank both institutions for their cooperation in preparing this volume. They bear, however, no responsibility for the views expressed therein.

PART I

THE THREAT
OF TERRORISM
TO THE BUSINESS
COMMUNITY

1

THE THREAT:
SOME TECHNOLOGICAL
CONSIDERATIONS

Robert H. Kupperman

Thus far, terrorists have rarely used more than pistols, submachine guns, and bombs. Compared with the tools of modern warfare, terrorist assaults are usually primitive. Yet, terrorists have achieved considerable tactical success. However, we cannot guarantee that the terrorists will be satisfied to restrict themselves to using small arms and crude bombs. Thus, we must consider the possible arsenals available in the future, should terrorism advance in sophistication and audacity. Minimizing the effectiveness of terrorism has many facets. In this chapter, we consider the particular contributions of technology.

An increased degree of sophistication of the terrorist arsenal could be marked either by the use of more advanced weaponry or by the use of the present crude weapons to attack more technologically sophisticated targets. Man-portable antitank and surface-to-air rocketry, chemical and biological agents, and nuclear weapons would fall into the first category. Use of explosives to knock out a main transformer of the electric power grid, sabotage against crude oil or natural gas pipelines, and destruction of critical computer installations fall into the latter category.

Although we expect that terrorism will assume new and more harmful forms—and the possibility of irrational acts of mass destruction cannot be excluded—we do not anticipate mass destruction terrorism. We view the very ambiguity concerning possible terrorist weapons and the consequent opportunities

---

This chapter is based upon a forthcoming book by Robert H. Kupperman and Daniel M. Trent, *Terrorism: Threat, Reality, Response* to be published in 1979 by the Hoover Institution Press, Stanford University.

The views expressed in this chapter are the author's and do not necessarily reflect the views of the U.S. government or any of its agencies or departments.

for implicit or explicit extortion as posing an important issue. This chapter is therefore largely devoted to a discussion of some of the more awesome possibilities.

Our purposes are to acquaint the reader with the damage that a small band of terrorists can wreak. We assume—as is clearly the case for the Germans, Palestinians, Basques, and some South Americans—that terrorists have access to machine shops and university-level laboratory facilities and that they might employ a handful of Ph.D.-level scientists and engineers.

TODAY'S TERRORIST WEAPONS

It is difficult to predict the actions of terrorist groups. Similarly, it is difficult to know which weapons they might use. Because of availability and previous use, however, there are certain weapons that we should expect to find in terrorist hands.

The most readily available weapon to a terrorist organization is the crude homemade explosive. Next in popularity is the automatic weapon. Such weapons have been used extensively in terrorist operations. Light antitank rocket launchers, principally the RPG-7, are known to be in the hands of terrorist groups. For example, the RPG-7 was used in the January 1975 attack on El Al Airlines at Orly Airport, Paris. Other antitank weapons, such as the US LAW and the French Strim F-1, have been issued in quantity to the military forces of various nations. They are man-portable and easy to conceal. Surface-to-air missiles, while the least readily available of the weapons discussed, are known to be in the possession of Palestinian groups.

Explosives

Terrorists, as a rule, employ two types of bombs: explosive and incendiary. Explosive bombs are of either fragmentation or blast type. The most commonly encountered fragmentation bomb used by terrorists is the black powder pipe bomb.

The effectiveness of explosive charges can be significantly increased by the employment of the shaped-charge (or cavity-charge) principal—namely, to "focus" the force of an explosive in a desired direction. The charge can be either conical for penetration or linear for a cutting effect. An air space is required between the explosive and the target for this principle to work effectively; the charge is usually placed a short distance from the target.

Fire bombs are quickly and cheaply constructed, easy to use, and capable of inflicting extensive damage. The typical fire bomb consists of a glass bottle filled with an inflammable mixture (usually gasoline containing thickening additives, such as motor oil, to cause it to adhere to the target). A fuse is attached to the bottle, being designed to ignite the flammable mixture when the bottle is shattered against the target. No matter how crude, explosives and fire bombs are the most common terrorist weapons. Used by terrorists here and abroad, they vary in sophistication from time-delay fused and barometric bombs to the primitive truckload of fertilizer mixed with fuel oil, which destroyed the U.S. Army Mathematics Research Center at the University of Wisconsin. Other than the risks inherent in dealing with explosives, bombings are relatively safe hit-and-run operations. They are difficult crimes to solve; witness some 70 bombing attacks against Pacific Gas and Electric (PG&E), the Fraunces Tavern tragedy, and the LaGuardia Airport bombing of 1975. It appears that as terrorist groups mature and gain experience and polish, they turn from bombings to more difficult acts, such as hostage taking. This is especially true of European and Palestinian terrorists. Other than the kidnapping by the Symbionese Liberation Army (SLA) of Patricia Hearst, U.S. terrorists have relied almost exclusively upon bombs.

Automatic Weapons

The automatic weapon is basically an antipersonnel weapon; however, it can penetrate the skin of a commercial aircraft or automobile. It is a favorite of terrorist groups because of its concealability, high rate of fire, and impact on lightly armed security forces or unarmed civilians. There are two basic types of automatic weapons: the military assault rifle and the submachine gun. The submachine gun and its miniaturized cousin, the machine pistol, are especially attractive terrorist weapons because of their short overall length. These weapons can be concealed in hand baggage, in an attache case, or under a suit jacket. Fortunately, the arc-shaped or long rectangular-shaped magazines used in the automatic weapons leave a distinctive signature when X-rayed.

Precision-Guided Munitions and Light Antitank Weapons

Possibly the most dramatic recent development in individual weaponry is in the area of precision-guided munitions (PGMs). PGMs are devices that can launch missiles whose trajectories can be corrected in flight. On noncloudy days, their accuracy is very high. Many PGMs are man-portable, that is, they are very lightweight and can be carried and operated by one or two men. Generally speaking, they have two operational purposes: the destruction of aircraft and tanks. Obviously, the man-portable PGM can meet terrorist requirements as well.

In fact, terrorists have attempted to use them, especially the Soviet-made SA-7 (Strela).*

There are a number of man-portable surface-to-air rocket systems, the most important of which are the U.S.-made Redeye and its successor, the Stinger; the Soviet-made SA-7; and the British Blowpipe. Sweden has developed the RBS-70, which is a tripod-mounted antiaircraft system, but the bulkiness of this weapon makes it less attractive to terrorists than the SA-7 or Redeye.

The SA-7 and Redeye employ infrared devices—heat-seeking sensors that guide the missile to a heat source, such as an aircraft engine. They weigh under 35 pounds and their effective range is on the order of several kilometers.

America's Dragon and the TOW missiles are precision-guided antitank weapons that are in the operational inventory. (The TOW system was used successfully in Vietnam.) Similarly, the Soviets employ the Sagger. These missiles are wire-guided in order to make in-flight corrections. They use lasers for target acquisition. They are relatively lightweight and have ranges of several kilometers. The projectiles, employing shaped charges, can pierce several feet of homogeneous armor plate.[1]

Precision-guided weaponry are found in many countries. In the estimate of Jenkins:

> First-generation PGMs such as Strela and Redeye will be available to 30 to 40 countries in the Third World. It is not realistic to expect that all of these countries will maintain strict security interest; some may find it in their interest to make these weapons available to nongovernment groups. If we postulate a conservative loss rate worldwide, by theft or diversion, of one-tenth of one percent over the next five years, then man-portable PGMs will be "loose" in the hundreds by the beginning of the 1980s.[2]

Although PGMs represent an exceptionally great menace, terrorists have already used related, but less sophisticated, light antitank rocket launchers against armored vehicles and commercial aircraft. While not precision guided, the Soviet RPG-7 and US LAW can achieve deadly results at ranges of over 100 meters. These weapons are lightweight, compact, and self-contained and require no support equipment. The rocket launcher systems can be dismantled and easily transported in a suitcase or disguised as something other than a launcher tube.

---

*In 1973, in Rome, a Palestinian terrorist plot employing two SA-7s to shoot down an El Al airliner was foiled. Similarly, in 1975, in Kenya, an analogous plot was also thwarted. Most recently, a Rhodesian airliner was shot down with an SA-7.

They are particularly useful against such targets as limousines, aircraft, transformer banks, trucks carrying casks of radioactive waste, and pipelines. Unfortunately, these weapons are made available to terrorist organizations by some of the less responsible countries and through the black market.

Weapons of Mass Destruction

The development of radiological weapons (excluding construction of a nuclear explosive), the synthesis of nerve agents, and the culturing of small amounts of suitable biologicals are straightforward matters that are discussed today in the open literature,[3] especially in a now famous study, known popularly as the "Superviolence Study."[4] Moreover, dangerous agents such as cobalt-60, the insecticide TEPP, and specimens of anthrax are commercially available.

Although growing virulent biologicals is a hazardous activity for the amateur, and making large quantities takes considerable skill and judgment, there are many thousands of persons sufficiently trained to perform such tasks.

While it is easy to illustrate theoretical construction of nuclear explosives, as well as those of virulent toxins and live pathogens, there is a wide gulf between the theoretical and the practical. Though theoretical construction of nuclear explosives has become an armchair pastime, first popularized by Willrich and Taylor over four years ago,[5] the fabrication of a reliable nuclear explosive is a difficult and dangerous task that would not be undertaken lightly by a terrorist organization wishing to preserve its meager technical assets, especially its scientific personnel. Similarly, while idealized estimates of casualties from chemical, biological, and radiological attacks are easily made, the dispersal of these agents are not trivial matters. In large water supplies, such attacks are virtually impossible to affect; and if the agents were dispersed efficiently as an aerosol, the help of a competent engineer might be essential. Compared with nuclear explosives, and despite the many difficulties associated with efficient dispersal, effective chemical, biological, and radiological attacks are readily accomplished. Mass destruction, however reasonably measured, is technically feasible.

The balance of our discussion of nuclear, chemical, and biological agents is intended to expose the reader to a variety of weapons and the difficulties to be encountered in their fabrication and use. To repeat, mass destruction is achievable, but it is a myth that one can accomplish it by tossing a small quantity of a "supertoxin" into the water supply.

Nuclear Explosives

Recently, a great deal has been written about the clandestine fabrication of a nuclear weapon. It has been fertile ground for movies, novels, and TV shows. Possibly, there is enough open information available to make a nuclear bomb. To the physicist, the most important fact of all was learned when the first nuclear explosion was announced: supercritical masses explode.

The terrorist who intends to explode a nuclear device need only ensure that it goes "bang" and that a mushroom-shaped cloud is obvious to all. The need for high reliability and predictable yield is a requirement for the military, not the terrorist. Toppling one of the towers of the World Trade Center would suffice—lower Manhattan need not be decimated. It would be foolhardy to believe that a small, dedicated group could not build an inefficient atomic bomb, yielding between a few hundred tons and a kiloton in TNT equivalents, but this would not be a trivial challenge.

The ingredients of a nuclear weapon include a high explosive and a special nuclear material (SNM). Obviously, the first obstacle would be obtaining the SNM: uranium-233, uranium-235, or plutonium-239. Other than stealing the material or an actual nuclear weapon from a government installation, the primary source of SNM is the nuclear fuel cycle.

There are many nuclear reactors in operation, the most common being light-water reactors, which employ low-enriched uranium as a fuel. The low-enriched uranium cannot be used in a nuclear explosive. On the other hand, once the fuel has been processed by the reactor, it does contain plutonium-239, which can be used to fabricate a nuclear weapon. Fortunately, the spent fuel from the reactor is highly radioactive. The plutonium cannot be retrieved without sophisticated handling and chemical separation processes. These may be out of the reach of many small nations, let alone terrorists.

Plutonium-239 is the most widely available SNM. It is produced by neutron bombardment of uranium-238. Were a clandestine nuclear explosive produced, by all odds, plutonium-239 would be the fissile component of the bomb.

How easy is it to construct a crude nuclear weapon? The question is best answered by asking analogous questions: How easy is it to teach a bright, thoroughly inexperienced individual enough surgical procedure to perform an appendectomy?; or Would a patient be satisfied with his or her would-be surgeon, the "surgeon" having just read a surgery text for the first time? The same problems may beset the would-be nuclear weapons designer. At one extreme, Taylor, who is an experienced weapons designer, feels that an enterprising amateur could fabricate such a weapon.[6] Few would argue that another Manhattan Project would be required, but most would conservatively estimate that it might take a half dozen technically trained and mechanically adept people to accomplish the feat in safety. In addition to the SNM and high explosive, the project would take time, space, and money, as well as technological abilities. Individuals with training in nuclear chemistry, physics, metallurgy, and electronics, as well as those with some experience in handling high explosives, would be especially desirable. Once the SNM is obtained, which should be an exceedingly difficult matter in itself, the remaining tasks concern weapon design, engineering, reliability, and safety. Playing with near-critical masses of fissile materials is a dangerous matter, indeed. Moreover, high explosives are known to have detonated at the most unwanted moments.

Chemical and Biological Weapons

The threatened use of chemical and biological weapons could cause widespread panic. There are many chemical and biological agents of extreme potency, but their effective delivery as weapons of mass violence, whether by means of water supplies, food distribution, or aerosols, would be formidable obstacles to the amateur. In the hands of the technically resourceful, however, we can (partially) rank weaponry according to certain criteria. In terms of fatalities, conventional weapons, such as machine guns and small bombs, constitute the least threat. They can produce tens or hundreds of casualties in a single incident. Chemical weapons, such as nerve agents, constitute a substantially greater threat, being capable of producing hundreds to thousands of fatalities. A small nuclear bomb could produce 100,000 casualties, but biological agents—both toxins and living organisms—can rival thermonuclear weapons, providing the possibility of producing hundreds of thousands to several millions of casualties in a single incident.

CHEMICAL WEAPONS

There are tens of thousands of highly poisonous chemicals. Some are commonplace but generally unknown to the public, and others are exotic. We limit our discussion to the organophosphorous compounds, popularly known as "nerve agents," and the biologically derived botulinal toxin, which causes botulism and which is produced by a microorganism (*Clostridium botulinum*).

The most toxic chemical compounds, other than those that are produced by living organisms, are the organophosphorous compounds, the so-called nerve agents. The first one to be synthesized was tetraethyl phrophosphate. Commercially known as TEPP, it is among the most toxic organophosphates. Many organophosphates are available commercially as insecticides. TEPP is one of them. Another is Parathion, an insecticide that has posed hazards to agricultural workers.

The Nazis pursued the study of organophosphorous compounds for insecticidal and chemical warfare purposes, and the German chemical industry developed two of the most toxic substances known to man: tabun (ethyl NN-dimethylphosphoramidocyanidate) and sarin (isopropyl methylphosphono-fluoridate). There is a vast open literature on organophosphorous compounds. Partly because of military interest, but largely because of academic and commercial relevance, this family of compounds has achieved a considerable amount of economic importance as insecticides. The chemistry of these compounds has also been important to basic research on the electrochemical transmission of nerve signals.

Botulinal toxin is produced from living organisms; it is not synthesized in a laboratory.[7] (It is a toss-up whether to call this a biological or a chemical agent.) The toxin that causes botulism is produced by the organism *Clostridium botulinum*, which is found virtually everywhere. Improperly prepared sausage or canned tuna are classic sources of botulism. The virulence of the toxin is incredible. Compared to the most toxic nerve agents, botulinal toxin is a thousand times more effective. While the mean lethal dose is not known precisely, it is measured as a few tenths of a microgram.

As a terrorist weapon, it could be devastating; yet, there are limits to its usefulness. Dissemination is the hardest step. As with other agents, it would be virtually impossible to poison a large water supply: the required quantity of the toxin, hydrolysis, and chlorination are the inhibiting factors. Distribution via the food supply and aerosols are potential alternatives. As should be expected, the food-processing industry is intensely concerned about botulinal contamination. Although technically feasible, and very frightening, a terrorist attempt to contaminate canned products would be of limited effect. Aerosol dispersal would be a difficult and risky matter as well. Were terrorists to attempt an aerosol attack, other agents appear more likely to be used.

BIOLOGICAL AGENTS

Unlike terrorist weapons derived from plants or bacteria, such as *Clostridium botulinum*, terrorists could successfully employ live pathogens, potentially inflicting great harm. Some microorganisms, including certain bacteria and viruses, are of nearly incalculable virulence. A mass destruction attempt using live biological material against a populous, dense target might produce few casualties or it might produce millions of casualties. Depending upon the (average) particle size of the aerosol, meteorological conditions, vertical dilution, sedimentation, and so forth, a biological attack could be nearly uneventful or absolutely devastating. Even the "uneventful" attack, producing a few hundred casualties, could cause government disruption and public panic.

Unlike chemical agents, a small seed culture, when in the hands of a knowledgeable microbiologist having laboratory facilities at his or her disposal, could be multiplied into a large quantity.

The balance of our discussion of biological agents is limited to perhaps the most available (yet devastating) agent within reach of the terrorist. Pulmonary anthrax, caused by *Bacillus anthracis*, is virtually 100 percent fatal when untreated. Other than supportive therapy, the treatment is massive doses of penicillin. Unfortunately, by the time the symptoms of pulmonary anthrax appear, antibiotic therapy is useless. In that there would be few willing volunteers, its mean lethal dose is not known precisely. Various authors, including Rothchild, estimate it to be ten times more toxic than botulinal toxin—a respiratory dose of .01 microgram would be lethal.[8]

Nearly all microorganisms die quickly when exposed to sunlight. They are adversely affected by high temperatures and succumb easily to desiccation. Simply put, they are fragile. This is not the case for anthrax. It is a hardy organism. In spore form, it can live for decades, withstanding wide variations in environment.

NOTES

1. For an excellent unclassified discussion of precision-guided munitions, see James Digby, "Precision-Guided Weapons" (Delphi Paper no. 118), mimeographed (London: International Institute for Strategic Studies, Summer 1975).

2. Brian Michael Jenkins, *Terrorism: Trends and Potentialities* (Santa Monica, Calif.: Rand, 1977).

3. Robert K. Mullen, (Advanced Concepts research) *The International Clandestine Nuclear Threat* (Gaithersburg, Md.: International Association of Chiefs of Police, 1975); and Robert K. Mullen, *The Clandestine Use of Chemical or Biological Weapons* (Gaithersburg, Md.: International Association of Chiefs of Police, 1978).

4. B. J. Berkowitz, M. Frost, E. J. Hajic, and H. Redisch, *Superviolence: The Civil Threat of Mass Destruction Weapons* (Advanced Concepts research) (Santa Barbara, Calif.: Adcon, September 1972).

5. Mason Willrich and Theodore Taylor, *Nuclear Theft: Risks and Safeguards* (Cambridge, Mass.: Ballinger, 1974).

6. Ibid.

7. Hans Riemann, "Botulinum Types A, B and F," in *Infections and Intoxications*, ed. Hans Reimann (New York: Academic Press, 1969); and G. Hobbs, Kathleen Williams, and A. T. Willis, "Basic Methods for the Isolation of Clostridia," in *Isolation of Anerobes*, ed. D. A. Shapta and R. G. Board (New York: Academic Press, 1971).

8. Jacquard Rothchild, *Tomorrow's Weapons* (New York: McGraw-Hill, 1964).

2

DOMESTIC TERRORIST
MOVEMENTS

John B. Wolf

In 1976, there were an estimated 18,780 murders committed in the United States, of which 1,622 were reported to the New York City Police Department, 814 to the Chicago police, and 501 to the Los Angeles police. Firearms, primarily handguns, were used to perpetrate 64 percent of these crimes, which brought death to one person out of every 10,000 inhabitants of the country's metropolitan areas.[1]

However, the average citizen, although shocked by murder, is impassive toward the violence associated with this crime unless he or she is personally touched. The crime of murder usually involves the killing of a specific individual for a definite purpose by a lone person whose action is based on a readily discernible motive, for example, jealousy, revenge, or escape from the scene of a robbery. Murder, therefore, has a rational aspect. Although a horrendous act, its impact upon the inhabitants of a city, however, is not comparable to the shock action that traumatizes the residents of an area targeted by a terrorist group for a spate of seemingly unpredictable attacks—these are intended to frighten them to a degree that exceeds the level of fear usually associated with the act of murder as perpetrated by the criminal offender, whose heinous acts are reported daily by the media.

FALN BOMBINGS

Inhabitants of New York City and Chicago, therefore, were particularly alarmed when they read of pipe bomb explosions that killed or maimed innocent bystanders because a radical group sought publicity for its declared objective of "freeing Puerto Rican political prisoners and ending alleged mainland exploitation of the island's resources." The FALN Armed Forces of National Liberation for Puerto Rico) has consistently supported the demands of the Puerto Rican Socialist Party in its many communiques and armed attacks. Therefore, its operations are designed to emphasize causes related to the immediate independence for Puerto Rico or the release of the terrorists associated with the Puerto Rican Nationalist Party, who attempted to assassinate President Harry S. Truman and killed a guard in 1950. In 1954, this same group of terrorists also tried to murder several members of Congress in a wild shooting spree in the House of Representatives.[2] The FALN has claimed responsibility for more than 100 explosions in New York, Washington, Chicago, and Newark since 1974. These bombings have killed five persons and injured 75 and are part of the FALN's coordinated attack against "Yanki government, monopoly capitalist institutions," and "imperialism by multinational corporations."[3]

TERRORISM AND ORDINARY CRIMINAL ACTIVITY

It is shortsighted, therefore, for an analyst to try to minimize the threat of terrorism to the American people and their institutions by comparing the number of people killed each year in the United States by terrorist violence with the number of fatalities that result from acts of murder and nonnegligent manslaughter. There were 2,074 bombing incidents in the United States in 1975, but only 90 of these events, responsible for the deaths of ten persons, could be linked to terrorists.[4]

Yet three incidents that took place in recent years should be sufficient to remind authorities of the continuing terrorist threat to the domestic tranquility of the United States. The first event occurred in March 1977 and centered around the seizure of over 100 hostages in Washington, D.C., by Hanafi Muslims.[5] Event number two was the bomb explosion caused by unidentified terrorists at LaGuardia Airport in New York City on December 29, 1975, which killed 11 people and injured about 75 others.[6] The third event was the killing in Washington, D.C., of Orlando Letelier, who once served as foreign minister in the Chilean government of President Salvador Allende Gossens. Federal and local investigators, putting together the events that preceded the murder of Letelier, believe the recruitment of anti-Castro Cuban exiles from a terrorist organization known by the code name "Omega 7" and from another radical group, identified as the Cuban National Movement by members of the Chilean Intelligence Service, formerly known as the National Intelligence Directorate (DINA), was the key to the assassination.[7] Letelier and a young U.S. associate were slain when a bomb blew up in the diplomat's car on the morning of September 21, 1976, as it rounded a traffic circle on a busy Washington street.[8]

STRATEGY OF THE NEW WORLD
LIBERATION FRONT

Although the aforementioned incidents were perpetrated by people associated with terrorist organizations that advocate a cause tailored to elicit support from a limited audience, for example, advocates of independence for Puerto
Rico or others who want an end to Fidel Castro's control of Cuba, the threat of
a professionally directed campaign of urban terrorism attracting a mixed group
of sympathizers is always a danger. The New World Liberation Front (NWLF), a
Marxist-Leninist group advocating the destruction of the U.S. government and
private industry, boasts of a four-year bombing campaign in California and acts
as an umbrella organization for terrorists from other groups. It has claimed more
than 40 bombing incidents since October 5, 1974, including the $1 million blast
on February 12, 1976, at the Hearst Castle in San Simeon, California.[9]

Among the radical West Coast groups linked to the NWLF are the George
Jackson Brigade, which has claimed responsibility for the bombings of car
dealerships, Safeway stores, government offices, and power substations in Oregon
and Washington, and an assortment of additional groups, who conduct bombing
operations primarily against the facilities of PG&E in the San Francisco Bay
Area.[10] The California groups include Friends and Neighbors of the Poor (FNP),
People's Light Brigade (PLB), the Eugene Kuhn unit, and others.[11] NWLF
claims that Eugene Kuhn was a 74-year-old man who froze to death in his Ohio
home because his utilities had been turned off for nonpayment of an $18 bill.
Consequently, NWLF, in its effort to attract media attention and support from
the poor and impoverished, attacked PG&E in the name of Kuhn for the advertised purpose of forcing the California utility company to provide free gas and
electricity for persons over 65 living on a fixed income below the poverty level
and to emphasize its determination to continue its campaign against the "corporate bloodsuckers."[12]

Additionally, a revolutionary group calling itself the Lucio Cabanas Unit
claimed responsibility for the bombings during the summer of 1976 of the
South African consulate in San Francisco. Also operating under the control of
the NWLF's central command, this group tries to attract support from anti-
apartheid factions in the United States who oppose various domestic policies of
the Republic of South Africa.[13]

Consequently, by undertaking a protracted campaign of terror, the NWLF
has adopted Castro's "foco" theory—that it is not necessary to organize the
population as a whole to accomplish armed revolution—"a small group of armed
insurgents . . . can act as a focus for the various discontented elements . . . [to]
channel all the latent energy available into action for the defeat of the government."[14] Thus, the NWLF strives to become the focus for a structural revolution
in the United States by demonstrating the inability of the U.S. government, particularly its law enforcement agencies, to prevent it from bombing financial

institutions, utility power stations, government offices, and private residences, which it characterizes as symbols of the "evils of capitalism."

Strategically, therefore, the NWLF views its "armed struggle" as contributing to the disequilibrium of the state and causing the government to incur further losses in its authority, which will eventually result in the ignition of a widespread antigovernment movement. The Italian *Brigate Rosse* (Red Brigades) exemplified this strategic use of terror when its kidnapping of former Prime Minister Aldo Moro kept Italy in suspense, demonstrating the weakness of the government and of the official parties when confronted with a professionally led revolutionary group. Consequently, NWLF's apparent understanding of Leninist revolutionary principles and its sophisticated use of "armed propaganda" combine to make it an exceedingly dangerous group.

TARGET ANALYSIS AND
"ARMED PROPAGANDA"

According to a Puerto Rican spokesman in New York City, the FALN has decided that at the very least, its bombings of corporate targets in Chicago and New York—for example, Citibank, Gulf and Western Corporation, Bankers Trust, Chase Manhattan Bank, and Union Carbide Corporation—have reduced tourism to Puerto Rico, dissuaded U.S. corporations from further investments on the island, and sparked proindependence sentiment within the Puerto Rican community in the United States.[15]

The NWLF also includes an armed propaganda component in its strategy of attacks against U.S. corporations. Among its favorite corporate targets are Safeway stores, which it accuses of unfair pricing practices in minority neighborhoods, and PG&E, which it views as the key participant in a national conspiracy of major utilities seeking increased profits by constantly agitating for higher utility rates at the expense of the elderly and the poor.[16]

The primary input into NWLF's strategic plan are the studies performed by the Bay Area Research Collective (BARC), which once published a periodical called *The Urban Guerrilla* (*TUG*). One issue of *TUG* contained an article, "How to Research Your Target," which was actually a target analysis of PG&E, replete with the names and addresses of the company's board of directors and their ties with multinational corporations and financial institutions.[17] The same article, by describing the corporate relationship that existed between the West Coast utility and a major lumber company that exported forest products to Japan, set the stage for a future attack against the Potlatch Lumber Company by the NWLF. By advertising this act as a gain for environmentalism and a setback for PG&E, NWLF sought to gain tacit support from groups advocating a variety of causes, ranging from saving the redwoods to opposing higher utility bills.[18] The utilization of this targeting technique by terrorist groups indicates that they share with

Che Guevara his concept of a stalled economy as being among the best conditions for a revolution.

ETHNICITY AND TERRORISM

The most active U.S. terrorist organizations are the FALN, whose campaigns, confined largely to New York City and Chicago, are designed to have a direct impact upon the proindependence for Puerto Rico factions that reside in the cities it targets for attack and the NWLF and its affilitates, whose armed assaults take place in California, Washington, and Oregon. An assortment of anti-Castro Cuban groups—for example, Omega 7, El Condor, and the Pedro Luis Boitel Commandos—are busy in the conduct of terrorist operations designed to influence and gain support from Cuban exiles living in the New York metropolitan region and the greater Miami area. Additionally, the Jewish Armed Resistance, composed of a number of people who have been and are currently active with the Jewish Defense League (JDL) in some of its more peaceful activities, is involved in a plethora of violent acts in New York City. In addition, since the autumn of 1977, a paramilitary group, known as the Brown Berets, has been involved in marches and demonstrations that have attenuated ties between the police and members of the Mexican-American community of Houston and other Texan cities.

The very real possibility of a handful of radicals undertaking some spectacular act of terror intended to focus worldwide attention upon the aspirations of a particular irredentist group is a matter of utmost concern for law enforcement agencies. The hijacking of a Trans World Airlines (TWA) jetliner carrying 92 people on a New York to Chicago flight during the late summer of 1976 by five Croatian nationalists is an example of an act undertaken for this purpose.[19] Washington, D.C., or New York City, therefore, could become the scene of another episode similar to the "Croatian hijack affair" whenever an international event of political significance to a particular terrorist group requires the use of shock action to emphasize its meaning to a worldwide audience. Both cities house diplomatic staffs and foreign missions, which terrorists regard as excellent targets for attack to achieve this purpose, and both cities are enveloped in a multimedia environment, which has been exploited by terrorists for the purpose of demonstrating both their efficacy and their demands.

Black terrorist organizations that were active in the 1960s and early 1970s, for example, the Revolutionary Action Movement (RAM) and the Black Liberation Army (BLA), as well as other groups prominent during the Vietnam era, such as the Weather Underground Organization (WUO) and the SLA, have faded. The Prairie Fire Organizing Committee, a derivative of the WUO, however, is still active. Also, Black Muslim groups who have used terrorism to emphasize the extent of their disagreements with other Muslims, as the Hanafi Muslims chose to do in Washington, D.C., could opt to employ it against a target whose destruction or abduction would prove beneficial to their cause.

THE ALASKA PIPELINE

The trans-Alaska pipeline, extending 800 miles across Alaska, is vulnerable to attack by a terrorist group as it rests on the surface of the tundra for approximately 50 percent of its length.[20] Additionally, extremists from the high school population of Barrow, a settlement that has recently experienced an alarming number of criminal assaults, and other villages on the North Slope, in collaboration with environmentalists could threaten to destroy the pipeline unless, for example, the U.S. government agreed to execute a land claim settlement favorable to the natives of northern Alaska and conducive to the preservation of endangered species of wildlife.

On February 15, 1978, a two-inch hole was blasted in the pipeline about six miles east of Fairbanks. Crews from the Alyeska Pipeline Service Company, the operator of the pipeline, repaired the damage, and the pumping of crude oil south to Valdez was resumed approximately 20 hours after the detonation of the explosive charge.[21] A caller to United Press International (UPI) in Miami, purporting to represent the extremist Cuban exile organization El Condor, said the blast was triggered "in retaliation, and at the same time as a warning, to the United States government" to discontinue efforts to normalize relations with Cuba. But the Alaska authorities had a suspect in this case whom they claimed was not linked to El Condor.[22] In July 1977, another dynamiting of the pipeline took place at a point about 17 miles north of Fairbanks.[23]

Leonard Le Shack, president of Development and Resources Company in Silver Spring, Maryland, a consulting firm that has conducted a number of Arctic projects for government and oil company clients, mentions that "at present neither Alyeska Pipeline Service Company, the Alaska State Police nor any federal agency recognizes any meaningful responsibility for protecting the pipeline against attacks of a terrorist nature."[24] He also remarked that "the potential threat against the pipeline, whether motivated by foreign or domestic interests, clearly fits into the category of political terrorism."[25]

INUITS OF THE NORTH SLOPE

In June 1977, Eskimos of Canada, Alaska, and Greenland attended an international conference of *Inuits* at Barrow, Alaska. *Inuit*, meaning "the people," is the term by which natives of the Arctic regions prefer to call themselves. The term *Eskimo* is a Cree Indian word meaning "eaters of raw meat." The solidarity of the assemblage at the Barrow conference strengthened the Inuit cause and increased the credibility of their demands upon their respective governments, ranging from land claims to political recognition. The Eskimo Brotherhood estimates that 46,000 Inuits live in Greenland, 22,000 in Canada, and 39,000 in Alaska. Inuits from Soviet Siberia were invited to the conference but did not attend.[26] Thus, all of the necessary preconditions for an act of political terrorism are present in Alaska; a distraught native population, which could contain a few violent extremists; a vulnerable target; and a cause suitable for manipulation for the singular purpose of generating armed propaganda.

ENVIRONMENTALISM AND THE ARTICULATION OF A CAUSE

The construction of nuclear generating stations, naval facilities in coastal wetlands, support facilities for offshore drilling operations, and other installations that threaten to impinge upon a nationally advertised issue advocated by an environmentalist group could trigger an act of terror intended to enhance the political clout of its perpetrators. A terrorist group active in southern California and skilled in the art of the articulation of a cause, for example, the NWLF, could attempt to combine their anticapitalist campaign with the demands of a group of environmentalists who opposed, say, the landing route planned for the space shuttle (favoring instead the interests of the Brown Pelican and the Peregrine Falcon). The proposed route, by crossing the Pacific coastline at a point north of Los Angeles and terminating in the Mojave Desert threatens to disturb bird colonies and nesting sites on offshore islands.

Although the SLA is defunct, its members were sufficiently versed in mass media skills to permit them to choose a name for their organization that expressed their cause in a catchy but sophisticated style. According to the SLA, Symbionese is a name referring to two forces, black and white. living together for the purpose of eliminating "the insect who preys on the life of the people." Abalone, Armadillo, and Clamshell, which are currently being used as names for alliances of people who oppose the extension and further development of nuclear power in the United States, are representative of creatures that inhabit the natural areas threatened for despoilation by the construction of power plants.[27] The peregrine falcon, the bald eagle, or the name of another endangered species of wildlife could be chosen by a terrorist group for its label.

Protesters belonging to the Clamshell Alliance, organized by leaders of the antiwar movement and some young veterans of radical activity, demonstrated at a nuclear power reactor construction site at Seabrook, New Hampshire, where 1,414 persons were arrested on a spring weekend in 1977.[28] Meanwhile the Trojan Decommissioning Alliance is bent upon securing the permanent closing of the Trojan Nuclear Plant at Rainier, Oregon, and another group wants to stop the development of a Florida Power and Light Company facility in the Florida wetlands, as it threatens the habitat of an endangered species of sea mammal known as the manatee.[29] Since 1976, veterans of the activist movements of the 1960s have been joining the antinuclear campaign, the purpose being to assist in organizational efforts and to instruct in such tactics as civil disobedience and demonstration.[30]

Similarly, radical Japanese students fronted their loosely defined Marxist grievances with those of other groups with regard to air pollution, noise abatement, and the dangers of transporting shipments of fuel over an inadequate road network; they succeeded in manipulating and broadening a cause that originated with farmers and which was once restricted to opposition of the construction of the new Tokyo International Airport in a fertile agricultural region.[31] Unable to halt airport construction through the use of protest demonstrations, more than 300 radicals, throwing fire bombs at police officers from the rear of moving vehicles and wielding lengths of steel pipe, crashed a truck through an airport fence and siezed the control tower. Once inside the tower, the radicals used sledgehammers to smash equipment. Some 14,000 riot police officers, mobilized from all over Japan and deployed to protect the airport from attack, were unable to stop the assault, which was fast moving and well-coordinated.[32]

EXPLOITATION OF THE URBAN ENVIRONMENT

Although targets of opportunity and manipulatable causes are present in rural sections of the United States, U.S. terrorist groups are most active in urban areas, as they appreciate the political and economic importance of the cities as the administrative and commercial centers of regions. Also, they calculate that cities have a symbolic value: here, where the power of the government is most concentrated, it should be least vulnerable and most capable of maintaining order. A government that cannot enforce its will in areas where it is most powerful is shown to be inadequate as a governing agent.[33]

Other characteristics of the urban environment also are favorable for the conduct of terrorist operations. U.S. cities are as geographically complex as that of any rural setting: physical cover is multidimensional due to the walls, roofs, basements, and labyrinth of utility passages. Furthermore, the logistical problems are not as great as in the countryside, since food and medical supplies are readily available from the corner store, and although specific targets can be safeguarded, traffic, cable conduits, and normal business activities can be disrupted at locations and times of the terrorist's choosing.

Also, due to high illiteracy rates and large concentrations of rootless and frustrated people in cities, opportunities for terrorist propaganda and recruitment are enhanced. Of equal importance in cities, it is easier for terrorists to blend with the population; it is extremely difficult, particularly in a free society, to maintain an adequate check on transients who frequent urban neighborhoods.

Because the insurgent "can work through so many thousands of people . . . the enemy is made to feel him as an impalpable presence, until every ordinary pedestrian seems like a guerrilla in disguise."[34]

This constant uncertainty has a profound psychological impact on the police officer. He or she is constantly open to harassment, and yet, he or she can trust no one, for the most innocuous person or incident can deal him or her a fatal blow. Added to his or her constant anxiety is the extreme difficulty experienced in seeking to implement antiterrorist techniques in the city. The police cannot hope to initiate a comprehensive antiterrorist operation without arousing the ire of the people thus inconvenienced.[35]

In April 1974, for example, the residents of San Francisco were horrified by the twelfth "Zebra" killing—a designation derived from the "Z"—the radio band used by the police who were ordered by Police Chief Donald Scott to conduct a manhunt, which included a massive stop-and-search sweep. As a consequence of the sweep, hundreds of young black men were halted, interrogated, and "frisked" for weapons. When cleared, the blacks were given identification cards. As the police dragnet continued, however, a cry of bitter protest came from San Francisco's black community. Lawsuits demanding an end to the searches were filed by the National Association for the Advancement of Colored People (NAACP) and the American Civil Liberties Union (ACLU). On April 25, 1974, a federal judge granted a preliminary injunction severely restricting police action.[36]

Urban terrorists' actions are also likely to attract mass publicity because they are more difficult for the government to cover up or rationalize away.[37] The terrorist hopes that his or her action will cause the people to realize that their time is now and that by militant action they can mold their destiny. Through the demonstrated effects of sustained terror, the insurgents thus try to raise the revolutionary consciousness of an entire people. In Fanon's *The Wretched of the Earth*, this idea of political agitation and terrorism acting as the catalyst for the awakening of the masses and the subsequent forging of the revolutionary mentality through the carrying out of armed struggle received its most elaborate treatment.[38]

Although failing in all of their previous efforts to cause a structural revolution, the cadre element of various U.S. terrorist organization, the NWLF in particular, continues to agitate and probe for any manipulatable cause that its present and potential members have the capacity to exploit. Thus, their campaigns of terror are intended to attract and condition people who are advocates of an assortment of causes to serve as followers and supporters and eventually abandon their particularism and work for a "united front." Consequently, the leaders of U.S. terrorist groups are the type of people who are convinced that adequately funded and properly managed campaigns of social, economic, or political reforms will not satisfy the psychological urges of potential followers, who are aware that organization of the entire people or an entire class is not a necessary prerequisite for a campaign of terror, but who are aware that what is needed is a special organization of people—specialists in terrorist organizations. These specialists understand that the prerequisites for a campaign of terror are a charismatic leader of the Charles Manson type, ideas that can be gleaned from the writings of revolutionary authors, swindles or bank robberies that can raise money, and the development of a propaganda campaign designed to attract mass support for their cause.

ORGANIZATIONAL COMMUNICATIONS

Protracted campaigns of political terrorism in the United States are undertaken, therefore, within the boundaries of a few of the nation's large cities, for example, New York, Chicago, Washington, D.C., Miami, Denver, Seattle, San Francisco, and Los Angeles. However, the attractiveness of targets in rural areas to a terrorist group should not be discounted, particularly oil and gas pipelines and nuclear plants. Organizationally, domestic terrorist groups operating in urban areas perpetrate their crimes on a limited scale within the confines of two or three cities and are best described, therefore, as agitational terrorists. Although some terrorist groups advocate the violent overthrow of the existing political or economic system, they have not been able to realize this objective, although they continue to persevere. In addition, U.S. urban terrorists have abandoned, at least for the moment, the concept of a fixed base or safehouse and instead "live apart and fight together." By being gainfully employed or living on welfare, a terrorist has a permanent street address and, therefore, a reason for being present in a particular neighborhood. Habitual criminals also adopt this guise, as they are aware that its usage prevents arousing the suspicions of police officers assigned to the urban patrol function, who are trained to observe conduct of an exceptional or unusual nature.

Communication among terrorists within a cell and the horizontal and vertical exchange of information among cells and various echelons of command is accomplished through a predetermined system of "dead-drops." This system consists of a network of coin-box telephones, which facilitate verbal coordination, and storage lockers at transportation depots and elsewhere, which serve as deposits for manufactured explosive devices and as pickup points for bomb placers, as well as places for the storage of weapons, explosives, and other supplies. Utilization of a dead-drop system, therefore, permits a group to maintain its clandestine contacts and cut out physical contact except during the execution of an armed attack.[39]

On October 17, 1975, a luggage locker at Miami International Airport was apparently being used as a dead-drop by an unidentified terrorist group, and on December 29, 1975, at LaGuardia Airport in New York City, another container of a similar type was rented for the same purpose, also by a still unidentified terrorist group. Additionally, the leader of the Croatian hijackers who siezed the TWA jetliner at LaGuardia Airport on September 10, 1976, told authorities about his use of a rented locker at a subway station at Grand Central Terminal in New York City for the storage of a live bomb. Premature detonation of the Miami bomb blew a small hole in the ceiling of an airport lounge but caused no injuries. However, the detonation of the LaGuardia device, equivalent to 12.5 pounds of dynamite, was responsible for the killing of four people and the injuring of more than 70 others. The Coration bomb was removed from the subway locker by members of the New York City Police Bomb Squad and transported to the police bomb range in the Bronx. A police officer was killed trying to detonate the device at the range.[40]

Regarding caches, terrorists are aware of the necessity for regular surveillance of the places they select to hide explosives and other supplies, as a site chosen for this purpose could be inadvertently uncovered by police patrol or through a "stakeout" as a consequence of an informant's tip. A batch of dynamite stolen from a Deer Creek, Colorado, construction site by the FALN and hidden in a crypt in an old Denver cemetery was recovered by police. Members of the Crusade for Justice, a Denver Chicano political and civil rights organization that had received funding from the National Commission on Hispanic Affairs, which is also associated with known FALN members, worked in the cemetery.[41]

FALN BOMB FACTORIES

On November 2, 1976, the Chicago police and agents of the Federal Bureau of Investigation (FBI) raided an FALN bomb factory in the apartment of Carlos Alberto Torres, a former student at the University of Illinois. Torres, his wife Haydee Beltran Torres, and a friend, Oscar Lopez Rivera, are wanted by the FBI in connection with attempted bombings. In addition, Haydee Torres, identified through a fingerprint found at the site of an August 8, 1977, bombing that killed one person and injured several others at the Mobil Oil building in New York City, is wanted for murder.[42]

In the Torres Chicago apartment, police recovered more than 200 sticks of high velocity dynamite stolen from Deer Creek, Colorado, and (perhaps staged to Chicago through the cache in the Denver cemetery) 70 pounds of explosive powder, hand-held radios, propane tanks, blasting caps, and other incendiary equipment. Also found were letterheads from the Protestant Episcopal Church's National Commission on Hispanic Affairs, of which Carlos Torres was a board member.[43] (Among the projects funded by this commission were the Crusade for Justice in Denver; a Frontier Airlines schedule for Chicago to Denver flights was found in the Chicago "bomb factory" and bore the fingerprints of Oscar Lopez, also a fugitive; an "alternative" high school for Puerto Rican students in Chicago, named for Rafael Cancel Miranda, a Puerto Rican terrorist who attempted to murder members of Congress in 1954; and the Cooperative Agricola del Pueblo in Tierra Amarilla, New Mexico.[44])Dynamite used in several FALN bombs that failed to explode in Chicago and New York is believed to have been stolen from the Heron Dam site near Tierra Amarilla, New Mexico, in the late 1960s.[45]

On Wednesday night, July 12, 1978, an explosion blew away both hands and part of the face of William Morales, 28, as he assembled a pipe bomb inside a two-room apartment in a largely Hispanic section of New York City. Police said that the apartment was being used as an FALN bomb factory for a planned widespread attack. Three of the pipe bombs uncovered in the apartment were removed to the police range in the Bronx, where they exploded unexpectedly. Sixty-six sticks of dynamite, 200 pounds of a substance used to make incendiary devices of the type planted in Manhattan department stores by the FALN, and a supply of shoulder weapons were also uncovered in the apartment.[46] In addition to his FALN connections, Morales was a member of the National Commission on Hispanic Affairs during 1975 and 1976, and the dynamite he was handling, according to Colorado police, was traced to a batch stolen from the Deer Creek, Colorado, site, parts of which were also uncovered in Carlos Torres's Chicago apartment in November 1976 and from the crypt in the Denver cemetery.[47]

"CUTOUT" STYLES OF ORGANIZATION

The "cutout" style of organization was not adopted by U.S. terrorist groups as a matter of course but as a matter of necessity. In the late 1960s, terrorist organizations operating in the United States, for example, the Minutemen, RAM, and the BLF, lacked the organizational safeguards required to prevent infiltration by informers and police undercover agents. Eventually, therefore, they were penetrated by the authorities and finally dismantled by the police, who became the recipients of "inside information," provided to them on a regular basis by an assortment of covert sources.[48] In addition, computer-supported police patrol operations, facilitating the routine and regular checks of all motor vehicles, and crime prevention programs, intended to encourage dwellers of urban areas to observe and report suspicious criminal activity to their neighborhood precincts, restricted the size of terrorist organizations and curtailed their scope of operations.

Jo Anne Chesimard, regarded as "the soul of the BLA," has expressed her view regarding the dread that most terrorists share with regard to the expertise of U.S. police in the areas of communications, mobility, and information. "I want to apologize to you, my Black brothers and sisters, for being on the New Jersey Turnpike," remarks Miss Chesimard. "I should have known better. The turnpike is a checkpoint where Black people are stopped, searched, harassed and assaulted. Revolutionaries must never be in too much of a hurry or make careless decisions. He who runs when the sun is sleeping will stumble many times."[49] Assada Shakur, a name by which Chesimard prefers to be known, was sentenced to life in prison in March 1977 after being convicted of the murder of a New Jersey state trooper in a shootout on the Turnpike on May 3, 1973. The shooting began after the police stopped the car in which Chesimard and two male members of the BLA were riding for a motor vehicle check after noting the car's faulty rear lights and New England registration plates.[50]

Although the cutout style of organization is intended to preserve individual anonymity, safeguard the cell from infiltration, and prevent the reoccurrence of instances of terrorists traveling together on the open road, as described by Chesimard, it restricts operational flexibility, reduces the number of people who can be safely admitted to membership in a group, and imposes an inexorable burden upon the terrorists in the areas of operational planning and intelligence gathering, both of which are prerequisites to the successful conduct of terrorist operations. Furthermore, this type or organization is not designed to support the agitation, pamphleteering, and other overt political work that was responsible for the original commitment of many of the people to a clandestine struggle, although it is capable of sustaining the operations of a few cells which undertake periodically a spurt of bombings or which seize a group of hostages.

PUBLICATIONS AND MEMBERSHIP

Osawatomie, an organ of the WUO, has ceased publication as a result of a split in that group (announced in an issue of *Takeover*, an "alternative newspaper" from Madison, Wisconsin, in January, 1977). Additionally, BARC has ceased publication of *Dragon*, a forum for discussion between the "underground" and its supporters in the United States. BARC stated that "the revolutionary movement" (in the United States) "is not large. Those who support armed struggle comprise just a small segment of the larger movement." *Dragon*, according to BARC, gave the impression that "the strength and active level of the movement is more advanced than it is."[51]

Also, active membership in domestic terrorist organizations is at its lowest ebb in recent years, although a variety of causes susceptible to manipulation by a trained propagandist have proliferated. Not one of these causes, however, is comparable to the broad-based appeal that issues related to the Vietnam War or the Civil Rights movement had for various segments of the U.S. population during the late 1960s and early 1970s. Unable, therefore, to recruit a large number of members through the vehicle of an appealing aboveground propaganda campaign and reluctant to intiate such an effort as a consequence of the increased urbanity of the U.S. police, terrorist groups are careful to regulate and restrict their membership. Thus, the NWLF is believed to consist of about 40 members organized into approximately ten cells, each of which contains three to five members. The FALN, according to some law enforcement officials, consists of approximately 12 or 15 members organized into three or four cells: one cell in New York City, which is mobile and able to move to Washington, D.C., for an action; one or two additional cells fixed within the confines of New York City; and another cell in Chicago, which maintains the Denver "connection."[52]

THE WEATHER UNDERGROUND ORGANIZATION "INVERTS"

The delimiting factors imposed upon terrorists by a cutout form of organizational structure were responsible for the decision made by the WUO Central Committee, announced in a January 1977 edition of *Takeover*, to "invert." In 1975, Jeff Jones, a member of the Central Committee, hatched a plan to begin surfacing the WUO, which he described as "inversion," meaning the process of emerging from fugitive life. The strategic aspect of this plan was Jones's belief, eventually shared by the Central Committee, that the WUO, a group claiming responsibility for 25 bombings since it emerged from the antiwar movement in 1970, would be better able to enlist other radicals if they were organized into an aboveground group. Bernardine Dohrn, probably the best known of the WUO fugitives, and other dissident members, however, criticized the Jones faction for its willingness to abandon violence and concentrate on aboveground political work. Dohrn, in a taped message, stated that the Central Committee had "abandoned armed struggle," turned away from blacks, and diluted their ideology. She also referred to the WUO as "the old organization," indicating the group may have broken up over the plan to invert. "Why did we do this? I don't really know," Dohrn said. "We followed the classic path of so-called white revolutionaries who sell out the revolution."[53]

PRAIRIE FIRE ORGANIZING COMMITTEE

In a prologue dated May 9, 1974, and addressed to "sisters and brothers," the WUO announced plans to expand its operations to include both the continuation of its clandestine operations and participation in an aboveground support group, which it called the Prairie Fire Organizing Committee. "Here is Prairie Fire, our political ideology," states the authors of the prologue, "a strategy for anti-imperialism and revolution inside the imperial U.S. . . . A single spark can start a prairie fire."[54] However, the arrests in November 1977 of five members of the Prairie Fire Organizing Committee in Los Angeles and Houston underscores the foolhardiness of terrorists who disregard security in the interest of the aboveground recruitment of members for underground criminal work of a conspiratorial nature. Clayton Van Lydergraf, identified in the complaint to the police as the leader of the Prairie Fire Organizing Committee of the WUO, was charged with directing the activities of the four other defendants, who were seeking to recruit members for an underground group whose primary objectives were the assassination of public figures and bombings of public buildings.[55]

ANTI-CASTRO CUBAN GROUPS

Meanwhile, terrorism perpetrated by anti-Castro terrorists, as exemplified by the assassination of Letelier, has not abated and continues to be a matter of concern for U.S. businessmen and individuals charged with the formulation of U.S. foreign policy. Membership in the various terrorist groups, composed largely of Cuban exiles, is restricted to 300 or fewer activists, who are committed to carry out acts of terror against the Castro regime and anyone or anything that they identify with it. In addition, the Cuban terrorists, who were involved in a wave of bombings and ambushes in seven countries between 1974 and 1976, were led, almost invariably, by persons who were associated with the Central Intelligence Agency (CIA), recruited during the period 1960-61.[56]

Orlando Bosch, head of an exile umbrella organization called the Commandos of United Revolutionary Organization (CORU), and Luis Posada Carrilles were two of the significant leaders of the 1974-76 terrorist campaign. Bosch, presently held by Venezuelan authorities for complicity in the bombing of a Cuban airliner on October 6, 1976 (which crashed with the loss of all 73 persons aboard), received extensive training by the CIA and once served four years of a ten-year sentence in the United States for firing a bazooka at a Polish ship in Miami in 1968. Posada served in Battalion Number 7 of Brigade 2506, the CIA's exile army, and received intelligence training in the U.S. Army.[57]

After the defeat of the exiles at the Bay of Pigs in 1961, the militant Cubans split into several factions, only to be pulled together in 1974 by Bosch and his associates, who undertook a successful series of shootings and bombings, which served to eliminate many exile leaders in the Greater Miami area who were hostile to their cause. Once organized under the CORU umbrella, Bosch's group launched a campaign of violence, which included bombings of Cuban installations in North and South America and the murder or abduction of Cuban officials at various overseas locations.[58]

Targets bombed by the exiles in the United States during the course of this campaign included the Cuban Mission to the UN in New York City and a Soviet cargo ship docked at Elizabeth, New Jersey, which is part of the port of New York. A group called Omega 7, tied to CORU, claimed credit for the bombings in the New York metropolitan area. Members of the Omega 7 group included Virgilio Paz Romero and Jose Dionisio Suarez, both fugitives and both wanted by the FBI for involvement in the 1976 assassination of Letelier, and two additional New Jersey residents, Guillermo Novo Sampol and Alvin Ross Diaz, who are being held by authorities for complicity in the same crime.[59]

Anti-Castro Cuban terrorist organizations currently active in the United States are El Condor and the Pedro Luis Boitel Commandos. Omega 7 was decimated by the police during the spring of 1978. On September 7, 1977, El condor set off an explosive charge in Washington, D.C., which shattered windows near the Soviet embassy and blew up a cement pot near the White House "in retaliation for giving away to the Communists the Panama Canal." The Pedro Luis Boitel Commandos, indignant over a Florida-based corporation's announced intention to fly commercial flights to Cuba, bombed the office of Mackey International Airlines on May 25, 1977.[60]

THE WORLD COMMUNITY OF AL-ISLAM IN THE WEST

Violence that could have a major impact upon the U.S. black community may be in the process of evolving. In March 1978, some current and former members of the World Community of Al-Islam in the West, formerly known as the Nation of Islam (NOI), reported that their group had lost thousands of members and was trying to assuage an ideological cleavage that threatened to further polarize its followers. Elijah Muhammad, organizer of the NOI and its leader for 40 years, until his death in 1975, preached a doctrine of blacks taking care of themselves and building their own separate institutions. Under his leadership, the members of the NOI (estimated to have peaked at approximately 200,000) considered the whites as devils and enemies of blacks. However, Wallace D. Muhammad, Muhammad's son and successor, initiated a series of reforms intended to facilitate the efforts to members of his movement to work with whites toward improving the conditions of blacks.[61]

Louis Farrakhan, once a powerful associate of Elijah Muhammad and his son Wallace and appointed by the elder Muhammad to succeed Malcolm X as leader of the Harlem mosque in New York City, contends that blacks are losing many of the social and economic gains won during the 1960s as a result of a mistaken pursuit of integrationist goals. Black joblessness and a rise in black-against-black crime are regarded by Farrakhan as additional issues of concern to blacks. Consequently, in March 1978, Farrakhan announced his plan to reinstate the separatist policies of the Black Muslims, abandoned by Wallace Muhammad, and to restore a strict discipline formerly required by members.[62] The renewal of internecine rivalry among Black Muslim factions could spark an act of terror similar to the March 1977 action of the Hanafis—led by Khalifa Hummas Abdul Khaalis and intended to focus national attention upon a controversial issue of concern to blacks, for example, the recent Supreme Court decision in the "Bakke Case."

KU KLUX KLANS

Although the Ku Klux Klan (KKK) has maintained a low profile for the last decade, it is again active and likely to provoke public disorder. During the first week of July 1977, a group of blacks stormed an outdoor meeting of hooded Klansmen in Columbus, Ohio, and on July 8, 1978, members of a southern Klan monitored a protest march by blacks in Tupelo, Mississippi. According to the FBI's 1975 estimate, total membership in all Klans is about 2,200. The Knights of the Ku Klux Klan, headed by David Duke of Baton Rouge, Louisiana, and Robert Shelton's United Klans of America are among the largest of a dozen generally competitive Klans located in a number of southern and north central states.[63]

FOREIGN CONNECTIONS

Evidence of an exchange of ideas and information among domestic and foreign terrorist groups emerged during the early spring of 1972, when information filtered into the press about U.S. Weathermen, Irish Republican Army (IRA) gunmen, and terrorists from other groups attending joint summer training sessions at Palestinian commando bases in Jordan.[64] However, since 1969, Castro's Cuba has been the primary foreign connection for domestic terrorists, particularly young U.S. radicals who served in the Venceremos Brigades (VBs). Organization of the VBs was directed by intelligence officers assigned to Cuba's DGI (the General Directorate of Intelligence, Cuba's equivalent of the CIA). Cuba's interest in members of the VBs related to their need to develop future sources of information regarding aspects of political, economic, and military intelligence in the United States.[65] But the Cubans also provided instruction in the use of arms and explosives to VB members, who requested this type of training. WUO leaders Bernardine Dohrn and Mark Rudd (leader of the 1968 Columbia University revolt, who inverted on September 14, 1977, and surrendered to authorities) are venterans of the VBs. After the Weathermen went underground in 1970 (many of them were being sought by the FBI on criminal charges), Cuban intelligence officers were in contact with them from both the Cuban Mission to the UN in New York and the Cuban embassy in Canada.[66]

Czechoslovakia also has a connection to at least two U.S. terrorist groups. Weathermen wanted by authorities for questioning regarding an explosion of a bomb factory in New York City arrived in Cuba and then returned to the United States by way of Czechoslovakia rather than using the regular route through Canada.[67] Eldridge Cleaver, who in 1970 opened the Black Panther Party's international headquarters in Algiers, was photographed and publicly applauded in Czechoslovakia.[68]

While in Africa, Cleaver and his associates visited Peking, Hanoi, and Pyongyand, North Korea, and held conversations with Palestinian guerrilla leaders.[69] Meanwhile, Black Panther Party members in the United States had opened a channel of communication to members of the Front de Liberation du Quebec (FLQ) and planned to meet with a delegation of the Quebec terrorists in a converted barn near Montreal.[70] The activities of the Black Panther Party in North and East Africa, however, were monitored by a select group of agents carefully recruited by the CIA, who were sent to Algeria, Kenya, and Tanzania to keep close watch on the U.S. black radicals.[71]

Connections between the FALN and Cuba, through the aegis of the Armed Commandos of Liberation (CAL), is another example of a connection between a domestic terrorist organization and a foreign government. CAL, an organization of Puerto Rican terrorists who confine their attacks to their home island, issues political communiques, which are publicized in the Cuban government's magazine *The Tricontinental*. Through Eduardo "Pancho" Cruz—a member of the Puerto Rican Socialist Party and of a terrorist group active in New York City during the years 1970-71, known as the Armed Revolutionary Independence Movement (MIRA), CAL is linked to Cuban-trained Filiberto Ojeda Rios, also a member of MIRA. During the early 1970s, over 100 bombing and incendiary attacks or attempts on New York City public buildings and department stores were attributed to associates of MIRA. All of the devices used by the terrorists had distinctly similar characteristics and resembled those handled by the FALN. At the core of the various Puerto Rican revolutionary groups are the leaders who have been trained in Cuba to carry out guerrilla warfare (they were taught sophisticated sabotage techniques and how to create explosive devices).[72]

CONCLUDING REMARKS

Political terrorism is a matter of concern for all residents of the United States, but particularly for the managers of domestic corporations whose personnel and facilities are targeted for attack by terrorists and for law enforcement officials, who are charged with the protection of life and property in U.S. cities. Particularly vulnerable to terrorist manipulation are urban areas, which contain a large multiethnic population. The persistence of this form of violence is attributable, at least in part, to a variety of emotional causes, which the various terrorist groups have identified and linked diabolically, through the instruments of target analysis and armed propaganda, with a campaign advocated by a particular segment of the U.S. population that they seek to exploit.

Although some terrorist groups in the United States contain a few sophisticated and articulate members, they have reduced their conduct of protracted agitation and pamphleteering, which are prerequisites to the development of broad-based popular support and which characterized domestic terrorist operations of the Vietnam era. Instead, terrorists have adopted a cutout style of organization and use secretive means of communication to negate the effectiveness of routine but deliberate and community oriented police patrol operations. Although this style of organization enhances the survival of a small band of agitational terrorists, on the one hand, it serves to inhibit the extension of a terrorist movement, on the other hand.

It has become risky for domestic terrorists to maintain links with a foreign terrorist organization; conversely, it has become equally hazardous for members of terrorist networks from overseas or intelligence agents from hostile governments to exploit existing ties with terrorists in the United States. The probability of such an association being uncovered is quite high and, therefore, must be regarded as an unacceptable risk. Meanwhile, agitational terrorism continues to take its toll in human life and property damage in the United States, and although its perpetrators may be as few as 200 or 300 individuals organized into about a dozen active groups, it necessitates utmost vigilance on the part of all agencies of government responsible for its control and those elements of the private sector that have been previously targeted for attack or calculate their being assaulted in the future.

NOTES

1. Clarence M. Kelley, *Crime In The United States–1976* (Washington, D.C.: Government Printing Office, 1977), pp. 8–9, 77, 84, 105.

2. Robert Reinhold, "Elusive F.A.L.N. Terrorists, Believed 12 in Number Have Bombed Scores of Buildings in Recent Years," New York *Times*, August 4, 1977, p. 36.

3. "Bomb Factory: Accidental Blast Boosts Hunt for F.A.L.N. Terrorists," *Star Ledger* (Newark, N.J.), July 15, 1978, p. 4.

4. "Terrorists Activities Still Pose a Threat to Police," *The Finest* (New Jersey Patrolmen's Benevolent Association) (February 1977): 1.

5. Linda Charlton, "Gunmen Linked to a Moslem Sect Invade Buildings in Washington, Kill 1 and Hold Scores Hostage," New York *Times*, March 10, 1977, p. 1.

6. Peter Kihss, "LaGuardia Blast Yields No Leads in Investigation," New York *Times*, December 31, 1975, p. 1.

7. Robert Rudolph, "Jersey Link Detailed in Slaying of Chilean," *Star Ledger* (Newark, N.J.), June 3, 1978, p. 1.

8. David Binder, "Opponent of Chilean Junta Slain in Washington by Bomb in His Auto," New York *Times*, September 22, 1976, p. 1.

9. Les Ledbetter, "Terrorist Bombs in San Francisco Prompt Concern on Leader's Safety," New York *Times*, February 11, 1977, p. 14.

10. Les Ledbetter, "Coast Bombing Expected to Go on Despite Arrests," New York *Times*, March 24, 1978, p. 7.

11. Federal Bureau of Investigation Bomb Data Program, *Incident Summary for the Month of November, 1976* (Washington, D.C.: FBI, 1976), p. 7, and Federal Bureau of Investigation Bomb Data Program, *Incident Summary for the Month of October, 1976* (Washington, D.C.: FBI, 1976), p. 3.

12. "Underground Documents: Corporate Bloodsuckers," *Counterforce: The Monthly Newsmagazine on Terrorism* (March 1977): 15-16.

13. "Underground Documents: Good Hit, No Pitch," *Counterforce: The Monthly Newsmagazine on Terrorism* (November 1977): 33-34.

14. Frank Kitson, *Low Intensity Operations: Subversion, Insurgency, Peace-Keeping* (Hamden, Conn.: Archon Books, 1974), pp. 33-34.

15. Michael Kramer, "Will Puerto Rican Terrorism Work Here," *New York* (January 1976): 5-6.

16. The Central Command, New World Liberation Front, "We Have No Choice—Struggle Is a Fact of Life," *Sunday News* (New York), August 29, 1976, p. 67.

17. The New World Liberation Front, "Corporate Bloodsuckers," reprinted from *The Urban Guerrilla (TUG)* and appearing in *Counterforce: The Monthly Newsmagazine on Terrorism* (March 1977): 15-16.

18. Ibid.

19. "Jet with 92 Hijacked out of LaGuardia," New York *Times*, September 11, 1976, p. 1.

20. "Alaska Pipeline Back in Operation as Clues Are Sought in Bombing," New York *Times*, February 17, 1978, p. 14.

21. "Pipeline Flow Resumes After Alaska Blast," *Star Ledger* (Newark, N.J.), February 17, 1978, p. 8.

22. "Police Investigate Suspect in Bombing of Pipeline," New York *Times*, February 18, 1978, p. 9.

23. "Alaska Pipeline Back in Operation as Clues Are Sought in Bombing," New York *Times*, February 17, 1978, p. 14.

24. Leonard Le Shack, "Threat to the Alaska Pipeline," *Counterforce: The Monthly Newsmagazine on Terrorism* (June 1977): 10-12.

25. Ibid.

26. "Eskimos, 'United' by Alaska Meeting, to Press Claims," New York *Times*, June 28, 1977, p. 2.

27. Charles Mohr, "Antinuclear Drives: Diffuse But Effective," New York *Times*, June 24, 1978, p. 6.

28. Ibid.

29. Phillip Shabecoff, "New Battles Over Endangered Species," New York *Times Magazine,* June 4, 1978, pp. 39-44.

30. Mohr, "Antinuclear Drives: Diffuse But Effective."

31. Andrew H. Malcolm, "Protestors in Japan Storm New Airport, Ravage Control Unit," New York *Times*, March 27, 1978, p. 1.

32. "Japan Delays Debut of Protest-torn Airport," *Star Ledger* (Newark, N.J.), March 28, 1978, p. 4.

33. John A. Hoagland, "Changing Patterns of Insurgency and American Response," in *Revolutionary War—Western Response*, ed. David S. Sullivan and Martin S. Sattler (New York: Columbia University Press, 1971), p. 141.

34. Raymond M. Momboisse, *Riots, Revolts and Insurrections* (Springfield, Ill.: Charles C. Thomas, 1970), p. 283.

35. John B. Wolf, "Urban Terrorist Operations," *The Police Journal* (October-December 1976): 279.

36. "Frightened People and Frustrated Police," *U.S. News and World Report* (May 4, 1974): 37-38.

37. Carlos Marighella, *Minimanual of the Urban Guerrilla* (Havana: Tricontinental, January-February 1970), p. 22.

38. Frantz Fanon, *The Wretched Of The Earth* (New York: Grove Press, 1968), pp. 107-47.

39. Everett M. Rogers and Rekha Agarwala Rogers, *Communication in Organizations* (New York: The Free Press, 1976), pp. 135–38.

40. Details on the Miami explosion are reported in "U.S. Seeks the Return of Accused Bomber," New York *Times*, January 25, 1976, p. 38. The Croatian bomb episode is described by Max H. Seigel in "Croatian Hijacking Leader Takes Full Blame for Seizure and Bomb," New York *Times*, September 18, 1976, p. 12.

41. "F.A.L.N. Terrorists," *Herald of Freedom* (Zarephath, N.J.), June 17, 1977, p. 4.

42. Arnold H. Lubasch, "Woman Is Charged in F.A.L.N. Blast," New York *Times*, September 8, 1977, p. 1.

43. "'Bomb Factory' Site Combed," *Star Ledger* (Newark, N.J.), November 7, 1976, p. 4.

44. Mary Breasted, "3-Year Inquiry Threads Together Evidence, on F.A.L.N. Terrorism," New York *Times*, April 17, 1977, p. 1.

45. George Carpozi, Jr., "Fear F.A.L.N. May Kill Bomb Factory Victim," New York *Post*, July 14, 1978, p. 7.

46. Cathy Booth, "Blast Termed F.A.L.N. Setback," *Star Ledger* (Newark, N.J.), July 14, 1978, p. 55.

47. "New Violence Stalled by Bomb Factory Blast," *Daily Journal* (Elizabeth, N.J.), July 14, 1978, p. 6.

48. Anthony Bouza, *Police Intelligence: The Operation of an Investigative Unit* (New York: AMS Press, 1976), pp. 1–13.

49. Assada Shakur (aka Jo Anne Chesimard), a letter entitled "To My People" (Morristown Jail, Morristown, N.J.), July 6, 1973.

50. Walter H. Waggoner, "Chesimard Murder Trial Opens in New Brunswick," New York *Times*, February 16, 1977, p. B2.

51. "Underground Documents: Publications Dwindle," *Counterforce: The Monthly Newsmagazine on Terrorism* (June 1977): 21.

52. "On Top Of It All, More Bombings," New York *Times*, August 7, 1977, sec. 4, p. 1.

53. John Kifner, "Weather Underground Splits Up Over Plan to Come into the Open," New York *Times*, November 18, 1976, p. 12, and Jonathan Wolman, "Surrender Plan May Have Split Radicals," *Huntsville Times*, January 16, 1977, p. 2.

54. "Excerpts from the Political Statement of the Weather Underground PRAIRIE FIRE," in *Skeptic: The Forum For Contemporary History* (January/February 1976): 30–33.

55. "5 Held in Plot to Bomb California Aide's Office," New York *Times*, November 21, 1977, p. 6.

56. "Cuban Extremists in U.S., a Growing Terror Threat," *U.S. News and World Report* (December 6, 1976): 29–32; David Binder, "Some Exiles Are Still at War With Castro," New York *Times*, October 24, 1976, p. 3; and Juan de Onis, "Venezuela Depicts Intrigue among Exiles in Crash of Cuban Plane," New York *Times*, October 26, 1976, p. 4.

57. Ibid.

58. Ibid.

59. Robert Rudolph, "Jersey Link Detailed in Slaying of Chilean," *Star Ledger*, (Newark, N.J.), June 3, 1978, p. 1, and "F.B.I. Given Details in Letelier Killing," New York *Times*, June 3, 1978, p. 1.

60. "Airline Cancels Service to Cuba After Bombing," New York *Times*, May 26, 1977, p. 18.

61. The Honorable Elijah Muhammad, Messenger of Islam, "What The Muslims Believe," *Muhammad Speaks* (February 15, 1975): 24, and Paul Delany, "Black Muslims, Amid Changes, Consider Sale of Much Property," New York *Times*, February 26, 1976, p. 14.

62. Judith Cummings, "Black Muslim Seeks to Change Movement," New York *Times*, March 19, 1978, p. 37.

63. Wayne King, "Black Protest Is Monitored by Klan as a Mississippi Boycott Continues," New York *Times*, July 9, 1978, p. 26, and Wayne King, "More Than a Dozen Ku Klux Klan Factions Compete for Membership and Feud Over Predominance," New York *Times*, July 11, 1978, p. 14.

64. "The Terrorist International," *Newsweek* (September 18, 1972): 33–34.

65. Nicholas M. Horrock, "F.B.I. Asserts Cuba Aided Weathermen," New York *Times*, October 9, 1978, p. 1.

66. Ibid.

67. Ibid.

68. W. Cleon Skousen, "The Police Face a Cultural Crisis: The Black Panthers," *Law and Order* (June 1970): 9.

69. Seymour M. Hersh, "C.I.A. Reportedly Recruited Blacks for Surveillance of Panther Party," New York *Times*, March 17, 1978, p. 3.

70. Robert Trumbull, "Canada Says the Mounted Police Illegally Opened Mail from '54 on," New York *Times*, November 10, 1977, p. 1.

71. Hersh, "C.I.A. Reportedly Recruited Blacks for Surveillance of Panther Party."

72. U.S., Congress, House, Committee on Internal Security, 93rd Cong., 2d sess., *Terrorism, A Staff Study* (Washington, D.C.: Government Printing Office, 1974), pp. 162–63, and "F.A.L.N. Terrorists."

3

INTERNATIONAL NETWORK OF
TERRORIST MOVEMENTS

Yonah Alexander
Robert A. Kilmarx

Terrorism, the threatened and actual resort to ideological and political violence for the purpose of achieving limited or broad and imaginary or realistic goals, has become a permanent fixture of contemporary life.[1] Recognizing the dangers of terrorism, such as the safety of individuals, the pace of economic development, the acceptance of the role of law, the expansion of democracy, and the stability of the state system, nations have pursued various approaches in their opposition to terrorism.[2] Non-Communist countries spend billions of dollars annually in order to improve security. Increased protection is provided for ordinary citizens and civilian facilities. Special defensive measures have been developed to protect ambassadors and government officials. Over a dozen nations have set up special commando units to fight terrorists and rescue hostages. Multinational corporation executives receive instructions for protecting themselves and their families, and the private sector has spent millions of dollars to safeguard its domestic and overseas investments.[3]

But despite national and international efforts to control the dangers of terrorism, the level of nonstate violence remains high. The reasons for these conditions are diverse, but include at least ten factors: disagreement about who is a terrorist, lack of understanding of the causes of terrorism, the role of the media, the politicization of religion, double standards of morality, loss of resolve by governments, weak punishment of terrorists, flouting of world law, the support of terrorism by some states, and the existence of an international network of terrorism.[4]

While all these factors deserve serious consideration, this chapter will focus only on the last two, because of their relevance to the risk-perceptions of the business community.

It is evident that while the resort to ideological and political violence is centuries old, there has been a marked rise in terrorism across national lines in the past decade.[5] This expression of international extralegal violence has been undertaken primarily by two types of substate groups: first, by ideologically motivated movements in Third World countries and their imitators in the Western industrialized societies, and, second, by ethnically based or separatist groups in both developed and developing countries.*

The coincidence of time and the formation of these types of terrorist bodies suggest the possibility of common origins, common influences, or common contributing factors. For instance, unique political circumstances existed in the turbulent 1960s: the failure of the rural guerrilla movements in Latin America and the resort to urban guerrilla warfare and terrorism, the defeat of the Arbas in the June 1967 War and the subsequent rise of Palestinian terrorism, the Vietnam War and the widespread demonstrations against it, and the Paris students' revolt of 1968.[6]

The importance of technological factors in promoting international terrorism should also be recognized. Indeed, modern technology, particularly increasingly inexpensive and convenient air travel and the development of modern communications, has provided terrorist groups with a facility that did not exist in the past, that is, intensified interconnection among them across national boundaries. Collaboration among ideologically linked bodies and even among those without a common philosophy or political interest has increased rapidly and substantially.[7] Significantly, the strategy of terrorism does not prescribe instant victories over established regimes or adversaries. On the contrary, the struggle for fundamental political, economic, and social change is seen as complicated and protracted. Terrorist groups, by their very nature, are too small and too weak to achieve an upper hand in an open struggle for sheer power.

Because of this realization, many subnational movements have developed a "comradeship" disposition in their struggle against "imperialism," "capitalism," "international Zionism," and for the "liberation" of a people for independence. It is this shared ideology and commitment to revolutionary comradeship that often expresses itself in the exchange of aid and comfort among different terrorist groups. As Ulrike Meinhof's "Manifesto" clearly rationalized: "We must learn from the revolutionary movements of the world—the Vietcong, the Palestine Liberation Front, the Tupamaros, the Black Panthers."[8] Thus, most of the terrorist groups, with few exceptions, did not evolve directly from their own national antecedents but, rather, designed their organizational models and adopted their terrorist tactics from foreign sources, which did not always fit local circumstances. Although these models were foreign transplants, various ter-

---

*These are obviously terrorist groups that do not fit this classification. A case in point is Ananda Marg, an Indian religious terrorist group. It has an international membership with transnational support apparatus. It has conducted attacks on Indian diplomats on several continents.

rorist movements accepted them for practical purposes. For instance, many of the nationalist or separatist groups adopted Marxist ideologies as a "flag of convenience." They rationalized that Marxism provides a model for revolution against the state, denies the legal authority of the government, establishes a successful historical example of a revolution, grants some sort of respectable international status, affords a sense of affinity with other revolutionary movements, and guarantees some assurance of direct and indirect support by like-minded groups and Socialist states. With the adoption of a Marxist philosophy, however, some of these terrorist movements fall victim to internal ideological debate, division, and conflict emanating from different interpretations of ideology.[9]

Notwithstanding the lack of connectedness with their own historical revolutionary struggles and their reliance on foreign models of ideologies, organizational structures, and modi operandi, the fact remains that international linkages among various terrorist groups are profound on both a regional and global level.*

Interconnections among Castroite, Trotskyite, Peronist, and other opposition forces in Latin America has occurred over the years. The rationale behind this relationship was explained by a Montenero leader:[10] "We must unite at the continental level to free ourselves from the yoke of Yankee imperialism and the native oligarchies."[11]

This rhetoric has been translated into action. Thus, operations by one terrorist group in support of another in a foreign country have been common. For instance, in May 1970, a Tupamero was arrested in Santiago with 880 gold coins stolen from a Uraguayan businessman.[12] These coins apparently were intended for the Chilean Movement of the Revolutionary Left (MIR).[13] Moreover, the MIR, the Argentinian People's Revolutionary Army (ERP),† the National Liberation Army of Bolivia,‡ and the Tupamaro guerrillas of Uraguay were cooperating to the extent of being "prepared to do combat under a joint command." A declaration by the four groups in 1974 pledged to overthrow "imperialist-capitalist reaction, to annihilate counter revolutionary armies, expel

---

*Linkages between terrorist movements operating within one country also exist. For instance, the pro-Soviet Revolutionary Armed Forces of Columbia (FARC) and the pro-Castro National Liberation Army (ELN) have recently agreed on the urgent need for a coordinated plan of action and other strategic tactics in the country (reported by Bogota Cadena Radical Super, in Spanish, 1100, GMT, July 10, 1978).

†ERP was founded in 1970 at the Fifth Congress of the Trotskyite Workers' Revolutionary Party. It still remains a significant force in Argentine politics. See Brian Crozier, ed., *Annual of Power and Conflict, 1976–1977: A Survey of Political Violence and International Influence* (London: Institute for the Study of Conflict, 1977).

‡The National Liberation Army of Bolivia was originally set up by Ché Guevara. See Brian Crozier, ed., *Annual of Power and Conflict, 1976–1977: A Survey of Political Violence and International Influence* (London: Institute for the Study of Conflict, 1977).

Yankee and European imperialism from Latin American soil, country by country, and initiate the construction of socialism in each of our countries." Also, the Argentinian, Bolivian, Uraguayan, and Chilean terrorist groups set up a "Revolutionary Coordination Board" to finance "a new stage of military development," establish rural guerrilla movements to mobilize and organize the masses, and complement the operations of the existing guerrilla units.[14]

Other regional collaboration in the western hemisphere exists in Central America.[15] Apparently, some of the terrorist groups in El Salvador, Guatamala, and Nicaragua that have conducted kidnappings, bank robberies, and other profitable activities in the name of "higher" ideological and political principles have also tended to cooperate logistically and operationally.[16]

There are also instances of interconnectedness among U.S. terrorist groups and their counterparts in Latin America. For example, it is clear that Ché Guevara's *Guerrilla Warfare* and Carlos Marighella's *Minimanual of the Urban Guerrilla* have had an impact on the thinking of U.S. terrorists. The SLA patterned its violence according to these revolutionary models.[17] Also, many political extremists have traveled to Cuba for indoctrination and training. Others bombed Latin American diplomatic missions in the United States for the sake of the "oppressed" continent.

Interestingly, foreign terrorists located in the United States, as well as their U.S. recruits, have collaborated with Latin American comrades. A case in point is the Command of United Revolutionary Organizations (CORU), an anti-Castro umbrella structure, which is comprised of the Cuban Action, the Cuban National Liberation Front, the Bay of Pigs Veteran's Association, the April 17th Movement, and the National Cuban Movement.[18] These exile groups are based in Miami, the Dominican Republic, Nicaragua, and Venezuela. CORU is allegedly responsible for the murder of 73 persons who died in the October 6, 1976, explosion of a Cuban passenger jet following takeoff from the island of Barbados.[19] According to intelligence sources, some of the Cuban groups "use Dade County as a base for international terrorism against allied governments of Cuba, Cuban shipping, Communists, purported Communists and individuals who take a stand against their terrorist-type tactics."[20] Targets also include "capitalist" firms. For instance, on May 25, 1977, an anti-Castro group claimed credit for a bomb explosion at the Mackey International Airlines offices in Fort Lauderdale. The Miami-based company subsequently canceled its plans to operate regular flights to Cuba.[21]

Also, a 1978 report related that the 23rd September Communist League in Mexico (which had recently absorbed about a dozen guerrilla groups)[22] had plans to enlist radical Mexican-Americans with military experience. These recruits would assist the League to overthrow the existing Mexican government and to annex much of the southwestern United States.[23] Although this alleged scheme was rather unrealistic, the fact remains that crossnational terrorist activities continue to be considered.

Regional Contacts for moral, logistical, and operational support also exist in Europe. The IRA,[24] for example, has cooperated in arms deals with the Basque Fatherland and Liberty Movement (ETA) via East Germany.[25] There are parallels between the modus operandi of the two groups. Both movements maintain links with France's Front for the Liberation of Britanny (FLB).[26] The IRA also developed relations with the Free Welsh Army and German and Italian extremists.[27]

The ETA, for its part, has connections with several French anarchist groups, especially the Group of International Revolutionary Action (GARI).[28] Both groups had collaborated in arms smuggling, attacks against business targets (including the shooting of the Paris manager of the Spanish Bank of Bilboa and the Iberia Airlines office in Brussels), and abortive attempts to blow up trains running between France and Spain in 1973 and 1974.

Some contacts have developed among Swiss anarchist groups and German and Italian terrorists. For instance, on March 20, 1975, members of a Swiss group, which included a number of West German nationals, were apprehended in Zurich. This movement was responsible for the thefts from depots of the Swiss army. Some of the stolen explosives were found in terrorist safe houses in Germany and Italy.[29]

Finally, a report alleges that "a kidnapping plan has been devised by a group of international extremists composed of Portuguese, Spanish and Italian nationals who are preparing to start a series of violent actions in Portugal."[30]

While the foregoing examples of regional cooperation among various terrorist groups in the Americas and Europe are ample evidence to suggest the existence of some sort of crossnational "comradeship," it has become increasingly clear that the major global network of terrorism consists of some 30 terrorist movements in the Middle East, Asia, Africa, Europe, and North and South America. It includes, inter alia: Al Fatah; the Popular Front for the Liberation of Palestine (PELP); the Popular Front for the Liberation of Palestine-General Command (PELP-GP); the Saika; the Democratic Front for the Liberation of Palestine (DELP); the Arab Liberation Front (ALF); the Palestine Liberation Front (PLF); the Black June; Chad's Frolinat; the Eritrean Liberation Front; South African People's Organization (SWAPO); the Oman and Persian Gulf Liberation Front; the Popular Army of Turkey; the Iranian National Front; the Japanese Red Army (JRA); the Baader-Meinhof group (also known as Baader-Meinhof gang and Red Army Faction); the Italian Red Brigades; the IRA; the British Revolutionary Party; the Dutch Red Help; the ETA; Swiss revolutionaries; Scandinavian extremists; and various Latin American movements.[31]

The Palestinian Movement,* particularly the PELF,† through a framework known as the Organization of the Arab Armed Struggle (headed by Wadi Haddad),‡

---

*The Palestinian movement represents the Palestinian guerrillas, or the Palestine Liberation Organization (PLO). It serves as an umbrella organization for eight guerrilla became the catalyst and communications link with other revolutionary forces throughout the world, bringing them together into a collaboration and operational network of violence. One expression of this cooperation is through bilateral relationships. For example, in 1971, Yasser Arafat held meetings with a representative of the Central Command of the Eritrean National Front. More recently, in July 1978, Abu Hatim, Fatah's official in charge of foreign relations, met with a delegation from the Higher Command of the Eritrean revolutionary movements. (These movements consist of the Eritrean Liberation Front Revolutionary Council [ELF-RC] and the Popular Front for the Liberation of Eritrea [PFLE].) The clandestine "Voice of Palestine," reporting on this meeting, asserted that both the Palestinian and Eritrean "revolutions fight in the same trench and are strategic allies against imperialism, Zionism, reaction and backwardness."[32]

During the same year, other bilateral links were established between Palestinian and Latin American groups. A transnational terrorist agreement was signed between the Democratic Front for the Liberation of Palestine (DELP) and Nicaragua's Sandinist National Liberation Front (FSLN).* These movements joined in a "common cause" to fight Israel, "United States imperialism," and other anti-Communist governments in Latin America.[33] The Palestine Liberation Organization (PLO) and FSLN also signed a joint communique in Mexico City in which they stressed the bonds of solidarity that existed between them.[34] Finally, a delegation representing the Argentine Monteneros met with Fatah commanders in Damascus to review their joint cooperation efforts.[35] Moreover, the visitors were given a tour of military installations and training camps in Lebanon.[36]

Aside from bilateral relationships between terrorist groups located in different regions of the world, multilateral meetings have been held over the years

---

groups, including small ones that oppose any negotiated settlement of the Middle East conflict. See David Pryce-Jones, *The Face of Defeat: Palestinian Refugees and Guerrillas* (London: Weidenfeld and Nicolson, 1972), and A. W. Kawwali, *Palestine, A Modern History* (London: Croom Helm, 1978).

†The PFLP crystalized under the leadership of George Habash in November 1967. This Marxist-Leninist group consists of 1,000 to 1,500 members. It rejects a peaceful settlement in the Middle East. See New York *Times*, February 21, 1978.

‡Wadi Haddad was the mastermind behind the most notorious international terrorist attacks during the past decade, including the Organization of Petroleum Exporting Countries (OPEC) raid in 1975 and the Entebbe operation in 1976. He died on March 28, 1978. Haddad was eulogized by George Habash, who described him as one of the greatest fighters on behalf of the Arab cause.

*DFLP is a Marxist-Maoist group that split from PFLP in 1969. It is led by Nayef Hawatmeh, who is close to Syria. The membership is about 1,500 people (New York *Times*, February 21, 1978). FSLN is dedicated to the overthrow of the Samoza dictatorship in Nicaragua.

as well. For example, in the spring of 1970, representatives of a dozen groups met at a refugee camp in Lebanon in a PFLP-organized conference to explore the possibilities of collaboration across national lines. Since that initial meeting, several other gatherings have either occurred or have been planned. For example, in July 1974, the IRA sponsored an "Anti-Imperialist Festival" in Dublin and Belfast. Among the participants were Palestinians, separatists movements, and European Trotskyites. More recently, a Danish "League Against Imperialism" planned a "solidarity" conference with participation by a number of terrorist organizations, including the Fatah and the PFLP. Also invited to this meeting were the Southeast Asia Committee from Sweden; the Palestine Front and the Communist Workers Association from Norway; and the Palestinian Workers Union, the Arhus Middle East group, the Left Socialists, the Socialists' League, and the Communist League from Denmark.[37]

It is clear that these and other multilateral and bilateral meetings among various terrorist groups and their supporters have strengthened informal and formal linkages that facilitate an accessible machinery for violence on the national, regional, and global level. This network maintains a service industry in Europe that supplies terrorist needs from clandestine centers in Algeria, Iraq, Lebanon, Libya, South Yemen, and Syria. There are essentially seven levels of collaboration among them: financial support, training, supply of combat material, organizational support, attacks by proxy, coordinated attacks, and joint operations.

The following discussion describes in some detail the nature of such transnational interconnections.

FINANCIAL SUPPORT

The Palestinian movement has provided substantial assistance for various revolutionary organizations, such as leftist terrorist cells in Iran,[38] the Eritrean Liberation Front,[39] and the JRA.* Other recipients have included underground groups in Chad, Ireland, Panama, the Phillipines, Sardinia and Corsica, and Thailand, to name a few.[40]

The main source of income for the Palestinian groups emanates from certain Arab states. In fact, following the Arab summit conference in Rabat in December 1969, it was reported that

the Arab Kings and Presidents have decided to allocate £26 million to meet the financial commitments of the Palestine Liberation

---

*Funding was provided by the PFLP for the JRA operation at The Hague, September 13, 1974.

Organization in the coming year, including £12 million for the support of the Palestine revolution and £11 million for the support of citizens' resistance in the occupied territory. It has been learned that Libya has decided to contribute 25! to the Palestine revolution budget.[41]

Libya, which considers itself to be "the only moral government in the world" and therefore stands "only for helping oppressed people, wherever they are," alone has allocated some $73 million directly to terrorist groups in recent years.[42] For instance, according to Tehran sources, Libya, in 1976, had already disbursed $100,000 to Iranian terrorists and planned to allocate an additional $100,000 every three months.[43] The Libyan contribution obviously increased dramatically during the 1978-79 revolutionary struggle.[44]

Also, special bonuses have been offered by Libya to terrorist organizations for the successful completion of operations. For the murder of the 11 Israeli athletes in Munich in September 1972, some $5 million was donated. Between $1 million and $2 million was paid by Mo'ammar el-Qadhafi, the Libyan chief of state, to the "international jackel," "Carlos" (Ilich Ramirez-Sanchez) for the kidnapping of Saudi Arabian Oil Minister Sheikh Yamani and other delegates in the Organization of Petroleum Exporting Countries (OPEC) raid in December 1975.* Another participant in the operation, Hans Joachim Klein, the German terrorist, reportedly collected some $100,000 for his role. According to Egyptian sources, el-Qadhafi offered $16 million to the PFLP for the assassination of President Anwar Sadat.[45] More recently, a Norwegian terrorist received $1,000 from a terrorist organization supported by Libya as a fee for planting explosives in Jerusalem.[46]

Paradoxically, a substantial portion of financial aid to Palestinian groups is provided by moderate and antirevolutionary regimes, namely, those of Saudi Arabia, Kuwait, and some oil sheikhdoms of the Persian Gulf. These countries, under the threat of terrorist activities in their own lands, are therefore indirectly responsible for ideological and political violence elsewhere. Saudi Arabia, for example, is contributing $35 million to the Arab League's budget of $44 million for the PLO.[47] Indeed, special taxes are levied for the Palestinian movements as a whole, and government officials are called upon to contribute 5 percent of their salaries for the cause.

Aside from the direct financial support given by Arab states, Middle East groups have also obtained funds from contributions made by Palestinians living inside and outside of the region, blackmail activities (extortion and protection),

---

*Carlos gained attention as the "world's most wanted terrorist." A Venezuelan by birth, he joined the PFLP in 1970. For details, see Dennis Eisenberg and Eli Landau, *Carlos: Terror International* (London: Transworld, 1976).

kidnappings, hijackings, legitimate investments, and drug-smuggling opera-tions.[48] Regarding the latter source, it has been reported as early as 1970 that several Palestinian groups purchased Chinese and Soviet arms with funds secured by smuggling large quantities of hashish to the United States through Canada.[49] In June 1978, members of a drug ring were convicted in Great Britain for their role in a similar activity. It was discovered that cannabis grown in Palestinian camps in northern Lebanon was smuggled into Syria, Turkey, Bulgaria, and Yugoslavia in foreign meat trucks, broken up into smaller loads, and hidden in cars and vans. Other Lebanese hashish was shipped out of Cyprus to Europe. Cash for the initial purchase of the drugs from a Syrian wholesaler in Sofia was provided by a large-scale car-stealing racket in Great Britain. The money earned from the sale of the drugs in various European cities was used for the purchase of arms in Eastern Europe. These weapons, which were shipped back to the Mid-dle East along the Sofia trail, were hidden in the same compartments that held the hashish on the way out.[50]

To be sure, funds available to Palestinian groups and provided to non-Arab revolutionaries have not been the only shared source of money for terrorist operations. Movements outside the Middle East have also been generous with their foreign comrades. Terrorist groups in Argentina provide a case in point. They have collected hundreds of millions of dollars in the past several years, primarily from ransoms for kidnapped businessmen.[51] Some of that cash has been channeled to terrorist groups outside the country. According to one re-port, more than $2 million was traced to Europe, where it was spent by Chilean leftists who fled after the fall of President Salvador Allende in 1973.[52]

TRAINING

The majority of training camps available to terrorist groups are in the Mid-dle East. They have been located at different times in Algeria, Iraq, Jordan, Lebanon, Libya, and South Yemen. Some camps are controlled by governments and others by various PLO groups, particularly Fatah and PFLP. Libya, for ex-ample, administers camps where many hundreds of terrorists annually undergo training, including the use of small arms and antiaircraft missiles. It also provides naval and flight courses for revolutionaries. Libya often offers training in the techniques of executing specific terrorist operations abroad. For very advanced training, Libya sends her own and other volunteers to Syria and Algeria.

In general, thousands of Arab and foreign terrorists from some 15 coun-tries have passed through Middle Eastern camps. Carlos, who joined the PFLP after being recruited in 1970, spent his indoctrination and training in a Jordanian camp. He later sent other European and Latin American comrades to the Arab countries for training in sabotage, hijacking, and assassination.

Many non-Arab revolutionaires from the region have been trained by Palestinian groups. For instance, in 1972, Turkish authorities seized 14 nationals in a boat who were en route to Turkey after completing training in Syria. The following year, an Israeli army unit detained a Turkish terrorist in a military operation at Neharral Berad, a Fatah training camp. In another Israeli raid on two training camps in Lebanon, nine Turkish terrorists were killed. They had been trained to carry out operations against Israeli and Turkish targets.[53]

Similarly, practical training in the use of arms was also given to Iranian terrorists. Reporting on this linkage, a Lebanese newspaper stated:

> This aid first began in 1968, when a contingent of the Iranian revolutionary movement left Iran for training with the resistance movement. After their return to Iran, they began to train other members. Owing to the direct influence of the armed Palestinian struggle, revolutionary groups began to study armed struggle and to carry out armed actions inside Iran.[54]

Also, 18 members of the Cypriote Liberation Army (CLA) went to Lebanon for tactical training by some Palestinians in preparation for "guerrilla warfare" against Turkish occupation forces.[55]

Among Asian terrorists, the JRA, who developed links with the Palestinians in 1968, began receiving training at PFLP bases in Jordan in 1970. It was reported that the PFLP undertook the JRA training at the time because it was impossible for them to undergo such training in Japan.[56] Ukudaira, Yassouda, and Okamoto, members of the JRA who participated in the Lod operation in May 1972 on behalf of the PFLP, were trained in Lebanon.[57] More recently, the Japanese hijackers in Dacca in September 1978 were reportedly trained outside Beirut and Baghdad.[58] Likewise, European terrorists underwent training in the Middle East. Members of the Baader-Meinhof group, as well as other German revolutionaries, began to receive training in 1970 and 1971 at Fatah camps in Lebanon and Syria. Others were trained by the PFLP in South Yemen, including Peter Jugen Boock and Sieglinde Gudrun Hofmann, who were arrested and later released by Yugoslav police. These terrorists are believed to have participated in the shooting in July 1977 of Jurgen Pronto, chairman of the Dresdner Bank of Frankfurt.[59]

Italian terrorists, too, have been trained in the Middle East. A recent report relates that in the course of an investigation of arrested Red Brigade terrorists, the police found a map of Lebanon, showing the location of a terrorist training camp. Besides geographical details, the map contained information on who to contact upon arrival, as well as other instructions. On the back of the map was written a Libyan address.[60]

Other Europeans trained in the region have been Irish, Dutch, and Norwegian terrorists. For instance, IRA sent comrades to train in South Yemen (summer 1976) and in southern Lebanon (summer 1978).[61] Several members of the Dutch Red Help were trained at a PFLP camp in South Yemen (summer 1976) in preparation for perpetrating a series of attacks in Europe. Between 25 and 40 Norwegians were trained as terrorists by Palestinian groups in Lebanon (summer 1978).[62]

According to some reports, several hundred U.S. citizens and residents of Arab descent have passed through training camps in the Middle East. They then have returned to the United States "apparently to establish new contacts and perhaps to study various cities and airports for future operations."[63]

Other reports also indicate that terrorists are being trained outside the Middle East. "Guerrillas" have been sent to training camps in the Soviet Union and other Communist bloc countries, such as Bulgaria, China, Cuba, East Germany, North Korea, and Vietnam.[64] Recently, Czechoslovakia and Hungary have agreed to provide training to Palestinians who have joined the PLO since the end of the Lebanese civil war. During the summer of 1978, some 32 Palestinian pilots and 60 mechanics returned from advanced courses in Eastern European countries. Interestingly, Cuba, which provides terrorist training on the island, has also sent its advisors to the Middle East and Africa. For instance, Cubans were engaged in training members of the PLO in Lebanon[65] and Basque ETA separatists in Algeria.[66]

SUPPLY OF COMBAT MATERIAL

During the 1960s, terrorist groups had limited and often poor combat material. In the past five years, however, modern military equipment, including Kalachnikovs, Katyushas, Dutch machine guns, portable antitank launchers of the RPG-7 type, and SA-7 antiaircraft missiles, have reached underground movements. Although the major source of these weapons is Communist countries, the equipment is actually procured through various Arab countries and the Palestinian movement. For instance, in 1975, Libya signed a $2 billion arms deal with the Soviet Union. Some of these weapons reach terrorist groups with the direct involvement of Tripoli. According to documents found in a terrorist hideout in Tehran, Libya smuggled machine guns and hand grenades to Iran's desolate Persian Gulf coast for the use of opposition forces in the country.[67]

Frequently, Palestinian groups serve as intermediaries in the supply of weapons. On December 13, 1973, two Arabs, an Algerian, and ten terrorists belonging to the Turkish Popular Liberation Army were arrested in Paris. During the raid, the French police confiscated guns, grenades, letter-bombs, booby-trapped books, and plastic explosives. This equipment had been smuggled in from the Middle East by the PFLP, which, with Turkish terrorists' assistance, planned to attack the embassy of Israel in Paris, as well as other targets.[68]

Also, it has been reported that in November 1977, five tons of PLO hardware-mortars, rocket launchers, automatic weapons, and explosives were intercepted in Belgium. The arms were hidden in electrical transformers that were en route from Cyprus to the Irish Republic for the use of the IRA. Early in 1978, the IRA received a new supply of weapons from the Middle East, including a half dozen U.S. M-60 machine guns and explosives. This fresh equipment enabled the IRA to initiate a new offensive in the country.[69] During the same year, the Argentine Monteneros received Soviet-made RPG-7 rockets from Palestinian guerrillas.[70] Moreover, the weapons used by members of the Red Brigades in the kidnappings of Moro in March 1978 were comprised of a Czech Nagent pistol and an "unusual" Soviet machine gun.[71]

To be sure, the flow of military supply is reciprocal. The Baader-Meinhof group gave some M26 hand grenades stolen from a U.S. military depot in West Germany to the JRA and to Carlos. These hand grenades were used by the Japanese in a raid on the French Embassy in The Hague in September 1974 and by Carlos in an attack on a Paris "drugstore" during the same month. Some of these grenades and other weapons were stored by Carlos in his Latin Quarter Paris apartment, as well as in a villa outside the French capital, which was rented by the PFLP, the Turkish terrorists, and an Algerian leftist group. Both underground hideouts were subsequently uncovered by the French police.[72]

Similarly, during the 1975 attack on the West German embassy in Stockholm, members of the Red Army faction used weapons provided by an Italian woman terrorist who had stolen them from a Swiss national armory. Other stolen arms were discovered in terrorist hideouts in West Germany and Spain.[73] Finally, the IRA obtained three sets of U.S. electronic night vision binoculars that could detect infrared ray equipment used by the British army in after-dark surveillance. These binoculars were reported to have been stolen during a 1978 raid in West Germany by "sympathizers."[74]

ORGANIZATIONAL SUPPORT

Organizational support, including communication and propaganda, forging of documents, and providing places of refuge, is another dimension of the international network of terrorist groups. They communicate with each other frequently and as the need arises. For example, on May 11, 1972, two days after the hijacking of a Sabena aircraft, Arafat received a cable from the Eritrean Liberation Front in which the "front expressed its condolences for the three Fedayeen killed by the bullets of the Zionist at Lod Airport."[75] Some of the movements also provide assistance in the field of propaganda. A case in point is the United Liberation Front for a New Algeria (FLUNA).* It organized a series

---

*FLUNA is composed of Harkis (pro-French Algerians) and the Democratic National Council of the Armed Forces of the National's People's Army. These groups challenge the authority of the government of Algeria.

of press conferences in which African, Arab, Asiatic, and Latin American groups described their "liberation struggles."[76]

Often, countries supporting guerrillas have provided similar assistance. A delegation from the Argentine Monteneros gave a press conference to the national news media of Mozambique on March 31, 1978. A spokesman expressed their support for the struggle of the Rhodesian Patriotic Front, Polisario, the Revolutionary Front for the Independence of East Timor, and the PLO.[77] Also, in October 1978, a series of radio broadcasts on behalf of SWAPO were carried by Dar es Salaam, Luanda, Lusaka, and Brazzaville. These communications stressed SWAPO's Marxist commitment to the control of economic interests and "armed struggle" for achieving that goal.[78] Finally, during the same year, Iran's Islamic Liberation Movement, the prime organizer of resistance to the shah, opened an information center in Beirut.[79]

Another dimension of organizational support is the forging of documents. The PFLP maintains a sophisticated workshop for the forging of documents, and it is likely that its international terrorist affiliates also make use of this facility. The Palestinian terrorists also utilize documents stolen by their sister terrorist organizations. A Japanese courier who was detained in Paris on July 26, 1974, upon his arrival from Beirut had in his possession a quantity of forged passports and documents. Again, when some international network hideouts were discovered in France in December 1973 and June 1975, laboratories for forgeries and a large number of documents, including passports, driving licenses, seals, official visas of various countries, and forged flight alteration notices for airline tickets, were found. The forged or stolen passports were of the following countries: Ecuador, Chile, Peru, Pakistan, West Germany, the United States, and Venezuela. It thus appears as if the terrorists can obtain official documents of almost any state in the world.

Indeed, 14 Palestinians carrying Latin American passports were arrested in Rabat, Morocco, for a conspiracy by Al Fatah to assassinate participants at the Arab Summit Conference.[80] In 1975, an Iranian terrorist seized in an attack on a Tel Aviv cinema had in his possession a forged British passport. The Iranian connection is also seen in a recent incident. On July 16, 1978, a West German terrorist suspect, Kristina Bersten, was arrested at the U.S.-Canadian border. She was carrying a false Iranian passport, one of several stolen by radical Iranian students when they occupied the Iranian consulate in Geneva in June 1976.[81]

A third form of organizational support is the providing of refuge havens for foreign terrorists released from prison or escaping from an executed attack. It is evident that some Arab countries have offered this type of assistance. The five German anarchists released in Germany following the kidnapping of Peter Lorenz, the candidate for the mayor of West Berlin, were taken to South Yemen, where they were granted asylum. They later participated in attacks perpetrated by Hadad's terrorist organization. Also, in an Orly Airport attack in 1975, Palestinian terrorists took ten hostages from among innocent passengers, demanding and obtaining an escape plane. The government of Iraq gave the escape aircraft permission to land, and, after demonstratively arresting the terrorists, released them clandestinely and allowed them to join the camps of the PFLP in Lebanon.

Similarly, the five members of the JRA who participated in the raid of the U.S. embassy at Kuala Lumpur in August 1975 found refuge in Libya, together with five of their comrades who were released from prison in Japan as a result of the attack. Again, the six terrorists who carried out the attack on the OPEC headquarters in Vienna in December 1975 were flown to Algeria; from there, they continued on to Libya, where they were granted asylum. Finally, the assassins of Hans-Martin Schleyer, the German industrialist, found refuge in Sabra, the Palestinian camp near Beirut, and in Iraq.[82]

ATTACKS BY PROXY

Another pronounced feature of interregional terrorism is the frequent attacks by proxy carried out by one terrorist group in advancing the cause of other underground movements. This form of collaboration began as early as 1969.[83] On December 12 of that year, members of the Baader-Meinhof group planted explosives in West Berlin at El Al Airline office, American House, and the U.S. Officers' Club.

Indeed, over the past ten years, similar incidents had occurred. The following cases, selected at random, illustrate the nature of the threat.[84]

A car of the Israeli meat company, Incade, was blown up in Ethiopia on April 29, 1970, by the Eritrean Liberation Front. On March 25, 1971, members of the Movement of Youthward Brothers in War of the Palestinian People, a French pro-Arab group, threw stones and Molotov cocktails at the offices of the Bill Computer Company, a subsidiary of General Electric (GE). In April of that year, five French citizens failed in their attempt to sabotage hotels in Israel. Questioning by the police led to the discovery of a network of 55 persons, including Algerians, Palestinians, and French extremists. On May 23, the Israeli consul in Turkey was assassinated by members of the Turkish Popular Liberation Army. Following the murder, Fatah expressed support for the Turkish extremist organizations, praised their antiregime activities, and emphasized its alliance with the Turkish fighters.

In another instance, three Japanese anarchists of the United Red Army were recruited to execute the Lod Airport operation on behalf of Palestinians on May 30, 1972, after they had been contacted several years earlier by PFLP's George Habbash. The Japanese trio was equipped with weapons provided by Italian terrorists in Rome. The latter sent them to Israel by Air France for an attack that brought death and injury to some 100 people, most of whom were Puerto Rican Christian pilgrims with no direct involvement in the Arab-Israeli conflict.

Also, on June 3, 1972, an extremist Italian group bombed the offices of Honeywell, International Business Machines (IBM), and Bank of America in Milan and a Honeywell factory in a Milan suburb. Leaflets found at the damaged sites referred to the "struggle of the Vietnamese people against American imperialism" and the victories "of the revolutionary and Communist army in Vietnam."

The overthrow of President Allende in Chile resulted in several attacks by proxy. On December 31, 1973, a leftist Italian group put explosives at three offices of International Telephone & Telegraph (ITT) subsidiaries in Rome, causing heavy damage. Leaflets found in the area stated that "ITT organized the coup in Chile and it is made up of Fascist and reactionary elements." Similarly, a French group, "We Must Do Something," claimed responsibility for the fire destruction of the Sonolar factory, a French ITT subsidiary, on March 1, 1974. It was a "welcome" for the newly arrived Chilean ambassador to France.

Several incidents related to various causes occurred in the following years. In January 1976, a San Francisco terrorist group planted a powerful bomb that heavily damaged a new financial district skyscraper housing the Iranian consulate. The bomb exploded after a telephone warning to the UPI. The group said the bombing was carried out "in support of the Iranian people's struggle to rid themselves of the CIA-backed Shah." The group proclaimed solidarity with revolutionary groups in Angola, Greece, Puerto Rico, and Iran, as well as U.S. terrorist organizations. Two persons who had been in an office on the skyscraper were slightly injured by flying glass from the blast, which caused $200,000 damage. Bernard Hansman, a German terrorist who planted a booby-trapped suitcase that exploded at Ben-Gurion Airport in May, worked on behalf of the PFLP. Two Dutch nationals, members of the Marxist-Leninist Red Help group were dispatched in September by the PFLP to study Air France's Bombay–Tel Aviv air route, in preparation for a future hijacking mission. Both were arrested, and the terrorist hijacking plot was foiled.

Also, on April 11, 1977, the Revolutionary Commandos of Solidarity, a Costa Rican group, exploded the offices of Pan Am and Henderson & Company, as well as a building housing the U.S. military mission, in San Jose. The attack caused heavy damage but no injuries. Apparently, the bombing was a reprisal for the death of Carlos Aguerero Echeverria, a Costa Rican who was a leader of Nicaragua's Sandinist Front of National Liberation. In May, a Norwegian student was detained at Beirut airport en route to Frankfurt and Israel to carry out sabotage acts for the Popular Democratic Front for the Liberation of Palestine (PDFLP).

Finally, on January 19, 1978, a bomb exploded at the U.S.-owned Discount Bank in Paris. Pamphlets found in the area called for revenge for the October death of Andreas Baader, who had been held in a West German prison.

COORDINATED ATTACKS

Growing coordination in the planning and execution of attacks by terrorists groups is becoming apparent. Several examples will suffice.[85]

Black September terrorists who held several Western diplomats hostage in the Sudan in March 1973 issued an ultimatum that they would kill them within 24 hours unless, inter alia, members of the Baader-Meinhof group were released. The reason offered for this demand was that the German terrorists "supported the Palestinian cause."

Three Pakistanis, describing themselves as members of the Moslem International Guerrillas, a group known to be active in the Philippines and Indonesia, seized a Greek freighter in Karachi on February 2, 1974, and threatened to blow up the ship and kill its crewmen unless two Black September terrorists, who were sentenced to death for an attack on a crowd at Athens Airport, killing five people and wounding 53, were freed. Subsequently, the Arab guerrillas were deported from Greece to Libya and freedom.

On September 13, 1974, members of the JRA attacked the French embassy in The Hague and took the ambassador and a dozen embassy personnel hostage. The terrorists demanded the release of Suzuki Furuya, a member of their group, who had been apprehended by the French police at Orly Airport while carrying secret documents. Reportedly, Carlos and PFLP's European commander Mukharbel did reconnaissance in The Hague prior to this raid. Several hours after the attack on the French embassy began, Carlos was apparently involved in another operation linked to the Dutch incident. A hand grenade was thrown into "Le Drugstore" on Boulevard Saint Germain in Paris, killing two people and injuring 34. Telephone calls to news agencies indicated that the attack on Le Drugstore was in support of The Hague operation and that further violence should be expected. Subsequently, the Japanese terrorists in The Hague and their comrade in French hands were given "free passage" for the Middle East, with a ransom of $300,000 paid by the Dutch government.

The most dramatic case is the hijacking of the Lufthansa plane to Mogadishu in October 1977 by PFLP for the Baader-Meinhof group·to reinforce demands of the kidnappers of Schleyer, who was subsequently murdered. Interestingly, Japanese authorities believe that the Lufthansa incident and the JRA hijacking in Dacca a month earlier were carried out under a coordinated plan. They reached this conclusion after closely studying the two cases. The Japanese officials related, for example, "that in both cases, the hijackers called themselves by numbers instead of names and the plastic bombs used in both cases were of the same type."[86] Also,

the Japanese commandos forced all passengers to write their names and addresses and sent letters to them in May through July seeking their support. They also sent similar letters to Japanese imprisoned radicals. The hijackers in the Mogadishu incident also distributed envelopes among passengers and forced them to write their names and addresses on them. The German hijackers then told the passengers they would send letters to them, but the German commandos were later killed or arrested by the German authorities.[87]

Finally, "the Japanese and German hijackers treated the passengers in a similar manner. The hijackers collected passports, ID cards and other personal belongings of the passengers apparently to determine the order for killing them in case the hijackers' demands were not met."[88]

JOINT ATTACKS

A close examination of terrorist activities since 1970 reveals an increasing number of joint operations among different terrorist groups. In the first place, it is evident that some members of terrorist movements have joined the ranks of other groups and have "fought" alongside their "brethren." For instance, the Iranian revolutionary movement established a "Palestine Group," composed of 45 people, and participated in operations against the "enemy" in Palestine. Also, Turkish and Japanese "volunteers" participated in Palestinian guerrilla operations during the Lebanese civil war.[89]

Most of the joint terrorist attacks, however, have occurred outside of the Middle East.[90] On September 6, 1970, an American, Patrick Joseph Arguello, head of a Nicaraguan underground organization, joined Palestinian Leila Khaled in an attempted hijacking of an El Al plane in London. On February 2, 1972, the Black September, with the participation of a Belgian teacher, Stefan van den Bermatt, detonated gas works in Holland. In July of that year, a Japan Airline plane flying over the country was hijacked by the JRA and two Latin American terrorists carrying Peruvian passports. In the following month, the Black September and Italian extremists blew up oil tanks in Trieste.

Also, on July 20, 1973, a Japanese jumbo jet was hijacked on a flight from Amsterdam to Tokyo by Arab and Japanese terrorists. Later, the plane was blown up at the Tripoli Airport in Libya. Another joint operation was carried out by the PFLP and the JRA in Singapore on January 31, 1974, where four guerrillas seized a ferryboat in the Harbor with five crew members aboard after making an unsuccessful attempt to blow up refineries of Royal Dutch Shell. The terrorists stated that their attack on the storage tanks was in support of the "Vietnam revolutionary people and for making a revolutionary situation after considering the situation of today's oil crisis."[91] The Singapore government rejected the guerrillas' request to be given a safe-conduct to an Arab country. Meanwhile, PFLP terrorists in Kuwait took hostages at the Japanese embassy there and threatened to kill them unless the demands of the guerrillas in Singapore were met. Subsequently, a Japan Airline plane took all the terrorists involved in both operations to safety in Aden.

The raid on the OPEC headquarters in Vienna in December 1975 was carried out by a combined squad of PFLP members, together with Germans and Venezuelans. It was led by Carlos, who was accompanied by Gabriele Kroecher-Tiedman, a Baader-Meinhof gang member released from jail in exchange for the release of a West German kidnapped politician.

Another example of this cooperation can be found in the hijacking of an Air France airliner to Uganda on June 27, 1976. Individuals belonging to several extremist underground organizations participated in that operation: the commander of the four-man terrorist squad that seized control of the aircraft after its takeoff from Athens was a German, Ernst Wilfied Boese. An anarchist lawyer associated with Carlos, and a member of the PFLP, after his defection from the Carlos network. Boese later served two prison sentences, first in Paris and later in Germany, where he was in detention until 1975. A young German woman was also a member of the hijack squad.

When the plane reached Entebbe, the hijackers were joined by three other terrorists. One of these was Antonio Degas Bonia, a South American with an Equadorian passport, formerly head of the Carlos network in London. He took command of the operation from the moment the hijacked plane landed at Entebbe.

Finally, in April 1978, the Egyptian attorney general announced the exposure of an international network of terrorism in Egypt, in which Palestinians, Swiss, and Italian Red Brigade members worked together for Abu Nid'al, head of the pro-Iraqi Arab Liberation Front (it has been reported that this group has changed its name to the Palestine Liberation Front). This group allegedly was under "the control of an international network which operated throughout Europe and which extends its activities with the cooperation of radical subversive elements in the Arab World."[92] This group, apparently linked to previous terrorist attacks, was apparently involved in a scheme aimed at carrying out a series of assassinations and acts of sabotage in Egypt in an effort to undermine the Camp David Middle East peace accords.

In spite of these and other instances of collaboration among terrorist groups, it would be a gross exaggeration to assert that most subnational movements belong to an international network taking orders from a single clandestine centralized body. Each group acts within very different traditions, and these differing traditions prevent a single transnational conspiracy from developing. However, the widespread alliance to the lineage of revolutionary ideologists and strategists, as well as the sense of guerrillas' solidarity with other comrades waging an armed struggle for political and ideological ends, provides ample evidence of the existence of an expanding international violence zone. With the proliferation of modern weapons, coupled with further advances in communications, which would probably increase the level of collaboration among "have not" groups, the danger of terrorism will ultimately become unbearable.

Because of the factors that encourage terrorism, particularly the support of terrorism by Communist and Third World countries and the existence of an international network of terrorism, nations and people of the world can anticipate the occurrence of more explosions, hijackings, kidnappings, and assassinations, possibly through the 1990s. Most liberal democracies favor control, at least in principle, but unless they can find ways to deal realistically with factors that promote terrorism, they will be hostages of global blackmailers forever.

In view of this probability, there is an immediate need for the business community to ponder the future with grave concern and to determine appropriate strategies to counter the threat of terrorism to commerce, property, and profit.

NOTES

1. For recent studies on terrorism, see, for example, Yonah Alexander, ed., *International Terrorism: National, Regional, and Global Perspectives* (New York: Praeger Publishers, 1976); Yonah Alexander and Seymour M. Finger, eds., *Terrorism: Interdisciplinary Perspectives* (New York: John Jay Press, 1977/Maidenhead: McGraw-Hill, 1977); Jonah Alexander, David Carlton, and Paul Wilkinson, eds., *Terrorism: Theory and Practice* (Boulder, Colo.: Westview Press, 1979); J. Bowyer Bell, *Terror out of Zion* (New York: St. Martin's, 1976); J. Bowyer Bell, *On Revolt* (Cambridge, Mass.: Harvard University Press, 1976); David Carlton and Carlo Schaerf, eds., *International Terrorism and World Security* (London: Croom Helm, 1975); Richard Clutterbuck, *Kidnap and Ransom: The Response* (London and Boston: Faber and Faber, 1978); Ronald D. Crelinsten, Danielle Laberge-Altmeja, and Denis Szabo, eds. *Terrorism and Criminal Justice* (Lexington, Mass.: Lexington Books, 1978); John D. Elliot and Leslie K. Gibson, eds., *Contemporary Terrorism: Selected Readings* (Gaithersberg, Md.: International Association of Chiefs of Police, 1978), Alona E. Evans and John F. Murphy, eds., *Legal Aspects of International Terrorism* (Lexington, Mass.: Lexington Books, 1978); Richard W. Kobetz and H. H. Cooper, *Target Terrorism* (Gaithersberg, Md.: International Association of Chiefs of Police, 1978); Stefan T. Possony and L. Francis Bouchey, *International Terrorism—The Communist Connection* (Washington, D.C.: American Council for Freedom, 1978); Walter Laqueur, *Terrorism* (Boston: Little, Brown, 1977); Maurius H. Livingston, Lee Bruce Kress, and Marie G. Wanek, eds. *International Terrorism in the Contemporary World* (Westport, Conn.: Greenwood Press, 1978); *Terrorism: An International Journal* 1 (1977–78); Paul Wilkinson, *Political Terrorism* (London: Macmillan Press, 1974); and Paul Wilkinson, *Political Terrorism and the Liberal State*, (New York: Wiley, 1977).

2. See, for instance, Yonah Alexander, Marjorie Ann Browne, and Allen S. Nanes, eds., *Control of Terrorism: International Documents* (New York: Crane, Russak, 1979), and Robert H. Kupperman, *Facing Tomorrow's Terrorist Incident Today* (Washington, D.C.: Law Enforcement Assistance Administration, 1977).

3. "Terrorism and Business: Conference Report," mimeographed (Washington, D.C.: Center for Strategic and International Studies, July 1978).

4. For details, see Yonah Alexander and Herbert M. Levine, "Prepare for the Next Entebbe," *Chitty's Law Journal* 25 (1977): 240–42.

5. See, for example, National Foreign Assessment Center, *International Terrorism in 1977* (Washington, D.C.: CIA, 1978), and *Executive Risk Assessment* (November and December 1978).

6. "The Various Ideologies and Forms of International Terrorism," mimeographed (International Scientific Conference on Terrorism, (Berlin: Center for Strategic and International Studies, November 14–18, 1978).

7. See J. Bowyer Bell, *Transnational Terror* (Washington, D.C.: American Enterprise Institute, 1975). For a popular treatment, see Ovid Demaris, *Brothers in Blood: The International Terrorist Network* (New York: Charles Scribner's Sons, 1977).

8. New York *Times*, January 4, 1974.

9. "The Various Ideologies and Forms of International Terrorism."

10. The Monteneros profess allegiance to the Peronist ideology of economic independence, social justice, and political sovereignty. For details, see for example Ernst Halperin, *Terrorism in Latin America*, vol. 4 (CSIS Washington Papers) (1976); Ernst Halperin, *Terrorism in Latin America*, vol. 4 (CSIS Washington Papers) (1976); Ernst Halperin, "From Peron to Somoza," *The Washington Quarterly* 1 (Autumn 1978): 110–14; Rose E. Butler, "Terrorism in Latin America," in Alexander, *International Terrorism*, pp. 46–61; Richard Gott, *Guerrilla Movements in Latin America* (London: Thomas Nelson, 1970); and Kohl and J. Litt, *Urban Guerrilla Warfare in Latin America* (Cambridge, Mass.: MIT Press, 1974).

11. *Granma* (December 5, 1970).

12. The Tupamaros of Uraguay never elaborated a detailed political and economic program; nevertheless, it is primarily concerned with armed struggle against the system. For details, see Halperin; Butler, "Terrorism in Latin America"; Kohl and Litt, *Urban Guerrilla Warfare*; Gott, "Guerrilla Movements in Latin America"; and Robert Moss, "Urban Guerrillas in Uraguay," *Problems in Communism* 20 (September–October 1971).

13. MIR includes Moscow-oriented Communists and Trotskyists. See Brian Crozier, ed., *Annual of Power and Conflict, 1976–1977: A Survey of Political Violence and International Influence* (London: Institute for the Study of Conflict, 1977), pp. 134–36.

14. Lester A. Sobel, ed. *Political Terrorism* (New York: Facts on File, 1975), pp. 102–3.

15. Thomas P. Anderson, "The Ambiguities of Political Terrorism in Latin America," (unpublished paper, February, 1978).

16. New York *Times*, October 19, 1976.

17. For a popular treatment, see Les Payne et al., *The Life and Death of the SLA* (New York: Ballantine Books, 1976).

18. See Sobel, *Political Terrorism*, pp. 137–42.

19. Ibid.

20. Statement by Lieutenant Thomas Lyons, a member of the Dade County Public Safety Department and Raul J. Diaz, a member of the Organized Crime, Terrorist and Security Unit, Dade County Public Safety Department, before the U.S., Congress, House Judiciary Committee's Subcommittee on Internal Security, in May 1976. Quoted in Sobel, *Political Terrorism*, p. 141.

21. New York *Times*, May 26, 1977.

22. For details, see Sobel, *Political Terrorism*, pp. 151–54.

23. San Diego *Union*, September 7, 1978.

24. See J. Bowyer Bell, *The Secret Army: The IRA, 1916–1974* (Cambridge, Mass.: MIT Press, 1974), and Alan O'Day, "Northern Ireland, Terrorism and the British State," in Alexander, *Terrorism: Theory and Practice*, pp. 121–35.

25. The separatist ETA developed from a splinter of the Basque Nationalist Party and then itself split into Marxist and non-Marxist factions. For recent developments, see Sobel, *Political Terrorism*, pp. 240–46.

26. FLB is a Celtic group advocating separate independence for Brittany. For a brief survey of terrorism in France, see Crozier, *Annual of Power and Conflict, 1976–1977*, pp. 31–35.

27. For a discussion of political violence in Britain during 1971–77, see Richard Clutterbuck, *Britain in Agony* (London: Faber and Faber, 1978), and Gordon Carr, *The Angry Brigade* (London: Gollancz, 1975).

28. Sobel, *Political Terrorism*, pp. 240–46.

29. Reported by Hans Josef Horchem at a U.S. State Department Conference on International Terrorism, Washington, D.C., March 25–26, 1976.

30. Broadcasting of Lisbon Domestic Service, in Portuguese, 0800 GMT, December 15, 1978.

31. For details on these groups, see Jillian Becker, *Hitler's Children* (London: Panther, 1978); Richard Clutterbuck, *Guerrillas and Terrorists* (London: Faber and Faber, 1977); Albert Parry, *Terrorism from Robespierre to Arafat* (New York: Vanguard, 1976); Alexander, *International Terrorism*; and Laqueur, *Terrorism*.

32. Broadcast in Arabic to the Arab world, 1800 GMT, July 1, 1978.

33. *Business Conflicts Report* (August 1978): 6.

34. Broadcast by Havana International Service, in Spanish, February 5, 1978.

35. For recent activities of the Monteneros, see Halperin, and Sobel, *Political Terrorism*, pp. 87–118.

36. Broadcast by "Voice of Palestine" (clandestine), in Arabic, June 21, 1978. This meeting was also cited in *Business Conflicts Reports* (October 1978): 3.

37. *Berlingske Tidende* (Copenhagan), March 18, 1978.

38. Reported in *Al Anwar* (Beirut), May 22, 1976.

39. *Al-Hakika* (Libya), June 16, 1972.

40. *Times* (London), January 4, 1974.

41. Cairo Radio, December 25, 1969, BBC Monitoring Service.

42. Quoted by a high-ranking Libyan official of the Ministry of Foreign Affairs during an interview with the *Bangkok Post*, January 5, 1975.

43. New York *Times*, May 23, 1976.

44. *Business Conflicts Report* (August 1978): 3, and *Near East Report* 23 (January 10, 1979).

45. *Newsweek* (June 25, 1975).

46. Jerusalem *Post*, June 2, 1978.

47. Yonah Alexander, "Terrorism in the Middle East: A New Phase?," *The Washington Quarterly* (Autumn 1978): 116–17.

48. For details, see *Al-Gumhur al-Jadid* (Beirut), March 6, 1969; "Arab Terror in Europe," *Britain and Israel* (October 1972); *JTA Daily News Bulletin* (March 29, 1977); Philadelphia *Inquirer*, April 10, 1977; and *The Guardian* (Manchester), June 4, 1977.

49. *The Daily Telegraph* (London), September 4, 1970.

50. Alec Hartley, "PLO Arms Funded by Drug Smugglers," *The Guardian*, June 4, 1977.

51. For statistics and details, see "Executive Kidnapping—A Growing Threat," *Executive Risk Assessment* 1 (November 1978).

52. Philadelphia *Inquirer*, April 10, 1977.

53. *Al-Usbua al-Arabia* (Beirut), December 19, 1971.

54. *Al-Ahad* (Beirut), December 19, 1971.

55. Sobel, *Political Terrorism*, p. 102.

56. *Al-Usbua al-Arabia*, (Beirut), December 19, 1971.

57. *Three Minutes at Lod* (Jerusalem: Israel Information Center, June 1972).

58. Tokyo Radio, in English, 0313 GMT, July 12, 1978.

59. New York *Times*, June 26, 1978.

60. *L'Europeo* (Milan), May 19, 1978.

61. *Irish Times*, June 14, 1978.

62. Jerusalem *Post*, June 2, 1978.

63. Andrew McKay, "Arab-U.S. Terror Link Admitted," New York *Post*, April 6, 1977.

64. See *Al-Jadid* (Beirut), May 15, 1969; *As-Safa* (Beirut), June 20, 1969; *Ad-Difa'a* (Amman), July 29, 1969; and Possony and Bouchey, *International Terrorism.*

65. Alexander, "Terrorism in the Middle East: A New Phase?," p. 117.

66. *Interresearch*, October 6, 1978.

67. New York *Times*, May 23, 1976.

68. New York *Times*, December 14, 1973.

69. *Times* (London), February 12, 1978; *Chicago Tribune*, February 23, 1978; *Irish Times*, June 14, 1978.

70. *Business Conflicts Report* (October 1978): 3.

71. Washington *Star*, April 21, 1978; *Time* (April 3, 1978); and *l'Europeo* (Milan), May 19, 1978.

72. Eisenberg and Landau, *Carlos.*

73. Sobel, *Political Terrorism*, p. 247.

74. *Interresearch*, October 6, 1978.

75. Sobel, *Political Terrorism*, p. 52.

76. *El-Moudjahid* (Algiers), June 5, 1978.

77. Maputo Radio (Mozambique), in Portuguese, 1400 GMT, March 31, 1978.

78. *Business Conflicts Report* (November 1978): 6.

79. *Near East Report.*

80. *Al-Sabah* (Amman), October 27, 1974.

81. Los Angeles *Times*, July 28, 1978.

82. Hamburg Radio, 1212 GMT, November 11, 1977, and *Christian Science Monitor*, November 29, 1977.

83. For further details, see Charles A. Russell, "Transnational Terrorism," *Air University Review* (January–February, 1976): 26–35; Edward F. Mickolus, "Chronology of Transnational Attacks upon American Business People, 1968-78," Appendix B of this book; and Demaris, *Brothers in Blood.*

84. Illustrations are drawn from Appendix B in this book.

85. For further details see Russell, "Transnational Terrorism"; and Demaris, *Brothers in Blood.*

86. Radio Tokyo Kyodo, in English, 0313 GMT, July 12, 1978.

87. Ibid.

88. Ibid.

89. *Al-Sha'ab* (Algeria), October 22, 1971; *Al-Usbue* (Beirut) May 31, 1973; Washington *Post*, April 25, 1978; and *Christian Science Monitor*, April 25, 1978.

90. For further details, see Russell, "Transnational Terrorism"; Appendix B in this book; and Demaris, *Brothers in Blood.*

91. Sobel, *Political Terrorism*, p. 68.

92. Cairo Domestic Service, in Arabic, 0525 GMT, April 23, 1978.

4

TERRORISM AND THE CORPORATE TARGET

Bowman H. Miller
Charles A. Russell

ATTACK THE EXPLOITERS

Today's terrorists, nearly all of whom are self-proclaimed Marxists, have a simple explanation for their politics and the violent tactics that they utilize. Essentially, to them, society consists of the contradiction between the wealth and power of the "haves" (big business coupled with ruling oligarchies) and the greater numbers but impotence of the "have-nots."

> In the great industrial centers there is a great human mass ruled by the tyranny of private capital. Private capital concentrates and accumulates the direct products of thousands of craftsmen, laborers, peasants and other victims of capitalist production. . . . To make a social revolution it is necessary to overthrow by violence the old ruling class, to dissolve the old social relations between exploited and exploiting classes, to create a new mode of production (socialism in place of capitalism).[1]

The guerrilla, revolutionary, terrorist, or whatever else we may choose to call him represents (to himself or herself) the essential positive step taken to redress this imbalance. At the present time, the young intellectuals who lead and have led most contemporary terrorist groups realize they have a special role to play

---

The views expressed in this chapter are the authors' and do not necessarily reflect the views of the U.S. government or of any of its departments or agencies.

All statistical materials contained in this chapter, unless otherwise indicated, were derived from a terrorist incident data base belonging to Risks International, Alexandria, Virginia. The data and conclusions drawn therefrom are the property of Risks International and are under copyright of that organization. This material is reproduced in this chapter with the express permission of Roy Tucker, president, Risks International.

and cannot hope to win popular support for their actions overnight. By their would-be heroic exploits, these crusaders hope to become models for others—magnets to draw new recruits into revolutionary commitment and activity. "Marx, Bakunin, Lenin, Fidel, Che were not workers but revolutionaries—sparks destined to set the prairies on fire."[2] So it is with today's nonproletarian terrorists, whose roots lie in the middle and upper classes.

The "root of all capitalist evil" is the United States. Guillen refers to a "holy alliance of repression whose strategic epicenter is the Pentagon and whose economic resonance box is Wall Street."[3] Marighella talks of the need "to demoralize the militarists, the military dictatorship and its repressive forces, and also to attack and destroy the wealth and property of the North Americans, the foreign managers, and the Brazilian upper class."[4]

Any terrorist group worth its salt has its own statements or corpus of doctrine that captures its basic political thinking. One of the most lengthy and most recent such pieces is the "Resolution of the Strategic Directorate of the Red Brigades" (Brigate Rosse: Revoluzione della Direzione Strategica).[5] This impressive-sounding pronouncement dwells on the alleged collusion of multinational corporations, the Italian and other Western governments, and the state machinery of Italian law and justice, which in the Red Brigades' view sees to it that "the worker gets the least reward for maximal output."

> Hand in hand with the reorganization of the politico-military apparatus, the restructuring of the economic apparatus marches in line with the strategy of the great multinational conglomerates, which have already chosen as their main goal a rearrangement of the machinery for capital accumulation, already deeply mired in crisis; increasing their own profits; introducing still higher levels of exploitation and control over the working class and new patterns of domination over peoples in the developing countries; and thus placing socialist imperialism in a position of inferiority and impotence.[6]

HARASSMENT, NOT INDUSTRIAL SABOTAGE

With the corporate world at the top of the terrorists' hate lists and revolution the objective being pursued, one has to take a long look at how terrorist groups view corporations, their personnel, facilities, and other assets from the standpoint of targeting and tactics employed. The seemingly obvious objective of actually destroying a corporation does not find itself reflected often, if at all, in the way terrorists have gone about attacking business enterprises. Although many facilities have been bombed or in other ways attacked, few penetrations have been made into the core of any industrial production facility. There are, in fact, relatively few indications that this has been desirable in the terrorists' thinking. At the same time, the favored tactic of kidnapping offers great satisfaction to those who thirst for the opportunity to manipulate both powerful individuals and their parent companies. A kidnapping's direct impact on an entire corporation, thanks to the singleness of its human targeting, seemingly is much less than that of the potential destruction of a plant, depot, or office complex, which could employ hundreds and be a key facet of the whole enterprise. Harassment, the key ingredient in the terrorists' repertoire, again is the best description for their operations. The record of the last decade shows little of what one could term purposeful industrial sabotage. One reason for this apparent lack may be the notion of constituency. If a group considers itself to be working on behalf of a larger body, it must be mindful of those who labor in corporate offices, factories, mines, and so on. These individuals may not look at all kindly on revolutionary acts, which could cost them their means of existence.

Leaving aside for the moment any statistical overview, one can readily observe that three branches of business have felt the brunt of terrorist operations so far. These are the international air carriers, banks, and, to a lesser extent, the energy industries. Hijackings and attacks on airports and ticket offices account for the vast majority of incidents having an impact on the airlines. While not the ideal source of funds for groups capable of kidnapping, banks remain a major source of operating funds for terrorists. The rationale for robbing banks is pragmatic, regardless of the amount of effort devoted to justifying these actions on primarily political grounds. Marighella again has noted that "the Brazilian revolution was able to hit them [the principal enemies of the people] at their vital center, with preferential and systematic attacks on the banking network."[7] However, *expropriation* is to *robbery* as *execution* is to *murder*. The choice of semantic variants is a matter of convention and moral perspective.

THE ENERGY TARGET

A notable series of orchestrated attacks against a branch of the energy industry occurred in 1971 and 1972 when Palestinian terrorists, principally, the Black September Organization (BSO), waged a campaign of bombings and arson against oil and gas refineries and supply facilities in Europe. These included several pipeline and pumping station bombings in Rotterdam and Hamburg and the bombing and attempted arson of a pipeline near Trieste. In late January 1974, PFLP teamed with its Asian understudy, the enigmatic JRA, in an operation designed to set fire to a Shell Oil tank farm in Singapore. The operation coincided with the oil crisis in the West and was the first in Asia for the highly selective Japanese expatriate group. The attack failed. Some of the explosive charges ignited, but no large fire or series of explosions ensued. The avowed objective of the attack—"inflicting damage on Shell Oil, an international monopoly, by burning its tanks"—was not achieved.[8] In fact, the four-man commando team panicked and seized hostages and a small harbor ferry in order to save the situation.

The hostage standoff ended favorably for the terrorists after a second PFLP team seized the Japanese embassy staff in Kuwait to be held as a tradeoff. The rationale for selecting Shell in this incident was only partly due to its interest in the petroleum business. The JRA had wanted desperately to launch an operation in the Far East to focus attention on itself and to appease its detractors in Japan, who saw the group as prodigals from the revolutionary homeland. In essence, the operation combined Palestinian objectives in attacking an oil company with JRA goals in the selection of Singapore.

Other targets in the energy industries that have suffered from terrorist assaults have included both conventional and nuclear power companies. Within Spain, the protest movement against construction of Europe's second largest nuclear facility (at Lemóniz) has been exploited very effectively by terrorists in the ETA. Using the legitimate Coordinating Committee of the Antinuclear Commissions of the Basque Region, which represents over 13 Basque political groups and is led by respected members of the Spanish Cortes ("parliament"), ETA has played upon the fears of these groups concerning nuclear contamination to build generally strong support for its own terrorist acts against Lemóniz and Iberduero, the contractor and utility firm involved in building the facility.

Playing upon peasant fears of the reactor, alleging unreported radioactive leakages and charging that the facility would endanger the farmland, ETA—using the antinuclear commissions—has stirred up strong opposition to the installation. In this campaign, it has made particular use of strong Basque distaste for the central Spanish government and demands for regional autonomy from Madrid. Charges also have been made indicating the government placed the facility in the Basque region because of its inherent danger to life.

In this climate, demonstrations were launched in late January 1978 at Lemóniz, as well as in the nearby towns of Algorta and Guecho. Several were attended by more than 2,000 persons. A month later, ETA began a bombing campaign against Iberduero facilities in ten surrounding towns. In all, ten bombs were placed, and eight detonated. In addition, an Iberduero technician in Eibar was kidnapped and questioned by ETA members concerning the Lemóniz facility. After this operation, ETA took an active role in a demonstration in Lemóniz in March, which drew 60,000 people under the sponsorship of the antinuclear commissions. Among the chants shouted by the crowd was, "ETA, Lemóniz, dynamite." Five days after the rally, ETA launched an armed assault on the Lemóniz project, resulting in $5.6 million damage to the facility, 14 wounded, and three killed. In addition to serious damage to this particular facility, Iberduero offices in various cities within the Basque provinces sustained over $700,000 in damages in late 1977 and early 1978. There is reason to believe that a late December 1977 theft of 1,200 kilograms of explosives formed the prelude to the mid-March 1978 explosives assault and attack on the Lemóniz reactor site.[9]

Orchestration of the Lemóniz attacks and those on Iberduero facilities throughout the Basque provinces is an excellent example of how a terrorist group—particularly one motivated by nationalist-separatist aspirations and strongly rooted in the local populace—can play upon the legitimate concerns of a group to develop a climate favorable to terrorist offensives. Many Basques continue to endorse ETA terrorist operations against Lemóniz and related targets as justifiable acts carried out for the long-range benefit of the Basque people. It seems likely that precisely this type of linkage (and there are similar ones in West Germany and France) provides the greatest potential for terrorist activities in the future directed against nuclear facilities.

CORPORATE VULNERABILITY A DILEMMA

Businesses face an almost insurmountable dilemma when operating in a threatening environment. By its nature, part of any business enterprise is open to the public and wants to retain a favorable, receptive image before the consumer. Increases in security measures that restrict freedom of access for the general public are not taken without potential risks to that corporate image. While a government can post armed guards, examine parcels, use screening or detection equipment, and even restrict entry into its facilities, corporations are not as amenable to taking such stringent measures. Visitors, be they current or prospective clients, investors, or whoever, may be put off by encumbering security procedures they encounter. Worse yet, they may interpret them as cause to wonder about the corporation's standing as a whole, its future stability, and its ability to cope with what to them may seem to be nonexistent or inflated threats to its well-being.

These and other considerations weigh most heavily when seeking to secure those publicly accessible areas of a corporation against placement of explosive devices. Lobbies, elevators, reception areas, washrooms, cloakrooms, custodial closets, stairwells, parking areas, telephone booths, and many other parts of a building lend themselves to placement of a bomb, which, if undetected, can be timed to detonate precisely when the bomber chooses. The more heavily furnished the public areas, the easier it is to place a device under a table, in a chair, in a planter or flowerpot, behind a drape, or elsewhere. In extremely congested public areas, only the most attentive security detail could detect the bag, parcel, briefcase, or other unattended container that has been deposited. Placement of explosives in trash receptacles, in toilet tanks, in first aid kits, and in fire extinguishers has been commonplace and is virtually undetectable. The security officer's problems are compounded further if and when he must come to grips with the possibility of an operation that relies on inside employee assistance or perhaps originates within the corporation's own personnel. Despite the infrequency of this type of terrorist scenario thus far, Marighella and others have stressed its value: "Industrial workers acting as urban guerrillas are excellent industrial saboteurs since they, better than anyone, understand the industry, the factory, the machine, or the part most likely to destroy an entire operation, doing far more damage than a poorly informed layman could do."[10] In this context, corporate security finds it necessary to depend on internal sources of information, surveillance techniques, and on continuing personnel security programs.

BOMBING STATISTICS

One can no longer quantify the frequency of bombings along the entire spectrum from the Molotov cocktail to the most sophisticated remote-controlled or timed devices. While it is easy to dismiss an incendiary as only consisting of a bottle of gasoline and a burning rag ("amateurs' work") the fire started from such a simple Molotov cocktail can be as devastating as any explosion would be. The December 1, 1976, bombing of the U.S. Air Force Officers' Club near Frankfurt did minor damage; the ensuing fire caused the total loss of the $1 million structure. Likewise, the August 20, 1978, arson attack on a theatre in Abadan, Iran, left over 400 dead. Thus, such devices may well deserve inclusion in any set of statistical findings concerning bombings. At the same time, the frequency of their use and the irregular reporting of incidents at the lower end of the threshhold of violence all but rule out a reliable count of them.

The data base used as the foundation of the statistical portion of this chapter contains descriptions of 3,043 bombing incidents between January 1970 and November 1978.* Bombings amount to slightly less than two-thirds of all terrorist operations in these data (62 percent). Only those incendiary incidents were included that resulted in significant damage to the target or loss of life. These amounted to less than one-fourth of the bombings recorded. Keeping in mind that the inclusion of an incident is based on the same criteria regardless of its location of occurrence, the bombing incident breakout by region shows 54 percent to have occurred in Western Europe, 19 percent in North America, 13 percent in Latin America, and 12 percent in the Middle East/North Africa. The

---

*The incident data base in question contains detailed data on over 5,000 terrorist incidents since January 1970. Incidents are broken down by date, time, country and city, target, nationality of target (if an individual, the corporation and his/her position therein), group involved, number in group, weapons or explosives used, ransoms demanded or paid, hostages taken, disposition of hostages, and other demands. Materials are filed by incident types as follows: kidnapping, assassination, facility attack, maiming, hijacking, and bombing. Only selected bombings are included: those where the damage or casualties are significant, the device is unique, or the method of emplacement unusual.

remaining 2 percent took place in Asia, with very few so far in Sub-Saharan Africa. The year 1977 was the high point for bombing frequency, with 525 in Europe alone. The annual total reached 857—28 percent of all such bombing incidents in the last nine years. Through the month of October, the year 1978 has seen 448 such bomb attacks.

Businesses have suffered from 46.9 percent of all the bombings registered in this data base. One-third of these corporate victims have been U.S. firms. One in ten bombings is directed at a utility, and one in 11 is directed at some transportation system. Citing only the fixed dollar costs reported, bombings have caused at least $108 million in damages (with data available on less than half the 3,043 bombings in the data available). Of those direct losses, $42 million was registered in 1977. Deaths and reported injuries from all 3,043 bombings have been 745 killed and 2,530 injured. These figures specifically exclude the death toll in Northern Ireland's ongoing civil unrest.

ARMED ASSAULTS ON FACILITIES

In addition to explosives and incendiaries, terrorists rely on automatic weapons, grenades, and various kinds of standoff weaponry to attack facilities in order to inflict casualties, damage property, and create havoc and fear. The intent of these operations is more often directed at human targets within facilities than at the structures themselves. Looking at overall casualty ratios, there was one death for every four bombings. Since, as noted earlier, it is those bombings or incendiary attacks at the lower end of the scale of destruction that are excluded from the data base used here, the casualty rate from all bombings is in actuality much less than one death for every four incidents. In contrast, armed attacks on facilities have resulted in 1.7 deaths per incident, at least seven times the ratio for bombings.

Facilities targets attacked by groups using weapons also find business in the forefront. The delineation by target categories is as follows: corporate—39 percent (31 percent indigenous business, 5 percent U.S., and 3 percent other foreign corporations); diplomatic establishments—10 percent; other government—13 percent; police and military installations—16 percent (of which 14 percent are indigenous forces and 2 percent U.S.); and 6 percent transportation facilities. The other 16 percent include media firms, utilities, political party offices, universities, and so forth. Private residences are included under the category of their inhabitants. As was the case in bombing incidents, the worst year since 1970 in terms of casualties and dollar losses in damages was again 1977. That year alone saw 20 percent of all facilities attacks since 1970 and 53 percent of the total property damage reported. In the first three-quarters of 1978, we have recorded one-third more facilities assaults than in the previous (and highest) year, continuing an upward trend. While facilities attacks in which weapons have been used have the added characteristic of often involving hostage seizures, recent years have brought fewer mass hostage stalemates. The barricading of hostages within a business establishment by terrorists is infrequent and seldom has had the characteristic of targeting business employees per se but rather the general public. News accounts have listed a minimum of 3,286 hostages seized in the course of such assaults since 1970.

TRENDS IN TACTICS

Corporations and their security managers have a major concern with trends in terrorist targeting, tactics selection, and new refinements in techniques. Comparing bombing frequency with the execution of armed attacks on facilities, the trend in the former tactic is more level than is the rising incidence of armed facilities attacks. Sixty-eight percent of all armed attacks have come since January 1975. The same three-year period accounts for 72 percent of the bombings; but 1978 shows a decrease thus far by almost half over last year. From a purely analytical perspective, the bombing tactic is considered to be the simplest, least sophisticated form of terrorist operation. If it is not increasing in terms of frequency, we have to ask ourselves why. Several possible reasons come to mind. Newly formed terrorist groups, which routinely rely on the bomb in their early development, are often short-lived. There appear to have been fewer new group entrants into terrorist operations in the last several years than was the case earlier in the decade. Likewise, groups concerned with their image tend to favor more sophisticated operations, which will garner more publicity than do explosive attacks. If coercive leverage is the objective, hostages are decidedly more valuable and command more media coverage than do bombing incidents, which lack the advantage of lasting leverage.

Tactically speaking, an armed assault team relying on hand-held weapons is much better equipped to adapt to changes in target configuration or location, to fluctuating conditions during an operation, and to unforeseen opportunities to seize additional advantage. Based on their flexibility and control of the situation, they can be more effective than the bomber who deposits his or her charge for some delayed and remote destination. While this operational security brings distinct advantages to the bomber, it also leaves him or her ignorant of the identity of his or her ultimate victims and incapable of altering the course of the operation once commenced.

FUTURE CONSIDERATIONS

Bombings and fire team assaults on buildings are obviously frightening incidents. The terrorists' methods and their inhumanity—the callous targeting of human victims (seldom individually selected) and the deliberate destruction of property—strike us as abhorrent. Despite these feelings, however, one should also pause to consider those other plausible developments in the range of terrorist tactics that heretofore have been all but ignored. Let us look briefly at only two: the notion of disruption-oriented terrorism and the perhaps presumptuous terrorist objective of subverting organized labor for action against the corporate employer.

Taking infiltration of labor first, most terrorists who draw their motivation from Marxism and who operate in industrial societies entertain the hope that they will be able to recruit workers for action within the group's political support apparatus and, perhaps, as the internal saboteurs recommended by Marighella. Guillen writes: "It is not enough that the Brazilian guerrillas have kidnapped consuls and ambassadors in order to negotiate with the military regime; they must also mobilize the masses to act out of self-interest."[11] Ulrike Meinhof, Renato Curcio, Marighella, and other terrorism advocates have all written of the absolute necessity of awakening the mass of workers to support the revolution, beginning with the need to convince the common person that he or she should not provide active cooperation to authorities attempting to take action against the terrorists.

With the possible exceptions of Nicaragua and, of course, Northern Ireland, no other recent cases of internal instability have seen workers in numbers rally to the terrorists' side. Depending upon the society in question, the individual laborer either is relatively well-off and content with his or her lot or considers himself or herself lucky to be among the employed at all in those areas with lower standards of living and less powerful trade unionism. The latter type of worker normally feels he or she can ill-afford the luxury of revolutionary notions and is often among society's most conservative strata in this regard.

Another puzzling question concerning terrorist operations, against corporations in particular, is why there has been so little actual industrial sabotage and few, if any, attempts to accomplish nationally disruptive acts. The potential for crippling a business seems almost limitless. A determined, innovative group of intelligent operators could well be able to seriously disrupt the major systems or services upon which entire technologically based societies depend. Computers, electronic banking and other key financial systems, mass transit, water resources, and many other crucial facets of life in a technocracy appear vulnerable to attack. One wonders whether terrorists are less convinced of this vulnerability or may be uninterested in attacks that only disrupt and which lack the violence against human targets that many seem to crave. Groups such as the second-generation German Red Army Faction, which appears to have no real political underpinnings in terms of people or doctrine, may well approach this type of activity, as nihilism comes to best characterize their natures.

Terrorism is presumed by most analysts to be designed (as a set of tactics) to have an intimidating effect on a large body of frightened observers. Potentially nationally disruptive acts certainly fit that assumption. In West Germany, terrorists have sabotaged mass transit lines and automated fare-card machines. Those protesting the opening of Tokyo's new Narita Airport have disrupted rail service to the airport several times. The Red Brigades have talked of and then later attacked major computer producers in Italian cities (both U.S. and European firms), citing the reliance of Italian police and judicial agencies on computerized holdings as part of their targeting rationale. Basque separatists have all but halted the Iberduero firm's construction of a nuclear power facility at Lemóniz, using bombings, gunfire assaults, kidnapping, and other tactics.

It seems likely that the time will come when a terrorist team of well-trained operators will seek to penetrate to the heart of a major facility, bent on major disruption or even its complete destruction.[12] The use of insiders in such an eventuality is very probable. Even fire, often overlooked in the midst of kidnappings and armed assaults, could prove amazingly effective in this type of scenario and is certainly not uncommon in the corporate sector. Access to the target and intimate knowledge of its operation and nerve centers is vital to any operation predicated on covert penetration of a facility. Terrorists have already been convincing in their abilities to collect quality intelligence on all types of targets. In the future, we may not only see more of the same in the use of proven tactics but perhaps attempts to affect the entire public with nationally-disruptive actions, no doubt relying on particular assistance from comrades recruited or placed inside the targeted facility.

NOTES

1. Abraham Guillen, *The Philosophy of the Urban Guerrilla: The Revolutionary Writings of Abraham Guillen*, trans. Donald C. Hodges (New York: Morrow, 1973), pp. 235, 237.

2. Ibid., p. 259.

3. Ibid., p. 229.

4. Carlos Marighella, *Minimanual of the Urban Guerrilla* (Havana: Tricontinental, January–February 1970), p. 17.

5. *Brigate Rosse: Revoluzione della Direzione Strategica*, February 1978, p. 13.

6. Ibid.

7. Marighella, *Minimanual of the Urban Guerrilla*, p. 22.

8. Masao Kitazawa, "Exclusive Interview with Fusako SHIGENOBU," *Shukan Gendai*, January 30, 1975, and February 6, 1975.

9. The information used in this summary was derived from the continuing coverage of the Lemóniz/Iberduero situation published in the Madrid newspapers *Ya*, *ABC*, and *El Pais*.

10. Marighella, *Minimanual of the Urban Guerrilla*, p. 45.

11. Guillen, *Philosophy of Urban Guerrilla*, p. 263.

12. For additional discussion of the potential for mass disruption terrorism, see also the authors' (together with Leon J. Banker, Jr.) study "Out-Inventing the Terrorist," in *Terrorism: Theory and Practice*, ed. Yonah Alexander, David Carlton, and Paul Wilkinson (Boulder, Colo.: Westview Press, 1979), p. 3–42.

5

TERRORIST TACTICS AND
THE EXECUTIVE TARGET

Charles A. Russell
Bowman H. Miller

Terrorism today is a fact of life for most multinational corporations, as well as for many national firms. Executives and corporate facilities are being attacked with increasing frequency. During 1976-78, 50 percent of all terrorist acts worldwide were directed against business personnel, equipment, and facilities. Today, there is little question that business organizations and personnel are the primary terrorist target.

The evolution in terrorist targeting to a focus on business is not accidental. It is a direct result of pragmatic and ideological considerations. It is not a sudden development but, rather, one that has grown gradually over the past eight years. This chapter examines this growth and some of the more significant tactics involved, particularly the abduction for ransom of corporate executives.

===============

The views expressed in this paper are the authors' and do not necessarily reflect the views of the U.S. government or any of its agencies or departments.

All statistical materials contained in this chapter, unless otherwise indicated, were derived from a terrorist incident data owned by Risks International, Alexandria, Virginia. The data and conclusions drawn from it are the property of Risks International and are under the copyright of that organization. This material is reproduced in this chapter with the express permission of Roy Tucker, president, Risks International.

The incident data base in question contains detailed data on over 5,000 terrorist incidents since January 1970. Incidents are broken down by date, time, country and city, target, nationality of target (if an individual, the corporation and his or her position), group involved, number in group, weapons or explosives used, ransoms demanded or paid, hostages taken, disposition of hostages, and other demands. Materials are filed by incident types. These are kidnapping, assassination, facility attack, maiming, hijacking, and bombing. Only selected bombings are included; those where the damage/casualties are significant, the device unique, or the method of emplacement unusual.

The priority targets for terrorist attack have changed substantially since 1970. A statistical analysis of the 5,310 major terrorist operations that took place between January 1, 1970, and November 30, 1978, indicates three separate and quite distinct stages in this process.

During the early 1970s (1970-73), terrorist groups in Europe and Latin America, as well as in most other areas of the world, focused their efforts on attacking police and government facilities and personnel. These groups seemed to believe that such acts would result in government moves to meet their demands. The failure of this strategy was quickly evident. Governments did not collapse, and police shot back. Accordingly, by 1973, terrorist targeting had shifted to assaults against diplomatic establishments and the abduction of foreign diplomats and ranking government personnel. Again, the terrorist belief was that incumbent governments would bow to their demands as a result of the leverage gained through these abductions.

Despite acute embarrassment in many cases, most governments did not give in. Instead, they often increased security measures and began active counterterrorist programs. As a result, by 1975, another targeting shift was evident. For the first time, corporations and their personnel became a top terrorist priority. As indicated earlier, for the succeeding three years (1976-78) 54 percent of all terrorist operations were directed against business targets. Particularly significant among these operations, from a financial, morale, and ideological standpoint, was a steady rise in the number of terrorist kidnappings featuring business personnel.

Although pioneered by Latin American terrorists, the idea of kidnapping businessmen for ransom quickly spread to Western Europe. Both there and in Latin America, this tactic has been used almost exclusively by terrorist organizations active within a limited region or single nation. Although such national groups may be capable of mounting transnational operations (crossing national boundaries), they rarely do so. The organizations that are viable on a transnational level—most of whom are linked with the Palestinian issues and tied to Middle East bases—have not favored corporate kidnappings as a basic tactic. In fact, over 90 percent of all abductions of corporate personnel during the 1970-78 time span have been by national versus transnational terrorist groups.

There are obvious reasons for the general rejection of corporate kidnapping by transnational groups and the priority role it has as a tactic for national terrorist groups. Among transnational organizations, a primary consideration is the fact that leverage gained by hijacking a planeload of passengers is substantially greater in attacking a target country than the abduction of a single businessman, no matter what his stature might be. In addition, such transnational groups receive continuing financial support from various patron Arab states and thus rarely suffer from an absence of funds. This is not, of course, the situation of most national level groups. These must rely on their own capabilities to obtain needed operational funds. One of the easiest routes to such funds is through the abduction for ransom of corporate personnel. These actions are substantially less risky than bank robberies or attacks against commercial facilities. In addition, they promise a much richer reward.

The use of kidnapping as a funds-acquisition technique is a pragmatic explanation for the move by terrorist groups toward increased corporate abductions. In the 370 terrorist kidnappings recorded between January 1, 1970, and November 30, 1978, 52 percent involved corporate officials; 49 percent of these 370 operations were in the last three years (1976–78). Ransoms demanded (in 110 cases where the data were available) totaled $290.18 million. Ransoms paid (in these cases) exceeded $145,209,000. Individual ransoms ranged from a high of $41 million to a current (1978) average of $1.2 million per incident in Italy. With a success rate of 94.3 percent over the 1970–78 time span, it is not surprising that kidnapping is a favored terrorist tactic both from an operational and financial point of view.*

In addition to its obvious importance as a source of funds, the abduction of corporate executives also has a very real ideological significance. Of the national level organizations active today, 80 percent are radical Marxist. (In Italy, for example, 80 of the 88 operational terrorist groups have been so inclined.) More strongly influenced by the simplified Marxism of Carlos Marighella, Abraham Guillen, Regis Debray, and Herbert Marcuse than the traditional texts of Lenin, such groups see "imperialistic capitalism"—directed by North American multinational corporations—as their primary target.

As succinctly stated by one Italian terrorist group, "Multinational imperialism thus emerges as a system of global domination in which various national capitalisms are merely its organic fingers and toes.[1] Since these national capitalisms are "at once an instrument for domestic repression and a national interpretation of the dominant imperialism headed by the U.S.A.,"[2] they can best be eliminated by attacking their very foundations—in-country domestic and foriegn business interests. In the words of terrorist theoretician Guillen, by making these interests "the object of permanent harassment, the foundations of the national economic system and the state itself can be destroyed.[3] As the terrorists have learned, one of the most effective (and financially rewarding) means of harassment is the abduction of corporate personnel. Thus, ideology and financial reward coalesce in a single act. The state is weakened, and terrorist coffers are replenished for future operations.

As pointed out earlier, the trend in terrorist kidnappings is up. Almost 50 percent of all such operations have been recorded in the last three years. Additionally, the locus of these operations has shifted dramatically. While tradition-

---

*Success rate is defined as abduction of the victim and successful escape from the kidnap site.

ally, Latin America has been a focal point for abductions, with 62 percent of all such incidents during the 1970–78 time span, Europe is now the key area. Within the past three years, 75 percent of all recorded terrorist kidnappings have taken place in Europe. As might be anticipated, Italy led the European nations, followed by Spain.

In the 370 recorded terrorist kidnappings over the past eight years, there have been a total of 567 victims. Excluding three cases involving an unusual number of multiple victims, the normal incident featured a single person (1.23 precisely). In almost all cases, this individual was a male. Only 41 females have been taken, and over half of these were dependent daughters of the actual target. Most of these abductions took place in situations where the real victim could not be reached for one reason or another. As a result, a dependent—able to provide useful ransom leverage—was selected as a substitute.

Reviewing the occupations of terrorist kidnap victims, business personnel head the list. Of all those taken, 199, or 54 percent, were corporate executives or businessmen. Of these individuals, 30.5 percent were indigenous to the country in which the action took place; 12.2 percent were foreign, non-U.S. businessmen resident in the country; and 11.1 percent were U.S. executives overseas. The next largest single category of victims was diplomats (14 percent), followed by foreign government officials (8.6 percent) and foreign police officers and military personnel (4.9 percent).

In the 73 terrorist kidnappings involving Americans (19.7 percent of the total cases), the above occupational ratios remained generally valid. Of the U.S. victims, 55 percent were businessmen, 28 percent diplomats, and 8 percent police and military personnel.

Once taken, the victim's chances of rescue or escape are minimal. Only a half dozen individuals have escaped over the eight-year period, and less than 20 were rescued successfully. At the same time, however, the odds of being killed by terrorist kidnappers are relatively low. Only 35 persons were executed by their captors, and these actions usually took place during the course of a police "rescue."

The actual site of most terrorist kidnappings has changed little over the eight years under study. Consistently, year after year, 95 percent of all such abductions take place while the target is en route from home to work or returning from work. In analyzing this route pattern, more than 60 percent of all these operations took place within a few miles of the victim's home. As the distance from this point increased, the number of incidents declined markedly. However, as the work site was approached, the incident rate climbed again.

In conjunction with this data, it should be noted that four-fifths of all kidnappings took place while the victim was in a vehicle. Another vehicle was involved in some form of blocking maneuver—against the victim's car—in all these cases. Additionally, in almost all instances, the kidnappers escaped with their victim in yet another vehicle. In short, from a statistical analysis of all terrorist kidnappings during the last eight years, it is very clear that the potential victim is most vulnerable when in a vehicle, a few miles from home, and en route to or returning from work. Should the time of day be added to this equation, morning kidnappings far outnumber those at any other time.

A terrorist tendency to follow the above pattern is a direct function of available manpower. Terrorists are few in number. No national level group operating today exceeds 250 to 300 persons. Most have fewer than 100 members. In any such organization, only a limited number of individuals can be mobilized for a single operation. Accordingly, few if any terrorist groups can afford the luxury of several alternate ambush sites. Only a single location can be chosen, and it must be one where the victim is sure to pass at a preselected time.

In choosing such a site, two useful constants in the daily routine of most corporate executives and government personnel are an established time of departure for work and a normal route of travel. Both can be verified via preoperational surveillance. For example, in the September 5, 1977, kidnapping of Schleyer, chairman of the board of Daimler Benz, terrorists in Cologne, Germany, had him under surveillance from at least early July to the date of abduction. Once such a surveillance has been conducted, two of the most difficult variables in any kidnapping have been controlled. By subsequently establishing the ambush point as close as possible to the victim's residence (Schleyer was taken within two blocks of his home), route variation possibilities are further reduced. By so eliminating critical unknowns, operational success is virtually assured (it is well to remember the terrorists' 94.3 percent success rate), and manpower requirements for the abduction are reduced substantially.

In connection with manpower involved in the actual kidnapping act, it is interesting to note this has increased over the 1970–78 time period. During 1970–71, the average terrorist kidnapping team worldwide totaled 4.1 persons. Females were involved in 6 percent of all abductions. By 1977–78, team size had increased to 5.2 persons, and female participation had jumped to 18 percent.

The growth in team size—despite terrorist desires to keep this at a minimum for security and manpower purposes—seems to be a direct result of the increased protection provided potential victims. Police escorts and private bodyguards present the modern terrorist with problems that did not exist in the early 1970s. An additional team member—armed with a submachine gun—is now almost essential to break through this increased security. In this connection, it is very interesting to note that during 1970–71, submachine guns (or other automatic weapons) were used in only 14.7 percent of all terrorist kidnappings. By 1977–78, this figure had jumped to 30 percent.

Increased female participation in the physical act of abduction appears less a function of "Women's Lib" than might be supposed—it is really due to some very hard thinking by terrorist leaders. Despite accelerating female involvement in all aspects of terrorism, many police officers still tend to view women as the "docile companions" of male terrorists. As one European police official reportedly stated: "This is a relatively new phenomenon . . . hard to grasp. It was one thing to view these women as submissive companions of terrorist men. It's quite another to see them rob, shoot and kill just like other members of the band."[4] Taking advantage of this view, terrorist leaders in all countries have been using more and more females in operational kidnapping and assassination teams rather than in their traditional roles as intelligence collectors, couriers, or safe house keepers. Thus, in both the kidnapping of former Italian premier Moro by the Red Brigades and the German terrorist abduction of Schleyer, females were involved in operational roles. In this sense, terrorism has truly become an "equal opportunity employer."

With these general considerations in mind concerning terrorist kidnapping operations—particularly as directed against corporate personnel—the following case studies are useful in illustrating the minute planning, attention to detail, and professionalism displayed by most terrorist groups today.

At 9.10 P.M. on April 13, 1977, Luchino Revelli Beaumont, director general of Fiat France, was kidnapped in front of his residence at 183 Rue de la Pompe in Paris by four men carrying pistols and rubber clubs. The operation took place as Revelli Beaumont returned to his home in a chauffeur-driven Fiat. As his chauffeur opened the door for Revelli Beaumont, four men suddenly appeared. Two attacked the chauffeur, and the others forced the Fiat executive out of his car and into a yellow Renault, in which they drove off. The men who attacked the chauffeur also tried to abduct him, but he put up a powerful resistance. As a result, he was severely beaten and left sprawled on the hood of his vehicle. After the attackers had left, the chauffeur made his way into the Revelli Beaumont residence and called the police.

Investigation disclosed that the escape car had been stolen and carried false license plates. Police also learned that for approximately 15 days prior to the abduction, neighbors had seen several men at various times watching the Revelli Beaumont home.

At 11:00 P.M. on April 13, a telephone call was received by a Paris radio station (Europe 1), and the following conversation took place:

> (Kidnapper) Hello, ready Europe 1? Listen. Good evening. I am calling you but this will be very brief. I don't want you to establish a tap. We claim responsibility for the kidnapping of the Director General of Fiat France. We are the Committee of Defense for Italian Workers in France and we require that 3,000,000 in old francs be supplied in the form of medicines and food supplies to the Italian workers on strike in France. You can send out this information in your first bulletin. Tomorrow at 6.30 A.M. in the morning we will call again.
>
> (Radio Europe 1) Why have you done this to the Director General of Fiat France?

(Kidnapper) We are not going to say anything more. Tomorrow
we will call again. Pass on our communique now.
(Radio Europe 1) What is the health of Mr. Revelli Beaumont?
(Kidnapper) Sorry, we have to terminate now.

The kidnappers did not call back at 6:30 A.M. as they had promised.
Rather, they sent letters to various Paris newspapers reiterating their demands
and enclosing Polaroid photos of Revelli Beaumont to show he was in good
health.

Late in June, Fiat reportedly arranged to deposit an estimated $10 million
in Swiss back accounts for use in a ransom payoff. The actual ransom was paid
in cash, not in medicine and food, and came to about $1.9 million. Revelli Beau-
mont was released July 11, 1977, in Versailles after being held for 89 days.
Seven Argentines and an Italian were arrested for the crime on July 23/24 in
Malaga, Spain. Much of the ransom was recovered in Switzerland.

The Argentine connection in the Revelli Beaumont case raises some interesting possibilities.

The headquarters of the IV International (Trotskyite) is located in Paris.
A member of the executive committee of that body is Julio Santucho, brother
of Mario Santucho, slain leader of ERP. The ERP had direct ties to the IV International. Until Mario Santucho and a number of his associates were killed in a
fire fight with security forces in July 1976, the ERP was the most effective terrorist organization in Argentina. One of its specialities was the kidnapping or
assassination of foreign and Argentine businessmen.

It was the ERP that kidnapped Victor Samuelson of Esso Argentina in
1973 and obtained $14.2 million in ransom for his release. The ERP also was
responsible for the 1972 kidnapping and subsequent murder of Oberdan Sallus-
tro, who headed Fiat operations in Argentina. On April 4, 1974, the ERP also
kidnapped the chief of personnel for Fiat Argentina (Roberto Francisco Kleber)
and later killed him.

In this context, it should be noted that Revelli Beaumont had been involved in Fiat Argentina operations in Buenos Aires in the course of 1970–74.
In view of the ERP operations against Fiat, the presence of Revelli Beaumont in
Argentina during the targeting of Fiat, the connections between the ERP and the
IV International in Paris, the Argentine nationality of those allegedly responsible
for the operation, and the fact that ERP exiles and other members had been
known to go to France, it would seem that this operation may well have been
conducted by former ERP activists.

Slightly over a year following the abduction of Revelli Beaumont, the kidnapping of the manager of Texas Petroleum operations in Colombia illustrated
again the resourcefulness and attention to detail exhibited by terrorist organizations.

Nicolas Escobar Soto, manager of Texas Petroleum in Colombia and chairman of the board, Bank of Colombia, was taken in Bogota on May 30, 1978, at 11:45 A.M. in front of a building on 44th Street. Having business at this address and in the area, Escobar Soto was obliged to park in a space in front of the building, between two occupied cars. In the Toyota camper ahead and the Renault behind were seven terrorists. Two were women, who sat with one man in the Renault. Apparently, the team had inside information, as they were able to set up in advance at a location not regularly visited by Escobar Soto. After he had parked, one of the women terrorists identified him to the men in the Toyota.

The four men in that vehicle immediately approached the target car and tried to force an entry. Escobar Soto closed the doors, locked them, and closed the wing vent on the hand of one of the men as he tried to reach inside. The attacker then shot out the window, and the four men grabbed the executive in full view of passersby. He was taken into the Toyota camper and driven off.

Escobar Soto had been aware of being targeted and, in fact, several weeks earlier, had eluded an attempt to kidnap him in the northern part of Bogota. He was armed and had radio communication with his office from the car at the time of his capture. Escobar Soto, married and with two children, was, at age 48, one of Colombia's most prominent businessmen. He had held several high corporate positions and had been head of Texas Petroleum operations in Colombia for ten years.

In addition to the abduction of corporate executives—which unquestionably is the primary terrorist tactic used against business personnel today—assassination and maiming also are of interest, but to a much lesser degree.

The planned assassination of businessmen is relatively rare. Of the 581 terrorist assassinations recorded during the past eight years, only 13 percent were targeted against business. As might be expected, the highest number of assassination operations (42 percent) were directed against police officers.

Quite clearly, the murder of a businessman by terrorists generally is counterproductive. Corporate officials are of great value when alive and available for ransom. As assassination victims, they are valueless as a source of income for the group. Accordingly, in those few cases where corporate personnel have been assassination targets, the operation usually was carried out "to teach others a lesson." In some cases, the lesson may have been to end corporate cooperation with the police or government counterterrorist forces. In other situations, it may have involved failure to pay a "revolutionary tax" levied by terrorists on all business operations in a given area. One of the more recent terrorist murders of an executive in the Basque provinces of Spain was precisely for this purpose. With these and possibly a few additional exceptions, however, corporate assassination is an infrequent terrorist tactic.

Within Italy, and to a much lesser extent in other nations, the deliberate maiming of businessmen has been a favorite terrorist technique. As in "kneecapping" (shooting off the victim's kneecap), a tactic originally used in the IRA against traitors, leg shooting (*azzoppare*—"laming") in Italy is designed to intimidate, but not kill, the victim. It is reserved primarily for business and government executives, who are viewed by Italian terrorists as vital parts of the state structure they are attacking. The intent is to create fear within the key target groups (businessmen, government officials, the media, and politicians) and to render members of these groups incapable of acting against the terrorists.

This tactic has been confined almost exclusively to Italy. Corporate personnel have been targets in over 47 percent of the 87 leg shootings that took place between May 1975 and mid-November 1978. With 37 such operations recorded between January 1, 1978, and November 15, 1978, these took place primarily in the metropolitan centers of Rome, Milan, Turin, and Genoa. Targets included the plant manager of Fiat Mirafiori, Turin; director of foreign operations, Pirelli Tire, Milan; manager of Chemical Bank, Milan; personnel manager of Italsider Metals Corporation, Genoa; manager of Alfa Romeo Plant, Milan; and so forth.

Carried out on busy city streets, at bus stops, and in apartment buildings, the tactic usually requires at least two persons, often women. One normally approaches the victim and asks an innocent question, such as, "Do you have a light?" or "Do you have the time?" While the victim is momentarily distracted, the other terrorist approaches him face-to-face, often points to his legs, and fires point blank anywhere from one to eight rounds. Usually a 9-millimeter pistol is used, sometimes with a silencer. In other cases, two or three terrorists approach a victim and simply fire, without any preliminaries.

To ensure hitting the proper target, at least one terrorist unit temporarily adopted a procedure of checking the victim's identification before shooting. With a wry sense of humor, several other groups—including the well-known Red Brigades—have sent notes of condolence to victims hit not only in the legs but also in the stomach, groin, and chest. In these, they have apologized for their poor marksmanship. With a trend toward the use of submachine guns in such operations and with the less than excellent shooting skills of many Italian terrorists, more and more intended leg shootings are now turning into fatalities.

In looking at the future of terrorist operations targeting corporate personnel, there seems little question that kidnapping will remain the primary tactic above all others. With a continued need for funds, terrorist groups see this tactic as a proven revenue producer. Additionally, based on eight years experience, it has been almost foolproof in execution. Coupling these factors with terrorist knowledge of the substantial kidnapping and ransom policies carried out on key corporate executives, there seems to be a feeling that "this particular well is not about to run dry." If true, such an attitude may well portend increased terrorist targeting of business personnel for abduction. In this same context, just as terrorists have come to rely on the tactics of violent crime, we also are likely to see the increased kidnapping of businessmen for purely criminal purposes, but with all the outward trappings of a political terrorist act in order to increase the problems of negotiation and the probabilities of favorable resolution for the kidnappers.

NOTES

1. *Brigate Rosse: Revoluzione della Direzione Strategica*, February 1978, p. 2.

2. Ibid, p. 41.

3. Abraham Guillen, *The Philosophy of the Urban Guerrilla: The Revolutionary Writings of Abraham Guillen*, trans. Donald C. Hodges (New York: Morrow, 1973), p. 295.

4. Washington *Star*, September 27, 1978, p. A-8.

PART II

CORPORATE RESPONSE TO TERRORISM AND THE ROLE OF GOVERNMENTS

6

CORPORATE VULNERABILITY—
AND HOW TO ASSESS IT

Brooks McClure

In the waning months of the 1970s, the international business community can look back upon a decade of turbulence and can contemplate an uncertain. legacy for the balance of the century. Trade imbalances and dislocation, currency fluctuation, inflation, rising operating costs, growing concerns about pollution, overpopulation, hunger, and revolutionary disruption in the Third World—all have matured as problems over the past ten years and none with a glimmer of hope for easy solution.

Then, in the midst of it all is the perplexing phenomenon of political terrorism—a true problem child of the 1970s—which seeks to become an instrument of world revolution in the 1980s. It has little chance of achieving this goal, based on its record so far, but it may be capable of causing costly damage and disarray in both the political and economic life of a number of countries. It has links with most of the basic problems of the times, being able both to capitalize on and promote social distress of all kinds.

Urban political terrorism, as it has now emerged, dates back to 1968, shortly after the death of Che Guevara and the collapse of his attempted revolutionary insurgency in Bolivia. A number of Latin American terrorist groups, following the lead of the Tupamaros in Uruguay, shifted the focus of their guerrilla operations from their traditional rural bases, sanctified in doctrine by Mao Tse-tung and Castro, to the cities. This proved spectacularly successful, especially in Uruguay, which became the model for militant extremists elsewhere in Latin America and in Western Europe.

Political targets, and particularly diplomats, were popular in Latin America as the urban guerrillas took hold, and large numbers of "political prisoners" were released in exchange for hostages. Funds were obtained, at first chiefly through bank raids. But early in the 1970s, the targets shifted more toward businessmen, as governments increasingly refused to pay ransom for kidnapped officials. By

1974, company executives had become favored kidnap victims, yielding ransoms far greater than the sums obtainable from bank robberies, and at less risk. In 1972, Esso paid a record $14.2 million to recover its manager from terrorists in Buenos Aires. Later, the Argentine conglomerate, Bunge & Born, paid a reported $60 million to ransom its two managing directors.

Risks International of Alexandria, Virginia, which keeps the most extensive computer record available on terrorist incidents worldwide, estimates that more than $290 million in ransoms have been demanded and about half that amount collected since 1970. This projection is based on information about payments reported for 30 percent of the 370 terrorist kidnappings recorded, involving a total of 567 hostages. Businessmen have been victims in more than half the cases—with the proportion rising steeply in recent years—and of these, more than a fifth have been Americans.

For international terrorist acts of all kinds—that is, incidents in which the perpetrators and victims are of different nationalities—U.S. property or personnel have been the primary target. A CIA report covering the period 1968–77 lists a total of 2,690 cases, of which 1,148, or 42.6 percent, involved U.S. targets.[1] Other principal targets were Western European (32.6 percent) and Latin American (14 percent). By type of international terrorist incident, U.S. property was targeted in 18.9 percent of the incendiary bombings and 53.6 percent of the explosive bombings, according to the CIA report.

By geographic area, the incidents involving Americans occurred most frequently in Latin America (39.6 percent), followed by Western Europe (26 percent), the Middle East and North Africa (16.9 percent), Asia (7.3 percent), North America (6.8 percent), and Sub-Saharan Africa (2.4 percent).

The CIA study for 1977 shows a dramatic drop of worldwide international terrorist incidents from a year earlier, with incendiary bombing down by more than one-third, explosive bombing and kidnapping by one-quarter, assassination by more than one-half, armed attack by one-third, and letter-bombing by four-fifths. But this does not take into account such purely internal terrorist incidents as the kidnap-murders of Moro by the Red Brigades in Italy and of Schleyer by the Red Army faction in Germany.

The more comprehensive file of Risks International, with a record of more than 5,500 cases since 1970, shows that political terrorist incidents have not declined recently—they have just been more domestic than "international" in character. For measuring general terrorist activities, therefore, the record of only those cases involving two or more nationalities is misleading, although it does reflect the incidence of violence affecting international business.

The dramatic downturn of international incidents in 1977 compares roughly with the record for 1975—in other words, 1976 stands out as a high point in a saw-toothed line graph, which shows that there is almost no predictable pattern in this type of terrorist targeting. For terrorist actions of all kinds, the overall totals have been growing, although the proportions among different kinds of attacks are constantly shifting.

This, then, is the general nature of the threat that confronts international business. There is little comfort in the recent slack in targeting of foreigners; the threat remains, and the techniques and tactics of terrorist groups are being refined. Given this state of the art, how can corporations evaluate their vulnerability to attack?

Evaluation of vulnerability is anything but an exact science. It does not lend itself to quantification, and one must be wary of mathematical models and comparisons—the variables are too numerous. But there are certain considerations that, when examined, each in its own context and then in combination, can give a valid overall picture of a company's exposure to attack. At the same time, such an evaluation sometimes suggests where specific improvements in defense can be made.

Following are five general factors in corporate vulnerability that can be systematically analyzed for any facility that might be targeted. The components under each major heading are necessarily limited by space considerations here, but they indicate areas that should be examined in detail. When the whole exercise is completed, the potential exposure of the facility to targeting will be evident.

COMPANY VISIBILITY

The first factor to consider in assessing a company's vulnerability to terrorist attack is its general visibility. Since political terrorists rank propaganda and other psychological effects high among their objectives, any conspicuous symbol of capitalistic enterprise offers an attractive target. Among the questions one should ask are these:

1. *Is the facility obviously American?* If so, it may well have a better-than-average chance of being hit (in Italy, for instance, and in several Latin American countries). This is not because organized terrorists need a sign to point out U.S. interests; they have rather sophisticated intelligence methods to help in their targeting. The low-profile U.S. company abroad, with a local name and perhaps local management, is not invisible to political terrorists, but it is not likely to be a prime target because of its relative obscurity.

When a U.S. subsidiary "flies the flag," however, it risks providing a propaganda incentive for attack because terrorists can make the point of striking at "U.S. imperialism." Depending upon popular attitudes in the host country, this type of target may be selected to reinforce a growing xenophobia or otherwise to stimulate anti-"capitalistic" sentiments. The target thus can provide a rallying point for radical agitation. The fact that two of every five international terrorist incidents in the past decade have involved U.S. property or citizens as targets testifies to the symbolic appeal of anything conspicuously American.

Certain company names are synonymous with an obviously American product (Coca-Cola) or suggest superior U.S. technical achievement (IBM), or otherwise project a distinctly American image. Firms of this kind tend to be choice targets of terrorist groups seeking to demonstrate opposition in U.S. political power, or even just to *any* foreign influence. Despite spectacular inroads into world markets by West Germany (which also has been targeted by terrorists abroad) and Japan—and the traditional commercial role of such countries as Great Britain, France, and The Netherlands—the United States remains the preeminent symbol of "capitalism" and "imperialism" to Marxist-oriented extremists.

2. *Is the company regarded as a "multinational?"* Although all companies with operations in several countries are by definition "multinational," some are clearly more so than others for political propaganda purposes. Firms engaged in extractive operations (oil production or mining, for example), or in plantation-type food cultivation (pineapples or bananas, for example) are singled out by radicals as being particularly exploitative. So are companies involved in defense-related production or in the computer-electronics field.

Large companies with high visibility as multinational corporations in recent years have been criticized in liberal, non-Communist circles in industrial countries because of their ability to "shop around" for favorable production or marketing conditions in developing countries and for being able to operate largely beyond control of national governments. To capitalize on this negative sentiment and to suggest common cause with moderate Socialist and Social-Democratic groups, terrorists have found the multinational corporation an especially attractive target.

Beyond this consideration, however, the international corporation is seen universally by Marxists as a key element of capitalism and a source of economic power to the developed Western nations. The degree to which any company can be portrayed as a "typical multinational" therefore has a bearing on its vulnerability to targeting by left-wing terrorists.

3. *Is the product symbolic?* Certain products, as already noted, have developed a negative social connotation among political critics, who often use and enjoy the very same products. Thus, one hears of the "Coca-Cola (or Pepsi) civilization," denoting an all-pervasive, materialistic, Philistine culture (of the United States) being exported around the world. Radical propagandists are quick to exploit any such symbolic linkage, trying to reduce complex attitudes toward the United States to simple slogans.

Other product associations that are singled out for attention by radicals—and, hence, by terrorists as well—center on military production of any kind. Thus, a chemical company that produced napalm during the Vietnam War is constantly identified with that product, although its product line includes hundreds of items with a vast range of utility. Likewise, in Italy, the Red Brigades in their strategy papers focus attention on computers, contending that modern computer technology imported from the United States is enabling the "repressive" Italian authorities to set up a data bank designed to ferret out and destroy the "Socialist revolutionaries." They have, consequently, caused heavy damage to Honeywell and IBM facilities and destroyed one whole Italian Army computer complex.

Automobiles are particularly symbolic of the country of origin; probably a car "carries the flag" more than any other product. It is no accident that Fiat and Alfa Romeo are favorite targets of leftist terrorists in Italy—as foremost symbols of the establishment and pillars of the Italian economy. Likewise, Daimler-Benz was targeted in both Italy and France after the suicide of Meinhof in 1976 and the suicide of Baader and other imprisoned terrorists after German commandos foiled the Lufthansa hijacking in Somalia in 1977. What could be more German than a Mercedes? Other factors also make automobile companies particularly vulnerable: the great size of their plants and storage areas and the relative ease with which their showrooms can be firebombed. Privately owned vehicles are of course the easiest targets; U.S. cars have frequently been fire-bombed around the world during violent political demonstrations.

4. *Does the company have local management?* If so, this is no guarantee that the plant will not be hit or the manager himself targeted. In Italy, for example, both the Red Brigades and Front Line terrorists have struck at Italians "serving the multinationals." But the locally run subsidiary generally is a less inviting target than a branch run by expatriates, when the aim is to emphasize the "foreign" enemy. Much depends on how the local population perceives the enterprise and identifies with it. (Of course, any native company can be hit by terrorists in its own right, as the statistics show.)

IMAGE FACTORS

Another set of criteria for measuring corporate vulnerability is what might simply be called *image factors*, or how the company is regarded by the community around it. These might be broken down into four categories for analysis.

Labor Relations

Are there any current union difficulties, or have there been any significant strikes in the past that have left emotional scars? What about layoffs? Have these been accomplished with minimum worker bitterness? What sort of cushion exists to tide over those temporarily out of work? Answers to these questions may reveal possible seeds of trouble.

Political agitators are quick to exploit any festering dissatisfaction among workers, and the company should ask itself how well prepared it is to detect early signs of such agitation and what it can do to blunt the effect. In this regard, the level of plant vandalism and sabotage should be watched carefully.

Even if the damage is relatively small, a growing incidence of such activity can indicate the beginning of an orchestrated campaign by political terrorists, which can spell serious trouble ahead.

Health, Safety, and Environmental Impact

This is an area of particular importance because it involves the entire social panorama around the company plant or facility. What about past accidents, in which there may have been loss of life or community property damage? Have the social and emotional effects been outlived? Is the company still blamed for some past incident, such as a mine cave-in? Are there embittered individuals who feel they have a score to settle with the company, no matter how unreasonable this attitude may be? Here may lie fertile grounds for agitprop exploitation and a chance for a terrorist group to penetrate the plant with spies or saboteurs.

On another plane is the question of continuing occupational hazards. Has the company taken steps to minimize the sometimes inevitable consequences of dealing with toxic or other harmful substances? What is the general employee view of the company's measures to protect workers and take care of them if they develop occupational disorders?

Environmental concerns affect not only the "company family" but the surrounding community as well. Does the plant generate water, soil, or air pollution? Is this pollution within tolerable limits, or is the condition likely to get worse? To what degree is there local political or academic-professional opposition, and how much publicity is being given to the problem? Within the past three years, there has been a discernible growth of political violence in Europe around environmental issues, centering on antinuclear sentiment but extending to other pollution and contamination charges. Terrorist organizations have also shown tendencies to exploit these broader-based protest movements.

Community Relations

The role and general relationship of the company to the community around it is of the utmost importance in determining the potential terrorist threat. Again, there are no simple answers. A company with fine community relations may be targeted in order to intimidate the population as a whole or to cause the townspeople, out of fear, to avoid contact with the company. (The political counterpart to this tactic is to attack municipal officials, suggesting in the process that any ordinary citizen who has contact with them may also become a target.)

In general, however, strong community relations will help any company and cannot possibly hurt it. In societies which have not reached a point at which terrorist activity is so massive and pervasive that it can exercise a counter-government authority (as has happened at different times in sections of such countries as Uruguay, Argentina, and Italy), communal social pressure can minimize the terrorist threat to respected institutions and industrial facilities in the neighborhood.

Usually, terrorist groups seek to exploit existing grievances and identify with a popular cause, thus earning the grudging support of persons otherwise repelled by their violent methods, and perhaps also winning recruits from among disgruntled youth. If one plant does not offer much opportunity for such exploitation, there is always another that will.

Some touchstones for evaluating community relations with the plant include: (1) company tax contributions—Does the populace consider these to be reasonable and fair?; (2) social services—Is the company seen as contributing to them or drawing excessively from them?; and (3) role as an institution—Is the firm socially integrated with the community, or does it stand physically and institutionally apart?

To raise all these questions is not necessarily to imply a remedy. The optimum role of a company in any society depends upon cultural, sociological, psychological, and even historical circumstances. Overparticipation in community activities in some cases can arouse popular concern about company domination or dictation. Excessive support for certain projects—such as building a community center—can lead paradoxically to resentment and rejection of the company's self-assigned role. This is the lesson learned on a larger scale, incidentally, by foreign aid programs of large countries in the developing world. Institutional largesse must be handled with great care to avoid creating an intolerable psychological obligation on the part of the recipient—which can be a whole community.

As a rule, however, reciprocal benefits between company and community can operate effectively within the economic sphere. When the population at large regards the company's contribution to the community as commensurate with the benefit the company receives (in labor availability, public services, and so forth), a firm basis for good relations is established. If there are further offsetting factors, such as plant-generated pollution or the inhibition of other commercial development because of the nature of the company's operations, still other compensation from the company side may be in order. Beyond this point, there are perhaps other modest company contributions that can enrich community life without appearing overly paternalistic or intrusive. As long as the relationship is a partnership between the community as a whole and the company, with each making its proper contribution to a mutually profitable endeavor, the danger of psychological rejection can be avoided.

While popularity of a company within its community is no assurance it will be spared by either terrorists or radical agitators, the likelihood of trouble is certainly significantly reduced.

Political Symbolism to the Left

Akin to the direct product symbolism already mentioned is the political propaganda image of certain companies that is nurtured by international left-wing movements. Thus, ITT has been targeted by both radical groups and terrorists in various countries because of its reported financial support of opponents of Allende in Chile, in cooperation with the CIA. The attempt here has been to exploit whatever moderate Socialist dissatisfaction exists against ITT while perpetuating and reinforcing the company's negative political image. This tactic extends as well to firms that provided munitions and other materiel during the Vietnam War or which operate plants today in South Africa. Such targeting is also appealing to left-wing extremists, who stress what they call the worldwide "fraternity of liberation" movements.

NATURE OF THE THREAT

External threats to a company come in many forms and vary in nature from place to place. It is therefore vital that the general security climate be correctly evaluated for each separate facility. Only on the basis of a sound assessment of the local threat can cost-effective and workable defense measures be developed.

Political violence tends to follow predictable patterns—although there can always be surprises. In general, radical activists start with relatively mild, nonviolent actions (demonstrations, leaflet distributions) and then move on to more intimidating measures (blockades, sit-ins)—feeling their way and measuring the reaction at each step. When the political terrorism stage is reached, the activists tend to start with less sophisticated operations, then gradually escalate as experience and opportunity warrant.

In terms of organizational skill and technical competence involved, terrorist actions rank roughly in this order: petty vandalism; small group "picketing" and distribution of radical literature; mass demonstrations (which usually enlist the participation of basically nonviolent, liberal, but nonrevolutionary students); firebombing; sabotage in easy-access areas; explosive bombing; felonious assault of targeted individuals; professional sabotage of key functions; assassination; and kidnapping.

Seldom does the violence escalate abruptly from the lower range of operations—say, from mass demonstrations or small group picketing—to the upper level of sophistication, such as kidnapping or assassination. This is due in part to the group's lack of readiness; it must train itself to take more complex and dramatic measures in turn. But perhaps even more important is the need to prepare the public at large to accept a high level of violence as a *political* rather than an ordinary *criminal* act.

The abrupt assassination of a company official by a political group, without having first passed through lesser stages of violence accompanied by political propaganda, might cause a strong shock reaction from the public, which could result in a concerted action with the authorities to crush the revolutionary movement. But a long period of slowly accelerating political violence can condition the public to accept such measures as a fact of life.

Several other things happen in this graduated process as well: the public loses confidence in the police, who are unable to end the trouble; it gradually feels more vulnerable to the threat itself (although wise terrorists carefully avoid harming "innocent" persons at the outset and try to isolate the targeted institution); and it is "educated" by the terrorists' propaganda to recognize their actions as political rather than as criminal. By the time the kidnapping-assassination phase comes, the public feels both helpless and intimidated. It is no longer prepared to respond wholeheartedly and spontaneously against even cold-blooded murder. The history of the Provisional IRA, as an example, largely illustrates this process.

The corporate security analyst can be guided by the principles outlined here to determine the level of threat directed at any plant or facility around the world. First, it is important to determine the general condition of stability and control in the society at large and what the record has been for political (and, indeed, for organized criminal) violence. A simple checklist for evaluating the level of threat might include the following:

Groups Operating in the Area

What are their political motivation, their modes of operation, their weapons-and-tactics sophistication, and their size? Also, what is the nature of their support mechanisms? Aside from members of the group itself, who provide safe houses and specialized technical and professional services, there is frequently a sympathizer element within the general population that gives invaluable moral and material support. The extent and influence of this support element—often found in professional, artistic, and academic circles—may determine how far the terrorists are likely to go.

Nature of the Violence

Where along the spectrum of possible violent acts has the terrorist group arrived now? If it is at the mass demonstration stage (which might be predominantly of a nonviolent radical nature rather than incipient terrorism), the threat may be contained at that level. If there is bombing, does it seek to take casualties, or is it confined to causing property damage at night? In the context of prevailing public attitudes, would the group be encouraged to escalate to a more lethal form of violence? (Most terrorist bombings by indigenous groups in the United States, such as the NWLF on the West Coast, have for several years now avoided bloodshed. The Puerto Rican extremist FALN, on the other hand, has not hesitated to take casualties. The difference reflects the degree of dependence by each group on American public opinion.)

The kind of current terrorist activity indicates, of course, what immediate defensive measures are needed. In addition, some precautions should be taken against the next likely level of violence, and contingency plans should exist for meeting any conceivable escalation of the threat in the future. But it is important to avoid excessive defenses, for the cost can become prohibitive and a siege mentality can be created, which will reduce the operating efficiency of the plant. The art is to meet the current level of threat, to have some excess capacity to meet a sudden rise in the threat level, and to be ready to cope with more serious dangers in the future—all without making a gross overinvestment in security.

How Have Others Coped?

No opportunity should be lost to profit from the experience of other companies in the area of one's plant, either of foreign or domestic ownership, which have suffered terrorist threat or attack. One should learn in detail what tactics were used by the terrorists, what countermeasures were taken by the company, and what the response was by the authorities. In some respects, the basic circumstances of one's own company may differ from those of the other targeted company, requiring modifications of the lessons learned. But the information gained will be valuable both for ascertaining the probable nature of the threat to one's facility as well as for determining what measures are effective against it.

Available Outside Assistance

If one's plant is attacked, how quickly and effectively would the police respond? Would there be military and other reserves to call upon? Terrorists always evaluate the effectiveness of the authorities in making their plans, and the possible victim should do likewise. Deficiencies in police protection or in the ability of the police to respond to an emergency might have to be made up by the company itself. Any evidence that the plant has compensated for inadequate police support—which would become evident to the terrorists through surveillance when they planned their attack—would tend to discourage an attempt.

The quality of fire-fighting services should also be assessed. In most places, the company is wise to have a considerable capability of its own to cope with arson or fire bomb attack. Even the quickest response of the community fire department may be too slow to deal with an incendiary assault.

In the case of either police or fire services, it is well to remember that well-organized terrorists frequently turn 'in false alarms to divert emergency services to a distant place just before they attack, thus assuring that help will not be readily available.

PHYSICAL SECURITY PROFILE

Surveys of building security are routine for every large corporation, and many of the precautions taken against criminal acts or industrial sabotage apply equally well against possible terrorist attack. But the terrorist poses a threat beyond the limits of either conventional criminals or vengeful individuals trying to cause damage to the company.

Criminals normally seek personal gain; they are trying to get something of value. The amount of damage they do is therefore usually circumscribed by this objective (although they might in some cases cause an explosion or start a fire as a diversion). The terrorist group, on the other hand, is not seeking what is normally thought of as "selfish gain"; the aim, rather, is to cause damage, attract attention, create an illusion of strength, and generate fear. This is an easier mission to accomplish than that of the criminal, and the consequent destruction or loss caused can be many times greater.

Furthermore, terrorists generally have greater resources at their command than do criminals—or the individual saboteur. Often, the terrorists have excellent intelligence from spies within the plant; they can draw on a variety of technical skills from among their members and sympathizers; they are usually well-financed; and they frequently have access to particularly effective weapons and technology.

When considering defense measures against terrorism, therefore, one must look far beyond established security precautions. A physical security profile for any facility or installation under potential terrorist threat must take into account the following factors.

Relation of the Plant to other Possible Targets

In politically motivated mass disturbances, a facility may come under attack as an alternate or incidental target: the primary target may be nearby and less accessible, or it might draw an attack that results in the damage of other property in the neighborhood. In early 1978, a Nicaraguan mob, protesting what was conceived as a government-directed assassination of an opposition news-paper editor, attacked and fire-bombed a blood plasma factory in north Managua, in which President Anastasio Somoza was reported to have an interest. On the way, the mob passed a Chevron gasoline station, which it wiped out—apparently only an incidental target at best. In Paris, at around the same time, TWA offices were demolished by a terrorist bomb directed at a nearby fashionable restaurant. Security planners should take such possibilities into account.

Relation of Plant to Target

Space between the company building and the nearest point of public access (normally a street screened off by a fence) constitutes both a warning time and a territorial buffer in an emergency. Often, it is not until the fence is breached and the company's "territory" invaded that a serious threat is recognized, so generally, the greater the distance from the building to the front fence the better the possibility of defense against some kind of assault.

In mob actions, it is possible to perceive a threat and use both the time and space afforded by the distance from the street to take defense measures. Obviously, the danger from this kind of threat is greater if there is no buffer zone or if the public has casual access to the facility itself. Retail establishments and automobile showrooms are afforded much less natural protection, and special precautions must then be taken for them in high-risk areas.

Situation of Facility on Grounds

Certain features of the plant layout can be important to security. If the building is less than 35 yards from the nearest public access area, for example, it might be hit by a hand-thrown Molotov cocktail. Within that range, then, certain other circumstances must be considered: (1) Are there large front windows (which might be wire-screened or inexpensively reinforced with Mylar or some other invisible sheet-plastic coating)?; (2) Is it advisable to move workers from the immediate window area to prevent possible injury?; and (3) Is there material in the front of the building that is especially volatile or inflammable and which can be moved elsewhere?

In any case, it is wise to consider how the building might be evacuated during a bomb threat, or even if an explosion occurred. Is there space in which to evacuate personnel in the case of an explosion, and are there suitable exits to the rear of the building? Since about three-quarters of all actual bomb plants have been either in the public-access areas of the target building or immediately outside it, one must always consider the danger of evacuating people directly into the explosion. Rear areas are generally less accessible to strangers than front areas (and should where possible be kept clear of receptacles, where a bomb might be hidden). Escape to the rear, preferably out of view from the street in front of the building, might be necessary if a mob threatens to attack from the front. Existing fire evacuation plans, which bring the employees out of all the exits, have to be modified for bomb-threat and mob-threat evacuation to avoid exposed areas.

Other points of vulnerability for a facility involve the elevation of the building and the general character of the surrounding terrain. Blind approaches; ground undulation; location and character of the shrubbery; the positioning of fences, gates, and other possible obstacles; and the layout of parking areas and access walks or roads—all of these should be examined in the light of any possible hostile approach or infiltration.

Structural Characteristics

Particularly if fire or explosive bombing is a danger, the facility should be analyzed for fireproofing and blast resistance. Such factors as the thickness and composition of exterior walls, size and design of windows, materials used for nonstructural partitions, and load-bearing capacity of floors determine what contingency plans might be developed for various kinds of threat. The division of work functions is particularly important for limiting possible damage; Fiat in Turin suffered particularly heavy plant damage a couple of years ago when its upholstery division was fire-bombed because the section was not segregated from the rest of the building by fireproofed partitions. Some small adjustments in work organization, establishment of relatively safe areas, and avenues of quick and easy exit can help minimize casualties and damage in the event of a serious incident.

Location of Key Elements of Facility

Certain functions constitute the very (organic) substance of a plant and are particularly vulnerable to attack.

Fuel Storage

Many factory complexes have fuel tanks on the periphery of the industrial estate, where they can readily be resupplied and pose no danger to the rest of the compound. Since terrorists frequently target fuel depots, such tanks should be relocated deeper within the fence. From a production standpoint, there should be a standby reserve, which can be drawn upon if the main tanks should be attacked.

Power Source

With respect to the power source, one should ask the following questions: (1) Is it located near the fence, thus relatively accessible to the outside?; (2) Is there a reserve transformer if the main one goes out?; and, (3) If the facility uses community power, is there an emergency backup system, which would permit at least partial operations if the transmission lines are cut?

Communications

With respect to the area of communications, one should ask the following questions: (1) Is there a radio or other backup system that could maintain external contact if the telephones went out? (even a citizens' band [CB] radio in a vehicle parked on the grounds would be a help in an emergency); (2) Is there at least one direct line that does not run through the switchboard?; (3) Is the switchboard room kept locked to all but authorized persons? (Incidentally, are the phone operators properly instructed on handling bomb warnings and other threats?)

Sensitive Records

With respect to sensitive records, the following questions should be asked: (1) Is the computer in a safe area and kept under proper security control?; (2) Are duplicates of important automatic data processing tapes available off the premises?; and (3) Are key papers kept secure, with access limited to designated persons? Penetration of sensitive files, both in industry and government, has been accomplished by terrorist groups in virtually every country.

Volatile Materials

With respect to volatile records, the following questions should be asked: (1) Are these kept in specially shielded areas, with quantities in the plant limited to the amount necessary for current production?; (2) Are reserve supplies also kept in a reasonably well-protected place?; and (3) Are critical spare parts likewise secure? It must be assumed that any terrorist group contemplating sabotage will know the potential squeeze points and bottlenecks of the plant and its processes.

Basic Security Precautions

Most of the measures to safeguard against theft and sabotage generally apply to the terrorist threat. The danger of political violence, however, calls for a new dimension to conventional security doctrine, enlisting the help of the personnel and public affairs departments. Terrorism is largely a psychological weapon directed at people. Effective countermeasures must therefore involve everyone who can be reached by terrorist propaganda. Among the special requirements are the following:

Personnel Security. The staffing of key functions has to be reevaluated. Is all sensitive information handled on a need-to-know basis? Is there limited access to executive files? Are secretaries and other clerical personnel properly vetted for security? (At the height of terrorist violence in Argentina, one U.S. company hired only married women over 30 for key secretarial positions, since nearly all terrorists and their sympathizers were young and single.) In some countries, the investigation of staff members is resented, and in Italy, it is forbidden by law. But most companies could scrutinize their key staff more carefully than they have in the past.

Rationalization of Functions. Restructuring of administrative procedures and the division of labor in the executive suite might be advisable if leaks of information are suspected or to avoid the concentration of sensitive data in the hands of certain clerical personnel.

Briefing of Employees. Probably a variety of orientation classes on the terrorist threat is required for such persons as secretaries of executives, phone operators, security personnel, safety officers, and so forth. One must avoid engendering undue fear, but in high-risk areas, key staff members must be informed of their role if emergency contingency plans are to work. It is helpful as well for everyone in what might be termed a *pivotal role*, down to the receptionist at the front desk, to be sensitized to danger signs. This provides an early warning system to detect impending terrorist actions. Not the least of these needing training are executives—potential kidnap victims—who should be advised on how to detect terrorist surveillance, to evade seizure, and, if need be, to survive as a hostage.

Intraplant Access and Security. Since sabotage is often most easily accomplished by someone from outside a critical area but who has casual access to it (the principle of "neighborly sabotage"), it might be well to declare such areas closed to routine visits. Color-coding identity (ID) cards and the screening of movement from one part of the plant to another—at least for the most vulnerable areas—could facilitate this control.

Executive Movement. Nearly every company can improve its measures for protecting top executives, although some of the executives themselves resist changes in their routine or work habits, which would improve their security. Again, in light of the oft-demonstrated ability of terrorists to penetrate corporate head-quarters, it is wise not to make general distribution around the office of the executive appointments schedule. Use of the "core day"—which assures that a top executive will be on hand for the same few hours every day (permitting scheduled in-house meetings) while he varies his arrivals and departures at either end of the day in irregular fashion—is another measure that greatly reduces his exposure to possible ambush, while not totally disrupting his daily routine. Random choice of routes to work or to other predictable stopping places also adds materially to his safety. Such "soft security" measures are indispensable to any company's protection system.

CRISIS MANAGEMENT CAPABILITY

The ability to determine—and correct—weaknesses in the company's defense against terrorist attack is the greatest possible insurance that there will be no attack at all. This is not a foolproof precaution, however. While studies of political terrorism show attackers usually pick the least protected among desirable targets, well-organized groups can bring to bear the resources necessary to hit a truly prime target almost regardless of defense. Thus, open battles were fought with armed escorts during the height of the ERP-Montenero violence in Argentina, and even a town was seized by the Tupamaros in Uruguay. When a particular target is sufficiently important for psychological or symbolic reasons, it must be assumed that terrorists can, and very well may, overwhelm the defenses to accomplish their mission.

What remains, then, is the ability to deal with an incident when it occurs, despite all reasonable precautions to prevent it. This requires additional contingency planning, backed by a top-level company command unit to handle such emergencies. It should be stressed that the requirement here goes beyond the need for a crisis management system to deal with natural disasters or major accidents—nonpremeditated, impersonal events. A terrorist incident is a planned hostile act that has anticipated the probable reaction of both the company and law enforcement agencies; there are plans for further psychological exploitation of the incident, and any countermeasure will encounter a further (and usually well-planned) terrorist response. The situation frequently constitutes a series of engagements—a dynamic, evolving campaign—built around the original attack.

How does a corporation prepare for such a problem? First, it must recognize that its normal management machinery is not able to cope with this threat. The typical business enterprise is not equipped to conduct hour-by-hour operations against a cunning and violent adversary or to "negotiate" for the return of a kidnapped executive. But with proper foresight and realistic planning, it can develop the necessary capacity.

Steps to establish this kind of capability might be outlined as follows:

1. Determine the extent of the problem. Based on the history of terrorism worldwide, what would realistically be the worst possible case in each category of terrorist attack to contend with? How might these threats be applied against the company's assets, either at home or abroad? Any one of several consulting firms could develop this more fully.

2. Develop basic policies for each contingency. What should be the general response to threat/extortion? Will the company pay ransom for kidnapped executives, and if so, what should be the limit? What is the policy for handling the family of a kidnap victim? Should a kidnapped executive automatically be replaced, or should his job be kept open until he is returned? Should the company "negotiate" with terrorists without involving the police? (Separate judgments have to be made here, depending on conditions in each place of operation.) (These are among the matters that should be settled before a crisis develops, in an atmosphere free from tension and anxiety, and they should be methodically thought out. It is exceedingly difficult to make sound decisions during an actual emergency, particularly if someone's life is at stake; it is even harder to get the necessary consensus of board members or other top management officials when no basic principles have been agreed upon in advance.)

3. Inform managers in the field of the policy. This includes informing key executives of the company in general terms of the plans for handling a kidnapping—whether ransom will be paid, whether the family will be removed from the scene (usually a good idea), and whether the victim will be automatically replaced. By knowing the general tactics of the company, the victim is less susceptible to psychological pressure by the kidnappers, who usually try to destroy his confidence in the company and convince him he has been abandoned.

4. Delegate necessary authority to the field. Branch managers should be instructed on how to respond to a sudden terrorist action and be given authority to act immediately when necessary (particularly in a kidnapping). Such crises cannot be managed from the outset by corporate headquarters. The very first steps taken by management at the scene in response to a kidnapping might well affect the outcome.

5. Establish a corporate crisis-response unit. This can be built upon whatever apparatus already exists for dealing with emergencies, but everyone must be aware that terrorist acts are not "normal" crises. At a minimum, the group should include the senior representatives of security, personnel, finance, and legal and public affairs. It should be headed by an executive vice president or a comparable official with a clear mandate from the chief executive officer. Proper organization and training of a crisis-response unit is a complex matter. Effectiveness depends upon the soundness of the corporation's basic policy for dealing with terrorism, the degree of mutual confidence and respect between the crisis-response unit and the corporate leadership, the extent to which the unit melds with the organizational structure and management style of the company, and the experience it has gained (through crisis-simulation exercise, among other things)

in working together under stress. Ideally, the crisis-response unit should have two basic functions: to staff out the problem and provide options for decision by top management and to supervise the execution of the decisions then reached.

Political terrorism is a fact of life in the world today, and after a decade of development and demonstration, it shows no sign of going away. Companies with international operations must contend with this phenomenon as one more problem to be solved or mastered—and at additional inconvenience and expense, which must be chalked up to the cost of doing business. Nothing has happened so far—despite spectacular terrorist events in Latin America, Western Europe, and the Middle East—to indicate that this mode of violent disruption will materially affect the flow of international trade. But the individual corporation wishing to continue to operate abroad (and, to some extent, at home as well), must adjust to the terrorist component of the world's life-style, which is certain to continue into the 1980s and perhaps beyond.

NOTE

1. *International Terrorism in 1977—A Research Paper* (RP 78-10255U) (Washington, D.C.: National Foreign Assessment Center, CIA, August 1978).

7

COUNTERMEASURES: SOME TECHNOLOGICAL CONSIDERATIONS

Robert H. Kupperman

Technology is but one means of countering terrorism—it is not offered here as a panacea for an advanced society lacking the commitment to remain vigilant in its own defense. Counterterrorism must necessarily use intelligence, police, and military operations, as well as psychological, medical, and behavioral science techniques before, during, and after threatened or actual incidents. Technology has a role to play in support of these efforts.

In order to make judgments with respect to the relative usefulness and breadth of application of various technologies, counterterrorism should be divided into functional tasks. The discussion and evaluation of technology can then be furthered by comparing these functional tasks with various scenarios. Though not mutually exclusive, we suggest that the job of counterterrorism can be divided into four functions:

1. Prevention: the avoidance of terrorist incidents, by denying access to suitable instruments where possible, by successful protection of critical targets should an incident be attempted, or by deterring incidents through a combination of denial and protection

2. Control: the timely establishment of mechanisms for command and control of government resources to assure an efficient response to an incident, with adequate informational and decision-making provisions, designed to seize the initiative from the terrorists

This chapter is based upon a forthcoming book by Robert H. Kupperman and Darrell M. Trent, *Terrorism: Threat, Reality, Response* to be published in 1979 by the Hoover Institution Press, Stanford University. The views expressed in this chapter are the authors' and do not necessarily reflect the views of the U.S. Government or any of its agencies or departments.

3. Containment: emergency measures taken to delimit the terrorist act in a physical sense and to "decouple" it in a psychological sense from the intended political consequences, with actions to limit damage and provide emergency health care included

4. Restoration: deliberate actions to conclude the incident and restore the situation, lasting until the situation is returned to normal and routine services are again available

CONCEPTUAL FRAMEWORK FOR RESOURCE ALLOCATION

For purposes of discussion, the management of terrorism problems are divided into four phases—prevention, control, containment, and restoration. Although the ways by which these phases are managed—and the concomitant technologies—are interrelated, the requirements that systems and devices must meet are quite different in the various phases. A further useful distinction is that between broad general purpose measures and specialized devices tailored to a particular type of incident or threat.

Raising Barriers

The first and last phases we mentioned—prevention and restoration—primarily involve general purpose measures. Screening of passengers and baggage at airports, fences, guards, and alarms serve to deter terrorists by making their activities more difficult. Although there can be no guarantee against circumvention by a skilled and determined effort, screening limits potential terrorism to the most talented groups (a high-pass filter) and so tends to inhibit terrorism. Such measures, to be effective, must be generally applied lest they merely divert terrorists from one opportunity to another, where the protective measures are lacking. (For instance, international air pirates, such as those involved in the Entebbe incident, arrange to board at points where security is known to be lax.) When the opportunities are numerous, the protective systems and devices used must be of relatively low cost if they are to be economically feasible. Multipurpose systems are preferable to a proliferation of single-purpose systems. Installing a sophisticated, single-purpose cobra venom detector at each U.S. airport, for instance, would be ludicrous. On the other hand, a device that could detect a wide variety of poisons, explosives, and drugs with moderate reliability might be useful if its cost was not too high.

Many of the emergency measures that would serve to restore well-being and tranquility in the wake of terrorist events would not be substantially different from those normally associated with natural disasters.

Measures intended to prevent terrorism will typically be costly, since they must be generally applied if they are to be effective. Most of the restorative measures have a joint utility in alleviating other sorts of calamities. Restorative measures related directly to disasters would not cost as much as preventive measures, because they would be applied after the fact to deal with a particular incident and would not need to be ubiquitous. Thus, such restorative measures might be feasible at a relatively high unit cost (per installation) in contrast to preventive measures.

Attempting to allocate counterterrorism resources on a marginal analysis basis poses extremely complex problems due to the vast number of potential targets and variety of possible countermeasures, leading to a great number of investment alternatives. These, of course, can be grouped, but they then must be compared with a combined utility function of lives and property saved and sovereignty preserved. Ultimately, one must fall back on sensitivity analysis and professional judgments.

Specialization

The control and containment phases of terrorist problems contrast sharply with the prevention and restoration phases. In prevention and restoration, generality of purpose is a desired feature. In controlling or containing a terrorist incident, precise tailoring of the response to the nature of the threat is needed. If it becomes apparent that a terrorist is credibly threatening to use cobra venom, the availability of an antidote becomes crucial. Moreover, it does not need to be ubiquitous. Subject to obvious logistic constraints, a limited antidote supply, matched to the terrorists' resources and their capability of using them, would suffice. The point here is that it may be worthwhile to invest in developing highly specialized technology on a very limited basis (in terms of numbers of devices produced) to deal with particular cases that may occur.

All contingencies cannot be covered, so the possibility of rapid access to a wide variety of experts and equipment is the principal strategy to adopt. Nevertheless, the high initial investment for the masses of ubiquitous equipment necessary for prevention is not involved here. Thus, we can aspire to a higher technology than would be feasible in the prevention mode and can develop more specialized devices for dealing with the threats we judge most likely.

Joint Usage

From our abstract viewpoint, the technology of containing the consequences of a terrorist incident differs from that of controlling the incident, primarily in its being more adaptable to dual purposes. Just as restoration from the effects of terrorism has much in common with restoration from the effects of other disasters, so with containment. Containing the effects of a chemical or biological terrorist threat has much in common with containing the effects of accidental events of these kinds. The havoc wrought by terrorist bombing of an aircraft does not differ much in its immediate physical effects from that of aircraft accidents and industrial explosions. Both the control and containment phases of antiterrorism technology can be highly specialized and fairly costly, but the containment can often depend on systems that are present anyway, such as ambulances and fire engines at airports and disease control resources.

The control phase of the antiterrorism problem appears to be the one most amenable to the application of highly specialized technology. It is interlinked with the prevention phase, at least in the case where extortion is attempted, through the credibility of the terrorist's threat. The Croatian hijackers of a TWA 727, for instance, were deterred by the airport security precautions from taking actual bombs aboard. Confidence in the system by the crisis managers, however, was not sufficient to allow them to call the terrorists' bluff. In general, the assessment of the threat credibility will depend on the preventive measures that are in effect and on their perceived reliability. Moreover, the willingness to act on a judgment that a threat is probably a bluff will depend on the means available for mitigating the consequences if the judgment proves faulty, that is, on the resources devoted to the containment and restoration phase.

A quantified analytical approach to dividing resources among various phases of antiterrorist activity or among the various possible threats that terrorists might mount does not appear possible. One must rely, ultimately, on estimates of comparative worth and probability of occurrence. We have tried in the above paragraphs to furnish some qualitative background context for making the judgments.

HARDENING THE TARGET

"Hardening the target" has a prophylactic value. It entails denying terrorists access to arms and explosives, as well as denying them access to their intended targets. The objective is to make the potential terrorist act so difficult that the amateur is defeated and the professional finds the cost too high. Thus, hardening the target is synonymous with establishing barriers, some of which are managerial and some of which are physical. The physical methods of hardening are to reduce the terrorist's ability to damage a specific installation and, for networks, such as the electric power and communications systems, to increase the number of critical nodes. Here, we consider two types of barriers: denial of means and security devices and procedures.

The rapid pace of modern technology has permitted significant improvements to be made in methods of detection and materials suitable as terrorist instruments and as well as in methods for preventing access to potential terrorist targets. None of the present or anticipated devices has a long-range detection capability. None of the present and anticipated barrier concepts are impenetrable. Sensors are most useful in preventing terrorism, by making it difficult for potential terrorists to obtain and transport arms and explosives, as well as chemical, biological, and radiological agents.

Denial of Means

The most effective preventive measure is to deny terrorists the means to strike, but our basic political, social, and economic values make this an unattainable goal. Much can be done in a technical way, however, to limit opportunities without taking repressive actions that would alter the very nature of our government. (Indeed, the terrorists' objectives may include goading the government into such unpopular acts.)

Tightened controls over access to commercial explosives through regulation of purchases and improved procedures to bar thefts would be of some use, but the wide availability of constituents (such as fertilizers) suitable for clandestine manufacture of high explosives makes it impossible to deny high explosives to terrorists. A capability to detect such explosives would help provide some protection to selected targets that are either particularly vulnerable or particularly valuable.

A number of techniques for automatic detection of the characteristic vapors given off by many explosives are under active development. There is considerable variation among explosive compounds in the amount and detectability of vapors emitted, but the most common ones emit detectable vapors. The two most useful and promising detection methods are specially trained dogs (which are expensive to train and manage) and electron-capture vapor detectors. Neither of these is completely satisfactory. The broad utility of such detectors in preventing a wide range of terrorist threats indicates that their development and procurement should receive priority.

Another technique for combating the use of explosives in terrorism is impregnating detonators with distinctive chemicals at the time of manufacture so that the presence of an explosive can be detected easily. If widely advertised, this technique has a deterrent value. Of related value is the tagging of explosives with "coded" microspheres. While not aiding in detection, tagging can be of immense value in the investigatory phase after a terrorist bombing has occurred.

The case of small arms is parallel to that of high explosives. Despite all that may be done to limit access, terrorists can almost certainly obtain them, while only a relatively small number of potential victims can be protected by detecting devices. While technical measures can serve to frustrate the marginal terrorist and protect key targets, they will not eliminate the problem.

Metal detectors, such as those used to screen passengers before boarding airliners, have become familiar. These detectors are useful in locating small arms. X-ray machines are presently used to inspect airline carry-on baggage. Their increasing use for inspection of checked baggage and cargo is expected, but the interpretation of X-ray shadowgraphs of large volumes of luggage will be tedious and imperfect. Developing and acquiring contrast enhancement and automatic pattern recognition attachments could be especially useful.

The situation with heavier armaments is rather different, for few sources of supply exist, and the level of technology required virtually precludes clandestine manufacture. On the other hand, protection against them is virtually impossible. The key to thwarting terrorist use of these weapons thus lies in denying them access. The chances for such a policy are fairly good. Although sophisticated ground-to-air and antitank weapons are widely dispersed in the hands of various national troop units (and significant quantities have found their way into clandestine arms traffic), this traffic is somewhat vulnerable to interdiction. Increased customs vigilance, new physical devices, and better procedures for tracking and locating stolen weapons appear to be the most promising measures to limit terrorist access to them.

In the United States, measures have already been taken to protect U.S. military stocks and to screen baggage and cargo entering the United States. The possibility of tagging military stocks in order to place them under stricter control has been investigated. Although there are a number of promising principles, each has some drawbacks. Further development is needed to determine if an acceptable method is possible, and if so, what costs and operational problems might be encountered.

Intelligence, inspection, and tagging are necessary but inadequate means to disrupt the clandestine arms traffic in advanced man-portable weaponry. Weapons like the Soviet SA-7 surface-to-air missile and the Soviet RPG-7 antitank weapon are already in the hands of terrorists. International agreements are needed to limit distribution, as well as to set physical security and "trackability" standards for them. In addition to international agreements, we must examine the question of their true military need. Heavier, jeep- or truck-mounted surface-to-air rockets might fulfill military requirements, while denying the terrorist ease of weapons transport and operation. Admittedly, this thought is ironical when the typical goal of fixed weapons performance at minimum weight or cost is considered. Yet, Sweden has adopted this philosophy in the design of its RBS-70 SAM, a bulky, tripod-mounted system, which would be difficult to conceal.

Chemicals of great toxicity are so widely used on the farm and in the factory that preventing access to such agents by potential terrorists is an unachievable goal. Moreover, the potential targets are so diverse and the mode of attack can be so subtle that protection does not seem possible either. At best, chemical detectors could interdict selected chemicals or give warning of an attack. It may be possible to further reduce this threat by developing and using sensors capable of detecting trace amounts of hazardous substances. Since it is nearly impossible to remove all traces of some agents from the outside of a sealed container after filling, trace detectors could be useful. A considerable amount of development is still needed because there are many potential toxic chemical agents.

There are numerous hazardous biological agents that could suit a terrorist's purposes. Unlike chemical agents, however, they are not generally available on a commercial basis. Although bacterial cultures can be obtained in many ways, isolating and subculturing the desired organisms can be a time-consuming, technically sophisticated matter. Sources of pure cultures of the more virulent pathogens are rather limited and, hence, would be easier to control. The existing controls over access appear to be loose, and only limited knowledge is required to breed a large amount of bacteria from a minute sample. As with chemical agents, protection of possible targets from biological attack is extremely difficult, and the particular measures that can limit the effects of an attack depend on rapid diagnosis of its nature. Here, there is an opportunity for technological innovation.

The techniques for control and detection of nuclear materials are much better than those for chemical or biological agents. Improvement, however, would be difficult and expensive, for much has already been accomplished. Fissionable and radioactive materials, such as could be used to construct crude nuclear weapons or cause a significant radioactive hazard, come from very limited sources and are strictly controlled. Denying access to such materials to unauthorized personnel has been a major concern of governments since the advent of the nuclear age.

Fissionable materials are guarded by the most sophisticated technical systems and are undoubtedly the most difficult materials for a terrorist to obtain in significant amounts. Should he or she succeed in doing so, however, protection of potential targets would be at least as difficult as with the other modes of terrorist attack. Moreover, the mere explosion of a crude nuclear bomb in a desert area by a terrorist group would cause panicky public reaction and form a basis for extreme demands.

Security Devices and Procedures

In the absence of specific intelligence about terrorist plans, the task of preventing terrorism falls upon such general purpose measures as fences, guards, alarms, and the screening of passengers and luggage at airports. There can be no guarantee that skillful terrorists will not circumvent such measures, but their use can discourage all but the most talented and determined. To be effective even to this extent, however, these barriers must be ubiquitous. If they are not, terrorists will simply shift their operations to unprotected targets. Potential air hijackers, for instance, will board planes at airports where security is known to be lax. (The Entebbe terrorists boarded the Air France plane at Athens, then a known weak point in the airport security system.)

Because they must be applied universally to all the potential targets to be effective, these preventive measures must be relatively inexpensive when the number of targets to be protected is large. This would tend to rule out a high level of technological sophistication in measures to prevent terrorism except in isolated instances, where a few extremely vulnerable targets exist. A technology directed against a broad spectrum of possible terrorist activities may be economically feasible in situations where few opportunities of relatively great vulnerability exist, but even in such a case, the necessary broadness of the measures militates against use of high-technology countermeasures to specific threats. A device that could detect remotely a wide variety of poisons, explosives, and drugs with moderate reliability might be useful in screening airline passengers if its cost were reasonable.

Access to potential terrorist targets can be made more difficult by erecting fences and barriers, using intrusion sensors, and increasing the effectiveness of guard forces. Many existing defenses were designed to be effective against the curious interloper or petty thieves. While any barrier serves a useful purpose, by excluding the less determined potential intruders, defenses against a determined, well-equipped terrorist group must be sophisticated and strong to have significant value.

The chain link galvanized steel fence, sometimes topped with a few strands of barbed wire, is probably the most common perimeter barrier. If it is backed up by a guard force, it is quite effective against casual and even some determined intruders. Intruders using wire cutters, ladders, or even heavy vehicles can penetrate such barriers. Nevertheless, a well-maintained, well-lighted, and well-patrolled chain link perimeter fence is probably the first priority as a defense against saboteurs. When such a perimeter is frequently patrolled or monitored by closed-circuit TV or intrusion sensors, it can be effective against surreptitious attack.

The category of intrusion sensors spans a wide variety of uses. Among the less sophisticated devices are the widely used door switches, conductive tapes, and photoelectric detectors used for home, store, and factory alarm systems. At the high end of the spectrum are sensors developed for the war in Southeast Asia, sensing vibration, sound, and heat. Experience with these devices has shown that they are very useful for sounding the alarm, but they must be accompanied by quick investigation and a backup guard force. Furthermore, alarms are often installed with inadequate attention given to protecting the alarm system itself. Although intrusion sensors can increase the effectiveness of a guard force, they require continual testing for malfunctions and other weaknesses.

Closed-circuit TV has become fairly widely used to expand the surveillance area of a guard force. The cost and reliability of such systems have been improved, so that we may anticipate their increasing use. The number of cameras that can be monitored effecitvely by a single guard is limited. Moreover, cameras can be blinded in a number of ways.

There are a great many examples of installations using advanced sensor systems, but the Sinai effort is possibly the best-known application.

The U.S. established and operates an' early warning system in the Sinai, which is intended to monitor the approaches to the Mitla and Giddi Passes. The system uses advanced types of intrusion sensors (acoustic, seismic, and so forth) emplaced in arrays to detect all intrusions. There are also devices designed to monitor the sensor fields; these include day-and-night imaging systems to determine the nature of the intrusion.

8

A STORY OF INADEQUACY: HIERARCHICAL AUTHORITY VERSUS THE TERRORIST

David G. Hubbard

Two stories with a common theme are told. In the first story, a little old lady was heard to complain, "Damn this dress! I've cut it off twice, and it's still too short!" In the second story, a workman arrived at a great insight, which he phrased as, "You can't drive a square peg into a round hole with a hammer." His solution was to use a sledgehammer instead. Both stories dramatize the angry, repetitive use of *force* as opposed to *logic*. In many ways, society's responses to terrorism have been similar to the illogical attitudes of these two souls.

Society is built upon the model of hierarchical authority. It is a pyramidal structure—broad at the base and narrowing gradually as it ascends to its apex. At the apex is the president (or chairman of the board). One level below is the cabinet (or board of directors). At level three, the structure branches out and broadens, because each person on level two, in turn, has dominion over a department. Stability of the foundation is dependent on the consent of the governed, the group forming the broad base of the pyramid. This consent may be approval of, or submission to, the system. Individuals who move upward in the pyramid power structure tend to be those who can most ably work within the system, manipulating its concepts and tools into ladders. Indeed, the person sitting on the capstone is usually the most agile climber. Those who hold power all along the line are efficient problem solvers—so long as the problems follow established pathways. Problems arising from the base up through channels or programs filtering down through channels can be handled very effectively.

The hierarchical authority model is one of mankind's oldest social organizations, dating back to the first "council meeting" inside some cave. The model crosses national boundaries, language barriers, and political divisions (that is, representative governments, federalist systems, or authoritarian dictatorships); all use some variation of this pyramidal structure. The structure has been tested and, under normal conditions of mass control, is a satisfactory tool of society.

I do not wish any reader to jump to the simplistic conclusion that because I point out certain shortcomings in the classical governing bodies' ability to manage some crisis situations, I recommend the overthrow, or indeed a complete overhaul, of these institutions insofar as principal function—the orderly distribution of mass product and the administration of mass government—is concerned. Although the discussion in this chapter will be confined almost totally to the limitations of committees in the pyramidal structure, by no means is that the only weakness in the hierarchical authority model. There are many other areas of comparable failure.

In the hierarchical authority model, the primary concern of both government and industry is the plural society rather than its individual members or small groups. Governments make and administer laws for the orderly protection, control, and taxation of the masses. Businesses produce, market, and sell to the masses. The pyramidal structure of hierarchical authority best serves this involvement with the masses.

At every level of the pyramid (below the apex), one finds study groups submitting reports to task forces, who, in turn, report to subcommittees, serve on committees, advise commissions, and make recommendations to cabinets—decisions, at every level, being made by consensus. Situations are studied, reports are made, positions are established, and ultimately, policy is formulated. But this policy is "watered down" at every level—each dilution facilitating smooth application to the "many" (and becoming less sensitive to the "few"). Policy is designed to capture the voluntary consent of the largest possible number of people who can be coerced as a group into submission to the authoritative top.

Careful committee construction strives to include in its membership every possible variety of ideological consanguinity that could conceivably belong to the group. Token outsiders may be tolerated to create the appearance of democratic or representational process. However, with few exceptions, those who are to be ruled are excluded from the committee.

Now, by and large, such cumbersome collections of committees (and the policies they produce) are useful, but not for the commonly accepted belief that they do something. The actual case is exactly the opposite. Principally, committees are designed to provide a special form of social friction that delays, diminishes, or prevents too rapid or too radical change—at the same time, providing a safety valve to discharge dissatisfaction.

Without committees to bolster the bureaucrat, it would be difficult to refuse requests (it is difficult for most people to say no directly to another person).* For the bureaucrat with committee support, the answer is easier: "*I* can-

---

*In this chapter, the authoritative figure will be called *bureaucrat*. For purposes of illustration, a caricature will be drawn that is, perhaps, unkind in exaggeration.

not honor your request—it is against *our* policy." (Voices from above have spoken.) Although policy is not a holy word, it can be as operative as if it were. For example, the Englishman who states in reference to this or that act that "it simply isn't done" is only referring to some distant all-powerful public totem which dictates behavior. Committees represent miniaturized versions of broad public opinion.

So, in the day-to-day functioning of government and industry, committees serve a useful purpose. If one correctly understands their inhibitive purpose, it is clear that they function efficiently and with creditable results. (This efficiency is thwarted, however, when one individual refuses to participate within the pyramid—an individual who will not consent to be ruled and who forcibly questions the right of legitimate rulers to rule—but more on this later.)

Because the committee approach to problem solving has served government and industry well in the past (in the control of mass function), it is easy to see why, when confronted with the "problem" of terrorism, their first reaction was to turn the problem over to a committee—a typical response to an atypical situation. In most cases, an already established management committee first undertook the task—and failed. In response to this failure, immediate, positive action was taken—and a new committee was formed.

Enter the crisis committee—approved of by the old, unsuccessful management committee (which, in this case, probably served as the nominating committee and appointed familiar faces to the new committee). The new/old committee then convenes, wearing shiny new hats and titles, filled to the gills with new importance and old inadequacy. Gertrude Stein said it best, "A rose is a rose . . ." Labeled by any other name, a committee is still a committee.

The crisis committee, which is currently in vogue for the management of acute situations, such as kidnapping, hostage taking, aircraft skyjacking, bombing, and assassination, is doomed to failure. Given their success at establishing workable policy in other areas, why should not such a committee be able to manage terrorist events?

Practical experience indicates that although major corporations and government bodies spend large amounts of time and money creating crisis committees, these committees seem to remain alive and viable for only short periods of time for a mutiplicity of reasons.

The first reason is philosophical in nature. One tenet that undergirds the pyramidal structure of the hierarchical authority model is the essential role of the manager in the prevention of emergencies. No self-respecting bureaucrat can admit having a crisis beyond his or her control. The policies established to avert catastrophes have no provision for recognizing, much less dealing with, those miscreants who precipitate the crisis. Administrative skills are expected to produce smooth, even function; eccentric function is disallowed. It is not possible to train people how to act in relationship to an event whose very existence they cannot philosophically acknowledge. Terrorists create situations that the individual and collective mind of the committee cannot comprehend.

Another reason group solutions to terrorist events are ineffective is that the problems ordinarily faced by committees are not immediate, single items. They are repetitive problems that were there yesterday and today and will still be around tomorrow. Consequently, there is no necessity for the committee to arrive at decisions quickly or formulate flexible policy. In contrast, the terrorist event is fast moving and as changeable as quicksilver. The unpredictability and irrationality of terrorism is almost incomprehensible to the committee—made up of rational beings accustomed to dealing with repetitive (and therefore predictable) events.

Still another factor dooming the crisis committee to failure is that despite the fact that committee organization was approved of at the very apex of the pyramid, when crisis occurs, almost without exception, the senior officer feels obliged to take over. When human life (or corporate image) is in jeopardy, the deliberately prepared policy of the committee proves inadequate, and the man at the top assumes command. The moment he does so, real operational problems are created.

First, nascent rivalry and conflict among various members of the disbanded committee come into the open, as individual members retrench to protect their positions. These maneuvers are often at the expense of the individuals whose lives are at stake. Without exception, the state, the industry, and the individual are all minor considerations compared with the career of the endangered dignitary. Society covers these moral lapses with the characteristic phrase, "That's politics."

Second, the final outcome of these crisis events tends to be catastrophic. Not infrequently, the offender sets into motion a chain of events he cannot control or makes serious miscalculations of his own ability, the nature of the situation, and the response of the authorities. In at least one out of every eight occurrences, regardless of the intentions of the offenders or the efforts of the authorities, the outcome is tragic. Inasmuch as the odds favor tragedy, one must question the advisability of gambling the future usefulness of a virtually indispensable executive on an individual response. The senior officer need not be victim or villain in such a tragedy, nor need he be "tarred" by association.

Also, government and industry should realize that the more able the senior officer is at administration and mass control (a skill of great value and the officer's primary responsibility), the less able that same officer will be at dealing with this type of crisis.

Additionally, the senior officer, by the nature of the position, is a political figure—viewed as such by employees and outsiders. This political visibility severely hampers objective action, and by accepting a leading role in the drama the presence of the officer elevates what might have been a small criminal act to a major event. Dramatic action by subordinates, who feel this importance, can create chaos.

Even if the senior officer remains in the wings and the committee continues in charge, following established policy, such policy is effective only so long as it can be applied to individuals who (1) voluntarily agree to submit to the group, (2) can be coerced to submit to the group, or (3) have no "force" through which to express their disagreement. Terrorists, then, are the nemesis of committees, because they refuse to submit voluntary or by coercion and have no hesitancy about exercising a force not employed by reasonable men—indeed, this use of force may be a psychologically appealing goal in itself. The terrorist breaks the social compact between ruler and ruled, refusing to respond to the wishes and implicit force of group function (government or corporate). At their own time and place, they confront the behemoth through terrorist threat and action.

When confronted by this violent and dissocial individual positioned outside the establishment, the committee proves inadequate. The essential agreement that gave the committee its accustomed illusion of strength is broken. Those who refuse to be ruled become unmanageable by the specialized tools invented to rule those who consent. At base, every terrorist act intends to question those who rule and their rights to do so.

In order to understand the reactions of the committee as a whole when confronted by a terrorist event, we must better understand the common psychological characteristics of committee members. It is probably fair to say that those who tend to align themselves with gigantic bureaucracies (government or corporate) are hardly "loners"; some part of them admires and feels safer with corporate function than with entrepreneur or soloist function. Years of working within the pyramid reinforces the bureaucrat's need to belong to a reasonable group in which problems are discussed and decisions are reached jointly. A lifetime of this adaptation leads to large cohesive groups of individuals who, by experience, learn to avoid high visibility, where their opinion or voice will be noted (other than when recommending caution or further thought). Rash behavior is so ill-thought-of in such circles that every negative voice recommending caution, delay, or further evaluation is acceptable and can be safely identified with the individual. Bureaucrats tend to raise only those questions for which they already have the answer. No sensible career bureaucrat can afford to appear stupid by raising an unanswerable question. Furthermore, recommendations for prompt, immediate, and positive action bear sizable risks. No one wants to be remembered as the "father" of plans that might fail; such plans quickly become "bastards." Inaction is less dangerous to bureaucratic careers than action that fails, particularly individually authored action. This hesitation to act leads to committee paralysis.

The actions of terrorists—solitary individuals or small conspiratorial groups—demand an immediate, creative, and often unconventional or unpopular response. In the past, committees have generally responded to such demands in one of four ways:

1. Acquiescence: in which even most outrageous terrorist demands were met without demurring; the spectacle of such gutless compliance whetted the appetites of potential miscreants.

2. Abstinence: the committee's lumbering motions of studying, evaluating, and reporting resulted in no action—thus, events careen to their own conclusions.

3. Abdication: the decisions were made by others: either the senior officer took control of the event, or an uninvited outside agency moved in.

4. Assassination: in a single, convulsive, desperate act, the authorities played in "the theater of the streets" for the support of the public, hoping to rescue "face," which had been lost in earlier negotiations and stalled conclusions. (The jeers of the public must be stilled, even if hostages die.)

The Aberrant Behavior Center in Dallas, Texas began its studies in connection with skyjackers. We conclude that matters such as final outcome and incidence were often more nearly related to the actions of functionaries in the establishment than to the perpetrators. For example, during one brief period (1968-69), the principal social drive responsible for the crime was hysteria generated by the space effort, which represented an undesirable "fallout" from a significant technical development. While such costs must be borne, they can be reduced. Another example would be the high success rate of skyjackers attempting to flee this country, which came to be seen as directly related to the assistance given by pilots, at the direction of airline management, rather than to the skills or determination of the offenders who started the event. This support and encouragement by the industry was unwise. Another example would be the sporadic increases in incidence resulting from the police policy of executing skyjackers in airports or aboard planes, which tended to attract potential suicides. These stimulated individuals were unusually inclined to take fatal risks, and the policy must be considered counterproductive. Also, the tenor and concentration of some media coverage encouraged imitative skyjackings. The "need of the public to know" must be distinguished from entertainment. Errors in judgment regarding aviation industry publicity accounted for some increased skyjacking activity. These errors were easily corrected. Finally, severed diplomatic relations handicapped efforts to extricate and prosecute skyjackers. Pertinent data-based materials were supplied to Congress, making a new treaty possible.

We encourage further studies of the hierarchical authority model rather than an endless preoccupation with the offenders. We submit that there are three productive approaches to the study of terrorism.

1. Study data related to incidence, targets, and so forth. This is the *only* study done routinely, and the information gathered is often useless, since it

rarely comes from original sources but, rather, from newspaper reports (incomplete and often inaccurate) or police records (accumulated not with enlightenment in mind but prosecution).

2. Study the terrorists themselves. What did they do? When? How? Where? Why? The Aberrant Behavior Center has demonstrated the value of firsthand information gained by the direct interview of the terrorist.

3. Study society itself and its responses. Our studies strongly indicate the importance of this factor. The terrorist does not act in a vacuum. As the establishment responds, and the terrorist reacts, the plot becomes more involved, and the action often escalates.

From studies completed thus far, we conclude that the hierarchical authority model—useful as it is in the orderly distribution of mass produce and the administration of mass governments—is improperly designed to meet the challenge hurled by terrorists outside the structure. Perhaps, crisis management should be assigned to one person who is also from outside the structure.

There are specialized safety personnel whose training and practice are based on the assumption that unpredictable emergencies can and will occur. Repeated drills are executed without undue reliance upon the guards and hardware of the policy model or the policies of the management model. This sort of preparation for urgent circumstances is most commonly seen in the aviation industry and in medicine. Both the pilot and the physician routinely practice drills in connection with anticipated emergencies that they concede will happen. Such training and drill for all individuals or groups who might encounter the terrorist emergency is impractical—the odds favoring need and application of such skills does not warrant the effort and expense.

If the management of a terrorist event is assigned to an outside specialist, then that person needs the authority to act. This authority carries with it total responsibility for management of the event, the outcome, and the aftermath. The person for such an assignment must be uniquely qualified, specially trained, and dispensable. This dispensability prevents irreparable damage to the system's structure in the event of disastrous developments.

Historians tell us that over 2,000 years ago the Roman general Agrippa said, "In important affairs it is necessary for success that the principal authority should reside in one man only." Machiavelli elected to quote this statement with clear support for the thesis.

This chapter offers no final answers, but it does raise definite questions. Hopefully, others will be stimulated to examine the subject. Shall we form a committee? I think not.

9

PREPARING FOR
TERRORIST VICTIMIZATION

Frank M. Ochberg

INTRODUCTION

An increasing incidence, worldwide, of both targeted and randomly perpetrated terrorist activities[1] has underscored the psychological, as well as physical, needs of victims[2]—and potential victims[3]—of terrorism. How will the
stress of an incident affect the behavior of the perpetrator and the victim? How
should a victim behave to protect his or her life? What psychological strategies
might be employed before, during, and after an incident in the best interest of
the victims?

These are complex questions, for which no pat answers exist. In the terrorist arena, each situation is staged differently, and each character has idiosyncratic
ways of coping with trauma. On the other hand, behavioral science has, over the
past few decades, generated considerable knowledge regarding adaptations to
stress,[4] mechanisms of psychological coping,[5] and the effects of personality and
temperament on behavior. More recently, observation of victims of terrorism
and similar trauma has provided a sharpened focus on the psychological needs,
risks, and successes of victims.[6]

This chapter will provide a brief overview of research on general and individual adaptations to stress and then will address more specific issues—coping
mechanisms, preparations and preventive strategies, and rehabilitative concerns.
Though the chapter will focus on the victim, an appreciation of these issues will
contribute to assuring that intervening authorities and victims alike respond
effectively to volatile and unpredictable situations.

The author gratefully acknowledges the valuable assistance of Marjorie Hoagland and
Paul Sirovatka.

GENERAL RESPONSES TO STRESS

Stress describes a physiological state of an organism responding to a provocation. Humans, like animals, are biologically equipped to assess and respond to danger. Neuronal pathways, hormonal mechanisms, and sensory circuitry allows appraisal of threat and emotional and behavioral arousal. Humans, however, while possessing basic biological assets for facing danger, exceed the automatic responses found among lower animals. The manner in which a human might choose to fight or flee is complex, a function of signs and symbols that are often subtle and unrecognized. Still, despite the variation in individual response to threat, there are common characteristics of that response. There is a tempo of response and stages in adaptation to stress, which were first described by Selye.[7]

First, there is *alarm*. The autonomic nervous system is triggered and aroused; the heart rate accelerates, increasing the amount of blood circulated to the muscles; and the adrenal gland functions at a much augmented rate. Each of these physiological mechanisms moves the organism toward a state of maximal preparedness to handle an adverse environment.

A middle phase of adaptation entails *resistance*. This marks the height of readiness, with the organism on "high gain," prepared now for total expenditure of energy. This phase can be maintained for only a discrete period of time; with some people, it could be days, with others, weeks, depending both on the fitness of the individual and the intensity of the situation.

Depletion of the energies required for resistance leads to the third phase of adaptation to stress, *exhaustion*. Thorough exhaustion can be lethal. Laboratory studies of animals exposed to prolonged stress have shown their adrenal glands to be ablated or hemorrhaged.

Any individual involved in a prolonged threatening situation, such as a terrorist siege, risks experience of these three stages of stress. If the duration of the threat is excessive, terrorist, victim, and negotiator may become exhausted.

In this context, it is useful to understand *panic*, a frequently misunderstood term. Panic occurs when the chances of a favorable outcome diminish rapidly with time. In the event of a sudden shock—an earthquake, for example—people sense the danger; given adequate time to respond, the panic reaction is unlikely to be prevalent. But when it is impossible for an individual or group of people to flee or to make decisions improving chances of survival over a period of time, panic may occur. Advance preparation can help people avoid this extremely maladaptive response to a stressful situation.

INDIVIDUAL RESPONSES TO STRESS

Within the context of general response to stress, each individual maintains a personal behavioral repertoire.[8] Early learning, personality, and life experiences, as well as physiology, contribute to response patterns in threatening situations. Moreover, different provocations prompt particular responses. Danger differs from failure as a provocation, for example, and while a police officer may typically have little difficulty dealing with the former, he or she may find the latter extremely stressful.

For many individuals, isolation poses a risk of stress; this may be particularly pertinent when considering hostage victims. Research on birth order that was conducted in the 1950s indicated that younger sons were often better able to cope with anxiety in isolated situations than were older sons.[9] Some of this research was stimulated by observations that fighter pilots in World War II and Korea who often experienced prolonged stress successfully were younger rather than first-born sons by a ratio of five to one. It appeared that during childhood, the younger sons received considerably less attention from their parents than did their older siblings; forced to learn to cope on their own, they developed the capability to handle stress by themselves, and subsequent behavior in isolation and under stress was less of a problem.

Another variable in an individual's adaptation to stress may be found in ethnicity. A study conducted in a New York City hospital that involved Anglo-Saxon Protestants, Jews, and Italians found that members of each ethnic group collectively demonstrated distinct psychological reactions to surgery.[10] All subjects received the same type of surgery for the same spectrum of ailments. The Anglo group reported the least amount of pain and required the least amount of narcotic medication. The Jewish patients were comparatively more concerned about the effects of their hospitalization on family members, about who was "minding the store," and the symbolism of their illness. They worried more and required more medication. The Italian patients required the greatest amount of medication: less bound by cultural stoicism, they were freer to express the pain they experienced.

In a terrorist situation—a hijacking, for instance—individual and ethnic differences might be expected to influence how all the participants, captors and captured, handle stress. Apprised of the identity of the perpetrators, authorities might key their responses to characteristic traits that might escalate or diminish the volatility of the situation.

Perhaps the single most significant finding of these and other studies of individual response to stress is that a person should not attempt to assume a role. Rather, an individual should become familiar with his or her own set of stress responses and adhere to that behavior—be yourself is a well-advised strategy. In assuming an alien personality, one is less human, less predictable to oneself, and less able to cope.

COPING MECHANISMS

Clearly, being held hostage in any situation is likely to induce a great deal of stress. By definition, successful coping in this situation will entail preservation of self-esteem, keeping anxiety within tolerable limits, problem solving, and maintenance of relationships with significant others. Of course, such clearcut and successful coping is not always feasible, and alternate strategies emerge.

The Stockholm Syndrome

One of the most recently defined coping strategies is seen in what has come to be termed the *Stockholm syndrome*, wherein captives become emotionally involved with their captors.[11] The term takes its name from the first recorded instance of this phenomenon, during a bank robbery and hostage taking in that city.[12]

It appears that the Stockholm syndrome is a coping device that most frequently is specific to the hostage. It is doubtful that the involvement is a conscious process, in which the victim intends manipulation of the captor through personal identification. In fact, reports indicate that victims who experience the Stockholm syndrome try to resist feelings of compassion for their captor, albeit unsuccessfully.

Some behavioral scientists consider identification with a captor a primitive attachment that stems from death imagery—a powerful force about which little is known. It may be related to an individual's anticipation of death. A hostage is extremely vulnerable and might be expected to express attachment and even affection toward other persons present. While it may be difficult to feel compassion for a captor, particularly one whose behavior has been brutal, that captor may represent to the hostage the continued existence of authority and ability to deal with the situation. In certain group situations, where a degree of interpersonal cohesiveness exists among the hostages, they may attend to one another's needs and not demonstrate reliance on the captors.

If the positive feeling expressed by hostage toward captor is reciprocated, the victim obviously will be better off. The outcome of an incident may be affected if the reciprocation occurs without manipulation, that is, if there is either a conscious or subconscious genuineness to the relation. If a victim attempts to encourage a captor to feel some attachment, it would be important to allow the necessary feelings of natural warmth, empathy, and understanding to occur over time. Here again, the importance of the dictum be yourself is obvious.

PREPARATIONS

Recent work with victims of terrorist activity has begun to illustrate a number of coping strategies that may be useful in terms of prevention, as well as in the event, of an incident.[13] Though terrorist activity may often involve an apparently random selection of persons who happen to be in a particular setting at a critical moment, other potential victims may be at discernible risk by virtue of geographic, occupational, and ideological factors. For this latter group particularly, but for others as well, specific preparations should be considered.

First, individuals ought to discuss the potential for involvement and the implications with significant others. Consider as concretely as possible what might happen and realistic ways of responding to the danger. With respect to emotional preparation, it may be helpful for members of a family to acknowledge and discuss the feelings of anxiety and depression with which they may have to cope. Families can identify in advance those who would be called upon for psychological and social support, as well as those family members and acquaintances who might require particular attention. Depending on roles that might emerge during the course of an incident—for example, if family members were called upon in some way to help, and failed—they might experience unnecessary but debilitating guilt.

Most tangible preparations should also be made. Wills should be polished, and needed trust funds planned for dependents. While such activities may seem morbid, they also are significant in relieving one measure of anxiety when trouble does occur. An individual who is held hostage for any length of time and has to cope with the psychological and physical onslaught of that experience does not need the additional worry and guilt of having left a family or loved one unprepared.

Health is another crucial factor in coping with stress. Though common sense dictates limitations on physical heroics, physical conditioning is nonetheless important. If a corporate executive is assigned to a danger zone—for instance, a locale where personnel have been attacked previously—he or she should attempt to assure that he or she is in sound physical health. Individuals such as Sir Geoffrey Jackson and Claude Fry, who survived captivity and reported on their experiences, emphasized the importance of preconditioning, as well as exercise that is possible during captivity.[14]

Increasing amounts of vital information are available to businessmen at risk of terrorist attack and should be sought before exposure to high-risk settings. Several public and private agencies have compiled considerable intelligence on terrorist group activities—identification of groups, probable timing and location of attacks, operational procedures, and trigger events.[15]

In some cases, simulation of a dangerous incident may be of value to persons at risk—for example, representatives of multinational corporations, ambassadors, or other government officials. For maximum effectiveness, such "dress rehearsals" should be sufficiently authentic that participants will experience the same reactions that a real incident might engender. Short of such authenticity, a rehersal may be little more effective than reading a book on the topic. Already, police training often involves rehersals in which officers are taught how to think and behave under such extremely stressful situations as hostage bartering or other types of negotiation. These practice sessions are realistic, with colleagues monitoring their activities, TV camera lights blazing, and reports to be written during the simulation and afterwards. The payoff of acclimating individuals to the strain and stress of such events has been proven in real-life situations.

Another preventive measure aimed specifically at hostage taking involves "kidnap insurance." Certainly controversial, the practice has been outlawed in some countries because it is felt that payoff to criminals indicates that payment is less of a financial hardship and thus increases the likelihood of kidnapping. On the other hand, kidnap insurance can relieve companies of both the cost of ransoming executives and the burden of difficult policy decisions under stressful circumstances. Also, proponents of these policies argue that they provide the victim a bargaining device with captors.

Despite the arguments that are made in favor of kidnap insurance, it appears that increasing numbers of governments and private organizations are turning away from the idea, considering it an inducement to kidnapping.

A strategy that has been used in the recent past involves systems of predetermined coded "signals" that may be used if the opportunity presents itself in a hostage situation. Key words can be used in messages, tonal inflections in telephone calls, and grammatical structure in written messages can convey a great deal of information. A primary advantage of all of these means of preparation lies in the psychological benefit that these and other techniques of self-control may offer in an emotional and stressful situation.

Target Hardening

Techniques described so far, while of proven value, are also of very broad applicability. Though it is impossible to anticipate every site of potential terrorist attack, for particularly high-risk settings, a more specific preventive strategy is that of *target hardening*.[16] The term simply describes the process by which a likely target of terrorist activity—whether a person, vehicle, or building—is made more difficult to reach. In the commercial world, target hardening has been employed by the airlines industry through use of metal detectors, luggage clearance, and similar techniques. With the military, of course, target hardening is a common practice.

For the individual businessman at risk of terrorist attack, strategies of target hardening exist also. Variation of the commuting route and desystemization of the work schedule and, even, manner of dress can contribute to making an individual less easy to identify and more difficult to reach. With an increasing number of attacks occurring while a businessperson is in transit, analysis of commuting patterns is advisable. Evidence of the growing awareness of this need is seen presently in more stringent security clearance of chauffeurs, instruction in defensive and high-performance driving, and commercial production of armored standard vehicles.

In many instances—most notably, perhaps, politics—target individuals cannot maintain a low profile. At one extreme, the danger of terrorist activity may ultimately necessitate dramatic changes in methods of political campaigning and other public appearances. Short of that, the public, law enforcement agencies, and public officials, in particular, will have to mutually recognize the need for, and the constraints of, security practices.

THE HOSTAGE SITUATION

In the first moments after an attack, an individual will probably act more instinctively than rationally. It is at that time that the greatest chance of escape may present itself; it is also at that time that action may be most lethally risky. Balanced judgments regarding response are most critical during these moments, and it is a period that warrants considerably more research and simulation training.

Recent incidents have indicated that a person may increase his or her chances of survival if he or she is able to establish himself or herself immediately as someone to whom the attackers can relate. Captors frequently find the murder of someone who has established a human identity more difficult. Given the information that a hostage may be a husband, wife, parent, musician, or lover of sports, the risk of being a nameless, faceless symbol diminishes. The hostage is a human being, a self rather than an object—and as indicated previously, the self that a victim can portray most convincingly is the true self.

Once a hostage allows such personal exposure, it may be that empathy between captor and hostage will be established, and it is likely that some effective dimension will be brought into otherwise cold and rational logistics. But again, personal interaction should not be attempted manipulatively. A victim clearly is confronted with numerous pressing anxieties, fears, and inner needs; attempts at interpersonal manipulation will be perceived of as superficial and are likely to produce untoward consequences.

Work with former hostages, some of whom have spent hundreds of days in captivity, suggest that an honest recognition of the need for self-attentiveness can be critical. Physical and mental exercise is important for the long haul. Individuals who have sustained prolonged captivity and who did not know how to occupy their minds productively have not seemed to fare as well as others who were more imaginative. One man who coped successfully with captivity had designed a new house in his mind; he literally worked out architectural plans and resolved problems that the plans presented. Interviews with another man who did not fare as well psychologically indicated that during captivity, he had focused solely on the size and construction of his cell.

During captivity, close observation of the attackers can provide the hostage with a sense of purpose. Interviews suggest that in large measure, the trauma of being a captive stems from the apparent purposelessness of it all. If he or she survives, the observant victim can contribute significantly to the identification, arrest, and prosecution of his or her captors. Seemingly trivial details can be crucial to the authorities.

Obviously, there are times when escape attempts are advisable. In a group hostage situation, if individuals are removed from the group under threat of death and not returned, the risk of being hurt or killed during resistance or attempted escape may balance against the threat. Realistic appraisal of the threat and of the captives' resources may be the most effective weapons.

PSYCHOLOGICAL AFTERMATH

Reports uniformly suggest that a variety of physical and psychological problems are apt to emerge among former hostages.[17] Posttrauma anxiety may appear in the form of nightmares, nightsweats, startle reactions, and phobias. Health problems may result if anxiety is turned inward, making biological systems more vulnerable to such illnesses as respiratory and gastrointestinal disorders, complaints of backache, headache, and so forth.

Some ex-victims have become profoundly, clinically depressed. Often, depression seems to come on when the victim is no longer sought after by the media or attended to by health or other public authorities. Long after the immediate crisis is resolved, the victim may be left carrying the "emotional baggage" of the trauma. He or she may be reliving the events constantly, but the interest of the public audience is lost. Also, "survivor guilt" may be a potent contributing factor to depression, if a hostage survived while others did not.

Other former hostages may develop paranoid patterns of thinking and behaving, fearing capture again. It is possible that a person may be victimized again, though unlikely. Not infrequently, however, such fears and anxiety become so consuming that normal functioning is disrupted.

Given this range of potential problems, reunion of hostages with family or significant others is often delicate and psychologically dangerous for all parties. Like the hostage, family members have experienced substantial and often physically debilitating anxiety while awaiting the outcome of the incident. Hostage and family should be aware of the danger—and the ease—of either over- or underestimating the others' feelings. Experience has shown that such basic precautionary measures as medical and psychological screening that are provided to released hostages should be offered to family members as well.

Beyond these basic services, the extent to which rehabilitative and supportive social service follow-up should be provided to released hostages is a yet unresolved issue, which requires policy consideration and working guidelines. Should persons coming out of a hostage situation be left alone for a period of time, or should they be encouraged to interact with other people? Should those "others" be family members, fellow hostages (in the case of a group release), or health or government personnel?

Following release of a large group of hostages of terrorist attack in Holland in 1977, physicians and psychiatrists planned to hospitalize the victims.[18] These individuals had been subjected to physical duress—cramped quarters, severe heat, and hunger—as well as psychological strain during 20 days of captivity. In the hospital setting, nutritional problems could be medically monitored and treated, and a large day room was intended to allow gradual reentry to the everyday world. The hostages could be visited by family and friends, and staff, for the most part social workers, were to be on hand to observe patterns of interaction. The idea was to avoid overstructuring but to encourage the victims to stay together and share in the process of physical and psychological "decompression."

As it turned out, very few of the released hostages would accept the services that were being offered. They wanted to go right back to their families; there was a pronounced need for reunion. Yet it is a fair assumption that in a number of cases, subsequent family relationships were difficult. The Dutch authorities had warned family members that the ex-hostages might prove to be somewhat sympathetic to the attackers and their cause. While a family member might be experiencing fear and bitterness, the victim might express empathy and understanding for his captors, thus aggravating existing tensions.

Research and pilot studies would be useful in determining individual and group needs and suggesting practices that would allow choices to be made by the parties involved between immediate affiliation or graduated decompression.

Research is needed, also, on means of assisting victims to work out most effectively social and psychological aftereffects of the experience. Two schools of thought predominate: the first holds that the victim should be allowed to forget and that need of psychiatric assistance should not be implied. The other viewpoint contends that the victim has suffered and that efforts to prevent or alleviate further stress should be offered and, in fact, should be financed by the government, for which the hostage may have been an unwitting political symbol.

SUMMARY

Individuals who have reason to consider themselves at risk of terrorist attack ought to prepare themselves, both psychologically and physically. Simulation of potential situations, discussion of the implications of attack with loved ones, financial arrangements, and accumulation of information about potential terrorist groups are useful preventive measures.

While all individuals are biologically equipped to respond to threat and stress, persons cope in accordance with personality and physiology, life experience, and training. Special training and educational programs may strengthen a person's capabilities in the event of various types of attack.

Until further research sharpens our answers to the obvious questions of preparing for captivity and coping with the problems associated with survival, these straightforward approaches must suffice.

NOTES

1. Edward F. Mickolus, "Chronology of Transnational Terrorist Attacks upon American Business People, 1968–1978," *Terrorism* 1 (1978): 217. See also *International Terrorism in 1977* (Washington, D.C.: CIA, National Foreign Assessment Center, August 1978).

2. Frank Ochberg, "The Victim of Terrorism: Psychiatric Considerations," *Terrorism* 1 (1978): 147.

3. Risks International, *Executive Risk Assessment* 1 (November 1978).

4. Richard S. Lazarus, *Psychological Stress and the Coping Process* (New York: McGraw-Hill, 1966).

5. David A. Hamburg and John E. Adams, "A Perspective on Coping Behavior," *Archives of General Psychiatry* 17 (1967): 277.

6. Ochberg, "Victim of Terrorism."

7. Hans Selye, *The Stress of Life* (New York: McGraw-Hill, 1956).

8. Benjamin Weybrew, in *Psychological Stress*, ed. Mortimer H. Appley and Richard Trumbull (New York: Appleton-Century-Crofts, 1967).

9. S. Schacter, *The Psychology of Affiliation* (Stanford, Calif.: Stanford University Press, 1959).

10. E. Gartley Jaco, *Patient, Physcians, and Illness: A Source Book in Behavioral Science and Medicine*, 2d ed. (New York: The Free Press, 1972).

11. Thomas Strentz, "Law Enforcement Policy and Ego Defenses of the Hostage." (unpublished manuscript available at FBI Training Academy, Quantico, Va.).

12. Daniel Lang, "A Reporter at Large: The Bank Drama," *New Yorker* (1974): 56–126.

13. Paul Fuqua and Jerry V. Wilson, *Terrorism: The Executive's Guide to Survival* (Houston, Tex.: Gulf Publishing, 1977).

14. Sir Geoffrey Jackson, *Surviving the Long Night: An Autobiographical Account of a Political Kidnapping* (New York: Vanguard, 1974), and Claude L. Fly, *No Hope but God* (New York: Hawthorn, 1973).

15. Risks International, *Executive Risk Assessment.*

16. Robert Kupperman, *Facing Tomorrow's Terrorist Incident Today* (Washington, D.C.: Government Printing Office, October 1977).

17. Brian M. Jenkins, Janera Johnson, and David Ronfeldt, "Numbered Lives: Some Statistical Observations from Seventy-Seven International Hostage Episodes," mimeographed (Santa Monica, Calif.: Rand, 1977), and Ochberg, "Victim of Terrorism."

18. W. Van Dijk, personal communication and author's on-site observations, January 1978.

10

COUNTERTERRORIST MEDICAL PREPAREDNESS: A NECESSITY FOR THE CORPORATE EXECUTIVE

Martin Elliot Silverstein

The world is threatened by a particularly dangerous, vicious, and unique form of disaster—that which occurs not as an act of God but as planned and executed by human agencies grouped under the general category of terrorists.

Disaster medicine, the treatment of mass casualties occurring in an unusual manner and at an unexpected time, is an incompletely studied field in itself. The terrorist-engendered disaster subset shares with the wider field of disaster the possibility of mass casualties but embodies a peculiar mixture of the elements of civilian and military disaster.

Unlike flood, earthquake, or tornado, poorly handled terrorist attacks contain an additional potentiality for loss of confidence in authority and the ultimate destruction of society. In preparing for terrorist casualties, we face the peculiar situation of a military event in a civilian milieu.

Some of the medical features of a terrorist attack are the following: (1) the potentiality for a variable number of casualties, ranging from a single corporate executive and his or her bodyguard to the biological, explosive, or chemical threat to whole communities; (2) the probable use of standard or homemade weaponry without regard to international humanitarian conventions; (3) the high probability of anticipation of attack—some targets are aware of their special status or, in some cases, an overt threat has preceded an attack.

These features represent special problems and opportunities in medical preparedness. Foreknowledge of the site and anticipated casualties allows for the advance deployment of medical equipment and professionals. This is especially important, since the very nature of the terrorist attack may prevent transportation of the victims to fixed base hospitals, and appropriate medical management places greater emphasis on early life support and extended on-site care.[1] Indeed, the potential corporate or political target is well advised to provide himself or herself with paramedical personnel and life support equipment.

The prudent corporation ensures its continuing function by protecting the health of its key personnel and maintaining its corporate profits. Indeed, every intelligent individual, whatever his or her occupation, makes every effort to care for his or her physical and emotional well-being. The most elementary fact of life is that longevity and the ability to function depend upon the prevention of disease and the treatment and cure of disease when it does occur.

Terrorism represents a form of injury that threatens life and limb of specific sectors of society. In the same way that vaccination and the automobile seat belt represent preventive medicine against infectious disease and physical trauma, the protective fence, the bodyguard, and other security measures are valid modes of preventing morbidity and mortality from the disease of terrorism.

Specialized surgical care also represents a security aspect for the individual terrorist target. Since terrorists inflict emotional and bodily harm through the use of specialized weaponry, specific medical preparedness is an intrinsic part of protection for the corporate executive target. No realistic individual expects to live out a full functional life totally exempt from ordinary disease. While prudence demands that the potential terrorist target provide himself or herself with optimum security and intelligence, prudence and realism demand an acceptance of the vulnerability of protective security and the significant probability of successful attack and injury. Appropriate medical preparatory measures can diminish the degree of injury and the incidence of mortality when protective measures fail partially or completely.

Involved is the military principle of acceptance of losses and the optimization of damage limitation applied to the corporation and its individual executives. In 1975, the author of this chapter was assigned as a mission the assessment of probable human injury by terrorists and research into optimum methods of diminishing mortality and morbidity by specialized preparations and specialized medical care in the Office of the Chief Scientist of the U.S. Arms Control and Disarmament Agency.[2]

The threat of bodily harm is, of course, a real one, both overseas and within the territorial United States. The terrorists' take has passed the $100 million line, and, according to FBI Director William Webster, they are "coming closer to our shores." The FBI estimates of hard-core political terrorists in the United States are reported to include up to 16 groups. Attempted assassination, arson, hostage taking, and bombings have occurred, and more than 100 political bombings are projected for 1979.

At first look, it would seem that all the advantages are with the terrorists. Prior to our research, there was a common, if unstated, opinion among law enforcement personnel that if a terrorist attack broke through the protective shield, subsequent medical aid would make little difference and that standard civilian medical care systems were optimum and appropriate.

Both these concepts are untrue. As we have learned in both warfare and aggregate civilian highway threats to life, specialized care systems cannot save every life and limb, but they can diminish the damage done by both physical and emotional trauma and can significantly decrease the number of deaths in any given situation. The key process is specially designed medical care systems.

Despite our inability to predict which of the wide range of physical, chemical, or biological weapons may be used, a study of these weapons and the injuries they cause revealed that the body's biological reactions to such injuries are limited, thus permitting a fairly standardized and economical, if highly specialized and systematized, medical treatment response. The scientific reason behind, and the details of, this "common model" theory of the biology of terrorist attack and its treatment has been described by the author in detail elsewhere.[3]

We believe that the myths of overwhelming weaponry and the hopelessness of large disasters can be disproved by the research facts of modern medicine. Further, we believe that a superior system of medical rescue can be devised to produce a 20 percent or higher salvage rate than is presently obtained by acceptance of the myths of hopelessness and capitulation.

Our conviction is based on three concepts:

1. The common weaponry model: despite the apparent disparate effects of various weaponry upon the human body, the initial injuries follow a common model. The individual effects of specific weaponry are secondary in importance during the initial time period.

2. The common injury response: the mammalian body can be considered as a system of interacting organ subsystems: brain, heart, lungs, kidney, liver, intestines, and aggregate muscle mass. Barring the complete destruction of any one of those organ subsystems, the body can be kept alive by providing the cells of each organ with sufficient water, oxygen, and certain other blood components and by maintaining within the subsystem's circulation the necessary volume-pressure relationships, whatever the nature of the injury.

3. The common resuscitative model: implicit in the common injury model is the potentiality of sustaining life by supporting the organ subsystems. In general, this is achieved by external oxygen supply, maintenance of adequate filling of the arteriovenous pipeline for oxygen and other transport, and maintenance of the cardiac pump to drive the circulation.

The practicalities of the common model approach and medical damage limitation depend upon the following: (1) specialized but fairly simple support measures, which, when instituted within five or six minutes of the injury, whatever its nature, have a good chance of sustaining life for quite a long time (until more specific and detailed medical and surgical measures can be begun); (2) nonmedical or paramedical personnel, who can be taught to effectively institute such life support in 80 to 200 hours of specialized training; (3) the equipment and materials for such life support, which can be packaged in 25-pound containers and transported in blackpacks or other suitable cases at a currently estimated price of $500 or $1,000; (4) second-stage postimmediate life support containerized multibed intensive care units and third-stage surgery urgent operative subsystems, which can be deployed and transported to the scene of the incident by ground vehicle semitrailers or cargo helicopters, thus overcoming the lethal physiological time limitations and the potential traffic or terrain obstacles to transportation of the wounded; (5) civil and military surgeons, physicians, nurses, and technicians of local hospitals or of the corporation's own medical department, who can be educated and trained to provide the deployable personnel teams necessary to man the stage two and three containerized multicasualty units; (6) the staffs of the nearby hospitals, who can and should be trained in the types of special trauma inflicted by terrorists. Arrangements can be made for corporate medical personnel so trained to function cooperatively within these hospitals.

For practical purposes, it is recommended that the bodyguard team or the barricade assault team be additionally trained as paramedics in life support procedures. Aside from the economy in personnel, these are the individuals who are most likely to be on the scene in the immediate postinjury time period. For the same reason, families, close working associates, and neighbors can and should receive such training. It will stand them in good stead in nonterrorist emergencies, including industrial accidents and cardiac crises, which constitute more than 50 percent of all civil medical emergencies.

The author has devised an aluminum-cased package, the size of a medium suitcase, which contains all the elements necessary for 30 minutes of life support, including the provision of positive pressure oxygen, the restoration of lost blood volume, the maintenance of cardiac function, the control of limb hemorrhage, and the care of nonlife-threatening but long-term disabling injuries, such as fractures. Such portable kits should be available in the trunk of the potential target's vehicle, the trailing bodyguard vehicle, and the office and home. Personal backpack editions should be part of the equipment of assaulting law enforcement teams.

Additional semiautomatic electronic portable diagnostic and monitoring equipment has also been devised and packaged in an accompanying 25-pound medical "black box." This has the capability of transmitting the victim's condition to a radio base station for specialist advice and consultation, but it is not an essential part of the system. The system can be expanded to handle mass casualties (indicated in Figure 10.1). Elements of the system have been tested by us utilizing highway accidents as a casualty model. Installation of the containerized second intensive care and third-stage surgical subsystems is in process at a major airport in at least one U.S. city.

Essential to this system is a prearranged transportation system—ground or air vehicles and routes to nearby civilian hospitals. But the personnel of these hospitals, like the corporate medical personnel, must have specialized training in

FIGURE 10.1

Sequence of Care

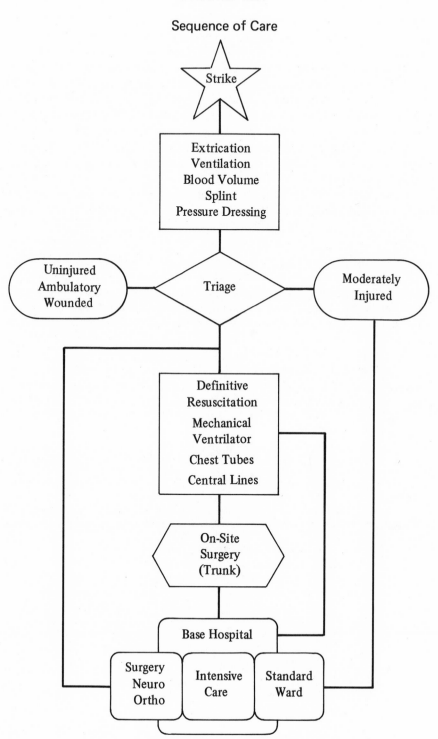

the weaponry and injuries of terrorism, as well as prearranged contingency plans for the care of such casualties. This is not a difficult task, and experience has demonstrated that civilian medical personnel are only too eager to add to their skills and to assist in counterterrorism.

One of the simplest and most effective measures to be taken by the executive at risk is wearing at all times a bracelet engraved with all significant medical information—allergies, blood type, and any significant medical disease. These insignia are recognized internationally, and the information they carry may be lifesaving in preventing the administration of drugs to which there is an allergic reaction and minimizing the time required for the typing and cross matching of blood.

A physically salvaged but emotionally injured executive is a personal and corporate loss. There is good reason to believe from our experiences in The Netherlands, as well as from other terrorist incidents, that there is truth in the phrase, "Once a victim, always a victim." The corporate target deserves appropriate psychological and psychiatric preparation and counsel, and the actual victim requires long-term but not necessarily intensive psychiatric counsel. The family of victims will also require continuing psychiatric assistance during and after an attack. The more preparation the family of a likely target receives in handling anxieties and fears, the easier and more effective will be his or her day-to-day life.

I cannot conclude a discussion of medical preparedness without an appeal to executive realism and a note of reassurance to the corporation and its key personnel that appropriate preparedness is economically feasible, practicable, and will provide a high level of survival and recovery.

NOTES

1. Martin Elliot, Silverstein, M.D. "Emergency Medical Preparedness," *Terrorism* 1 (1977): 51–69.

2. M. E. Silverstein, "The Medical Survival of Victims of Terrorism," mimeographed (Prepared for The Office of the Chief Scientist, U.S. Arms Control and Disarmament Agency) (1976).

3. Silverstein, "Emergency Medical Preparedness," p. 3.

11

THE AIRLINE RESPONSE TO TERRORISM

Thomas M. Ashwood

The first recorded hijacking took place in South America in 1936, but that remained an isolated incident until the mid-1950s, when there was a brief resurgence. There was little to be learned from these early occurrences, for they followed no discernible pattern and, geographically, were widely scattered.

Aircraft hijackings became a true phenomenon in 1970, and the United States and its carriers were the primary targets.

In the early 1970s, the motivation for these acts could basically be identified as falling into two categories: fugitive (escape) and extortion (money). The fugitive situation was essentially a jet-age update on the old Bonny and Clyde, Pretty Boy Floyd exercise of fleeing across state borders following a bank stick-up, with guns blazing and sheriffs in hot pursuit. The concept of fleeing the jurisdiction of the territory in which a crime has been committed is as old as the Old West, and it is only surprising that this very American phenomenon did not occur in aviation at an earlier date. Due to the introduction of federal laws governing most crimes, a criminal could no longer avoid justice by moving from Kansas to Oklahoma, but these modern-day gangsters were quick to realize that there was a line they could cross and be safe from prosecution. I refer, of course, to the territorial and political line that existed between the United States and Cuba—therefore, Cuba became the "hijacker's haven" of the early 1970s. The Castro government not only accepted these fleeing criminals but openly encouraged them, for it was a great embarrassment to their giant neighbor to the north, with whom they had no extradition treaty.

Hijackings conducted for the purpose of extortion of money were hardly a surprise when they became a fad. Airlines had huge financial resources, were vulnerable, and, in the early stages, paid the demands with alacrity. Extortion hijackings took a bizarre turn, however, with the introduction of the "jumper-jack," that is, the criminal who extorts money with a hijacking and then parachutes from the victim-aircraft into a remote area and then makes his or her escape. This was a new twist, for it allowed the criminal to remain in the United States, undetected and considerably wealthier. With the U.S. penchant for fads and provoked by a gleeful press, jumper-jacks became the "in" crime and its perpetrators the new U.S. folk hero. Happy to say, however, like the hula hoop, this fad was short-lived and quickly faded into obscurity.

Alarms were being sounded throughout the civil aviation industry by the airline pilots, but they largely went unheard. In retrospect, it is fairly understandable why the governments and industry adopted a negligent attitude. Essentially, fugitive and extortion hijackings, which only demanded transportation and/or money, were cheaper to live with than the expense of providing a preventative security system throughout the entire airline structure. It could be classified as an accountant's decision.

This attitude of benign neglect was abruptly altered when hijackings took a dangerous and deadly new turn. National and international political strife came into the picture. Aircraft were being hijacked by political terrorists, who killed and maimed for effect and demanded the impossible, that is, the release of convicted and imprisoned comrades. Civil aircraft became military targets in the Middle Eastern conflict, and new extortion demands for changes in a nation's foreign policies created agonizing dilemmas for governments not directly involved in the conflict. The message became clear: the hijackers had mutated from the common, criminal, sad psychotic type to the deadly, vicious, professional terrorist, organized into military units with the support and encouragement of states. Shocked and wounded by this new assault, the civil aviation industry began to react. The previously unheeded warnings and protests of the world's airline pilots had proved to be sadly prophetic. Unfortunately, we live in a time when a few warped and dangerous individuals can place the lives of hundreds of innocent persons in jeopardy.

Terrorists are usually willing—sometimes even eager—to sacrifice themselves for whatever cause they subscribe to. They have no concern for their hostages, regarding them only as mere aids in achieving an objective.

The growing supply of sophisticated weapons and explosives available today to terrorists make them even more dangerous. For example, we know there are small surface-to-air missiles available right now to various terrorist groups. We also know of at least two incidents in which terrorists with these missiles have been arrested near airports. It is only a question of time until someone uses such a missile to shoot down an airliner and murder the innocent persons on board.

Even more frightening is the prospect that some of the large amount of nuclear material available will find its way to a terrorist group. Sooner or later, innocent residents of a city will find themselves facing nuclear destruction, not from a hostile nation but from a small band of fanatics.

A terrorist group is usually considerably smaller than the forces it is trying to overthrow. Consequently, the war they must wage must differ from the conventional force-to-force confrontation. Terrorists have a great advantage over their larger opposition: they are able to operate undetected and can pick their targets of attack. They selected civil aircraft as their targets. An analysis of their choice indicates why they acted against international civil aviation. The reasons for this attraction include the following:

1. Airlines are highly indentifiable with their country. Most are government-owned, and even privately owned airlines, such as PanAm and TWA, are widely considered to represent their countries.

2. The place of attack can be selected from a variety of airports, depending upon such factors as security arrangements, closeness to the destination, and political stance of the government.

3. Modern airliners cost up to $50 million. Where else can something so valuable be taken so easily?

4. The aircraft are relatively fragile and can be easily disabled or destroyed with a few dollars worth of easily obtainable materials.

5. There will be as many as 400 passengers of different nationalities on a single flight. They make invaluable hostages.

6. The hijacked aircraft provides the terrorist with a fast, reliable means of escape to almost any part of the world.

7. One of the goals of terrorists is publicity. Aircraft hijackings and airport terminal attacks are proven worldwide attention getters.

With the exception of a few nations, such as the United States, Israel, and Great Britain, the world was slow to react to what they now recognized as a serious threat—a threat not only to airline crews and passengers but, also, to the very ability of the nations to govern. Political solutions were sought, but it was soon realized that the goal of international agreement would be difficult and that the prospects for its rapid accomplishment were very dim and probably unattainable. In the meantime, responsible governments began preparations to defend themselves and the civil aviation industry against attack. The form these initiatives took will be discussed later in this chapter.

Making predictions is an easy but dangerous exercise. It is easy, for predictions can be based solely on opinion. The danger lies in that if one's predictions do not come true, then one's credibility and effectiveness become impaired. Recognizing that fact and based upon many years of experience in the field of aviation security, I predict that political/terrorist acts of violence against civil aviation will not only continue but, periodically will escalate in both number and intensity, depending upon the fortunes of war being experienced by terrorist groups. It is conceivable and expected that as they suffer greater reversals and undergo philosophical and ideological splits within their organizations, the sub-groups will use an increasing "bodycount" of victims in an attempt to "outgross" the original parent organization. Possibly, the easiest and safest way of achieving this is to destroy a widebody jet with its complement of 400 passengers and crew.

As referred to earlier, political solutions are being sought, and defense systems are being developed and deployed. In the political arena, the UN seemed an obvious choice of forum for a resolution to the problem. Unfortunately, that body, originally created with the highest ideals and intentions of beating swords into plowshares, has become a public slander-pit, under the control and at the beck and call of a few oil-rich, Third World nations encouraged and prompted by elements from the Communist sphere. These are the very nations that have the greatest role to play in the promotion of international terrorism. International politics within the UN reached an all-time low when its General Assembly gave a tumultuous greeting to a self-confessed murderer, complete with gun on hip—the leading representative of those terrorist groups they are ostensibly committed to condemn and destroy. It is the author's belief that the UN, by its lack of action as much as by its dubious resolutions and positions, has completely lost any shred of credibility among responsible nations. Many believe that the damage is irreparable. We have been forced to conclude that the UN has neither the will nor the way to take effective measures against international terrorism. The only practical method, we have decided, is firm action by a few powerful nations.

Consequently, nations are turning more and more to bilateral and multilateral agreements on hijacking and terrorism, as evidenced by the agreement between the United States and Cuba and the more recent dramatic move in Bonn, West Germany, by the heads of state from the United States, Canada, Great Britain, France, West Germany, Italy, and Japan. It will only take a few more nations to join in this endeavor for the movement to total acceptance to be completed. Once the list of complying nations grows to a certain number, it will be impossible for those remaining to resist acceptance.

The representatives from the Air Line Pilots Association (ALPA USA) and the International Federation of Air Line Pilots Association (IFALPA) have been in the forefront of the war against terrorism. For almost the last ten years, they struggled to get recognition of the fact that a problem existed. Once that was accomplished, they successfully cooperated with, and advised, governments about the political and technical solutions and expended much of their energy and finances in research and development of techniques and equipment to defend themselves against terrorist acts against civil aviation. ALPA and IFALPA have also had a measurable effect in influencing many governments in the world to take legislative action with respect to international terrorism—in fact, it would be reasonable to claim that the world's airline pilots have been in the forefront from the very beginning. It is interesting to note that the efforts are still continuing and will continue until air piracy becomes a thing of the past, as did piracy on the high seas. It is this author's firm conviction that such a goal is an attainable one.

Meanwhile, international terrorism continues to grow like a cancer. Because we have an effective security system in this country, we tend to overlook the fact that aircraft hijackings are on the increase. There were 30 throughout the world in 1977, exactly twice as many as in 1976.

While the world seeks political solutions to the problem, it has become necessary to find a stopgap to stem the tide of terrorism as it relates to civil aviation. This has been accomplished in the United States and a few other nations by a system of mechanical screening procedures that have been introduced at airports.

Obviously, if one is able to prevent the introduction of weapons on board an aircraft, then its likelihood of being hijacked is decreased dramatically. It is significant that most of the hijackings which have recently taken place against airlines from "secure nations" have been the result of successful hoaxes, not the result of actual armed threat.

The Croation hijacking of a TWA flight in 1977 was an elaborately planned affair involving several people. Those on board constructed what appeared to be bombs from a variety of seemingly innocent components. What made this threat so effective was that the group had left a real bomb in a baggage locker at Grand Central Station in New York City. (A New York City bomb disposal police officer was killed by that device.)

All involved in this hijacking incident were aware of this and consequently were prepared to believe that the hijackers had somehow circumvented the security system at LaGuardia Airport (the original point of departure of the flight).

That the aircraft threat was subsequently found to be a hoax did not detract from the terrorist act, for many peoples' lives were placed in grave jeopardy. The aircraft was a Boeing 727, which had insufficient range to cross the North Atlantic to Europe (the stated destination of the hijackers). The captain literally had to hop across the top of the world, stopping in Newfoundland, Iceland, and northern Europe in an aircraft with no long-range navigation aids or equipment. It was a minor miracle that the aircraft was not lost at sea.

This case clearly illustrates that even the best of security systems can be circumvented. That notwithstanding, as can be seen from the semiannual report to Congress on the effectiveness of the Civil Aviation Security Program by the U.S. Federal Aviation Administration, the number of people caught attempting to smuggle weapons aboard aircraft is still frighteningly high.[1] It is not unreasonable to assume that many of these attempts would have resulted in a terrorist act had they not been thwarted.

The costs of security are staggeringly high, however, and airlines and governments are most reluctant to expend money on what is essentially nonproductive equipment. It is difficult to convince people that not only is it necessary to institute an effective security system but it is also necessary to maintain it and not be lulled into a false sense of security by its success.

By their very nature, security systems are prophylactic in nature. They are preventive, and, consequently, it is difficult to quantify their effect. This is much like the assumption that the worldwide dissemination of the birth control pill has caused a number of babies not to be born, though we cannot prove how many. We can assume it is a large number, but how large is it? Is it 5 million, 50 million, or 20 million?

Security has another cost, and that is debited from the personal freedom and rights of law-abiding citizens. In other aspects of life, how many times is it assumed that everyone is a potential criminal and checked for that discovery?

If we are to survive as a civilized society, how much curtailment of our personal freedom can we sustain? I suspect that the answer is "not very much."

Fortunately, thus far, we have not instituted airport-type security at bus and railroad stations, movie houses, sports events, and all the other myriad of public activities and institutions. To do so would, I fear, accomplish the goals of the terrorist, that is, turning the people against a "dictatorship" and leading, in the end, to a proletarian victory or total anarchy.

The choices are few and sometimes painful, and they must be selected with utmost care.

APPENDIX: REPORT OF THE INTERNATIONAL FLIGHT SECURITY COMMITTEE

Security activity in the international forum has been at an all-time high for the past two years. Due to the experience and expertise existing in ALPA, we have found ourselves deeply involved in, or at the forefront of, events in both the international aviation and political fields.

As often predicted by ALPA, the problem of hijacking has mutated into the much broader spectrum of what is now referred to as *international terrorism.* In terms of ALPA's involvement, we expanded our terms of reference in concert with the expansion of the problem, for it became increasingly difficult to isolate the narrow field of aircraft hijacking from the whole problem. Hijacking has become only one of the battles in a global war.

· For ease of reference and hopefully a better understanding of this report, we shall break it down into three major areas: (1) activities—United States; (2) political situation—international; and (3) IFALPA.

This report was prepared by Thomas M. Ashwood and submitted to the 25th Biennial Board of Directors Meeting of the International Airlines Pilots Association held at Bal Harbour, Florida, October, 1978.

Because of the international aspect of aviation and the ebb and flow of world events, it is difficult to ascertain in which area some of the activities fall. As a general rule, however, all the events taking place are inexorably intertwined and invariably interdependent; therefore, that is important only from an administrative viewpoint.

We also caution that much of the following is dependent upon subjective analysis (except those portions supported by actual data). Since the subject matter has an illegal, complex foundation, it is extremely difficult to present an array of specific problems and resultant recommended solutions.

Activities—United States

Since the last report to the board of directors, significant progress has been made in this area. Senator Abraham Ribicoff (D.–Conn.) introduced an anti-terrorist bill in the Senate earlier this year. From the very outset, the senator and his staff worked and collaborated with ALPA with the result that an extremely effective piece of legislation is on its way to enactment as legislation. For the first time anywhere in the world, this bill calls for specific sanctions against nations who harbor, train, promote, or give sanctuary to terrorists. The sanctions include provisions to deny trade (commerce), military hardware, technical assistance, and, importantly, suspension of air service between the United States and the offending nation.

As ALPA has long claimed, legislation without enforcement provisions is virtually worthless. The bill contains very strong enforcement language. ALPA testified strongly and effectively before several Senate committees and subcommittees in favor of the bill and involved itself in some high-interest public relations efforts in support of it. It is our belief that the bill will pass virtually intact. It is important to recognize that the bill requires other nations to establish and maintain adequate, preventive security procedures at international airports for the purpose of prescreening passengers and carry-on baggage.

Prompted by this Senate action, Congressman Glenn M. Anderson (D.–Calif.) introduced companion legislation in the House of Representatives. It is interesting to note that there was an almost unseemly scramble by congressmen wishing to co-sponsor the bill. The original bill has and is still undergoing changes at the time of this writing; thus far, however, those changes do not cause significent or adverse effects upon the basic elements, which we support. The one major difference between the House and Senate bills addresses itself to the matter of *explosive taggants*. As a brief explanation of the term, explosive taggants come in two types: (1) a chemical element placed in all manufactured explosives that enables *identification* of the manufacturing source to be obtained—this enables the explosive to be traced after an explosion; and (2) a chemical element placed in all manufactured explosives that enables a greater degree of *detection* either by dogs or mechanical devices.

If this section of the bill passes into law and U.S. manufacturers are obliged to comply with both of the above, it is obvious that such capabilities will be a great help in the future, especially with the possibility of the development and aircraft installation of a mechanical "sniffer" at an aircraft outflow valve, which could sample all the air in an aircraft and electronically alert the crew to the presence of explosives prior to leaving the gate. While it is recognized that such a device or situation is several years away, the committee considers it an important prospective protection.

ALPA testified in support of the House bill and, at the time of writing, has some hopes of its passage before the end of the present congressional session. Thus far, little opposition has been engendered against either bill, and there are no divisions along partisan lines.

ALPA is also working on an arrangement whereby security agreements will become a part of our commercial aviation bilateral negotiations with other nations. We feel that this effort will be successful.

In recent times, the United States has been most fortunate in that the level of terrorist attacks has been fairly low. The upheavals of the Vietnam and immediate post-Vietnam eras have largely subsided. The Weathermen, Students for a Democratic Society (SDS), Black Panthers, and the SLA, for instance, have faded into obscurity. We would caution, however, against any relaxation of our vigilance or efforts, for there are strong indications that some of our domestic terrorist groups are only dormant, not dead. The FALN has started to come into prominence recently and is credited with several bombings and subsequent deaths. As its attempts to gain independence for Puerto Rico are successfully thwarted, it is likely that aggressive acts will escalate both in number and intensity. There is no reason to believe that they will not turn to the airlines as terrorist targets; therefore, our vigilance must continue unabated.

Political Situation—International

In concert with the actions taking place in the United States, there has been a flurry of activity internationally, much of it within the last six months. There are two basic reasons why other nations have finally begun to move against terrorism. First, acts of terrorism against European countries have increased dramatically in the last year. What was long considered to be a U.S./Middle East problem is now coming close to home for many nations: Great Britain (IRA), France (Communist Party), Italy (Red Brigades), West Germany (Baader-Meinhof), Japan (JRA), for example. A network of small but highly effective terrorist groups are springing up throughout Europe. While their goals, individually, are parochial in nature, alliances and federations have been formed for the purpose of mutual assistance, logistic support, and so forth. The *total* number of terrorists involved probably number in the few hundreds, but the very nature of Western society, that is, freedom of movement, human rights, capitalist economic structure, and so forth, and the relative fragility such elements create has given these few terrorists a greatly disproportionate effect on the order of things.

The West German government passed legislation this year that is aimed at combating terrorism. While the necessity for such legislation is clear, it is felt that the government acted emotionally and with an excess of zeal. The resultant law cuts deeply into the civil rights of citizens and greatly increases the rights of the state over them. Some view this with alarm, as they see it edging West Germany back to the extreme right-wing stance of the Nazi era. This committee fears that such a move is in accord with the terrorist goals of ultimately turning the people against a right-wing "dictatorship," and leading, in the end, to a proletarian Communist victory or total anarchy.

ALPA is closely monitoring these individual "antiterrorist laws" and, through its contact and participation with the pilots of these nations, continues its efforts to ensure that we win the war as well as the battle.

A recent development occurred in July at a summit meeting in Bonn. Seven nations (United States, Japan, France, Canada, Great Britain, West Germany, and Italy) passed a surprise resolution against hijacking. While ALPA welcomes any move toward eradication of this menace, we must caution against expecting too much. The summit meeting was called for economic reasons, and as it progressed, it began to crumble under its own weight. Pressed with the necessity of bringing something back from the meeting, the seven leaders hurriedly agreed to a sweeping, general resolution on hijacking and sanctions against nations who harbor and abet those who conduct them. As this subject matter was not on the prepublished agenda, the resolution produced the designed effect of becoming a media event. While the foregoing analysis may appear to be somewhat cynical, it is based on long experience in dealing with governments on this subject.

Notwithstanding this viewpoint, ALPA publicly endorsed the Bonn resolution and subsequently participated as observers at the lower-level diplomatic meetings. The purpose was to first determine what the resolution meant and then to establish details and guidelines of formal protocol. We briefed the U.S. State Department officials prior to their departure for the first meeting, but we declined to attend the session in Bonn for we feared that what would be seen as labor involvement by the other six nations would inhibit the discussions. Few nations enjoy the relationship that exists between the U.S. government and ALPA. Pilot associations, for the most, are viewed as being "industrial" in nature and are generally excluded from their government's activities on their behalf. To assure the best possible chance of success, we felt it necessary to downplay the leadership role of the United States. It is very clear that with the tremendous amount of antiterrorist expertise existing in the United States, the United States will be pushed to the forefront in this multinational effort. With the close relationship and mutual respect existing between ALPA and the Department of State, we will have a strong input into all the proceedings.

There is no question that the legislative activity described in the section "Activities—USA" is the other part of the catalyst that promoted international interest in antiterrorism legislation. One may be justifiably proud of the leadership role our country has taken in this regard. Once again, through our IFALPA connections, we are able to press our foreign colleagues to get their own governments to follow suit.

IFALPA

Our participation in the IFALPA Flight Security Study Group has provided ALPA a great opportunity to accomplish three basic goals:

1. The first goal is to shape IFALPA policies to conform with ALPA policies on flight security matters.
2. Educate the members of the study group (which includes pilots from 34 nations) by means of symposia on preventative security, in-flight management of explosives, crew training, and so forth. The Federal Aviation Authority (FAA) Technical Security Division has given continuing assistance in these symposia and has provided the necessary finances and personnel to conduct them.
3. Because of our leadership role in IFALPA, we have successfully utilized our position on the study group to obtain international recognition and support for the U.S. antiterrorist legislation, which greatly enhances its chances of success and which has also given ALPA great credence and stature with Congress and the administration.

It is evident that the initiatives taken by the seven nations in the "Bonn Agreement" will spread to other nations. Through IFALPA, it is expected that this process will be greatly accelerated, and the prospect of getting widespread acceptance of an international agreement on air piracy is closer now than ever before.

Conclusion

While the problems of international and domestic terrorism remain with us, our means of combating it are improving rapidly. The system in place in the United States is working well, as will no doubt be reported by the ALPA Flight Security Committee (domestic) in its report to you. We are hopeful that a similar system will be in place throughout the rest of the world within the next few years.

Recommendations

We recommend that all master executive councils from time to time remind their membership of the need to be continually vigilant. Because of our success since the almost daily hijacking events of the late 1960s, we must assure that apathy does not lead to a recurrence of the hijacking and terrorist acts of the past.

NOTE

1. See Semi-Annual Report to Congress on the Effectiveness of the Civil Aviation Security Program (July 1–December 31, 1977). Washington, D.C.: Department of Transportation, Federal Aviation Administration, Civil Aviation Security Service, 1978.

12

THE RESPONSE OF
THE BANKING COMMUNITY
TO TERRORISM

David Godfrey

How does a financial institution react to the kidnap/extortion demand of $500,000 to $1 million or $10 million in exchange for the safe return of a wife or child of a staff member—or a senior executive?

Do you just pay up, refuse to pay, or negotiate? There is no one answer to this question, because circumstances vary; however, it is widely recognized that this can happen and that payment guarantees nothing except repetition.

The same questions can be related to bomb threats—"There is a bomb in one of your branches, in a safety deposit box." This is a tough decision for somebody to take—but who, how, and on what basis? How do banks react to a crime wave, to a police strike, or to a swindle of crisis-making proportion?

But let us examine this more closely—starting with the threat and its content—Is it valid, or is it just a confidence trick?

How corporations prepare and to what degree they are able to handle the crisis situation varies enormously for both conventional and historical reasons.

At a broad level of generality, a financial institution's response to sociological change tends to be governed by how quickly it can identify the elements concerned and to what extent these are immediately applicable to its own situation. To date, few banks have separated their many criminal-related problems to a degree where they take specific steps to protect themselves against terrorism.

If three masked bandits arrive at a branch pointing automatic weapons or sawed-off shotguns at tellers and customers, there is an immediate element of terror in the most literal sense. This is not perceived as the emergence of a terror situation because banks have been robbed since their inception. The incidence of bank holdups has gradually increased over the past century, and the banking communities responses have related to this. However, this has to be taken in the context of an increased population, the size of banking institutions, and numbers of branches. Dollar losses are lower than ten years ago, even though the value of money in itself has greatly depreciated in terms of buying power. Be that as it may, there is no evidence whatever that there is any connection between the high crime incidence and political terrorist or separatist activity. It may simply be that banks are no longer perceived as impregnable bastions and are regarded as easy targets.

Basically, the factor common to all terrorist incidents is coercion—this principle can be applied to a single holdup or to one that develops into a hostage situation or into its cousin, the kidnap/extortion event, whereby an individual hostage is confined while demands are made. Of course, in a kidnap/hostage situation, the action is drawn out and may well be the result of advanced planning, while the robbery that develops into a hostage-holding incident may well occur as the result of effective preventive measures, which have initially succeeded.

H. H. A. Cooper, former director of European and Middle Eastern Studies of the Aberrant Behavior Center in Dallas, Texas, and one-time staff director of the National Advisory Committee Task Force in Disorders and Terrorism, has written extensively about terrorism and has examined the meaning of the term, which he outlines as follows:

> Some criminal activities generate terror incidentally. Such terror facilitates the commission of the crime, but serves no other purpose for the criminal. For the terrorist, however, terror is an end in itself. This is what he seeks to create by the activity undertaken; this is what he will use for his special purposes.
>
> Terrorism is fear for effect. It has a theatrical quality that is designed to impress. There is an immediate and a remote audience for terrorism. The impression upon those who feel its effects directly is intended to make itself felt on those farther from the scene.
>
> Terrorism requires a responsive audience. All its manifestations are attention-getting devices. By means of these destructive activities, the terrorist seeks to establish a relationship with the person whose conduct he wishes to influence. Terrorism cannot be ignored. The degree of exploitation of the notice he receives is the measure of the terrorist's success.
>
> Terrorism is a bad word; few, nowadays, call themselves terrorists. One man's terrorist is another's patriot, freedom fighter, or revolutionary hero. Terrorists seek to justify or rationalize what they do so that in the process it is not terrorism. Thus the essential ingredient of a definition of terrorism becomes a matter of perspective. Definition, therefore, rests on a judgmental factor.

These remarks are particularly pertinent when reviewing the attitude of banks and their reactions.

The question of whether or not the perpetrators of crime are politically motivated is purely academic. It is often difficult to determine whether this is so, and it is usually totally irrelevant because armed kidnappers carrying out a criminal act are equally unpredictable and potentially dangerous, whether they are social misfits, mentally deranged, or calculating groups of individuals concerned solely about creating "theater." It may be that the bandit's sole aim is to make money and that kidnapping is merely a more sophisticated form of armed robbery, or it may be that the bank is symbolically a social target, presenting a useful medium for advertising a cause and for pressing demands, such as publicity, release of other criminals, and so forth.

In the majority of incidents, globally, it is impossible to determine how often financial institutions are under attack by organized dissidents who wish to inspire terror or by a terrrorist—within the meaning of that term which is applicable to this book. It must be borne in mind that the terrorist is possibly unbalanced, and it should not be assumed that espousing a political cause is some guarantee of sanity. The mental asylum is seldom filled with politicians, although it has been suggested that political institutions consist mainly of lunatics—the point being that emotional stability has absolutely no relationship to political persuasion. It is, therefore, extremely dangerous to attempt to categorize, for example, three types of hostage takers or extortionists, namely, criminal escapee, terrorist activist, or deranged individual. Many elaborations and variations exist. In practice, it is entirely possible that all these elements apply in varying degree. Further, the nature of a criminal act can quickly alter. A hijacking resulting from a jail escape, which involved Southern Airlines and was perpetrated by three deranged individuals, suddenly developed into an ad hoc plan to crash dive on either the White House or an atomic reactor. Despite the preparation of detailed plans for hijacking and hostage taking, an obsessive-compulsive is perfectly prepared to switch at a moment's notice.

The CIA Research Study on International and Transnational Terrorism, dated April 1976, uses the following definitions:

> *Common Characteristics:*
>   The threat or use of violence for political purposes when (1) such action is intended to influence the attitudes and behavior of a target group wider than its immediate victims, and (2) its ramifications transcend national boundaries (as a result, for example, of the nationality or foreign ties of its perpetrators, its locale, the identity of its institutional or human victims, its declared objectives, or the mechanics of its resolution).
> *International Terrorism:*
>   Such action when carried out by individuals or groups controlled by a sovereign state.
> *Transnational Terrorism:*
>   Such action when carried out by basically autonomous non-state actors, whether or not they enjoy some degree of support from sympathetic states.

Many of those elements that have taken part in group attacks on banks have never been fully identified. It is reasonable to suppose that financial institutions are favorite targets if only because the requirements of either terrorist or criminal activity necessitates the raising of funds for arms, escapes, and bribes, as well as a personal reward. The infamous Carlos is alleged to have accumulated a considerable personal fortune following the OPEC raid, which presumably is at odds with claims of high flown motivation. It is conceivable that the task of saving mankind becomes secondary to lining one's pocket. On occasion, bank robbers have subsequently claimed affiliation with extremist groups, the most publicized example being the French bank robbery described extensively by the press as "the Heist of the Century." A very sophisticated group of burglars tunneled into the Nice branch of the Société Generale, one of the largest banks in Europe, during July 1976, making their entry through a sewer. After extensive police inquiries, the leader of the gang was arrested, and it was discovered that he had some nebulous connection with extremist movements earlier in his career. He suggested at the time of his interrogation that all the proceeds of the robbery had been donated by himself and his companions to a secret organization called the Catina and claimed that raising funds for the organization was the purpose of the robbery. However, nothing further was ever heard of the Catina, and French police inquiries failed to reveal any trace of such an organization. It can therefore be assumed that this was merely an attempt to mitigate his crime and reduce his sentence.

In Canada, the Front Liberation de Quebec (FLQ) demanded the release of 23 so-called political prisoners as part of the ransom demand for the release of the British Trade commissioner, James Cross; two of these individuals were bank robbers, and one used the court as a platform to deliver a political harangue during his trial in 1964. After release from prison, both individuals resumed their bank-robbing careers; their connection with the FLQ was never fully established. It was at one time suggested that prior to 1970, this particular organization did carry out bank robberies in order to raise funds for the movement, but there is little hard evidence. It does not follow that if a bank robber belongs to an extremist political group, he or she is committing crimes for political purposes or that all of the take goes to the party fund (as opposed to his or her personal gain).

In the United States, the SLA robbed banks as a means of self-support, while the West German Red Army Faction (Baader-Meinhof gang) carried out a series of raids from 1972 onward, which included bank robberies, along with bombing, murders, and kidnappings, presumably, again, to finance their operations. Nevertheless, these were basically criminal actions, and the purpose was to achieve financial gains, using common criminal methods.

Motivation for bank robbers that ultimately developed into hostage-taking situations have included such bizarre requirements as needing money to complete a sex change operation of a girl/boyfriend in New York or to commandeer a military aircraft to fly a bandit to Uganda from Toronto. Both situations had common factors, the most apparent being the potential for violence, which was out of proportion to the occasion. In a large metropolis, the impact of a downtown shoot-out quickly accelerates and is perceived as becoming an international incident.

Prolonged terrorist battlegrounds tend to breed total subcultures. It is reported that a so-called Mexican blood bank was set up to accommodate capital gains from ransom payments made to Latin American terrorists, while the principle of protection money as insurance has apparently been well-established in Northern Ireland.

Unfortunately, incidents can be blown out of proportion by the media, and this has played an enormous part in creating a public forum for the sort of spectacle that audiences attended in Roman arenas. The coverage of hijacking and hostage-taking situations where human lives have been involved has often been marked by enthusiasm rather than by objective reporting. In many instances, as the Dallas psychiatrist G. D. Hubbard has stated, public reaction and media response created a new form of "social pornography." Fortunately, this has now been recognized by responsible media elements, who have made conscientious efforts to ensure that lives of hostages are not endangered by sensational coverage and that police activities are not hindered. In the past, some reporters and editors have compounded problems, on the assumption that their prime responsibility to themselves, their employers, and the public was to write a good story and be first with the news. In one instance in Canada, the wife of a bank manager was kidnapped and arrangements made with kidnappers to make the "drop." Because approximately six police forces were involved, it was easy for the press to pick up this information from police broadcasts. The first people to arrive at the scene of the proposed drop happened to be reporters, which, understandably, discouraged any attempt to collect the money and hampered law enforcement activities. However, while the reporter needs his story, the banker needs no part of news accounts that provide a guide to would-be extortionists and an invitation to the "copy-cat criminal."

Realizing the issue is a rather complicated one and in an effort to develop better understanding and rapport with the news media, the chairman of the Canadian Bankers' Association's Bank Security Committee, R. A. McElwain, of Canadian Imperial Bank of Commerce, recently participated in a panel discussion on hostage taking and the media's responsibility during a seminar presented to Toronto journalists.

More than 150 students and working journalists heard McElwain say that generally, there has been good cooperation and a high degree of responsibility shown by the media in reporting such events. As far as the banks were concerned, their prime concern was for the safety of customers and staff. This represents an accurate statement of fact.

While there is room for improved perception by the media and the banks of each other's needs, an understanding that the media's requirement for news must be balanced against considerations for the safety of those concerned.

Some appreciable difference of opinion exists among senior executives, and even among managers, of financial institutions as to how they are perceived by the public at large, and the media in particular, with the result that this is often reflected in a withdrawal type of public relations approach, which varies from "No comment" to "Ask the police." Unfortunately, such a reply tends to exasperate the media, who, rightly or wrongly, feel entitled to be informed of the facts; if not informed, they are bound to dig elsewhere, particularly if they do not feel that they are being frankly told what the situation is.

The most effective deterrent to kidnapping is visible lack of success, followed by rapid conviction of offenders and demonstrably heavy sentencing. This can only be achieved when publicity following an occurrence is equal to that during the course of the incident—in this respect, a workable media relationship is essential. Corporations that are victims of extortion owe it to themselves to ensure that accurate and full media coverage is provided, with the rider that it must not ever endanger the life of the hostage or increase the elements of hazard.

In the United States and Canada, police forces have achieved a very high level of apprehension rate, and the courts take serious views of the offence. In the United States, it still carries the death penalty in certain states, and in Canada, extortionists have been receiving sentences of 18 years or more, depending on the circumstances. Conversely, the irony of the situation is that the more successful law enforcement agencies become, the more willing the target is to pay even higher ransoms, on the assumption that a successful termination will lead to restitution and release—again, assuming that money is the major bargaining unit.

Kidnapping, hostage taking, and various forms of extortion are crimes that the public abhor. With the danger of imitation and the increasing popularity in the criminal world, there is a greater risk to staff and customers. While the public often have a good deal of sympathy for the vault burglar, who has ostensibly outwitted a giant monolith by skill and daring, an extortionist is recognized as what he or she really is—a cowardly pest. The offender who holds guns to the heads of infants and wives or takes photographs and then terrorizes the husband so that he will raise the money will never be regarded as a minor folk hero, such as the second jumping-jack Cooper (a hijacker with a parachute—the first was a Canadian, Paul Cine). Banking associations have recognized this fact and established close liaison with police forces in order to develop procedures, which are designed (1) to protect customers, personnel, and their families; (2) to ensure that the incident terminates without loss of life; and (3) to discourage future repetition. To this end, large rewards have been offered and published for information leading to the arrest and conviction of extortionists, as well as to a lesser but more regular degree for bank bandits. Many police forces of all sizes have allocated and trained special extortion and hostage squads and have devised game plans, based on trial and error, which greatly enhance the chance of an early arrest. Bank security personnel have learned how to prepare for and handle a crisis, often setting up special committees to cope with sudden or unforeseen threats. Like other corporate executives, senior bankers and their families have always expressed an ambivalent attitude, namely, "It can't happen to me," but "it might," and "Logically, why not?" The creation of a crisis management group is indicative of an attitude change at the senior level and an essential prerequisite for the creation of a successful security program. Equally important has been the willingness of senior executives to allocate their time to study potential problems outside their normal business experience and to create an organizational capacity, that can respond or delegate during emergencies. These vary from kidnap/extortion to police strikes, bomb threats, power failures, and so forth, including planned terrorist penetrations of their organization.

The intention of banks is to avoid the situation whereby executives are suddenly confronted with a major decision and finds they are on their own. They may have to react, on little or no information, to such matters as a serious bomb threat in a high-rise building, and this no longer can result in the immediate confusion of a mass evacuation. Unless there is reasonable cause to do so, such activity could in itself be dangerous, apart from any nuisance value and loss of time. Executive officers and their families now attend protective driving courses with increasing frequency and learn from specialists the principles and tactics of evasion. They have conceded that their homes and behavioral styles must be influenced by security implications because they have recognized this as an inherent necessity, both at home and abroad. This is not inevitably as tedious or constricting as suspected, nor does it invariably cost as much as some security directors have previously predicted. In desperate efforts to influence their superiors, the latter have deliberately endeavored to create a state of apprehension in order to ensure concurrence by overstating the case and overestimating the precautions needed. Indifference and a low rating in terms of priorities more often than not encouraged security personnel to the "doom and gloom" approach, which was extraordinarily self-defeating. Most financial institutions, like the aviation industry, have now recognized that they are confronted by increasingly serious problems.

At one time, in many countries, managers were reluctant to notify their superiors or law enforcement officials when they were under coercion. If their families were in jeopardy, the prospect of homes being surrounded by Special Weapons and Tactics (SWAT) teams armed with high velocity weapons was sufficient to discourage them, as they regarded this as an unwarranted intrusion of violence into their lives. Starsky and Hutch may be great on TV, but nobody wants them to drive out of the TV set into their living room. However, by tactful and effective handling, extensive educational programs, and successful police work, a relationship based on mutual confidence has been created in many countries, which has assisted law enforcement agencies to hastily mobilize their resources, both externally and internally. Procedures ensuring immediate response to a crisis have been developed by many banks, with the intention of ensuring that maximum attention is afforded to staff and customers, based on close cooperation with law enforcement agencies.

The widely held assumption that extortionists are mental giants, capable of extensive planning, and that payment must immediately be made in the exact denominations demanded has been replaced by the realization that corporations are not necessarily helpless victims. Banks, like many others, have talented and resourceful managers. They are flexible organizations and are basically disciplined. The resources available are almost limitless, and the capacity to preplan and defeat an adversary without loss of life or assets is boundless. Once the initial confusion has been overcome and a well-prepared mechanism put into operation, law enforcement agencies and banks will be more successful in terminating kidnap/extortions than criminals will be in executing them. Would-be kidnappers may sometimes plan carefully, carry out surveillance, and, like hijackers, develop sophisticated techniques, but the statistics in Canada, for example, have indicated a substantial reduction of the offence: namely, 14 kidnap/extortions against chartered banks in 1975, 11 in 1976, four in 1977, and two in 1978. Conversely, arrest figures have risen in proportion, and in all but one instance, the hostage has been released unharmed. This cannot be taken to indicate that banks are now complacent, and it is recognized that there will be more incidents and that some of these will be more successful, but at least bankers are prepared and their executives know how to react, acknowledge their limitations, and closely scrutinize their areas of vulnerability.

Contrary to popular misconception, large sums of money are not available for payment, and a deliberate mechanical delaying element is an integral part of the protective program. The most dangerous time to the hostage is in the early stages, when excitement runs high, with resultant confusion. Initially, the hostage is merely a symbol and a tool of coercion, not a fellow human being. Banks recognize that hasty payments can mean quick deaths and will ensure only that there will be an early repetition of the demand.

Having stated all this, it must be admitted that this chapter deals in a high level of generality and covers a variety of countries and an infinite variation of financial institutions, who inevitably respond in many different ways. The chapter is therefore addressed in the main to the North American experience. No attempt is made to cover the rapidly changing Latin American scene, where in places such as Colombia, over 200 kidnappings for fun and profit have taken place during the past few months, without any particular indication of organized terrorist influence. Nor does it refer toward Middle East or Europe specifically, as the problems of international banking in particular areas have resulted in the implementation of extreme measures to protect staff—residents or visitors. This includes such specialized security problems as the study of the operation of executive jets, executive pretour briefings, and, in some cases, advance reconnaissance of routes. In Lebanon, banks recently reestablished themselves after some hair-raising, even bizarre, experiences, ranging from negotiation with terrorists for readmission to their vaults to terrorist attacks on buildings by anti-aircraft guns.

This has been a very broad-based summary of past and current responses that have evolved as a result of rising crime rates, terrorist activity, and special problems, featuring the popularity of financial institutions as targets. The success of these attacks has diminished gradually in response to protective measures and preplanning, but future prospects do not appear encouraging. The capacity of law enforcement agencies and intelligence-gathering units have either been enormously eroded or alarmingly enhanced, so that the question to be asked is, inevitably, How far will society submit and modify its response, indeed its very structure, to the deliberate manipulation of emotion by extremely small but increasingly powerful groups, whose aim apparently is only to further the growth of terror as an "ism" in its own right?

In summary, then, the response of the banking community to the threat of terrorism, including large-scale nonpolitical crime, has been to (1) identify major problems; (2) alert senior executives to the potential situation; (3) set up a crisis-planning mechanism; (4) strengthen security groups internally; (5) question, review, and examine existing security measures and equipment; (6) ensure adequate executive security measures are taken for staff and families; (7) institute internal security awareness programs; (8) arrange close liaison and relationships with police forces; (9) examine the media conundrum; and (10) plan and prepare for emergencies and delegate authority beforehand.

Each of these preparations could be elaborated upon (and, indeed, frequently will be) at various seminars and in a number of security-oriented publications. The somewhat gloomy but justifiable predictions of the Rand Corporation studies will doubtless act as an incentive to corporations to spend more money and effort on security, possibly at the cost of physical protection to structures, which are already the most expensive part of an ordinary bank branch. The Rand study, which was partly incorporated in a work on international terrorism, "Trends and Potentialities" by Brian M. Jenkins, did not foresee mass violence as being an inevitable development but predicted the emergence of "semi-permanent subcultures." These would consist of sympathizers, lawyers, propagandists, and chroniclers—all in some way dependent on the survival of the terrorist group and the continuation of its activities—it might become a political underworld that would be able to survive the fate of any specific terrorist group. It might develop its own service industries, providing illegal documents and weapons, as well as fences for stolen cash or ransoms. Terrorism itself may become its ideology.

Jenkins believes that today's terrorist groups may become tomorrow's new Mafias, as political objectives become secondary to maintaining a cash flow. The IRA, for example, is deeply involved in extortion: it runs protection rackets, participates in defrauding insurance companies, and also is acquiring ownership of legitimate businesses.

Society's reaction to this has been to gradually build up the office/home fortress concept for executives, with a high degree of protection afforded the executive while in transit between the two. Undoubtedly, banks will be influenced by this development in varying degree, according to local circumstances; indeed, in Europe, bankers are already heavily protected, and the armored car industry is flourishing. Like other industries, training has been given to bank drivers, and even to executives and their families, to ensure that adequate steps are taken to avoid kidnapping on the road. A large number of bankers in senior positions no longer sit in the back seat and have an easily identified chauffeur in a uniform, but the degree of reaction is clearly directly related to the perceived situation. The caged executive concept has not yet been accepted and, hopefully, never will be necessary. Most financial institutions have adopted common-sense approaches to the practical application of security measures, particularly in terms of cost and inconvenience. It is not feasible to expect the bank staff to radically alter their life-styles or to anticipate that rational security personnel can advocate a never-ending series of measures and gadgets designed to defeat would-be attackers. However, there is a definite and continued movement toward self-reliance, which is greatly encouraged by law enforcement agencies, who feel that big corporations should play a major part in helping themselves. This, in turn, has created an ever increasing number of security specialists in the banking field, whose status in the organization has risen from being a security officer with investigative experience and functions to a senior vice-president, who speaks on a regular basis to the board of Directors and provides up-to-date analysis of the overall security situation, criminal trends, and the potential threat. The liaison between financial agencies and the police, as well as the relationship, both nationally and internationally, between financial institutions, has become much more apparent. Sometimes, this is done bank to bank or sometimes through banking associations or, in the case of police, through Interpol and other agencies. Response on the international field has varied enormously. Some countries, such as the Scandinavian ones and other European nations, have sponsored a more regular and accepted form, but this relates more to fraud and forgery than to terrorism.

The fact is that sophisticated crime is far more profitable than a "sledge-hammer" approach, which is more apparent in North America. Internal problems match external threats, and this may be attributed to changing social values, which will require a gradual, but analytic, alteration of security emphasis, related to current and predicted local conditions. It is indeed impossible to provide even an estimate of total bank losses or security-related expenditures.

Terrorism, as defined earlier, is only a small portion of the total problem confronting financial institutions, but it is an obvious aspect that can be overemphasized by the ill-informed and by media reference, which accepts other bank crimes as being a normal business risk but mirrors public interest in more unusual or sensational aspects (which puts more importance on certain matters than they merit in proportion to such matters as staff reaction and the creation of protective measures).

13

THE INSURANCE COMPANIES' RESPONSE TO TERRORISM

Julian Radcliffe

Societies faced by the threat of assassination, kidnappings, or other misfortunes, whether politically or criminally inspired, look to the governments for protection; then, realizing that total security is not possible and is very expensive, they seek to shift the losses of the few to the shoulders of many by means of insurance. Some of the first risks underwritten by Lloyd's in the early part of the eighteenth century included the loss of vessels through piracy and other similar perils, as the wording of the Lloyd's standard marine policy, still used today, explains.

> Touching the adventures and perils which we the assurers are contented to bear and do take upon us in this voyage: they are of the seas, men of war, fire, enemies, pirates, rovers, thieves, jettisons, letters of mart and countermart, surprisals, takings at sea, arrests, restraints, and detainments of all kings, princes, and people, of what nation, condition, or quality soever, barratry of the master and mariners, and of all other perils, losses, and misfortunes, that have or shall come to the hurt, detriment, or damage of the said goods and merchandises, and ship &c., or any part therof. And in case of any loss or misfortune it shall be lawful to the assured, their factors, servants and assigns, to sue, labour, and travel for, in and about the defence, safeguard, and recovery of the said goods and merchandises, and ship, &c., or any part therefor, without prejudice to this insurance; to the charges whereof we, the assurers, will contribute each one according to the rate and quantity of his sum herein assured.

Dutch shipowners at a similar time formed mutual insurance companies to collect ransoms from their members to release crews held hostage by priates in the East Indies. There has therefore been a recognized market for war risks and similar perils for ships and cargoes for several centuries, and the hijacking of jets has been written in the London Insurence Market since the first incidence of air piracy. During the hijacking by Palestinian terrorists of the two jets to Dawson's Field and the hijacking of a third to Cairo, in 1970, Lloyd's Underwriters and the Insurance Market responded for the hull values for several million dollars; if all the passengers had been killed, the losses would have been enormous.

Insurance companies have also realized that there was a requirement for them not to take on liabilities for potential losses that could affect their own solvency. Hence, during the 1930s, when the possibility of large-scale bombing became a reality during the Spanish Civil War and the threat of a world war in Europe loomed, the Insurance companies agreed among themselves as to what risks should be covered by both fire, marine, and liability policies, so that all war risks, as such, were excluded. It was felt reasonable that ships, aircraft, and cargoes should continue to be covered in a specific market, since as they were mobile, the chances of enormous aggregate losses were diminished, as they could be moved from a danger area. By concentrating the coverage in a specific market in London, the insurance industry was able to keep an exact track of liabilities assumed, which would not have been the case if these types of war risks had just been added to every normal insurance policy.

Under the voluntary agreement negotiated in the late 1930s, insurance companies agreed not to insure any war risks on land but only ships, aircraft, and cargoes; however, even in regard to the latter, they agreed that any damage occurring through a war in which one of the five major powers (USSR, China, United States, Great Britain, and France) was involved or any damage in a war in which a nuclear weapon was exploded would be excluded even from their own war risk policies. The reasoning behind this was fairly clear: it would have been unethical for an insurance company to accept a premium for a risk, the magnitude of which was so great that the insurance companies might not be able to pay (even if the client was not in a position to collect either). However in fire policies for factories and other fixed investments, policies included riots, strikes, and malicious damage, but these were not extended to cover politically motivated losses, such as sabotage.

With these voluntary limitations by the insurance companies, it was inevitable that governments would produce indemnity schemes to cover risks that their citizens faced and which the insurance companies could not cover. Examples of these have included a riot damage scheme run by the U.S. government in the aftermath of the race riots of the late 1960s and a similar one run by the British government to indemnify losses in Northern Ireland caused by terrorist action. The latter scheme extends to the damage of property, consequential business interruption, and injuries to personnel. In a similar fashion, at times, governments have felt that the war risk premiums required to insure the hijacking of aircraft against terrorism have been so high that they have been prepared to give an indemnity to their own national airline rather than to allow it on the private market. In the nuclear field, liabilities from ordinary nuclear accidents are still greater than the private insurance markets can bear, and there is therefore a government indemnity scheme that comes in once the capacity of the private insurance market worldwide is exhausted.

One obvious aim of terrorist action is to reduce the efficiency of an economy by frightening away foreign investment, disrupting sources of supply, preventing labor from operating, and generally reducing confidence, which is a precondition for any successful economy. This problem has been recognized by many of the Western nations as one of the aspects of political instability, which affects the Third World in particular. About 20 governments, including the United States, Great Britain, and West Germany, set up schemes to insure overseas investments by their own nationals in order to encourage private investment, which was felt to be the most effective form of overseas aid. Under these schemes, such as the Overseas Private Investment Corporation in Washington, D.C., the government will insure an investment against damage due to war, confiscation, or the inability to remit funds. These policies could well respond to a loss caused by civil war started by terrorist groups, if their confrontation theory had worked to the extent that civil war was caused. In the same way, Lloyd's underwriters, and now other insurance companies, insure investments for similar perils. Terrorism can also frustrate export contracts, which could be insured either under the government scheme, such as the Foreign Credit Insurance Association/Eximbank (Export-Import Bank) or by the private market, which will give coverage against political risks, which could include the consequences of terrorist action.

It is perhaps fortunate that with very few exceptions, terrorist groups, on the whole, have been unable to overthrow the government to the extent that the previous government's policies have been so directly reversed that large losses have been suffered by such government or private insurance markets. However, one has to be alive to the possibility that this could happen, and indeed, the aggregate values at risk in an area such as the Middle East, in which the entire area could be affected by a successful terrorist campaign, would be extremely serious.

This is a brief historical survey of what the insurance companies had already done before the waive of terrorism of the late 1960s. It is instructive to look at one or two case studies before going on the talk about risk management in depth and the most recent developments, as well as our predictions for the future. The typical effect of terrorist action on a corporation can be seen by the Owens-Illionis case. This glass-making company, which was considering a further investment in Venezuela, had one of their executives, William E. Niehous, kidnapped. One of the demands in return for the release of this victim was that Owens-Illinois should pay for the advertising of a guerrilla manifesto in a number of international newspapers. This they did, and the effect on the Venezuelan government was to cause the latter to threaten to expropriate Owens-Illinois's assets in Venezuela, which were worth some $20 million. Subsequently, Owens-Illinois paid a ransom reported to be in the order of $2 million—sadly, the victim has not yet been returned and must be presumed to be dead. Not only was there a significant cost in terms of the ransom, the advertising costs, and the disruption to the operations in Venezuela, but the effect on morale throughout the corporation must have been considerable. The largest ransom ever paid was some $60 million, when the two Born brothers were kidnapped on their way to work in Argentina. The negotiations continued over some six months, and eventually a payment was made in a number of installments, together with gifts of food and other political concessions.[1]

A corporation must take the same steps to mitigate these risks as they would for any other. Through a logical process of risk management, the risk must be identified, analyzed, evaluated, reduced, and either transferred or accepted. Insurance has played a major part in this process, since the losses tend to be unpredictable, large in nature, and difficult to avoid entirely.

Various governments have questioned whether the availability of kidnapping insurance was against the public interest on the grounds that it may have encouraged those covered by such insurance to pay higher ransoms than they would have otherwise been able to afford. It has therefore been argued that kidnappings that have been made successful by the existence of insurance would encourage futher attempts and, also, provide finance for criminal and political actions of an illegal nature. In fact, this argument is founded on a number of basic misconceptions, which have arisen primarily because the full implication of kidnapping insurance on a worldwide basis has been, in the main, available only to the underwriters concerned in London, their advisers, and a limited number of government agencies.

First, one must examine what effect an insurance policy has on the payment of a ransom. Although this type of insurance has only risen to significant proportions during the past five years, it has been written by some underwriters at Lloyd's since before the second world war. Despite considerable research, Lloyd's has been able to find no evidence whatsoever that the granting of insurance has either increased the ransom amount paid or the incidence of kidnappings; on the contrary, it can probably be demonstrated that the advice given by Lloyd's representatives prior to, during, and following a loss has, in almost all of the cases insured by Lloyd's, led to the safe return of the victim, as well as a substantial reduction in the amount that would otherwise have been paid. Second, a kidnapping is an event that generally only happens once to any given group, so that without advice, the negotiators are operating under extreme duress and are invariably warned by the kidnappers of the dire consequences that will follow any disclosure of the ransom demand to the police or the press. Without the benefit of past experience, it can be shown that on receipt of such a demand, most people cannot think beyond securing the immediate release of their colleague or relation and, therefore, simply set about collecting the sum demanded.

The existence of the policy is secret between the insured, brokers, and the underwriters, thereby preventing any possibility of the criminals trying to select their victims on the ground that those who are insured would pay more easily. As far as is known, there is no evidence of this type of selection by criminal gangs. Indeed, the presence of the secrecy clause appears to have engendered in the insured genuine fear that discovery of the policy may lead to its cancellation. Moreover, underwriters only give policies to corporations or families whose assets exceed the sum insured.

The policy is also one of indemnity only. A corporation must raise the money from its own resources without using the existence of the insurance policy as security for a loan and will be subsequently reimbursed only if the underwriters are satisfied that the policy conditions have been observed. Some corporations may have felt that a decision to buy insurance was a tacit admission that they would pay up, but since virtually all corporations have paid up when faced with a kidnapping situation but not all corporations were insured, this is not a valid argument.

Because of the importance that Lloyd's attaches to professional help during negotiations, consultants from Control Risks—a company formed in 1975—retained at Lloyd's expense, are available on immediate notice to monitor and assist with postkidnapping negotiations and to inject reason and a range of experience into the decisions. Their advice is only offered to the client, who still has responsibility for all decisions made; the whole philosophy of negotiating is described later in this chapter.

Underwriters offer sophisticated security measures, particularly in the more exposed countries, and will give a discount on the premium of a company if it can implement the recommendations made in the survey program, which is outlined below.

One further advantage of kidnapping insurance is that underwriters can insist that the police must be informed that a kidnapping has occurred, and this can be extremely helpful to the government in certain countries where the police are severely handicapped by a large number of incidents that are not reported. This situation has sometimes arisen because the police are known to be corrupt, and there is some concern by risk managers that the policy condition of informing police may lead to the death of the victim if the police have been infiltrated. This problem can usually be averted by finding a senior government official or policeman whose integrity is unquestioned and through whom all information, suitably vetted, can be passed to the local police.

It appears that kidnapping insurance, as in other fields, such as fire and burglary, is now the main factor in introducing greater security awareness. Governments have often proved to be incapable through international cooperation of countering terrorism, and it would seem to be unreasonable for them to deny to corporations or families the ability to be reimbursed for the substantial losses that may suffer as a result.

There is obviously a great onus on the press not to give details of the way in which kidnappings are undertaken in order to prevent other groups being encouraged to try the same system. In the same way, those handling insurance on behalf of Lloyd's, such as the broker, are discouraged from panic selling or using such methods as direct mailing or advertising, which may be both in bad taste and counterproductive in the long term.

A number of countries have looked at the possibility of making kidnapping and ransom insurance illegal, including Northern Ireland and Argentina, as well as the state of California. In all cases, they have eventually found that to make insurance illegal would probably be counterproductive for the reasons previously mentioned. Indeed, in many countries, they may now welcome the role of Lloyd's representatives, who have far more international experience in the prevention of kidnapping and the problems of negotiations than many individual police forces.

Governments have also considered outlawing the payment of ransom or even negotiations themselves. It may be tempting to do so, since the initial reaction of many responsible citizens when they are faced with the demand for ransom and negotiation under duress is to stand firm in the belief that sacrifices must be made to prevent terrorism or similar criminal activity from spreading.

The U.S. State Department has publicly endorsed this policy with respect to its own employees; it has also encouraged the same policy for U.S. corporations. The State Department adopted a no-pay policy early on in the attacks on U.S. diplomats in Latin America. It is probably the correct policy for a government to take, but it is worth considering whether corporations or families could adopt the same policy and what other measures the State Department took at the same time as they made their stand against payment or political concessions.

Security precuations at embassies were strengthened, special vehicles were purchased, and security precautions taken at a level that few corporations or families could afford. The U.S. government was also in a powerful position in relation to the local government to obtain help from their security forces. If an attack occurred, the criminals and terrorists responsible knew that all the local resources of the U.S. government would be directed against them. This has had the classic result of making the corporation or family, as opposed to the diplomat, a more attractive target, both for criminals seeking money and for the terrorists, who can obtain as much political capital out of kidnapping a U.S. multinational executive as they can out of kidnapping a U.S. diplomat.

The problems for corporations in implementing the same policy are greater. First, public servants, such as diplomats, recognize particular duties inherent in their careers and particular advantages, such as job security. An executive has less security and no implied obligations for his corporation. Second, the U.S. embassy can afford far greater protection than a U.S. executive, and the local government will be more embarrassed by the kidnapping of a U.S. diplomat than they would be by that of a businessman. Third, there are usually far more corporate executives than there are diplomats, and therefore, businessmen are a more difficult target to protect. Fourth, the legal position of a corporation is different from the U.S. government in that it can be more easily sued by the family of a kidnapping victim, with the consequent risk of adverse publicity.

However, the key difference is that the U.S. government is a single decision-making entity, whereas for a similar policy to be effective among corporations, there would have to be absolute confidence that thousands of companies would hold the same line. If it was known that any one corporation was likely to give in, then there would be no effective deterrent at all. Furthermore, this policy would have to be adopted by all the overseas subsidiaries of U.S. corporations acting under different local laws, and it is questionable whether they could take the same line for a non-U.S. citizen. The outcry can be imagined if the first victim of the new no-pay policy was not the local chief executive, a U.S. citizen, but the local non-U.S. postboy or postgirl. Ultimately, all non-U.S. corporations would have to agree to the same policy if it were to be effective, and all families would have to do the same as well.

Considering how some governments, such as Japan and Austria, have continued to give in to terrorists' demands, it is denying the natural dictates of human nature to expect families not to do so. Efforts have been made to make negotiations illegal, and police have tried to seize ransoms when they were due to be paid. The effect of these measures has been to make certain that families conducted secret negotiations without informing the police, and this is obviously the worst of all possible worlds. It is probably just as unrealistic to try to make the payment of ransom illegal as it would be to forbid a person to hand over his or her wallet if he or she was mugged on the street. Nevertheless, the public stance of the government must often be to discourage companies from paying, although their private advice in a particular case could well be different.

It would therefore appear to be difficult to maintain either voluntarily or legally a policy of no payment or no concessions. Generally, there is no argument in favor of no negotiations (except perhaps tactically at certain stages during negotiations), since negotiations give both time and intelligence, which are essential factors to the police if they are to have a chance of detecting those responsible.

The responsibility, therefore, cannot be shirked by corporate executives, even if the police take charge of negotiations—the company will probably have to provide the ransom, and very few police forces are prepared to try and conduct negotiations without any reference to the view of the corporation or family.

It is only in a dictatorship that there is no theoretical conflict in the duties and rights of the individual and the duties and rights of the state. The whole response of terrorism must be to balance the repressive measures required to defeat terrorism with the preservation of the democratic state. There are, of course, different priorities among the different parties after a kidnapping: the family will wish the release of the victim as their first priority, the police to capture those responsible, and the government to preserve its credibility. It is therefore necessary to provide a coordinated response and this is the main task in which Lloyd's representatives advise. The government must continue to respect the rights of the individual kidnapping his or her victim, family, and the corporation; it must not impose laws that will not be respected. Without the cooperation of the individual, terrorism will not be defeated unless a police state is formed, which is, of course, the aim of the terrorists in the first instance.

In theory, it is simple to favor a no-pay policy, particularly for an unknown individual. In practice, few would deny that they would be prepared to pay a ransom for their own eight-year-old daughter, particularly if it only amounted to about $10,000. There is no doubt that the greatest deterrent to kidnapping is a high detection rate, and this is the policy that is being followed by the FBI, who have not usually intervened in the negotiations or the payment but have allowed the victim to be released before moving in to make arrests.

It is comparatively easy to work out the philosophy of how kidnapping insurance should be made available, but it is a good deal more difficult for the practical experience to be gathered together in order that advice can be given to corporations by Lloyd's representatives in crisis management situations, as well as in preventive assessments.

It has been apparent since the late 1960s that little expertise was available outside government departments in this area and that the assistance which can be given by any government department to an individual corporation abroad is strictly limited. In Great Britain, the expertise in the government in counterterrorist warfare was particularly concentrated in one unit of the British army, which has not been the case in many other countries, where a larger number of different agencies may be involved. This unit has provided considerable expertise for the training of other similar organizations, and it was from this expertise that Lloyd's was able to obtain expertise. Control Risks, a company that was formed in 1975, has now advised in over 50 kidnapping negotiations in several different countries. They have also undertaken extensive survey work (on preventive measures with regard to kidnappings) of overseas subsidiaries in particularly hazardous countries and of corporate headquarters in order to implement crisis management plans; they have also run crisis-management exercises. They also undertake detailed threat assessment work, both for Lloyd's and corporations. At the time of writing, Lloyd's was unique in offering this service at its own cost, that is, it paid for it out of the premium and allowed a discount after the survey work had been done if the recommendations could be complied with. In the same way, Lloyds' would pay for the cost of advice during crisis-management negotiations, although the advice was in no way binding on the corporation that had suffered the loss. One of the executive directors of the company,

Richard Clutterbuck, produced a book *Kidnap and Ransom: The Response,* which was the first serious work that concentrated in this area of counter-terrorism.

The response of the insurance companies must obviously follow the pattern of terrorist attacks of the future. Indeed, good advice given to corporations by the insurance industry may go some way toward preempting points of potential weakness. There is still considerable scope for underwriting those risks that are currently excluded by market practice, from ordinary insurance policies, and for which no special market has yet been developed. It is possible that this could be done in conjunction with a government scheme and might include the physical damage of property from terrorist action, consequential losses following sabotage, and perhaps an insurance policy to reimburse companies for the increased costs of protecting themselves should they become specific targets rather than merely reimbursing them for out-of-pocket expenses after an event.

The parallel to this is the way in which, in certain countries, such as West Germany, individuals insure themselves for legal costs in the event of being involved in court action.

One has to be careful of identifying publicly possible terrorist tactics of the future. The sort of problems may include the product liability risk for producers of consumer goods, who may find themselves liable for slow-acting and virtually untraceable sources of contamination. The same problems could affect pharmaceuticals or, indeed, sources of energy.

There will be an extremely interesting court case in the next few years, where judgments will be made on what is "reasonable care" in relation to protecting facilities against terrorist attacks. There may yet be a further, more important role for the insurance industry—as an international collector of statistics on damage, standards of protection, and certain aspects of intelligence. This is already the case for technical standards of safety for ships, which is undertaken by the various national societies, such as Lloyd's Registry of Shipping. It may well be that the insurance industry could begin to insist on certain protective requirements being taken, although in a highly competitive industry, there is a limit to their ability to enforce high standards.

If nations feel unable to cooperate together as they should in the area, (countering terrorism by swapping information) since they suffer from the paradox that one nation's terrorist is another nation's freedom fighter, then it may well be that the insurance industry will have to provide a growing focus for international cooperation between corporations rather than between governments. There are parallels for this in the ordinary crime field, where loss adjusters already provide considerable sums of money for the police to reward informants and to trace stolen goods. It has already been demonstrated that a private company working for the insurance industry and its clients has been able to develop a recognized expertise in the field of advice on kidnapping negotiations, and this type of role may well be expanded.

NOTE

1. For further examples, see Richard Clutterbuck, *Kidnap and Ransom: The Response* (London and Boston: Faber and Faber, 1978).

14

TERRORISM:
SUMMARY OF APPLICABLE
U.S. AND INTERNATIONAL LAW

Louis G. Fields, Jr.

For most of our recent history, our societies have been able to deal with terrorism as a variation of common crime. We have relied on our existing laws to prosecute and punish terrorists for their criminal acts, and we have acted with the assumption that this prosecution and punishment would deter others from committing similar crimes. But too often in recent years, this institutional optimism has been challenged and jeopardized by those determined to prove through repeated and often inhuman criminal acts that the rule of law cannot protect our societies.

The dimension of terrorist crime has caused many countries to reevaluate the application of their laws to meet this new form of malevolence within society. The targeting of civilian aviation by terrorist groups and their indiscriminate attacks against civilian facilities, populations, and officials has led to the development of international conventions to deal with these manifestations of terrorist activity. This chapter will survey the development of U.S. law and codified international law to meet this new threat to society.

U.S. LAW

The U.S. Criminal Code (Title 18, U.S.C.) includes traditional crimes utilized by terrorists in their efforts to influence government policy or action, that is, murder, kidnapping, assult, arson, and so forth. Recently, however,

---

The views expressed in this chapter are the author's and do not necessarily reflect the views of the U.S. government or any of its agencies or departments.

Congress has taken account of particular manifestations of terrorism and enacted laws to deal with this specialized criminal behavior.

Crimes against Internationally Protected Persons

Public Law 92-539, October 24, 1972, amended the Criminal Code (Title 18, U.S.C.) by adding crimes directed against foreign officials and official guests of the United States. These crimes include (1) murder or manslaughter (Section 1116); (2) conspiracy to murder (Section 1117); (3) kidnapping (Section 1201); (4) assults, including harassment (treated as a misdemeanor) (Section 112); and (5) injury, damage, or destruction of real or personal property, owned or utilized by a foreign government, international organization, or foreign official or official guest (Section 970). This law antedated the Convention on the Prevention and Punishment of Crimes Against Internationally Protected Persons, adopted by the UN General Assembly on December 14, 1973. Public Law 94-467 (October 8, 1976), implementing the UN convention, further amended those sections of Title 18 that were changed by Public Law 92-539 by adding "internationally protected person" as a third category of individual entitled to the special protection of the law. Public Law 94-467 added Section 878 to Title 18, a new section that provides felony punishment for (a) willfully threatening to kill, kidnap, or assault a foreign official, official guest, or internationally protected person, and (b) making any extortionate demand in connection with any violation of Section 878(a) or actual violation of sections 112, 1116, or 1201. It also confers jurisdiction upon U.S. federal courts to try alleged offenders present within the United States for offenses under sections 1116, 1201, 112(a), and 878 that were committed outside the territory of the United States. The new law also authorizes the attorney general, in his enforcement of sections 1116, 1201, 112(a), or any conspiracy or attempt to commit those sections, to request assistance from "any Federal, State or local agency, including the Army, Navy, and Air Force," thus providing an exception to the prohibition against use of military forces as *Passe Comitatus* (18 U.S.C. 1385).

Crimes against Aviation

The Antihijacking Act of 1974 (Public Law 93-366, August 5, 1974) was enacted in implementation of the Convention for the Suppression of Unlawful Seizure of Aircraft (The Hague Convention) adopted at The Hague on December 16, 1970. This law amended the Federal Aviation Act of 1958 (49 U.S.C. 1301 et seq.) to redefine the "special aircraft jurisdiction of the United States" and to modify the offense of aircraft piracy to conform to the requirements of The Hague Convention. It also conferred extraterritorial jurisdiction upon U.S.

federal courts to try alleged offenders under this statute and provided for the death penalty when the death of another person resulted from the commission or attempted commission of the offense.

Aside from the criminal provisions of the act, it gives the president authority to suspend

(1) the right of any air carrier or foreign air carrier to engage in foreign air transportation, and the right of any person to operate in foreign air commerce, to and from [any nation that he determines permits the use of its territory as "a base of operations or training or sanctuary for, or in any way arms, aids, or abets, any terrorist organization which knowingly uses the illegal seizure of aircraft or the threat thereof as an instrument of policy"], and (2) the right of any foreign air carrier to engage in foreign air transportation, and the right of any foreign person to operate aircraft in foreign air commerce, between the United States and any foreign nation which maintains air service between itself and [a nation subjected to the determination referred to in (1) above].

Thus, the president has, under specified circumstances, authority to suspend air service rights, both primary and secondary, and the act makes it unlawful (civil penalty) for any air carrier to operate aircraft in foreign air commerce in violation of the suspension order. It should also be noted that a notwithstanding clause relieves the secretary of Transportation and Civil Aeronautics Board of any statutory obligation to exercise their powers and duties (in granting certificates of public convenience and operation) pursuant to any treaty obligation of the United States and to take into consideration applicable laws of foreign countries.

The act provides for the maintenance of the minimum security measures in foreign air transportation and grants to the secretary of transportation (subject to the approval of the secretary of state) authority to "withhold, revoke, or impose conditions on the operating authority of the airlines of [any nation he finds 'does not effectively maintain and administer security measures . . . equal to or above the minimum standards established pursuant to the Convention on International Aviation'] ."

Part II of the act (known as the Air Transportation Security Act of 1974) provides for the establishment of screening procedures and promulgation of rules and regulations for aircraft security. It confers upon the Administrator of FAA *exclusive* responsibility for the direction of any law enforcement activity affecting the safety of persons aboard aircraft involved in the commission or attempted commission of aircraft piracy and prohibits, except as otherwise provided by law, the transfer or assignment of those responsibilities. "Other Federal departments and agencies" are required, upon FAA request, to "provide such assistance as may be necessary to carry out the purposes [of the law enforcement activity] " [49 U.S.C. § 1357(e)(2)] .

It should be noted that the United States is a party tó the Convention on the Suppression of Unlawful Acts Against the Safety of Civil Aviation (Sabotage) (the Montreal Convention); however, implementing legislation is needed to enable full discharge of obligations under this convention. The U.S. criminal code (18 U.S.C. Ch. 2) established felony offenses involving the destruction of aircraft and aircraft facilities; however, these offenses do not conform completely to the offenses described in the convention, nor is there extraterritorial jurisdiction in the federal courts to try such offenses. Legislation has been submitted, but Congress has not acted upon it to date.

Sanctions against Countries that Aid or Abet Terrorists

The International Security Assistance and Arms Export Control Act of 1976 (Public Law 94-329, June 30, 1976) contains a prohibition of assistance to countries granting sanctuary to international terrorists. Section 303 of the act ("Wolff Amendment") adds a new section (620A) to the Foreign Assistance Act of 1961 requiring, except where national security dictates otherwise, the president to terminate for one year "all assistance under this Act" to a government that "aids or abets, by granting sanctuary from prosecution to, any individual or group which has committed an act of international terrorism." Assistance affected by this section includes economic, military (including training), and security supporting assistance, all granted under the Foreign Assistance Act of 1961, as amended. It would not affect foreign military cash or credit sales, disaster relief assistance, international narcotic control assistance, any economic preferences or loans not under the Act, or commercial sales.

The 94th Congress, in its final days, adopted the "Javits resolution" (Senate resolution 524), which urges the president to (1) direct U.S. ambassadors to encourage host governments to suspend air service to countries aiding or abetting terrorism, (2) undertake international negotiations to strengthen and improve aircraft and airport security, and (3) exercise his present authority to suspend aviation rights as conferred under the Antihijacking Act of 1974. Moreover, it urges the president "to conduct a comprehensive review of all U.S. trade and diplomatic relations to determine what further appropriate actions, including specific sanctions, might be taken to discourage any further support of international terrorism." The Javits Resolution is advisory in nature and does not have any binding effect upon the federal government. It does, however, convey a strong congressional interest in a more innovative and forceful policy to deal with governments that encourage and support terrorists.

The International Security Assistance Act of 1977 (Public Law 95-92, August 4, 1977) amended Section 3 of the Arms Export Control Act to require the president, unless he "finds that the national security requires otherwise," to "terminate all sales, credits, and guaranties" under the act to "any government which aids or abets, by granting sanctuary from prosecution to, any individual or group which has committed an act of international terrorism." It establishes a one-year "embargo" under the act from the date of initial presidential action to terminate such assistance and provides for an additional one-year extension of the embargo for any intervening grant of sanctuary by the offending government.

Section 509 ("Heinz amendment") of the Foreign Assistance and Related Appropriation Act of 1978 (Public Law 95-148, October 31, 1977) provides that

> none of the funds appropriated or otherwise made available by this Act to the Export-Import Bank and funds appropriated by this Act for direct foreign assistance may be obligated for any government which aids or abets by granting sanctuary from prosecution to, any individual or group which has committed an act of international terrorism, unless the President of the United States finds that the national security requires otherwise.

On October 25, 1977, Senator Ribicoff (D.–Conn.) introduced a bill entitled the "Omnibus Anti-Terrorism Act of 1977 (S2236). He characterized the legislation as an effort to combine "diplomatic initiatives with a strong unilateral United States policy to combat terrorism."[1] Major features of the bill included (1) reorganization of executive branch responsibilities and capabilities to combat terrorism; (2) reporting requirements regarding terrorist incidents; (3) a List of Countries Aiding Terrorist Enterprises (LOCATE) together with a range of sanctions against such countries, unless the president waived application on national security grounds; (4) a List of Dangerous Foreign Airports, with sanctions against foreign governments whose airports were so listed; and (5) implementing legislation for the Montreal Convention. The bill was considered reported by the Government Affairs, Foreign Relations and Select Intelligence committees of the Senate. The committee process made several changes to the bill, namely: (1) eliminating reorganization provisions; (2) modifying the listing of countries supporting international terrorism (the LOCATE acronym was dropped); (3) reducing the range of sanctions applicable to listed countries; and (4) dropping the dangerous airport provisions. Although cleared for floor action in the Senate, it was not acted upon before the expiration of the 95th Congress.

The 95th Congress passed two bills designed to assert U.S. influence within international financial institutions against loans or other assistance from those institutions to any country which "provide[s] refuge to individuals committing acts of international terrorism by hijacking aircraft" (Public Law 95-118, Section 701), or permits terrorists to enter its territory, or supports, encourages, or harbors them, or fails to take "appropriate measures to prevent [them] from committing [acts of international terrorism] outside the territory of such country" (Public Law 95-435, Section 6). Section 701 requires U.S. executive directors in such international financial institutions to oppose loans to such countries, unless the loan serves "basic human needs"; whereas, Section 6 instructs U.S. executive directors "to work on opposition to any extension of financial or technical assistance" to such countries.

CODIFIED INTERNATIONAL LAW AND INITIATIVES

Civil Aviation

There are three conventions that address the question of offenses against civil aviation; these were prompted by terrorist attacks against aircraft engaged in civil air commerce. These conventions were adopted under the aegis of the International Civil Aviation Organization (ICAO). The first to be enacted was the Convention on Offenses and Certain Other Acts Committed on Board Aircraft (Tokyo Convention) of September 14, 1963. The convention applies to offenses against penal laws and to acts, whether or not they are offenses, which may or do jeopardize the safety of the aircraft or of persons or property therein or which jeopardize good order and discipline on board while the aircraft is in flight or on the surface of the high seas or of any area outside the territory of any state (Article 1).

The convention is concerned with ensuring that at least one state has jurisdiction of the alleged offender, but contains only limited provisions for the trial of persons accused of offenses under it. Article 3 provides that the state of registration of the aircraft is competent to exercise jurisdiction over the alleged offenders and, further, that each contracting state is obliged to make necessary measures to establish its jurisdiction as the state of registration. Even though a contracting state is required to adopt the laws necessary to give its courts jurisdiction, it is not obliged to ensure that all alleged offenders will be prosecuted (Article 13).

The convention provides for a contracting state to take delivery of a suspected offender, but it places no extradition obligation on the receiving state. Article 16 merely provides that offenses committed on aircraft registered in a contracting state are to be treated, for the purposes of extradition, as if they had been committed not only in the place in which they had occurred but, also, in

This section incorporates portions of a report prepared for the U.S. Department of State by the Procedural Aspects of International Law Institute, entitled *Multilateral Conventions and Agreements Relating to the Punishment of Terrorist Acts* (September 1976).

the territory of the state of registration of the aircraft. Without prejudice to that provision, it is declared that "nothing in the Convention shall be deemed to create an obligation to grant extradition."

The second convention that was enacted was the Convention for the Suppression of Unlawful Seizure of Aircraft (Hague Convention) of December 16, 1970.* The convention obliges contracting states to make the offense of unlawful seizure of aircraft punishable by severe penalties (Article 2). Article 1 defines the offense as the act of any person who on board an aircraft in flight:

(a) unlawfully, by force or threat thereof, or by any other form of intimidation, seizes, or exercises control of, that aircraft, or attempts to perform any such act; or
(b) is an accomplice of a person who performs or attempts to perform any such act.

The convention limits itself to cases where an international element is involved, that is, that the place of take-off or the place of actual landing of the aircraft on board which the offense is committed is outside the territory of the state of registration of that aircraft. The convention does not apply to aircraft used in military, customs, or police services (Article 3).

The convention requires the following states to establish its jurisdiction: (1) state of registration, (2) state of first landing, and (3) state in which the lessee has its principal place of business or permanent residence (Article 4). Further, in an attempt to prevent the establishment of havens for hijackers, the convention provides that each contracting state is to take such measures as may be necessary to establish its jurisdiction over an offense in the case where the alleged offender is present in its territory and is not extradited.

Article 7 embodies the principle *aut dedere aut judicare*, that is, that a contracting state, if it does not extradite an alleged offender, is obligated to submit the case "without exception whatsoever to its competent authorities for the purpose of prosecution."

Although the convention does not contain an obligation to extradite, it does facilitate the extradition of an alleged offender by providing that the offense defined in Article 1 is deemed to be included as an extraditable offense in any extradition treaty existing between contracting states and must be included in every future extradition treaties between contracting states (Article 8). Further, it is provided that contracting states may consider the convention as an independent legal basis for extradition. Article 8, however, makes it clear that extradition is to be subject to the laws of the requested state, which may preclude extradition of nationals or political offenders.

---

*There were 101 contracting parties to the Hague Convention as of January 10, 1979.

The third convention that was enacted was the Convention for the Suppression of Unlawful Acts Against the Safety of Civil Aviation (Montreal Convention) of September 23, 1971.* While the Hague Convention is concerned only with the hijacking of aircraft as such, the Montreal Convention (Article 4 [2]) covers a range of offenses, which are punishable by "severe penalties":

(1) Any acts of violence against a person on board an aircraft in flight; destruction of, or damage to an aircraft in service; sabotage of an aircraft in service; destruction of, or damage to air navigation facilities or interference with their operation; communication of false information which is likely to endanger the safety of aircraft in flight;
(2) Any attempt to commit any of the aforementioned acts; and
(3) Any complicity with anyone committing or attempting to commit these acts.
The Convention applies only if:
(a) the place of take-off or landing, actual or intended, of the aircraft is situated outside the territory of the State of registration of that aircraft; or
(b) the offense is committed in the territory of a State other than the State of Registration of the aircraft.

Further, notwithstanding the above provisions, the convention applies if the alleged offender is found in the territory of a state other than the state of registration of the aircraft (Article 4 [3] and [4]). The convention does not apply to aircraft used in military, customs, or police services.

The convention attempts to establish a form of universal jurisdiction. It recognizes, in addition to the traditional territorial jurisdiction, the jurisdiction of (1) the state of registration, (2) the state of first landing, (3) the state in which the lessee has its principal place of business or permanent residence, in the case of an aircraft leased without crew, and (4) the state where the alleged offender is present and is not extradited (Article 5).

Like the Hague Convention, the Montreal Convention contains the principle of *aut dedere aut judicare*, by which the contracting states have an obligation either to extradite the alleged offender found in their territory or to submit the case, without exception whatsoever, to its competent authorities for the purpose of prosecution (Article 7).

The convention contains provisions (similar to the Hague Convention) for the facilitation of extradition, but it does not create an obligation to extradite (Article 8).

---

*There were 96 contracting parties to the Montreal Convention as of January 10, 1979.

Aside from whatever stigma there is that is attached to breaching one's international treaty obligations, there is little to compel a contracting state to honor its commitments under these conventions. There are no sanctions or enforcement measures in these conventions, and efforts to achieve an independent enforcement convention during the Rome Air Security Conference and the ICAO Extraordinary Assembly (September 1973) ended in failure.

The heads of state of the seven summit countries meeting in July 1978 in Bonn to discuss international economic issues made a dramatic announcement at the conclusion of their conference.* The following joint statement was read by Chancellor Helmut Schmidt at the Summit Press Conference on July 17.

> The heads of state and government, concerned about terrorism and the taking of hostages, declare that their governments will intensify their joint efforts to combat international terrorism.
>
> To this end, in cases where a country refuses extradition or prosecution of those who have hijacked an aircraft and/or do not return such aircraft, the heads of state and government are jointly resolved that their governments should take immediate action to cease all flights to that country.
>
> At the same time, their governments will initiate action to halt all incoming flights from that country or from any country by the airlines of the country concerned. The heads of state and government urge other governments to join them in this commitment.

The summit countries are major aviation powers, whose airlines carry two-thirds of the air passenger traffic in the free world. Thus, this statement of intent (referred to as the "Bonn Declaration") could have a profound influence upon countries that depend upon international air commerce to augment their economies and facilitate movement of goods and persons beyond their own borders. The full effect of the Bonn Declaration has yet to be tested; it represents the first multilateral effort to develop enforcement measures for use against countries that refuse to extradite or prosecute hijackers and/or do not return hijacked aircraft.

Internationally Protected Persons

Responding to increasing incidents of terrorism directed against diplomats and public officials, the UN General Assembly adopted Resolution 3166 on

---

*Canada (Prime Minister Pierre Trudeau); West Germany (Chancellor Helmut Schmidt); France (President Valéry Giscard d'Estaing); Italy (Prime Minister Guilro Andreotti); Japan (Prime Minister Takeo Fukuda); Great Britain (Prime Minister James Callaghan), and the United States (President Jimmy Carter).

December 14, 1973. The resolution adopted the Convention on the Prevention and Punishment of Crimes Against Internationally Protected Persons, Including Diplomatic Agents.

The convention obliges contracting states to make punishable by appropriate penalties the following acts against internationally protected persons: (1) murder, kidnapping, or other attack upon the person or liberty of an internationally protected person; (2) a violent attack upon the official premises, the private accommodation, or the means of transport of an internationally protected person or liberty; (3) a threat to commit any such attack; (4) an attempt to commit any such attack; and (5) an act constituting participation as an accomplice in any such act (Article 2).

Article 7, embodying the principle of *aut dedere aut judicare*, provides that "The State Party in whose territory the alleged offender is present, is obliged, if it does not extradite him, to submit, without exception whatsoever and without undue delay, the case to its competent authorities for the purpose of prosecution."

For purpose of extradition, the crimes referred to in the convention are deemed to be included as extraditable offenses in any extradition treaty existing between contracting states and are to be included in every future extradition treaty to be concluded between contracting states (Article 8). For states that do not make extradition conditional on the existence of a treaty, they are obliged to recognize these crimes as extraditable offenses between themselves, subject to the procedural provisions and the other conditions of the law of the requested state. Further, it is provided that contracting states may consider the convention as the legal basis for extradition.

State parties are obliged to "afford one another the greatest measure of assistance in connection with criminal proceedings brought in respect of the crimes set forth in [the convention], including the supply of all evidence at their disposal necessary for the proceedings" (Article 10).

The provisions of the convention do not affect the application of the treaties on asylum in force at the date of its adoption (Article 12).

The Organization of the American States (OAS) adopted on February 2, 1971, a Convention to Prevent and Punish the Acts of Terrorism Taking the Form of Crimes Against Persons and Related Extortion That Are of International Significance. There are six parties to the convention, namely, the United States, Mexico, Venezuela, Costa Rica, Dominican Republic, and Nicaragua. The focus of the convention is on terrorist acts, characterized in Article 2 as common crimes of international significance, namely, kidnapping, murder, and other assaults against the life or personal integrity of those persons whom the state has the duty to give special protection according to international law, as well as extortion in connection with these crimes.

The convention obliges states to include in their penal laws the above prohibited acts (Article 8). Article 5 embodies the principle of *aut dedere aut judicare*, that is, a state is obliged either to extradite an accused offender or submit his or her case to its competent authorities for prosecution. Extradition is to be granted pursuant to extradition treaties in force between the contracting states or, in the case of states that do not make extradition dependent upon the existence of a treaty, in accordance with the conditions established by the laws of the requested state (Articles 3 and 7).

Common Devices or Weaponry used by Terrorists

Among the destructive devices used by terrorists, perhaps the most invidious is the letter or parcel-bomb due to its maiming potential. The Universal Postal Convention (November 14, 1969) requires state parties to adopt measures necessary to prevent and punish the insertion, in postal items, of "explosive or easily inflammable substances, where their insertion has not been expressly authorized by the Convention and the Agreements" (Article 11 [e]). Article 29(e) prohibits the insertion of explosive, inflammable, or other dangerous substances in letter-post items. There are no penalties or sanctions prescribed in the convention for violations, nor is there an extradition or prosecution requirement; thus, it will be of little effect as either a deterrent or an international basis to acquire jurisdiction of terrorists who send letter- or parcel-bombs. (See discussion on letter- and parcel-bombs in section that follows on "European Convention on the Suppression of Terrorism.")

U.S. Draft Terrorism Convention

In 1972, the United States tabled a Draft Convention for the Prevention and Punishment of Certain Acts of International Terrorism in the Sixth Committee of the UN.* The U.S. draft was aimed at the "export of terrorism," and it sought to establish as an offense the unlawful killing, kidnapping, or bodily harm to another person if the effect of that act takes effect outside of the territory of the state of which the alleged offender is a national, the state against which the act is directed, or within the territory of a State against which the act is directed and the alleged offender knows that the victim is not a national of such state. Acts of armed forces, as perpetrators or victims, are exempted, and the act must be intended to damage the interests or obtain conecssions from a state or international organization. The draft convention employed the *aut dedere aut judicare* technique to bring alleged offenders to justice. Unfortunately, the draft convention was never adopted by the UN General Assembly.

---

*United Nations (document A/C. 6/L. 850) September, 1972.

European Convention on the Suppression of Terrorism

On November 10, 1976, the Committee of Ministers of the Council of Europe adopted the European Convention on the Suppression of Terrorism. It was opened for signature and ratification to the 19 members of the Council of Europe on January 27, 1977; to date, 17 states have signed the convention, of which five have ratified it, thus bringing it into force.

The preamble to the European Convention states that its purpose is to "take effective measures to ensure that the perpetrators of [acts of terrorism] do not escape prosecution and punishment." Extradition is the measure on which the convention principally relies, and it seeks to remove offenses under The Hague, Montreal: and UN Internationally Protected Persons conventions, as well as offenses involving kidnapping, taking of hostages, and use of certain lethal weapons (including bombs, rockets, automatic firearms, letter bombs, and so forth), from any political consideration or exception in the extradition process between contracting parties (Article 1). It has the effect of amending existing bilaterial extradition agreements between contracting parties to remove any incompatibility between them and the convention (Article 3) and to include offenses specified in the convention, if not otherwise included (Article 4).

The convention also requires contracting parties to "take such measures as may be necessary to establish its jurisdiction over an offense mentioned in Article 1" and to prosecute an alleged offender found in its territory if it does not extradite him (Article 7). There are requirements to provide "the widest measure of mutual assistance in criminal matters [relating to the convention]" (Article 8), to use the European Committee on Crime Problems for Coordination and Settlement of Disputes (Article 9), and to resort to binding arbitration as the final means of dispute settlement (Article 10).

It is interesting to note that the convention avoids the persistent problem of defining "terrorism" by merely listing offenses. Terrorism then, for the purpose of this convention, embodies their offenses *ad* referendum. The problem is that it makes all forms of kidnapping, the bulk of which is extortionate kidnapping, a terrorist crime.

The most serious problem, however, with the Convention rests with Article 5. That article appears to contradict the intent of Article 1 to declare the offenses under that article not to be political offenses. Article 5 allows a contracting state, to which an extradition request is directed, to deny that request if it "has substantial grounds for believing that the (extradition request) has been made for the purpose of prosecuting or punishing a person on grounds of his race, religion, nationality or *political opinion*, or that that person's position may be prejudiced for any of these reasons." (Emphasis added). The normal interpretation of this provision would have the effect of negating the intent of Article 1. Since there is no generally accepted definition of the term "political offense," each State is free to interpret it as it will. This then creates a serious lacuna in existing international agreements with respect to the extradition of persons accused or convicted of acts of terrorism. This point is raised in a paper presented to Parliament by the Secretary of State for Foreign and Commonwealth Affairs in December 1977. The paper comments as follows:

> The European Convention on the Suppression of Terrorism aims at filling this lacuna by eliminating or restricting the possibility for the requested State of invoking the political nature of an offence in order to oppose an extradition request. This aim is achieved by providing that, for extradition purposes, certain specified offences *shall never* be regarded as "political" (Article 1) and other specified offences *may not* be (Article 2), notwithstanding their political content or motivation.
>
> The system established by Articles 1 and 2 of the Convention reflects the consensus which reconciles the arguments put forward in favour of an obligation, on the one hand, and an option, on the other hand, not to consider, for the purposes of the application of the Convention, certain offences as political.
>
> In favour of an obligation, it was pointed out that it alone would give States new and really effective possibilities for extradition, by eliminating explicitly the plea of "political offence", a solution that was perfectly feasible in the climate of mutual confidence that reigned amongst the member States of the Council of Europe having similar democratic institutions. It would ensure that terrorists were extradited for trial to the State which had jurisdiction to prosecute. A mere option would never provide a guarantee that extradition would take place and, moreover, the criteria concerning the seriousness of the offence would not be precise.
>
> In favour of an option, reference was made to the difficulty in accepting a rigid solution which would amount to obligatory extradition for political offences. Each case should be examined on its merits.[2]

Italy, Norway, Portugal and Sweden have taken reservations to Article 1 as permitted under Article 13, which permits a State to declare its reservation of the right to refuse extradition in respect of any Article 1 offence which it considers to be a political offense. It is obliged, however, to take into consideration, when evaluating the character of the offense, any particularly serious aspects of the offense, such as danger to life, cruel or vicious aspects, or remoteness of victims to the political motives.

If this confusion is not resolved by some subsequent interpretation, the Convention will have lost a substantial degree of its effectiveness.

Draft Hostage Convention

On December 10, 1976, the Sixth Committee of the UN recommended to the 31st session of the UN General Assembly that it consider a resolution to conclude, under the auspices of the UN, an international convention against the taking of hostages.* The 31st session of the General Assembly adopted the resolution and established "an *ad hoc* committee to draft the requested Convention." The Ad hoc committee has been unable to date to adopt a convention for consideration in succeeding General assemblies. West Germany has made a major effort in behalf of its draft convention, but certain Middle Eastern countries successfully thwarted its adoption during a heated session of the committee in early 1978.

NOTES

1. U.S., Congress, Senate, Committee on Governmental Affairs, *Hearings* on S.2236, January 23, 1978, p. 4.
2. Miscellaneous No. 28 (1977): European Convention on the Suppression of Terrorism (with Explanatory Report), Cmnd. 7031, p. 13.

---

*This initiative was proposed by the Permanent Representative of West Germany to the UN (Ambassador Baron Rüdiger von Weichmar) in a statement to the Security Council on July 12, 1976.

15

THE U.S. GOVERNMENT'S RESPONSE TO TERRORISM

C. Allen Graves

The government's response to terrorism has been a series of unrelated actions and enactments. Unfortunately, these lack a coordinated locus to prevent or deter terrorism in the United States. The tightening of airport security has greatly reduced the threat of skyjacking; yet, this security system, like all others, is not impregnable. Skyjacking has been greatly reduced, but not eliminated. Another aspect is the lack of security in other countries where flights originate. As a result, at least 40 percent of U.S. planes are potential targets for skyjackers.

Another response to the threat of terrorism is the government's increased scrutiny of foreign travelers. This would be more effective if the members of the terrorist groups were known. As it is, only the leaders are known and the object of scrutiny. It is virtually impossible to involve all foreign travelers without limiting tourism.

Better protection of our diplomats is being effected, yet without a quasi-prison status, this effort is still far from adequate. The spontaneous nature of diplomatic kidnapping or assassinations all but precludes any effective defense. Unfortunately, the routines necessary for diplomatic endeavors make it easy for the terrorist to plan and execute his or her activities.

Washington officials have advertised a "no-ransom" and "no-prisoner release" in return for hostages. This has not been put to the ultimate test. It is difficult to conceive that the president or other high-ranking officials would not be exempt. This advertised policy also lacks any codification and remains merely a "stance," supposedly adopted as procedure. In order to be effective, this attitude should be more formally adopted by either Congress or by the president.

The UN has failed to respond to this world crisis. In 1972, the UN General Assembly Legal Committee failed to pass the tough U.S. proposal, which recommended the member nations return terrorists to the country where the action occurred for trial. Rather, the UN voted, 76 to 34, for a "status quo" policy and recommended that a series of studies be conducted.

It is obvious that any nation is a potential target for terrorism. However, it is the advanced nations that are the prime targets. Therefore, it becomes mandatory that these nations unite to coerce other nations to cease harboring these terrorists by canceling airline and even economic sanctions. Only in this way will all nations succumb to the need of joint action. This, in itself, would reduce the activity for a time. However, any effective antiterrorist plan must include more than apprehending the bombers and kidnappers. It must include "intelligence." This is the only truly effective counterweapon against terrorism and other clandestine operations. This means that the public must understand and support the use of spies, networks of informers, wiretaps, and so forth. The public must understand how vulnerable it is to the attack of the terrorist and other radical elements in the world today.

In 1957, the British Privy Council Committee on wiretapping stated: "The freedom of the individual is quite valueless if he can be made the victim of the lawbreaker. If these powers are properly and wisely exercised, they are in themselves aids to the maintenance of the true freedom of the individual."

Following his banishment from Moscow, Aleksandro Solzhenitsyn stated:

> Hijackings and all other forms of terrorism have been spreading tenfold precisely because everyone is ready to capitulate before them. But as soon as some firmness is shown, terrorism can be squashed forever. We will have to erase from human consciousness the very idea that everyone has the right to use force against justice, law and mutual consent.

The current trend in the United States is to protect the rights of all its people until some statute is broken. In most cases, this is adequate. However, when dealing with terrorism, it becomes an inefficient method to protect anyone. "Terrorism strikes without warning" is the hue and cry of the ultraliberal. No statement could be further from the truth. The terrorist group, obviously goes to great lengths to plan and execute its operations. The smooth operation of terrorist activities attest to the extensive planning undertaken. As a result of this, normal reactions to crime by law enforcement methods are ineffectual. It becomes increasingly more important to learn of potential and planned terrorist activities. This involves an extensive intelligence system, which is lacking in the United States at present.

Congress must enact enabling legislation to authorize the FBI and other agencies to apply wiretaps and other methods of collecting evidence. These methods, forbidden at present, are the only hope of anticipating potential terrorist activities.

As early as 1968, the United States began a series of antiterrorist responses. The problems had already become a major one. Small groups of terrorists, equipped with modern weaponry and communications, had developed a network of cooperative groups in different countries. The danger became more evident with the increasing incidence of kidnappings, bombings, and murders by Palestinians, Croatians, Tupamaros, Cubans, Turks, and others. Then, in September of 1972, the world was shocked by the killing of 11 Israeli atheletes and five terrorists in Munich. This was evidenced by the horror with which TV viewers watched reports of this incident.

The United States had, until then, pursued a number of preventive measures mainly aimed at the skyjacking operations. The advent of Munich stirred President Richard M. Nixon to adopt a more systematic approach. Nixon formed a special Cabinet Committee to Combat Terrorism, chaired by Secretary of State William Rogers. This committee was to have an operating army, called the Cabinet Committee Working Group. Originally, this working group was to consist of ten senior Cabinet committee members. Since then, 12 other agencies concerned with terrorism have been added. As a result of the work of these groups, a task force in the State Department's Operations Center has been formed. The latest terrorist activities have served to inform these groups with valuable data concerning the methods and goals of terrorism. While these measures are enlightening, they are wholly ineffective at present.

Based on the knowledge gained about terrorism, there are three basic ways to combat it. The United States should pursue all of these. The first of these is "intelligence." If plans can be learned prior to their execution, it is possible to forestall and even prevent the action. The federal and local authorities could and should coordinate their antiterrorist endeavors through the Cabinet Committee Working Group.

The second method of combating terrorism is "security of places and people." Although improved in recent years, the physical security of important places and people is still far from adequate. Every year, there are skyjackings, kidnappings, and bombings. Obviously, the existing measures are inadequate.

The third method of control centers on the apprehension and punishment of the terrorist. The key function here is international standards and cooperation. Unfortunately, only a few countries have established relations in this area. Additionally, there is no international stance as to the method of reaction or amount of punishment.

Dealing with intelligence is more than a cursory problem. It involves the institutional interpretations of such items as privacy. At present, the courts have precluded most intelligence-gaining activities through their decisions. The *Katz* decision laid to rest the longstanding "trespass" doctrine in police surveillance. The facts reveal that defendant Katz had been overheard in a public telephone booth by federal agents who had attached an electronic listening and recording device to the outside of the booth. Both the government attorney and the defendant's counsel focused their arguments on whether a public phone booth was a "constitutionally protected area," that is, a physical place legally insulated from law enforcement intrusion. The U.S. Supreme Court stated that this focus was incorrect because "the Fourth Amendment protects people, not places."[1] Applying this principle, the court denounced the trespass doctrine, which sanctioned surveillance as long as no physical penetration of the premises occupied by the suspect occurred. The court reasoned that

> once it is recognized that the Fourth Amendment protects people—not simply "areas"—against unreasonable searches and seizure, it becomes clear that the reach of that Amendment cannot turn upon the presence or absence of a physical intrusion into any given enclosure.[2]

The Court concluded that the government agents' activity in listening to the defendant's words "violated the privacy upon which he justifiably relied,"[3] while using the public phone booth, constituting an illegal search and seizure. Thus, the Court formulated a new standard: the reasonableness of the person's *expectation of privacy* when he or she converses, not solely the *location* of the conversation.

Although the courts are concerned with the individual's expectation of privacy, the courts scrutinize the nature of that expectation. An individual's expectation of privacy and secrecy, no matter how sincere, is not always "reasonable" by legal standards.* For example, an individual takes a calculated risk whenever he or she reveals information to another party. Even if the confidant or confidante has been sworn to secrecy, the courts will not hold that the speaker's expectation of privacy in such a situation is "reasonable" and constitutionally safeguarded. Therefore, "false friends" may be utilized by law enforcement agencies for surveillance in most instances.

The deception at the heart of the false friend doctrine has withstood repeated constitutional challenges. In *Lewis* v. *United States*,[4] the Supreme Court reiterated that the government is constitutionally permitted to conceal the identity of its agents and that a disguised government agent may accept a suspect's invitation to enter his or her home without violating the suspect's Fourth Amendment rights.†

---

*It has been stated that the *Katz* decision states a two-part test: "(1) that there be an actual, subjective expectation of privacy, and (2) that this expectation be recognized as reasonable by society" (Note 43 [1968] : 958, 982 [footnote omitted]).

†It must be noted that this case was decided before *Katz*, so that the focus was placed on whether the "home"—a traditionally protected area—had been "trespassed upon" by the federal agent when he concealed his identity to gain entry.

In another pre-*Katz* decision, *Hoffa* v. *United States*, the Supreme Court defended the false friend doctrine.[5] In *Hoffa*, the famed union leader was on trial in Nashville in the fall of 1962. Jimmy Hoffa told an associate, Partin, he could visit him in Nashville. Partin conferred with federal authorities before going and agreed to report any attempts by Hoffa to bribe the jury. Partin was invited to Hoffa's suite and there was told or overheard Hoffa's plan to bribe certain members of the jury. The Supreme Court affirmed Hoffa's conviction and commented on the false friend doctrine: "Neither this Court nor any member of it has ever expressed the view that the Fourth Amendment protects a wrongdoer's misplaced belief that a person to whom he voluntarily confides his wrongdoing will not reveal it."[6]

After the *Katz* decision, a question remained as to whether the new expectation-of-privacy rule formulated in *Katz* destroyed the false friend doctrine. In *United States* v. *White*, the question was posed and the answer divided the Supreme Court.[7] Defendant White's conversations with government informant Jackson had been monitored by federal agents over a transmitter concealed on Jackson's person. When the informant could not be produced for trial, the agents who had overheard the incriminating statements testified themselves, and White was convicted.

The Court of Appeals reversed the conviction, holding that the fact the informant instantaneously transmitted the conversation electronically to other agents violated *Katz* and the Fourth Amendment. A plurality of the U.S. Supreme Court, however, ruled that it did not.* The plurality of the Court reasoned:

> So far, the law permits the frustration of actual expectation of privacy by permitting authorities to use the testimony of those associates who for one reason or another have determined to turn to the police as well as by authorizing the use of informants in the manner exemplified by *Hoffa* and *Lewis*. If the law gives no protection to the wrongdoer whose trusted accomplice is or becomes a police agent, neither should it protect him when that same agent has recorded or transmitted the conversations.[8]

The plurality concluded that since the police agents' activities would have been "reasonable investigative efforts and lawful under the Fourth Amend-

---

*Four of the justices, Mr. Justice White, Chief Justice Burger, Mr. Justice Stewart, and Mr. Justice Blackman adopted this view. Mr. Justice Brennan, in a separate opinion, concurred in the result. Mr. Justice Black filed a statement concurring in the judgment. Justices Douglas, Harland, and Marshall filed dissenting opinions. For a critical discussion of both the plurality and Harlan opinions see Weinreb, "Generalities of the Fourth Amendment," University of Chicago Law Review 47 (1974): 67–69.

ment," the use of a recorder or transmitter did not make these same activities unreasonable.[9] In addition, "an electronic recording will many times produce a more reliable rendition of what a defendant said than will the unaided memory of a police agent."[10]

When the California Supreme Court was faced with the question of whether a false friend's surreptitious transmission of a suspect's conversation to police violated the Fourth Amendment, the court definitely sided with the plurality opinion in *United States* v. *White*. In the California case of *People* v. *Murphy*,[11] an apparent accomplice requested that his telephone conversation with the defendent be recorded by the police, and another possible criminal associate consented to wear a transmitter during his conversation with the defendant.[12] In upholding the covert tapings of the suspect by his false friends,* the California Supreme Court observed:

> We . . . perceive no distinction between the risk one faces that the person in whom he confides will later breach that trust by testifying about the conversation and the risk that such person has already betrayed him and is instantaneously transmitting their conversation electronically to police equipped with radio receivers.[13]

To the detriment of increased intelligence efforts, several bills have been introduced in Congress. As an example, on April 5, 1977, Congressman Herman Badillo of New York introduced H.R. 6051 (95th Congress, first session). This bill was labeled as a bill "to prevent abuses of power by the intelligence agencies of the Federal Government." In essence, it would emasculate the FBI and similar agencies. For instance, the bill would prohibit the federal government from engaging in "political surveillance," engaging in "preventive action," engaging in "selective investigation or prosecution," or engaging in cooperative efforts with state, local, or private agencies. Additionally, Section 114 of this bill would limit the time a case could be investigated to 30 days, with an authorized extension of 60 days. This whole bill is obviously conducive to the expansion of terrorist activities.

Other bills, such as H.R. 11245, introduced by Congressman E. P. Boland of Massachusetts on March 2, 1978 (and its counterpart, S. 2525, introduced by Senator W. Huddleston of Kentucky), do little to aid intelligence efforts. Under these bills, the Government Accounting Office (GAO) would have overall coordinating responsibility for the 12 investigating segments of the government.

---

*In *Murphy*, though law enforcement suspicion had focused on the defendant at the time of the conversation, no *Miranda* admonition had been given. The court, however, found no Fifth Amendment violation, reasoning that the defendant spoke voluntarily and was not deprived of his freedom of movement in any significant way. 8 Cal. 3d 362 (1972).

Other bills of a similar nature have been introduced. These include H.R. 4173, which is designed to reorganize the entire U.S. intelligence community. It provides that counterintelligence investigations inside of the United States would be conducted by the FBI, but they would be limited to the obtaining of evidence of violations of criminal statutes. This would eliminate any U.S. capability to combat the threat of hostile intelligence services operating within its borders in a manner that skirted the law.

It would seem that the drafters of this legislation were intent on denuding the United States of the ability to protect itself against its domestic as well as its foreign enemies. In their zeal to protect civil liberties of an individual to the detriment of society as a whole, they proposed repeal of legislation that originally was passed to strengthen the general welfare.

The Riot Act would be repealed, apparently to protect rioters. The laws relating to seditious conspiracy and advocating the overthrow of the government would be set aside, presumably to protect individual liberties. But, the First Amendment does not grant a license to riot or to overthrow the government.

Another bill, H. R. 4173, directs that "the Federal Bureau of Investigation shall have no function other than the investigation of specific acts which violate Federal Criminal Statutes." What would happen to the FBI law enforcement training programs? What about technical assistance and expert testimony afforded by the FBI during local trials? Would the millions of fingerprint cards collected as an aid to local law enforcement agencies and used as a means of assistance in national tragedies be no longer utilized?

Severe limitations would be placed on investigative techniques. One of the most serious would be the requirement of a court order to recruit, place, or use any informant or undercover agent, with the proviso that even then, the latter could be utilized for only 30 days. Ninety days after the termination of this order concerning recruitment or use of an informant, the subject of the case would have to be notified, and the court would have to make available to him or her the entire record of the surveillance. If the subject moved to suppress information derived from use of an informant based on any one of the defined grounds, the court, upon the initial *filing* of the motion, must reveal the identity of the informant to the subject.

It must be concluded that under the above requirements, the identities of informants and undercover agents could not be protected. In such circumstances, cooperation of confidential live sources would be nonexistent.

Court orders would also be required to obtain information from banks, financial institutions, communication common carriers, credit card issuers, and consumer-reporting agencies. A mail cover could not be placed without a court order.

One of the principal objectives of H.R. 10400 is to eliminate all intelligence-gathering functions of the FBI. While the two bills previously discussed would permit FBI investigations if a crime is being, has been, or is about to be committed, H.R. 10400 would prohibit investigation in the latter instance.

The only reason for the FBI's existence would be to gather evidence of crimes under way or already consummated. The bill would preclude the FBI from engaging in any law enforcement activities, except as expressly provided by act of Congress. Since the bill does not provide for any other such activities, the FBI would have removed from it such responsibilities as collecting and preserving fingerprint records, operating the FBI National Academy, cooperating with local law enforcement agencies—some 18 specifically defined responsibilities under Title 28, Code of Federal Regulations, Chapter I, subpart P.

FBI officials and employees would be personally liable if, acting under the color of federal law, they deprived any person of any right, privilege, or immunity secured by the Constitution. The final section of the bill provides for "Repeal of Certain Laws to Eliminate Color of Authority." The laws enumerated are the same as in H.R. 6051, the so-called speech crimes. These statutes relate to crimes that strike at the very foundation of domestic tranquility, and in proposing their repeal for the alleged purpose of eliminating color of authority, the drafters of this bill must be using a subterfuge. Certainly, if the statutes are repealed and no effective alternative ones are enacted, it will be the federal government, not the FBI, which is the ultimate victim.

By proposing their repeal, the drafters seem to be proclaiming loudly and clearly that a "politically motivated" person cannot commit any crime against the authority of the United States short of treason, rebellion, or insurrection.

As much as civil liberties must be protected, so must life and civil order. It is not a debatable item that law enforcement has violated certain civil rights over the years. It is equally not debatable that the Supreme Court and the legislature has overreacted to these overactions. It is time to step back and evaluate these recent events. Certain rights must be inviolate, but by the same logic, some are negotiable. Absolutes cannot exist if they are utilized to the benefit of certain groups, such as terrorists.

It is time for the legislature to enact laws that would aid, not hinder, antiterrorist intelligence. At present, 22 states allow court-mandated wire taps. Why not 50? If Congress enacts a law to allow authorities to use wire taps for terrorist investigation, this would be a start. It is essential to know of the plans of terrorists before they act. Only in this measure can effective countermeasures be realized.

Another factor, involving Congress, is that of punishment. Legislation must be enacted to deal with convicted terrorists. A minimum of life imprisonment must be levied as the sanction. At the present time, little, if any, legislation is available to deal with terrorists. The problem is real, and the heretofore soft line must be abolished. Terrorism is a national threat and must be recognized and treated in its proper perspective.

Simultaneously, strong sanctions must be imposed on countries that harbor or protect terrorists. Greater care must be taken in the issuance of visas in order to reduce the fluid mobility of most terrorist cells.

Time is of the essence. The United States must act, and act decisively. Terrorism in the United States and the rest of the world must be eliminated if the "freedom" held so dear is to survive.

NOTES

1. *Katz* v. *United States*, 389 U.S. 351 (1968).
2. Ibid., at 353.
3. Ibid.
4. 385 U.S. 206 (1966).
5. 385 U.S. 293 (1966).
6. Ibid., at 302.
7. 401 U.S. 745 (1971).
8. 401 U.S. 745, 752.
9. Ibid., at 753.
10. Ibid.
11. 8 Cal. 3d 349 (1972).
12. Ibid., at 361.
13. Ibid., at 360.

16

THE POLICE RESPONSE
TO TERRORISM

Robert L. Rabe

Terrorism has no place in a free society. To defend or protect its methods and goals is to glorify violence and encourage the terrorist. Further, it intimidates both the general public and local authorities into accepting irrational demands. In light of the disturbing increase in the number of terrorist acts, both domestic and international, it has become apparent that terrorism and violence are no longer a means of last resort. Now, they have become a common method of communication for real and imagined grievances.

In recent years, there has been an increase in this country of militant groups who have adopted foreign-bred terrorist tactics as their method of focusing attention on various political issues. For example, individuals affiliated with such groups as the BLA, the WUO, and the SLA have been linked with the killing and wounding of police officers, the assassination of public officials, kidnapping, racist murders, bombings, jailbreak attempts, prison riots, urban guerrilla warfare, and even posting public notices threatening death to anyone who opposes them.

In 1978, Director William Webster indicated that the FBI was taking steps to head off political kidnappings and murders, such as those that had hit European countries in recent months. He further stated that it was likely that international terrorist groups would target political leaders in the United States, as they had in West Germany and Italy.

Acts of terrorism over the past decade indicate a move from the urban arena to the national and international level. If we review recent incidents, we also can see the possibility of terrorism becoming a form of surrogate warfare. It does not appear that any long-range objectives have been accomplished by terrorists; however, their tactics have brought them enormous publicity and some concessions. These tactical victories, no matter how small, appear to be successful enough to preclude the abandonment of current tactics. It is a known fact that terrorist organizations study mistakes made by others and shift to softer targets to minimize risk.

Terrorism knows no borders. On August 5, 1978, four persons were killed in Pakistan in an international war between members of the PLO and pro-Iraqi radicals. The vendetta apparently began on July 28, in London, when a woman failed in an attempt to assassinate Iraq's ambassador. Several days later, the terrorist war shifted to Paris, where the Iraqi embassy was besieged for eight and one-half hours by Palestinians demanding the release of the woman jailed in London. Two days later, in Karachi, terrorists failed in an attempt to assassinate Iraq's counsul-general. On the same day, there was an abortive attempt to kill Iraq's ambassador in Beirut. The next day, again in Paris, terrorists murdered the PLO representative and his aide.

Most Americans, however, believe the United States is immune to such attacks and that we face little threat from terrorists. However, the involvement of the United States in such issues as the Middle East peace settlement, the return of the Panama Canal, and efforts to bring black majority rule to Rhodesia could prove to be a popular cause for a terrorist group either outside or within the United States.

Aside from being the center of world power and wealth, we have a rather liberal democratic society, which offers a fertile field for terrorist activity. With a free press, the terrorist is guaranteed instant recognition, with his or her cause or grievance televised around the world. Our Constitution also guarantees the terrorist a fair trial and equal justice under the law.

WHAT IS TERRORISM?

Terrorism has never been defined by statutes, as have homicide, robbery, burglary, and so forth. Law enforcement agencies deal with criminal statutes; therefore, the social and political issues usually associated with terrorism have no legal basis. By this, I mean that while law enforcement officials should be concerned with social and political issues, there are no criminal statutes in the United States that cover these issues.

First, in an effort to learn more about what terrorism may or may not be, we must look at those acts already committed that have been termed as terrorist actions.

One incident of importance was the kidnapping of Moro in Italy. His kidnappers, the Red Brigade, struck during the time 13 members of the group were on trial in Turin for various criminal charges. Their strategy was designed to disrupt, damage, destroy, and discredit the institutions of society by influencing the masses in an attempt to show that the responsible authorities were unable to effectively cope with the problem. By attempting to shift the balance through coercive violence, they developed the power to set up a bargaining situation.

The term *terrorism* has been used to describe a variety of acts. Idi Amin's actions in Uganda, the PLO's actions at Entebbe, Anthony Kiristis's actions in Indianapolis, and the SLA's actions in California are all encompassed under the heading of terrorist activity. Many believe terrorism will never be defined, because one man's terrorist may be another man's freedom fighter.

In an effort to find some legal language that could provide law enforcement officials with an insight into what a court may or may not consider terrorism, a civil case (*Pan American World Airways* vs. *Aetna Casualty and Surety Co.*) was located that may prove useful.[1] The case involved the hijacking of a Pan Am plane over London by two members of PFLP. The aircraft was subsequently flown to Cairo and destroyed by explosives. The trial court reviewed in detail the goals and structure of the Fadayeen in general and the PFLP in particular.

The claim was taken to court, and the insurers asserted that their policies did not cover loss or damage due to or resulting from:

1. capture, seizure . . . or any taking of the property insured or damaged to or destruction thereof . . . by any military . . . or usurped power, whether any of the foregoing be done by way of requisition or otherwise and whether in time of peace or war and whether lawful or unlawful . . . ;
2. war . . . civil war, revolution, rebellion, insurrection or warlike operations, whether there be a declaration of war or not;
3. . . . riots, civil commotion.

After careful deliberation, the court ruled that "the loss was not one 'due to or resulting from . . . (a) taking . . . or destruction . . . by any military . . . or usurped power.'. . . The loss was not the result of 'riot' or 'civil commotion'."

In upholding the trial court, the appeals court (*Pan American World Airways* vs. *Aetna Casualty and Surety Co.*) also addressing the area of insurrection, stated:

In the district court the all risk insurers relied on every term in clause 2 except "invasion." Thus, aside from "war" and "warlike operations," they claimed that the loss was excluded from coverage by each of "civil war," "revolution," "rebellion," and "insurrection.". . . "Insurrection" presents the key issue because "rebellion," "revolution," and "civil war" are progressive stages in the development of civil unrest, the most rudimentary form of which is "insurrection."[2]

Another case (*Home Insurance Co.* vs. *Davila*), although occurring some 24 years earlier, considered *insurrection* to mean a violent uprising by a group or movement acting for the specific purpose of overthrowing the constituted government and seizing its powers.[3]

If the language cited in the above cases is to be taken literally, it appears that terrorism, as we know it today, is not easily fitted into current constitutional or statutory law.

Careful review of the material outlined above indicates why defining terrorism is difficult. I will attempt to define terrorism in the language of a law enforcement official, taking into account the social and political issues, as well as the criminal aspect. However, I am sure that it too has some language that many will not accept, but at least it is more acceptable than most I have analyzed. Terrorism will be defined as a criminal act in violation of specific federal, state, or local statutes that causes a psychological reaction of intense fear in the victim(s) and is intended to intimidate, coerce, demoralize, or influence government or the civilian population.

Using this definition, a review of U.S. history reveals that we have experienced various forms of terrorism from domestic groups from time to time. Some may even go so far as to say that those who fought the War of Independence were terrorists, as well as the Ku Klux Klan of earlier times, the SLA, Black Panthers, and the WUO of the 1960s. Today, we have the NWLF, FALN, the Red Guerrilla Family, and the National Socialist Liberation Front (NSLF), to name just a few. Any one of the current left-wing or right-wing groups could become involved in terrorist activity given the incentive and a popular cause.

THE THREAT OF TERRORISM TO THE BUSINESS COMMUNITY AT HOME AND ABROAD

The most important consideration to establish at the outset of any discussion of terrorism and the business community is that there is no absolute or certain security from terrorist acts. While U.S. businesses are increasing their efforts, both at home and abroad, to minimize or prevent these attacks, there is no guarantee that anyone has the perfect program. Additionally, the terrorist threat poses a dilemma that is not easily resolved—how much security is a government or business obliged to provide against terrorism? This is a question facing many members of the business community today, and it also places many administrators in an awkward position. If you are overzealous in security, you may impede the overall organization to the point of frustration. But on the other hand, if you are lax, you will be subject to criticism.

While it is somewhat easier to control outright criminal acts against businesses through strict security measures, it is much more difficult to protect against terrorism. The very nature of terrorist acts, with their infrequency of occurrence and unpredictable timing, leave corporate security managers with no real indicators as to when a terrorist strike might occur.

I do not see any great changes in the terrorist acts of today and those that have been committed against U.S. businesses in the past. The bombing of business facilities at home and abroad, in addition to the kidnapping of executives overseas, appears to have worked well for the terrorists, if not politically, at least economically. Today's technology has given the terrorists new targets and capabilities. The airplane allows them to travel around the world at will, striking any place at any time. They will use dynamite stolen from the southwestern area of the United States to make bombs for use in New York City, the Chicago area, and the nation's capital.

The first report issued by the FBI's Terrorist Research Center indicates there were a total of 26 significant international terrorist incidents between January 1977 and March 1977. Included were the killing of a U.S. businessman in M xico City, a DuPont executive murdered in Northern Ireland; another U.S. citizen kidnapped in Colombia, and several U.S. business buildings damaged there as a result of bombings.

While the majority of attacks against U.S. businessmen have been in foreign countries, there have been incidents within the United States. The FALN, the NWLF, and the WUO have all claimed credit for some form of terrorist activity against U.S. business facilities.

One may wonder why a particular business facility or executive may be more vulnerable than another. It does not appear that the products they represent are the primary factors, since many have been attacked because of political affiliations and others because of their particular involvement with foreign governments. Businessmen would probably not have paid much attention to political issues just a few years ago, but today, it is an important issue—one constantly under review by many corporate executives.

Terrorist acts against a company or its executives cannot be prevented. If a terrorist group targets a U.S. company, there is little one can do to prevent it. However, there are reasonable preparations that can be made to minimize the attack in addition to preparing contingency responses. Business executives have a responsibility to provide reasonable security against terrorist attacks. The degree and form of protection established by that particular organization must be commensurate with its vulnerability. While public law enforcement agencies continue to increase their capabilities to manage terrorist incidents, those persons who may be targets of terrorist attacks also must be alert to this real and potential problem.

MANAGEMENT OF TERRORIST
AND HOSTAGE INCIDENTS

Crisis management of terrorist incidents raises complex legal issues for law enforcement officials responsible for the control of such situations. During past incidents, management authority has been maintained by both federal and local law enforcement agencies, depending on the target and nature of the event.

Foreign nations handle terrorist and hostage incidents on a national level, sometimes using military forces, but the response by law enforcement agencies within the United States would be quite different. Because the United States is composed of 50 states, each with its own autonomous government structure, the protection of its citizens is the responsibility of each individual state. There is no law enforcement agency in the United States that could be said to constitute a national police agency.

The present state of constitutional and statutory law controlling domestic military activities all but rules out their participation in a domestic terrorist incident. Remedial legislation is clearly needed, unless we intend to torture existing law to bring these situations within the heretofore narrow circumstances under which the president may order the intervention of federal troops in domestic law enforcement.

Terrorism is very realistic and extremely destructive. It is usually done without a plan for the future, and the act itself may not be related in any way to what the terrorists are trying to accomplish. By realistically analyzing terrorist and hostage incidents of the past, law enforcement officials, particularly those who are responsible for the management of these types of incidents, can prepare themselves to meet the challenge. By responding in an intelligent and positive manner, most incidents can be brought to a successful conclusion. By responding quickly, one is able to manipulate the time factor and cause the terrorists to lose initiative. Therefore, it is incumbent upon law enforcement officials to prepare both themselves and their organization to combat acts of terrorism commensurate with their responsibilities.

It is impossible to devise standard procedures for handling each situation—for each has its own characteristics and individual solution. The overall police attitude must be one of flexibility and adaptation of relevant experiences. Experience dictates that present operational plans are valid insofar as the initial allocation of manpower and material resources. The hard tactical decisions must be made in the street, on a moment's notice, and based on the best intelligence data then available.

The following guidelines are based upon similarities that exist in terrorist and hostage incidents. While they are intended primarily for law enforcement agencies, they will also assist those in the business sector faced with the same problems. The acronym or slogan Profit—P for patience, R for response techniques, O for organizational preparedness, F for future effectiveness, I for intelligence, and T for training—has significant meaning to both the law enforcement and business community:

Patience
1. Remember, hostages are taken solely for purpose of gain.
2. Be decisive and define the problem.
3. Do not act hastily, slow down.

4. This is one of the few police emergencies in which police can request specially trained personnel, organize police efforts, and embark on a planned course of action.

Response Techniques

1. Are your guidelines, general orders, and so forth known to those who are responsible for handling these type incidents?
2. Personnel must know their mission and who they take orders from.
3. Need for uniform control of tactical teams. Officers must cease acting as individuals and quickly unite as a team.
4. Success is geared to organizational coordination.

Organization Preparedness

1. *Policy*: Organizational policy must be formulated and known to all members responsible for the management of terrorist and hostage-taking incidents.
2. *Priorities*: What are your priorities and in what order—consideration of philosophy, people, property, and law?
3. *Planning*: How much are you going to spend for training, personnel, and readiness? There is need for public support.
4. *Preparation*: There must be adequately trained personnel, who are skilled and determined to completely manage and control an incident.

Future Effectiveness

1. Today's response and success can have a dramatic effect on reducing future incidents.
2. If possible, never allow the terrorist or hostage taker to gain safe haven. If allowed, they have demonstrated their power and show a weakness by government authorities by not being able to successfully manage the incident.

Intelligence

1. *Timing*: One of the dangers of dealing with terrorism and hostage taking is trying to deal with it the way we did in the past. The terrorist today is not the terrorist of yesterday.
2. *Organization*: Most terrorist groups are organization orientated. We may know their objectives, lines of authority, and to whom they owe their allegiance; however, we may not know all members of the group. Although it may have been possible to penetrate an organization in the past, it is becoming extremely difficult because the organization is usually constantly changing or merging with other organizations. There must be a concentrated effort to trace individuals from group to group.
3. *Place*: The world is a small place because of increased mobility. Some incidents are tied to certain localities, while others are place oriented. One must ask if the location of the incident is symbolic in itself or if the location has been picked to involve a weaker third party.

4. *Ideas*: Ideologically, terrorists are completely blind to accepting the world in any other way than he or she already sees it. They may be driven on by own ideas.
5. *Character*: One may not have the intelligence that would give one the necessary reference tools. There must be an attempt to see the terrorist as a person, subject to human frailties and with relationships, that is, with mothers, fathers, sons, and daughters. Terrorism is not a full-time occupation.

Training
1. Members of unit responsible for handling these type incidents must receive the best training and equipment available.
2. They must be allowed periodic training, updating themselves with proven methods.
3. They must have coordinated training with other local, state, and federal agencies if necessary.

WHY NEGOTIATE?

Recent terrorist and hostage-taking incidents, including both domestic and international incidents, have been successfully concluded through the negotiating concept. The word *negotiate*, as listed in *Webster's Seventh New Collegiate Dictionary* (1967 edition), is defined as: "to confer with another so as to arrive at the settlement of some matter." Isn't this the same thing police officers have been practicing for years? Haven't they been resolving family disputes between husband and wife, parents and siblings, and merchants and customers? While these may be negotiations of a lower order, the concept itself is not entirely new to law enforcement officials.

What is new to law enforcement is negotiating during hostage-taking incidents—situations that are much more complex and violent than ever before. This has caused most urban law enforcement agencies to train hostage negotiators—officers specially trained in conducting and controlling extended discussions with persons engaged in the coercive use of criminal violence. Nierenberg describes the successful negotiator:

> The successful negotiator must combine the alertness and speed of an expert swordsman with an artist's sensitivity. He must watch his adversary across the bargaining table with the keen eye of a fencer, ever ready to spot any loophole in the defense, any shift in strategy. He is prepared to thrust at the slightest opportunity. On the other hand, he must also be the sensitive artist, perceptive of the slightest variation in the color of his opponent's mood or motivation. At the correct moment, he must be able to select from his palette of many colors exactly the right combination of shades and tints that will

lead to mastery. Success in negotiation, aside from adequate training, is essentially a matter of sensitivity and correct timing.

Finally, the mature negotiator will have an understanding of
the cooperative pattern. He will try to achieve agreement and will
remember that in a successful negotiation everyone wins. And if this
is the case, why shoot it out, when we can still talk it out?[4]

Negotiating is a skill not unlike other police skills. There are rules to follow, techniques to master, and strategies to evaluate. Leaving it to chance will
severely reduce the probability of success, which, regardless of first impressions,
is extremely high.

In the report of the Task Force on Disorders and Terrorism entitled "Police Specialization for Prevention and Control of Extraordinary Violence," it
states:

Negotiation. Specialists in negotiation should be capable of *conducting and controlling extended discussions* with persons engaged in the
coercive use of criminal violence (or threats of violence). They
should be capable of developing and maintaining rapport with fa-
natical, disturbed, or abnormally excited persons. This function is to
be distinguished from preliminary or short-term efforts to bring
about a resolution of presently or potentially violent incidents
through communication with suspects, which should be within the
capability of every patrol officer who may be the first to arrive at
an incident scene and which, even if unsuccessful, may be the basis
for later efforts by negotiation specialists. Every police agency
should have a *minimum of two such specialists on call at all times*; in
addition, every department should have one part-time negotiation
supervisor who is fully trained in negotiation techniques and who
can conduct departmental training for other officers. Wherever possible, a negotiation unit should be able to call upon a trained psycho-
logist with practical experience in law enforcement problems to assist in training, candidate evaluation, and postoperational review.[5]

However, the use of law enforcement personnel as negotiators has raised
the question as to why we negotiate. Wasn't the previous practice of assaulting a
building quickly and rescuing the affected persons much better? By always being
ready to negotiate, rather than taking a more direct approach, don't we foster
more hostage-taking incidents? Further, most criminals now know that the
police are more likely to negotiate rather than take more drastic action (only
assaulting a stronghold as a last resort).

The question as to why we negotiate is a legitimate one—one that I will
attempt to answer in the reasons outlined below:

1. We negotiate because of the value we place on human life, including hostages, law enforcement personnel, and even the hostage takers themselves.

2. We negotiate in order to gain time. Time is the most important factor for the following reasons: (1) it allows for anxieties and tensions to ease and allows the hostage taker time to assess the situation more rationally by engaging him or her in conversation; (2) the more time a hostage spends with a hostage taker, the less chance he or she will become injured or killed; (3) the passage of time also gives the police an opportunity to prepare for various eventualities; (4) the more time a hostage taker has on his or her hands, the more likely at some point he or she will make a mistake; (5) it allows the police to more effectively allocate personnel and equipment; and (6) it allows the time to prepare an assault plan in the event negotiations fail.

3. Negotiations allow time to determine the necessary level of force to be used: (1) containment and negotiations, (2) chemical munitions, (3) selected fire power, (4) full fire power, or (5) direct assault.

4. Should negotiations fail, you can always escalate to the next level of force commensurate with the threat. However, once a direct assault is made, your chances of negotiating are drastically reduced, if possible at all.

WHAT TO EXPECT

Theoretically, terrorism has no limits. With a minimum exertion of power, sometimes only a handgun, a terrorist or hostage taker can bring about a chain of events that can challenge any government at the highest level. Broadly, you can divide terrorist acts into two classes: (1) those whose method is to bring the terrorists into direct confrontation with authorities, as in hostage taking and skyjacking, and (2) those who use covert methods and do not challenge the authorities directly, as in a bombing or extortion.

The ability of terrorists and hostage takers to carry out a successful attack, and for law enforcement to successfully defend the public from such attacks, depends on many factors. When hostages have been taken, the actions of law enforcement personnel must be clear, decisive, coordinated, and fully understood. The success of any hostage plan depends on the team approach, communications, and strict command and control under one commander.

Again, one must remember that hostages are taken solely for purposes of gain. Specific tactics employed by a hostage negotiator will vary with the type and explosiveness of the incident. Negotiations must be based on the negotiator's expertise in dealing with human behavior, which is obtained through training and experience. The terrorists and hostage takers of today are not the same as those of yesterday. For the most part, being a terrorist is not a full-time job. They do not carry computers containing their plans and alternatives. Not only do they share different ideas but different affiliations as well. It is important to view the terrorist or hostage taker as a person, examining his or her perspective, personality, outlook on life, and what he or she is attempting to accomplish. They are not superhuman beings; therefore, they are subject to human frailties. Because they have emotions, they will usually react to the situation around them.

Looking at terrorist groups may give you an opportunity to analyze their objectives and goals. You may find something that will give you an idea of who the members are. It is also important to be aware of the organization's structure, since some are tightly knit, having complete control, while others may have no control at all. Some groups are structured so that they always have someone in command away from the incident who is giving orders. You will usually find this condition present when the demands are escalating and are unreasonable.

The negotiator must approach negotiations with the idea that all parties must come away with something—in the case of a hostage taker, a way to save face for the release of the hostages. Whether we like it or not, face saving is important to them and should never be overlooked during negotiations.

In conclusion, negotiating requires the most intensive type of long- and short-range preparation. How do you foresee the strategy of your opponent, and how can you prepare yourself to cope with it? The answer is simple: do your homework.

NOTES

1. 368 F. Supp. 1098 (S.D.N.Y. 1973).
2. 505 F 2d 989 (2nd Cir. 1974).
3. 212 F 2d 731 (1st Cir. 1954).
4. Gerard I. Nierenberg, *The Art of Negotiating.*
5. *Report of the Task Force on Disorders and Terrorism*, Washington, D.C.: National Advisory Committee on Criminal Justice Standards and Goals, 1976, p. 419.

17

SWAT (SPECIAL WEAPONS AND TACTICS)— THE TACTICAL LINK IN HOSTAGE NEGOTIATIONS

Abraham H. Miller

INTRODUCTION

When a situation calls for extraordinary weapons and tactical support that cannot be provided by the regular police patrol, a specially trained and equipped unit is called to the scene. Such units are called "barricade squads," "emergency service units," "advance teams," and so forth. The most common name is "SWAT" (Special Weapons and Tactics) teams. Owing to a conscious attempt on the part of some police departments to downplay anything that resembles a military operation and owing to a strong desire to avoid being linked to the dramatization of police work portrayed in the television program "SWAT," this name has been formally eschewed in a number of departments. It has been replaced with what are considered to be more publically palatable euphemisms. Yet, the notion of a special weapons team clings, and even where a euphemism has been substituted, officers talk about the special weapons unit. For this reason, I have referred to such units as special weapons or SWAT units, even though in any particular case, a department may have gone to great lengths to call the unit by another name.

What follows is a discussion of some of the more prominent of these units and how they operate, the kind of tactical support they provide in hostage situations, and some of the issues that surround their operations. These observations are based on in-depth interviews with team leaders and members, close observa-

This research was supported by Grant number 76-N199-0108 awarded by the Law Enforcement Assistance Administration, U.S. Department of Justice. Points of view or opinion expressed in this chapter are solely those of the author and do not represent the official position or policies of the U.S. Department of Justice.

tion of a team in action, public reports in terms of film and media, and internal police reporting of specific incidents.

For several reasons, I avoided a city-by-city comparison of procedures. Most procedures are sufficiently similar so that distinctions are often of little practical significance. Moreover, I felt that such comparisons have the appearance of being invidious. Instead, I sought to highlight a procedure that appears to exemplify a given concept or tactic.

Some readers will be disappointed, inasmuch as incidents—even those described in the press—are alluded to without specifics. This was necessary to preserve the anonymity of respondents and because what happened is far and away more significant than where it happened and under whose authority. Disclosure of the latter information of necessity results in defensiveness and little learning. Police departments are always vulnerable to political intrusion. Police journals have a deliberate penchant for describing and analyzing good operations—such are the dictates of politics. Bad operations, however, also have a contribution to learning that is worthy of study and reflection. This can only occur when the parties involved are spared the need to be defensive. Consequently, even some operations that received formidable publicity are analyzed without reference to time and place.

THE PHILOSOPHY OF SWAT

"What we do is take a man who is oriented to act on his own and bring him into a situation where he acts in a team. He is trained not to be impulsive, but rather to act only when he is told." In that statement, a highly placed Washington, D.C., police official described the essential philosophy behind the special weapons and tactical units police have developed to deal with hostage and barricade situations.

If there is one common attribute in the personalities of the men and women who join the police, it is that they are action oriented. To be out there in the street where the action is taking place is the guts of police work. This is a commonly and repeatedly cited comment that came across in my interviews with police in various ranks and in various cities. What the special weapons units have done is to harness that individual ethic and bring it into an organized, effective, and well-disciplined team effort.

The single most important aspect of a special weapons team is discipline. This is inculcated through intensive training and buttressed by highly selective recruitment. It is further reinforced by a large number of officers on a team and a high ratio of supervisors to team members. In New York, the ratio of supervisors to personnel runs one to four—sometimes, even one to three. As one New York police official put it, "We impose a lot of supervisors because we are dealing with a lot of firepower and that firepower is useless, even detrimental, unless it can be controlled."

The concept of discipline and controlled firepower is so basic to the special weapons operation that there has been a general disdain on the part of all the special weapons personnel I have interviewed toward the TV program "SWAT." The program, which is set in Los Angeles, is a fictional depiction of the operations of the Los Angeles Police Department special weapons unit. Unfortunately, a segment of the audience was unable to distinguish between reality and fiction. In the minds of some of the audience, the TV "SWAT" program was inseparable from the operations of the Los Angeles Police Department. The Los Angeles Police Department received hundreds of letters asking for autographs from the various fictional characters in the show. To a large extent, the portrayal created an erroneous and improper conception of the nature and function of special operations units. As one officer in the Washington, D.C., police department noted, "We don't jump out of trucks and start killing people. There are more rounds fired on TV in five minutes than we fire in years."

Beyond the depiction of the special weapons unit as jumping out of trucks and killing people, many police objected to the portrayal of the unit as sitting around waiting for the next dramatic hostage or barricade situation to unfold. In real life, such units are assigned to anything from routine police work to special duties. The assignments vary with the needs of the local department. In the larger metropolitan areas, such units are drawn from members assigned to special operations work, such as the Emergency Services Unit of the New York Police Department, which does everything from rescue work to extrication of corpses.

The most dramatic contrast to the media and popular version of "SWAT" is the definition the police use of a successful operation. This is one in which the problem is brought to an end without casualties or loss of life—and that means the lives of the perpetrators, as well as those of the victims. Interestingly, this definition of success is widely adhered to by the police. One of the strongest resentments articulated by members of the Los Angeles Police Department SWAT team was against the cliche bandied about in police circles that if a person takes hostages in New York City, the police will talk the person to death, while in Los Angeles, the police will shoot the person to death. This erroneous and negative image of the Los Angeles Police Department operation is unfortunately so widespread that it is even held by members of other California police departments.

In point of fact, the current Los Angeles Police Department hostage negotiation operation is only different from that used by the New York Police Department inasmuch as some negotiators are directly assigned to SWAT and are not part of a separate unit. The advantages and disadvantages of this procedure are a subject of debate in police circles. The New York position is that the negotiator must be as "neutral" as possible. This is reflected in the decision of New York Police Department Chief Negotiator Frank Bolz to conduct negotiations in civilian clothes. This is also the position of Lieutenant Richard Klapp, head negotiator for the San Francisco Police Department.

HOSTAGE NEGOTIATORS AS SWAT MEMBERS

From the perspective of neutrality, negotiators as part of the SWAT operation are seen as being in role conflict. After all, negotiators maintain, while the basic definition of success is the same for both special weapons teams and negotiators in hostage situations, one cannot excape the fact that the special weapons units are primarily action oriented. Their training is geared toward the controlled use of tactical and strategic firepower, where objectively success means that no shots are fired or shooting only takes place under specific conditions. Despite objective definitions of success, subjectively, many negotiators argue that there is a strong desire on the part of every person to fulfill the mission for which he or she is trained—like the Israeli pilots who flew the Entebbe mission. When they were asked how they felt about being given the green light, they responded by noting that they had trained so long and so hard for such a mission that there was a great excitement in having the opportunity to execute it. Negotiators further maintain that in contrast to SWAT, the objective and subjective fulfillment of their mission resides in the same result—talking the perpetrator into surrendering.

The SWAT personnel, however, propose that such distinctions between subjective and objective fulfillment of one's role may be more true in theory than reality. After all, they propose, even the New York Police Department negotiating team maintains its strong skills in marksmanship should a hot pursuit situation arise out of a hostage situation. Moreover, while SWAT teams are action oriented, a good SWAT team is robotlike in its response to discipline and to its commitment that a successful operation is one in which a resolution is brought about without casualties or injuries to any of the participants—including the perpetrator.

It is further argued that having negotiators as part of the team is perhaps a response to the reality of police work—inasmuch as there are a large number of negotiations that are quickly brought to a conclusion by police arriving on the scene. These situations, being more common and less dramatic, do not make the headlines but constitute the bulk of police negotiations. Denver police inform me that their situations seldom last long enough for the negotiators to get to the scene—de facto, the negotiations are done by the SWAT team. Similar observations were also communicated to me by members of Scotland Yard, who noted that most negotiations are undramatic, of short duration, and accomplished by the beat patrolman. These observations lead one to conclude that the motif of crisis intervention is such a large component of police work that hostage negotiation training might be made more generally available, but this does not answer the question of how the more dramatic and long-term negotiations should be handled. Should negotiators called upon to perform in such situations be tactically part of a special weapons team, or should they be a separate unit?

Scotland Yard, in part, justifies their decision to use separate personnel on tactical grounds. Their weapons people are drawn from the weapons specialists at the Yard's academy. They work and train as a unit. Negotiators are generally drawn from the antiterrorism squad. They, in turn, will be more knowledgeable about the personalities and operations of the people likely to precipitate serious hostage situations. There appears to accrue here a natural division of labor based on training and work experience. Moreover, since none of the negotiators are armed and since all the negotiators are in civilian clothes, this means that any civilian in the controlled inner perimeter who is in fact armed is a perpetrator.

IMPLICATIONS OF THE DIVISION OF LABOR

Irrespective of the decision as to whether or not a fairly strict division of labor is created between special weapons personnel and hostage negotiators, one pattern that clearly emerged in some police departments that had separated negotiators from the weapons personnel was a lack of sufficient contact between the units to provide the best possible understanding of each others' roles. In one department, the negotiating unit perceived that the special weapons people had created what might have developed into a crisis in one hostage situation by placing personnel on a rooftop which the negotiators had ordered cleared as part of the exchange with the perpetrators. In my interviews with the negotiators, this incident was discussed with strong concern and alluded to as confirmation of the unprofessional mentality of some of the special weapons people. Actually, the incident was precipitated by two regular patrolmen, who on their own initiative had sought to establish a tactical advantage—and almost destroyed the credibility of the negotiators in the process. Since there is some mutual distrust between the negotiators and the SWAT unit—as there invariably will be in all separate units in any organization—the erroneous perceptions have not been resolved. One means of attacking this problem is to have elements of both units together during debriefings. This unfortunately is not always done.

In any situation where there is a creation of special units with complementary assignments, there is bound to be friction. Noteworthy throughout the interviews with some departments with separate hostage-negotiating and SWAT operations was the lack of knowledge the members of each unit tended to demonstrate concerning the training and operations of the other unit. Basic information on the recruitment and training of the other unit was sometimes absent. Negotiators seemed to be uninformed about the internal operations of the special weapons personnel and vice versa. This again appeared to be a problem that could be readily alleviated by better communication and joint debriefings.

OTHER CONFLICTS AND MEANS TO AVOID THEM

The basic organizational conflict emanating from the creation of SWAT units is the internal rivalries and jealousies that any elite unit generates. Although these conflicts are inevitable, there are mechanisms that have been adopted which ease the severity of conflict. New York, Los Angeles, and San Francisco, for example, have refrained from providing special weapons personnel with extra pay. New York has also removed the special weapons personnel from making any arrests. As one New York police official put it: "If we make some arrests and not others, they will say we only take the good ones. If the responding officers know we make 'collars' they will be less likely to call us when we are needed. We avoid the problems by not making any arrests. We turn the perpetrators over to the responding officers. It is their 'collar'—all the time."

In San Francisco, where the SWAT unit does make arrests, the underlying philosophy is still the same—that arrests will be made whenever the team responds and is in a position to make the arrest. There is to be no selectivity in determining which arrests will be made by the team and which will be made by responding officers. It is a question of who is in a position to do it. As a San Francisco Police Department special weapons officer put it: "We respond to anything we can, and we take *all* the arrests. That way, it cannot be said that we just take the good ones. This stops the animosities." Members of the San Francisco team further point out that they share the publicity with other units. This factor, and the absence of extra pay, they claim, are formidable aspects in restraining hostilities and jealousies between the rest of the force and an elite unit.

Resentments, however, are inevitable. Even without extra pay or arrests, SWAT is an elite unit, with more individuals wanting to join than there is space available. In Denver, for example, which has a total police force of 1,200 men and a SWAT team of 25 men, there are currently 200 applicants waiting for a position on the SWAT unit. Although Denver does provide extra pay to its team members, a similar demand for a position with SWAT can be found in any major police department.

RECRUITMENT AND TRAINING

Getting on the team anywhere is not easy. In Denver, there is a five-year minimum experience qualification, a physical requirement, and a demand for reliability and strict submission to discipline. After making the Denver team, an individual must be prepared for a strenuous morning of running, calisthenics, and physical conditioning. In addition, there is one full training day per month. This can include anything from practice assaults to gas drills. While experience, reliability, and submission to discipline are the primary ingredients in all special weapons teams, the emphasis on physical conditioning varies greatly. In some departments, there is no special physical conditioning requirement, while in others, such as in Chicago, there is a special emphasis on maintaining the special weapons personnel in a state of excellent physical readiness.

The Chicago program is largely the result of the direction of Commander Walter Valee. Under the tutelage of the Chicago Bears' athletic trainer, Commander Valee's special weapons teams are trained in aerobics and isotonics three days per week. The men who apply for the special weapons teams are generally found to be athletic and in good physical condition. Yet, there is usually a division of activity between the men. Some are found to be involved in isotonic-type exercise, while others are involved in aerobics. What the Chicago program does is to cross-train the men so that all are equally proficient in isotonics or aerobics. The program is highly demanding, and the men are tested every six weeks.

The function of the program is not simply to put the men in a state of physical readiness, which is vital to the demands of their occupation, but to develop the men's cardiovascular system to the point where the heart beat is lower under stress. The men are run and made to shoot after coming to a halt—with pulse rate increased. This firing under stress simulates real life conditions, and the athletic programs make the men more tolerant of the physical and emotional stress they are likely to encounter in real life situations.

The Chicago program, like many of the others, is supplemented with such training as night assaults, shooting and assaults under different weather conditions, and "hostage" shooting. Hostage shooting is accomplished against a double silhouette where one silhouette is imposed over another. Marksmen must qualify by being able to hit only the second (nonhostage) silhouette.

In San Francisco, specialized training sessions are generally undertaken by teams at least once a month. These often are done in competition with neighboring departments and under the supervision of the FBI. Praise for the FBI in taking an active role in such training was very strong. Members of the special weapons teams saw the FBI as playing a vital role in providing new training techniques and also in making possible joint operations, since the team trained with the FBI and relied on similar tactics.

SWAT TRAINING AND ITS IMPLICATIONS FOR NEGOTIATION PROCEDURES

One of the problems that appears to ensue from having an excellent special weapons operation where negotiators are part of the team and under its direct tactical control is that the training emphasis appears to be primarily on the weapons component of the team mission. In contrast, when one interviews a separate negotiating unit, one hears a great deal about the process and techniques of negotiating. There is even a concern for academic learning in psychology and behavioral sciences and how work in these disciplines might better assist the negotiators in their handling of subjects. Moreover, while SWAT teams spend training time on assaults and physical conditioning, negotiating units spend time simulating hostage situations, studying tapes from previous operations, and attending seminars that contribute to the enhancement of their negotiating skills. Since the hallmark of virtually every special operations team is that every man qualify for every position—except in some cases that of marksman—this puts a double load on the hostage negotiators assigned to SWAT. They must maintain their special weapons skills and still maintain their negotiation skills. It is obvious that the demands to maintain both functions in top condition are too great for any single individual. Moreover, if an individual is a negotiator and also a member of a special weapons team, the primary ethos to be found among his peers and co-workers will be one that places an emphasis on the proficiency of the action-oriented activities of the team. Consequently, the maintenance and updating of negotiating skills will of circumstance, and perhaps necessity, take a secondary place to the demands for maintenance of skills more directly related to the operations of the special weapons units.

There is another aspect of the special weapons operation that appears to reinforce the deemphasis on negotiation. At the bottom line, when all is said and done, even many experienced and sophisticated police negotiators believe that for the overwhelming majority of their experiences that involve interrupted felonies where hostages are seized as an afterthought, the primary role of the negotiator is invariably and eventually to convince the subject that if he comes out, he will not be harmed. For his part, the subject is confronted with an array of heavily armed, helmeted, and flack-jacketed police.

This specter causes the subject to face the prospect of his own vulnerability and imminent death. The felon is rational enough to decide to survive. The problem is to convince him that the awesome array of force will not be used against him if he surrenders. Many hostage negotiations eventually amount to this type of persuasion by the police and a quest for good faith and security by the subject. One nationally prominent hostage negotiator told me that most of what he does is to convince felons that if they come out and surrender, they will not be harmed. Since this accounts for the largest portion of police experience with hostage negotiation, it is easy to see why, in the case of men who serve as negotiators on a special weapons unit, negotiating skills can further be deemphasized. After all, the primary advantage to the negotiator appears to come from the efficient deployment of a heavily armed tactical weapons unit. Negotiation begins with a subject who for all practical purposes is himself a hostage, having been contained by the special weapons unit. The appearance of this unit and the efficiency with which it deploys itself are undoubtedly instrumental ingredients in the pressure being applied to the subject. Thus, it is possible for an individual who is part of the unit responsible for these activities to further emphasize in his or her own mind the importance of the unit's tactics, as opposed to the strategy of negotiation.

To some highly placed police officials, hostage negotiation is not even perceived as demanding a special set of skills. One high-ranking police officer, who had gotten favorable publicity from an episode that came out well despite some rather questionable, if not inept, procedures, told me that any police officer with experience understands the criminal mind and that hostage-negotiating units are unnecessary. During the episode in question, he did not even attempt to draw upon the resources of men in his own department who had formal training and experience in negotiation procedures. While the end result was a capitulation by the subjects and a release of the hostages, it happened for reasons that had little to do with good police procedure. Unfortunately, success is perceived as its own validation, and undoubtedly, future operations will continue to be handled in a similar fashion until such time as a major disaster results in some belated introspection. In the meantime, the need for a separate or even a trained negotiating unit will continue to be viewed as unnecessary in this community.

TACTICAL PROCEDURES

Where SWAT does not do the negotiating, its primary role is to maintain control of the inner perimeter. In any hostage or barricade situation, the primary duty of the special weapons unit is to establish control of an inner perimeter. Generally, the only police members in the inner perimeter are members of SWAT and the negotiators. The watchwords are "lock it in and stop the action." That is SWAT's immediate function. The perpetrators must be confined; the uniform patrol drops back to establish an outer perimeter. Here, the crowd control is established. Experience shows that the longer the operation is in progress, the greater the crowd. The uniformed patrol is not permitted within the inner perimeter. Between the two perimeters, depending on local policy, members of the press and public information officers are permitted. The press is generally prohibited from the inner perimeter, although some departments have taken the position that if the press wants to take the risk, they can go where the action is. Of course, the pros and cons of such policies are debatable. All civilians who are within the inner perimeter are, if possible, evacuated. If not, they are warned to stay inside and keep down, away from the windows.

The inner perimeter is generally about a block square, although some teams prefer, if possible, a two-block-square area. Within the inner perimeter, an observation and command post are established, and communication lines to the perpetrators are opened. The preference here has been for the use of army field telephones. This is a result of telephones being tied up by an overly eager press. In some situations, the press has tied up phones to such an extent that negotiators have had to request that they relinquish the line in order for negotiations to begin. In New York, as a result of press intrusion, special arrangements have been made with the phone company to have all incoming calls other than those initiated from the police phone stopped and all outgoing calls ending up only at the police phone. This procedure also prevents perpetrators from adopting dramatic forms of role behavior for publicity purposes.

As positions are assigned the special weapons detail, the marksmen take up their position on the site and also provide antisniper control. In San Francisco, the marksmen are drawn from the district and are supplemental to the special weapons team.

In all such situations, response time is a vital ingredient. For this reason, in all departments, the special weapons units carry enough gear in the trunks of their cars to respond to a call. In Los Angeles, when officers are off duty two members of each five man team are assigned equipped cars. The vehicles contain enough equipment to sustain a responding team, pending the arrival of the SWAT logistics truck. During normal working hours, a 15-minute response time is considered average. There is an attempt to keep off duty response time within 30 minutes.

Intelligence gathering is initiated as the team takes over from the uniformed patrol. It is important to obtain descriptions of the perpetrators and the hostages, as well as their respective numbers. If possible, the identities of both parties should be established. This provides information about the seriousness of the threat and likely reactions of perpetrators and hostages. Medical records are also vital if the use of gas is likely. Knowledge of the location is important if any assault or marksman action becomes likely. In one hostage episode that I witnessed in the Georgetown section of Washington, D.C., the location had been completely remodeled, thus obviating the information available from the building plans. Fortunately, the interior designer, realizing that knowledge of the interior layout might be vital to the police, rushed to the scene with his renderings.

PROBLEMS FACING SWAT

The need for a SWAT-type operation in our major metropolitan areas would appear to be accepted as a vital part of police work. The concept of SWAT, while of prime and visible political importance during a dramatic hostage or barricade situation, is unfortunately privy to little political support at other times. SWAT does require extra resources and specialized training, and this pulls men off the street. Teams complain that when an operation is in progress, politicians will sometimes violate the security of the command post to gain on-the-scene media exposure; yet, the same politicians are often so restrained in their fiscal support of the concept that some teams find it difficult to obtain necessary equipment and even to get enough ammunition to keep up their proficiency in the use of weapons. In a number of instances, the weapons proficiency of SWAT operations has only been sustained by the sympathy and largess of National Guard and Army commanders.

A SWAT commander also walks a public tightrope. The operations he is frequently called upon to handle are of strong press interest. They are highly dramatic—they involve life and death decisions, are imbued with deeply stirring and vivid emotions, and are played against a backdrop of sirens, fast-moving cars, and men poised for deadly action. The publicity rewards for a successful operation are virtually incalculable. But publicity is based on result, not procedure. No matter how professionally an operation is executed, there is always the possibility that it will turn out badly. As experienced police officers involved in hostage negotiations have noted, there are principles and procedures that are applicable to hostage and barricade situations, and there are obviously some regularities in such situations, but ultimately, each individual case is unique and, consequently, unpredictable. One can do everything by the book, follow all the rules and procedures, make all the right guesses, and still there is that crucial element of chance that one cannot control. There is that idiosyncratic aspect of each case and each subject that can turn a good operation into a bad one. When that happens, it does not make a difference how good the procedure was— those in charge will, in the public eye, shoulder the blame.

The converse, however, is also true. If an operation is totally inept but the end result is deemed successful, the press will be unrelenting in its praise for the skills and competence of the team. The unfortunate attribute of that outcome is that the team gets so caught up in its own press notices that it learns little if anything of what it should have learned from the operation.

In one such operation in a major metropolis, noted in the press as an outstanding example of police work, almost everything was done incorrectly. According to procedures governing the use of the SWAT team in that particular community, the district commander was in charge of the operation. A good, experienced officer who ran an efficient district, he was without any special training in the tactics of handling a hostage situation. Moreover, he felt that experience overrode all and that specialized training was neither vital nor necessary to the conduct of the operation. The special weapons team arrived on the scene to control the inner perimeter. In a manner that would have shocked most tactical units and sent a number of them packing their gear and wanting no part of the operation, regular patrolmen and plainclothes detectives were assembled within the inner perimeter with guns drawn. The situation was anything but locked up and sealed. When asked about controlled firepower, the commander responded by saying that he had such authority over his men that no one would have fired without his signal. That kind of confidence was misplaced, as some of his men went behind the building and threw stones at the windows where the subjects were holed up—in an attempt to get off a shot. This took place while negotiations were in progress.

To add disaster to ludicrousness, the perpetrators demanded they name their own negotiators—two well-known black members of the media. The perpetrators, being black, did not trust dealing with white policemen. The request was acceded to, but one of the media people came into the negotiations wired for sound, and all the major local television stations converged on the scene to transmit the encounter. Network transmissions were aborted, as the unfolding drama was carried live across the local airways.

After having been shot at earlier, the commander further acquiesced to the subjects' demands to stand out in the street in gun range with the two reporters and one of the subject's sisters, as a show of good faith. One reporter, who demonstrated excellent judgment under pressure, refused. The others responded to the request, and the perpetrators surrendered.

Fortunately, this operation, with its continual violation of established procedure, ended well. The media wanted heroes, and the reporters and the district commander were vaulted into the limelight. The two reporters informed me that the whole operation might have ended in disaster save for the persuasiveness of the subject's sister.

As things turned out, success embellished by the media resulted in its own reconstruction and creation of heroes. Both reporters actually wanted little of it. It did not serve them well. Both were prominent in their own right, and the additional media exposure, while useful to the station to which one belonged, was not needed or desired. As for many of the police involved, the incident only served to underscore a bad set of procedures that had fortuitously, and despite the best attempts of the police, worked out well.

SWAT AND THE MEDIA

It is always difficult to impute motivation in an episode such as that just described; however, one of the difficulties that both SWAT teams and hostage negotiation teams commonly encounter is the intrusion of politicians and high-ranking police officials seeking publicity. (What is ironic about the preceeding situation is that it took place in a community that had an exceptionally well-trained special weapons team.) Some examples of the disruptions that have taken place in operations as a result of the encroachment of politicians or higher-ranking officers seeking publicity are presented.

In one example, a well-trained and highly experienced negotiator wanted to go to face-to-face negotiation after a long and measured encounter with the subject. The negotiator felt the point had been reached where sufficient intimacy and trust had been established and this procedure was desirable. Although face-to-face negotiation is common and this negotiator had done it many times before, his superior, surrounded by the press, adamantly refused to let him do it. The scene had more to do with theater than a calculated command decision.

In another example, a potential skyjacker seized a private airplane at an airport in a large metropolitan area. A command post was set up and was soon overrun with the governor, the mayor, city councilmen, and various and sundry of their associates. Eventually, there were so many politicians and newsmen in the command post that the local SWAT team and the FBI had to move the actual command operation to the airfield.

In another example, a well-trained and well-led SWAT team in a major city was instructed to put a female on the team in deference to affirmative action constraints. The team leader asked to be able to select a female candidate from several of the outstanding female officers in the force. He was told whom to take. The female officer in question had never qualified for the team—although by administrative fiat she was a member. She had generated a lot of "good" press, which is exactly what the officials wanted. At present, the team was short one person, since the female member had yet to qualify for any position. In my travels from team to team around the country, there were many questions about this particular female officer, who had been the subject of very favorable but unrealistic press coverage. Unfortunately, for both the team and those female officers who would have qualified, police functions were placed in a posi- · tion subsidiary to the desire for publicity.

SWAT AS PUBLICITY AND FAD

Publicity, the idea of an elite unit, and the dramatiz tion of SWAT on TV have created other problems for the concept. It appears that every department throughout the country, irrespective of size and need, has an application before the International Association of Chiefs of Police to have a SWAT team formed. Few have the need, budget, talent, or training facilities to maintain such a unit. But SWAT is popular, and it appears everyone is interested in cashing in on the fad. Such quests appear to have the result of raising the question as to whether or not SWAT is a necessary concept anywhere.

The issue is easily resolved if one simply considers the history of SWAT. In Los Angeles, the concept developed out of the Watts riots of the mid 1960s. There, police found that a talented sniper with command of the terrain could tie up an entire police force. Similar knowledge through unfortunate experience was hammered home to the police throughout major metropolitan areas during the riots of the mid-1960s. The mass demonstrations of the same period forced the police to confront the need to develop new tactics to deal with mass confrontation, especially when mass demonstrations escalated from nonviolence to violence or when undisciplined police reactions produced the same results as escalation would have.

In Washington, D.C., the SWAT unit grew out of an ill-fated attempt by officers to respond to a scene in February 1969 where a man had barricaded himself with a shotgun. The first two responding officers sustained injuries, as did their backup. The department realized that a specialized set of tactics was required for this and other extraordinary situations. From this emerged the concept of what D.C. police call the "barricade squad."

One of the most dramatic incidents that highlighted the need for a SWAT-type operation occurred in New Orleans several years ago. A sniper atop a tall building held the entire police force at bay for several hours. Patrolmen with .38s were observed attempting to hit the subject by lobbing bullets up in the air. When police finally rushed the subject, a number of officers were killed and injured from ricocheting police bullets unleashed in a fusillade of fire. The subject had been dead hours before the assault took place.

With various forms of political terrorism on the rise, internationally and domestically, there is little doubt that SWAT-type units are vital and necessary. The problem appears to be one of gaining proper public acceptance of the concept and public support for its funding. SWAT teams are not vital to the police program of every city. Under mutual aid and assistance agreements, the services of such units can be obtained from neighboring metropolises or, in the case of violation of federal law, from the FBI. In the negotiation for hostages, the SWAT operation not only provides vital tactical support but important psychological impact as well. After all, hostage negotiation techniques are an extension of normal police tactics, not a substitute for them.

APPENDIX: TACTICAL PROCEDURES—
BASIC ELEMENTS

The existence of a special weapons team mandates a set of tactical procedures to be executed under emergency conditions. Although tactical procedures will have to accommodate circumstances and environments, it is important that certain predetermined guidelines be established. This is not to limit flexibility but to set out a series of functional responses that will most likely be applicable under a wide variety of circumstances.

The initiation of any procedure requires basic information as to what is happening at the scene. The first order of business for the tactical unit is to secure information from the uniform patrol. Such information would include:

1. Where is the action taking place?
2. Who is involved (description and number)?
3. What weapons do the subjects have?
4. Why are the subjects engaged in this activity?
5. What has happened thus far? Has there been any shooting? Are there any injuries, casualties, or hostages taken, and so forth?

Obtaining such information is vital to the function of creating an inner perimeter. Before the scene can be locked up and closed off, the men who are about to undertake that function must know what they are confronting. Even the size of the perimeter itself and the ability to exercise lateral and vertical advantage will be contingent on the disposition of information obtained. Moreover, it is imperative that the team establishing and maintaining the inner perimeter be protected from potential snipers or a hostile populace. Consequently, suitable positions will have to be established to provide covering fire on all sides. The establishment of these positions is also contingent on knowledge obtained concerning the disposition of the scene.

The establishment of the inner perimeter brings access to the scene under restriction, prevents the movement of the subjects from the scene, removes civilian personnel from potentially dangerous exposure, and stops the action so that necessary intelligence gathering can continue and a tactical plan can be devised.

As the tactical unit is establishing the inner perimeter, the uniformed patrol falls back to establish an outer perimeter. This perimeter functions to (1) restrict the access of all traffic and pedestrians that might come into potential conflict with the police in the performance of their duties, (2) establish the external boundaries of an evacuation area to protect civilians from possible gunfire, and (3) establish between the boundaries of the two perimeters an area for the dissemination of information to authorized members of the media.

Between the two perimeters is the tactical command post, or TCP. The TCP functions to direct the special weapons operation within the inner perimeter. In small operations, the TCP may also serve as the main or overall command post; however, in large operations, the TCP's control is limited to the tactical command, with an overall operational command maintained separately and under the direction of higher-level police personnel.

The operational command post, or OCP, has operational control over the entire operation and has final jurisdictional authority. However, once an order is given to the TCP, it is up to the tactical leader to decide how and when the order will be implemented. The OCP is responsible for the total direction, supervision, and decision making. As the command decision is its primary function, support functions are maintained through subsidiary sections, which are staffed by appointments made to the commander. These functions include but are not limited to the following:

1. Operations—this section is responsible for overall coordination of information and maintenance of pertinent records and data. Decisions and directions for the overall operation are transmitted from this section.

2. Logistics and communications—this section is responsible for providing logistics support in the form of equipment and manpower and in establishing and maintaining communications equipment. This section is also responsible for securing additional special weapons teams.

3. Intelligence and investigations—this section handles the gathering of pertinent intelligence data and investigates the situation at the crime scene. The dissemination and processing of intelligence data is only undertaken by this section upon clearance and direction from the operations unit.

4. Liaison—this unit is responsible for maintaining liaison with the news media. It conducts, under the direction of, and from information supplied by, the operations section, news conferences, and briefings. It also maintains and restricts the area to which the press has access. It directs the press to preestablished locations for major announcements and is responsible for coordinating efforts to keep the press out of the inner perimeter.

The structure and procedures outlined here are only one reconstruction of a mode of operation. Each situation and the basic policies of each police department will mandate their own procedures. There are, however, certain elements in the above procedures that would be useful under almost any circumstances and should most likely be incorporated in any set of operational and tactical considerations. These principles include the following:

1. Containment of the situation and the restriction of access should be the primary objective.

2. The special weapons unit should be completely and solely in control of, and responsible for, the security of the inner perimeter. This enables the maintenance of discipline and the control of firepower.

3. The tactical and operational command posts should be physically and hierarchically separated in a serious situation.

4. Ultimate authority and decision making resides with the OCP. However, the TCP must retain discretionary decision making as to how to implement the operational commander's decisions.

5. A division of labor should be maintained between the two commands. This centralizes authority in a single location and yet permits the discretionary authority appropriate to a commander with specialized knowledge and skills.

6. There should be a distinct means of providing for the centralization of operations, logistics, and communications functions, intelligence and investigative roles, and for liaison with the press. These functions should be executed under the supervision of the commanding officer but conducted in such a fashion that they do not interfere with the imperative of command decisions. The centralization of these functions means that incoming and outgoing information is regulated and disseminated through a single communications location. This tends to ensure that everyone has the same information.

7. Establishing the liaison section is imperative. This prevents the adverse effects that can result from the circulation of rumors. Liaison work, while directed at the community through the press, must at times result in communica-

tion directly with the community to defuse rumors that would turn a barricade situation into a riot.

These elements, then, appear to be essential ingredients of any operation, and mechanisms that incorporate them will of course tend to vary. The mechanism used for incorporation is less important than the fact that the function has been performed.

18

HOSTAGE RESCUE IN A HOSTILE ENVIRONMENT: LESSONS LEARNED FROM THE SON TAY, MAYAGUEZ, AND ENTEBBE MISSIONS

James E. Winkates

Continuing political instability characterizes much of the global environment. Weak governments, rising pressures of nationalism, ready access to compact, conventional weaponry, and the existence of antagonistic ideologies make terrorism possible. In addition, seizure of private and uniformed nationals by foreign governments for varying reasons has also occurred in recent years. Whoever the source or whatever the cause, political decision makers desire some flexibility in choosing among appropriate responses to citizen seizures. One such option is to mount a rescue mission to extract the hostage group.

This chapter focuses on what lessons—military, diplomatic, and political—have been learned from three dramatic rescue efforts: the Son Tay prisoner of war (POW) mission to North Vietnam (1970), the Mayaguez case (1975), and the Entebbe operation (1976). The conclusions in this chapter are derived from an extensive comparative analysis of the missions prepared for the Air War College Associate programs. The initial investigation also examined in some detail technical and legal aspects of the missions. The purpose of this chapter is to synthesize the strengths and weaknesses of these rescue missions so that they might serve as ready input in planning similar missions in the future. The summary judgments contained herein are based on documented research, unclassified accounts of the participants in the missions, and the often extensive media reportage that accompanied or followed the close of the operation.

A few caveats ought to be mentioned before proceeding. The three rescue missions were selected as much for their diversity as for their commonality. One

Views or opinions expressed or implied in this chapter are not to be construed as carrying official sanction of the U.S. Department of Defense, Air Training Command, the Air University, the Air War College, or any other government agency.

common element in all three cases is that a group of foreign nationals were captured and sequestered against their will for the political purposes of their captors. All captives were pawns or hostages held not because of their individual identity but because of their group value. A second element common to the rescues is that all three were military missions designed to extract the hostage group by using force. For purposes of analysis, U.S. POWs in North Vietnam are treated as hostages but it must be remembered their legal status was that of prisoner of war, and thereby, they were rightfully incarcerated under the prevailing laws of war.

Mission diversity is readily apparent. Time frame, hostage location and nationality, motivations of the captors, and mode of extraction varied widely. In considering various rescue efforts, a larger number of key variables surfaced than would be the case in examining similar missions. At the same time, such mission diversity makes analytical judgment dependent on the special circumstances of a particular case.

There is a distinct advantage, however, in mission analysis after some time has elapsed. One can bring together key aspects of a complicated, structured rescue that was often clouded at the time of execution because of classified information, reluctance of principals to discuss details, and the fact that not all facets of a sensitive military operation are rendered public for quite some time, if ever. Even in the rescue efforts reviewed here, comparison of their essentials remains hampered by these roadblocks. Ideally, the most constructive reassessment emerges when all pertinent information is accessible. Rarely is this possible when government policy, military dispositions, personal reputations, and sensitive sovereignties can be damaged by full disclosure. Although some key facts remain hidden and still others moot, there exists sufficient material on these missions to permit drawing operational lessons for similar future ventures. Inherent disadvantages in the investigation of these missions, and indeed there are some, must be viewed as acceptable hazards with such controversial events.

SYNOPSES OF THE RESCUE MISSIONS

In the fall of 1970, the Pentagon believed there were nearly 400 POWs, mostly downed pilots, held captive in North Vietnam.[1] The Defense Intelligence Agency (DIA) claimed that a minimum of 61 POWs were held at Son Tay, a prison compound 23 miles west of Hanoi.[2] A small U.S. joint service helicopter force penetrated North Vietnam in the early hours of November 20, 1970, in order to extract the American POWs from the camp and return them to freedom. The U.S. rescue force found no POWs in the camp, nor had any been there for several months. There was no U.S. loss of life, and the rescue force sustained only two minor injuries.

On May 12, 1975, Cambodian gunboats seized the U.S. merchant ship S.S. *Mayaguez*, an unarmed container vessel en route from Hong Kong to Sattahip,

Thailand, and incarcerated the captain and the 40-man crew on a small island near the Cambodian mainland. Three days later, a joint Air Force, Navy, and Marine assault recaptured the ship, which had been left unguarded. During the course of the U.S. assault, Cambodian military elements released the crew unharmed. U.S. forces sustained 18 killed in action, 50 wounded, and 23 other personnel killed in a related helicopter crash.

On June 27, 1976, four terrorist members of PFLP hijacked an Air France commercial flight with 257 passengers and crew en route from Tel Aviv to Paris and forced the plane to land at Entebbe, Uganda. Following the release of some Air France passengers, six days after the seizure, an Israeli air commando team flew into Entebbe Airport to free the remaining hostages. Of the 105 air hostages, three were killed in the assault, one remained behind, and five were wounded. The Israeli force suffered two killed in action and four personnel wounded.

Hostage rescue in a hostile environment is inherently a high-risk venture for the hostages, the rescue force, and the authorizing government. Despite the execution of several major hostage rescues in recent years, the limited experience suggests that each mission is sui generis. In each instance, the conditions prevailing and the military execution have necessarily varied. In dissecting the Son Tay, Mayzguez, and Entebbe operations, several key functional requirements appear to be most significant in the success or failure of the missions. These include the preliminary diplomatic efforts, intelligence appraisal, mission structure, and execution, logistics, command-control-communications (C^3), and public opinion. It is suggested that prerescue diplomatic efforts and postrescue public opinion bear heavily on mission success. At the same time, no rescue can be successful if the hostages are not extracted or if the loss of life is so prohibitive for hostage group or rescue force that final casualties exceed the number of hostages threatened.

DIPLOMATIC EFFORTS

The importance of diplomacy in addressing hostage seizures is twofold. First, of course, there is the real possibility that forceful hostage extraction with its concomitant risks can be avoided and the hostages freed unharmed. Second, demonstration of a serious diplomatic intent may well ensure more favorable postrescue public opinion. Domestic U.S. experience with hostage seizures has established the importance of lengthy negotiations with the captors. The most vulnerable time for hostages is immediately following their capture, when the perpetrators are proud of their success, edgy in their anticipation of hostile reactions, and as yet unacquainted with their captives. Particularly in terrorist seizures, prolongation of negotiations tends to enhance hostage survival prospects. Terrorism, it has been suggested, is a form of theater wherein each unfolding act contributes to the publicity of the terrorist cause.[3] It is the limelight and ideological exposure that often motivates terrorist seizures. There exists a spectrum of progressive measures in response to hostage seizure, and it rationally begins with diplomatic fact-finding and proceeds to negotiation and bargaining.

Among the three hostage incidents, serious diplomatic efforts were pursued toward the release of U.S. POWs from North Vietnam, modest but abortive attempts in the Entebbe affair, and very little U.S. effort extended in the Mayaguez seizure. The Johnson and Nixon administrations attempted on a number of occasions to negotiate the release of some or all of the POWs, but Hanoi insisted any discussion of prisoners had to be linked to termination of U.S. support to South Vietnam and complete withdrawal from Indochina. Only after the 1973 Paris Peace Accords were signed did 566 U.S. POWs gain their release from North Vietnamese prisons.

Hostage negotiation presumes some willingness for compromise and bargaining. The diplomatic postures of both Hanoi and Washington, however, were irreconcilable. For North Vietnam, U.S. POWs served as one of the few instruments outside the battlefield that could be used to pressure Washington. U.S. policy in Vietnam, on the other hand, required both a continuing U.S. presence and energetic support of the South Vietnamese government. Under these conditions, there could be no common ground for hostage negotiations and certainly not as long as both Hanoi and Washington could endure the costs of not negotiating.

In the Entebbe case, the PFLP hijackers, guided by an anti-Israeli terrorist ideology, demanded the release and delivery of 53 convicted terrorists who were imprisoned in Israeli (40), West German (6), Kenyan (5), Swiss (1), and French (1) jails. Although none of these governments pressed for capitulation to the terrorist demands, Israeli diplomatic resolve atrophied when all but Jewish captives and the aircrew were released.[4] When the PFLP hijackers required the exchange of imprisoned terrorists for Jewish hostages in Uganda, the Israeli government viewed a military rescue effort as no less dangerous than a prisoner exchange on hostile soil. Prior to some assurance that a commando penetration might succeed, the Israeli Cabinet had voted unanimously to negotiate the terrorist demands. In retrospect, this decision to meet PFLP terms—even though never executed—provided the precious time needed to mount a rescue operation and even to practice operational details of the insertion. Throughout the harrowing six days of the hostage scenario, Jerusalem maintained a two-track approach—pursuit of negotiation and planning for a military rescue. Depending on how events in Israel and Uganda unfolded, this dual planning permitted the Israeli government some flexibility in response to the seizure.

The Israeli diplomatic approach yielded other positive benefits as well. When the Israeli Cabinet voted unanimously to negotiate the terrorist demands and that decision was conveyed to the captors at Entebbe, 100 additional hostages were released. Upon their return to Paris, these hostages provided Israeli intelligence with vital information on the terrorist defenses.[5] Despite gloomy prospects for successful negotiation, the Israeli government made every effort to keep communications open and ongoing with the Ugandan government. Colonel Baruch Bar-Lev, former Israeli military mission chief in Uganda and confidant of President Amin, spoke repeatedly by phone with the Ugandan president in order to prey on his sympathies and gain whatever hard information it was possible to obtain. Israel used a wide range of intermediaries, both government and private officials, to ferret out scraps of information useful for continued negotiation or for a prospective military rescue. The decision to negotiate accomplished two critical objectives. First, it lulled the terrorists into a false sense of security. Second, it provided Israeli military planners with three critical days to plan, experiment, and operationalize a complex rescue mission 2,500 miles away in a hostile environment. Most importantly, Israel's diplomatic posture conveyed the signal to the terrorists that Jerusalem would bargain their demands in good faith. The Israeli government even created "special deception teams" to reinforce public perception of their negotiating in earnest.[6] Late in the capture scenario, the Arab League not only condemned the terrorist hijacking but the PLO chieftain, Yasir Arafat, sent an aid to Uganda to seek the release of the hostages.[7]

U.S. diplomatic initiatives in the Mayaguez seizure were few and extremely limited. Only 36 hours elapsed from the time the Cambodian gunboats seized the ship off Poulo Wai Island to U.S. initiation of military measures.[8] Diplomatic notes demanding release of the Mayaguez were given to the People's Republic of China's liaison representative in Washington, D.C., to the People's Republic of China Foreign Ministry in Peking, and to Prince Sihanouk and the Cambodian Embassy in Peking.[9] No direct contacts with the Cambodian government in Phnom Penh, where the United States had no representation, were made.[10] No radio or other media transmission was attempted to local Cambodian authorities near the area of the Mayaguez seizure. While Washington assumed that the gist of the diplomatic notes delivered in Peking had been conveyed to Cambodian authorities, no evidence exists to prove this occurred. There is, in fact, substantial doubt that the central Cambodian political and military authorities were aware that a ship had been seized.[11] Even if the central government in Phnom Penh knew of the events, intracountry communications were so limited that grave doubt exists that they could have contacted the perpetrators.[12] President Gerald Ford directed U.S. Ambassador John Scali to request the assistance of U.N. Secretary-General Kurt Waldheim, but only after the president had ordered the Marine assault on Cambodian territory to free the crew.[13] Fourteen hours before the Marine operation began, one foreign government informed Washington it was using its influence to seek the early release of the Mayaguez crew and expected some success in this effort.[14] The Ford administration opted not to give much weight to this effort.

When Cambodian authorities finally offered to release the Mayaguez, President Ford, on the advice of Secretary of State Henry Kissinger, decided to continue with plans for military rescue because the Cambodians made no mention of the ship crew.[15] To the extent diplomatic initiatives were employed by Washington, they were both incomplete and inadequate.[16] No attempt, for example, was made to contact Cambodian representatives in Paris or Moscow, two key Cambodian embassies with ready U.S. access. No effort by Washington to enlist the aid of governments other than the People's Republic of China took place either.[17]

Since both Moscow and Peking seemed essentially disinterested in the crisis, Washington could readily discount any fears that either state would take precipitous action.[18] Neither the president nor Congress seemed at all inclined to pursue diplomacy with an eighth-rate power and a nation of so little consequence.[19] Given the ignominious defeats of U.S. allies in Cambodia and South Vietnam only weeks earlier and the fact that the Mayaguez was President Ford's first foreign policy crisis, resort to diplomacy was not viewed as the appropriate U.S. response.[20] It was a time for muscle flexing for the American eagle. It was a time to show the world the United States could still act like a superpower. The Mayaguez seizure happened to coincide well with a nadir of U.S. power. *The Economist* of London suggested that the meager U.S. diplomatic efforts simply filled the time needed to get elements of the U.S. Seventh Fleet to the crisis area.[21] In retrospect, that judgment does not appear to be wholly inaccurate.

INTELLIGENCE AND RECONNAISSANCE APPRAISAL

Intelligence is at best an imperfect science. No one argues that it must be perfect, but it does need to be adequate for successful mission execution. Unlike most conventional military operations, however, hostage extraction can only succeed on the first attempt. Failure, for whatever reasons, alerts the captors to further military efforts and may, in fact, encourage the immediate execution of the hostage group. In hostage rescue, superior intelligence can override sloppy or inadequate preparations in other areas. On the other hand, inaccurate or incomplete intelligence appraisals can doom the lives of the rescue force, the hostages, or both.

These three rescue efforts offer rich and relevant material for postmission intelligence analyses. The Entebbe raid demonstrated outstanding intelligence preparation. The breadth of collection and the acquisition of details proved more than adequate for mission objectives. Even foreseeable departures from the raid plan appear to have been supported by appropriate intelligence. The Israeli intelligence program might even be called flawless. The Son Tay rescue attempt illustrated first-rate intelligence with respect to North Vietnamese military dispositions, air defenses, and prison camp details, but disastrous intelligence with respect to the location of the hostage group. In the Mayaguez effort, executing authorities appeared to dismiss the need for thorough and timely mission intelligence because mistake and error characterized the entire venture.

Only in the Entebbe instance was the hostage group facing an execution deadline. As the Israeli authors of *Entebbe Rescue* point out, "the main battle was against the hands of the clock."[22] Only six days of intelligence preparation time was possible given the final PFLP deadline for hostage execution. Israeli Chief of Staff General Mordecai Gur later admitted that the Entebbe raid's success hinged completely on reliable intelligence.[23]

Even under cloak of secrecy, Israel collected a striking body of intelligence in a short time. Key information on the terrorists was solicited from the Direction de la Surveillance du Territoire, the French intelligence arm in overseas departments and territories; Scotland Yard; the Royal Canadian Mounted Police; and the CIA and FBI. Other information flowed from police and military specialists in multiple Western capitals and the Pentagon.[24] Timely information from Uganda reportedly came from Israeli informants within Amin's government, from a Ugandan underground, and from sympathetic African observers.[25] Agents of the Mossad, Israel's CIA, deployed black Africans recruited in earlier years to penetrate Entebbe Airport for information on troop disposition, hostage location, terrorist routine, and airport layout.[26] Other Israeli agents and sympathizers collected intelligence as tourists in Uganda, as vacationers on Lake Victoria, and through private air flights in the Entebbe region.[27] Israeli Defense Force reconnaissance missions were executed from outside Uganda over the hostage location.[28] Commercial airline pilots and sympathetic technicians in the East African Directorate of Civil Aviation conveyed needed technical data.[29] The breadth of the Israeli consultation process in the search for bits of intelligence suggest a thorough but low-key effort of great magnitude.

Two other unique advantages aided the intelligence collection effort. In earlier years, as Israel became increasingly isolated as an outcast state in the international arena, Israel launched a small but wide-ranging economic and military assistance program, especially in Africa. As part of this program in Uganda, an Israeli construction firm, Sollel Boneh, designed and built the Entebbe International Airport in 1966.[30] While the facilities had been expanded in later years, the company's original blueprints and specifications provided basic technical data about the airport lounge and surrounding buildings. Photo and visual reconnaissance augmented and updated the old plans.

A second asset was the experience and personal contacts Israeli Defense Force personnel had derived while operating the military assistance program in Uganda (1967–73), until President Amin terminated the program in the wake of the 1973 Middle East war.[31] From this author's personal experience in Uganda, the Israeli presence in both the civilian and military programs were highly valued and no doubt later yielded additional intelligence data for the hostage rescue.

By far the most significant and crucial information, however, came from debriefing the two groups of released Air France hostages who were flown to Paris. The number and routine location of terrorists, Ugandan troops, and type of hostile weapons gave the Israeli Defense Force critical information if a split-second lightening raid were to succeed.[32] Even more importantly, Israel learned that the hostage group remained together and were now of a manageable size— 106 persons—to evacuate in a single rescue operation. It is noteworthy, also, that the Israeli Defense Force and the Mossad had prepared detailed strike plans for various African contingencies, a region where Israel anticipated potential terrorist threats to originate.[33] The Israeli Defense Force, moreover, tradition- ally operated with reliance on surprise tactical insertions, subterfuge, rapid mo- bility, and with particular expertise in special operations. Except for the 2,500- mile strike distance, the Entebbe circumstances conformed well with the conven- tional strengths of the Israeli Defense Force.

Situational circumstances, uncovered by Israeli intelligence collection, fortified the raid planning. As outgoing president of the Organization of African Unity (OAU), President Amin attended the annual OAU conference in Mauritius only two days before the ultimatum expired. Israeli military forces thereby gained additional time for planning the Entebbe strike. With Amin outside Uganda, there was some certainty that no hostage execution would take place until his return, which was on the evening of July 3. The PFLP ultimatum was set for 1:00 P.M. Uganda time, July 4. As a matter of routine, the Entebbe run- way lights and radio navigation aids always remained on at the airport. No scheduled air traffic into Entebbe interfered with Israeli rescue plans. Between early evening on July 3 and 2:30 A.M. July 4, when a British Caledonian flight refueled (bound for London), no traffic came into or out of Entebbe.[34] Routine Saturday night revelry and drinking occupied the Ugandan airport troops, par- ticularly in Amin's absence.[35] Raid timing ensured that upon arrival, Entebbe Airport was quiet and somnolent.

Unlike the concentrated and exclusive Israeli concern with the Entebbe hostage rescue, the Son Tay planning effort took place in the heat of the Viet- nam War, amid divided public opinion and political sympathies; it constituted one minor act in a much larger decision-making drama. In all fairness, it was a time in which U.S. intelligence capabilities were taxed supremely. By 1967, the Pentagon accorded the highest priority to intelligence collection on U.S. POWs and placed that responsibility upon the DIA, wherein the chief effort was car- ried out by the Interagency POW Intelligence Committee.[36] During a routine review of the POW situation in early May 1970, a special group within the Joint Chiefs of Staff (JCS) proposed the raid idea.[37] Brigadier General Donald D. Blackburn, USA, assumed planning authority for a potential rescue mission as special assistant for counterinsurgency and special activities (SACSA), and he reported directly to the JCS chairman, then General Earl G. Wheeler, USA.[38] Since the DIA Interagency Committee already existed to coordinate POW plans, the JCS delegated responsibility for raid intelligence to the DIA. The JCS never- theless retained the overall responsibility for the POW rescue efforts.

Intelligence for the rescue mission depended primarily on aerial recon- naissance, with minor reliance on North Vietnamese contacts and agent insertions. No reliable on-the-scene surveillance took place. In the first place, the United States did not operate an effective intelligence network in North Vietnam. Second, deploying intelligence operatives prior to the planned raid may well have compromised the mission.[39]

Problems that emerged in collecting necessary information for raid planning stemmed in large part from the nature of DIA. Unlike other U.S. and foreign intelligence organizations, it is not a full-service intelligence "bank." Much of what DIA is responsible for emanates from other elements of the intelligence community. In the case of Son Tay intelligence, DIA relied on high-altitude reconnaissance flights and drone missions of the Strategic Air Command (SAC) and on ground intelligence provided by CIA operators in Southeast Asia.

According to published POW accounts, the first group of 20 prisoners arrived at Son Tay prison on May, 14, 1968; a total of 55 POWs—the entire hostage group—was moved on July 14, 1970, to Dong Hoi, a converted army barracks 15 miles east.[40] When rescue planning first began in earnest in May 1970, the POW hostages were then incarcerated at Son Tay, but all had been removed a full four months prior to the rescue attempt. What then went wrong with the intelligence collection between July and November 1970?

In late spring and early summer 1970, high-altitude SR–71 strategic reconnaissance flights confirmed that Son Tay was indeed an active POW camp and that the prison compound had actually been enlarged in late spring. SR–71s mapped the prison environs, and photo interpreters estimated that the enlarged camp could accommodate as many as 100 POWs. At the request of DIA, the CIA executed a comprehensive photo reconnaissance study of the target area, which the agency completed in August 1970. On-site photography shot after June 6 revealed less than usual activity in the camp.[41] Between September and late October 1970, seven drone flights were launched over the Son Tay compound to confirm the presence of U.S. POWs. Of the seven, North Vietnamese gunners shot down two; four had mechanical malfunctions caused by maintenance, weather, or other operational problems; and the seventh drone banked an instant too soon and returned only with pictures of the horizon.[42] A final photo verification was attempted just 36 hours before the rescue mission departed on November 18. An SR–71 flew the route over Son Tay but suffered an airborne emergency, after the photos were shot, forcing the craft to land in Thailand, where there were no qualified photo interpretation facilities available. This film footage was neither processed nor interpreted until the rescue force had already departed for the target.[43]

The JCS had no hard evidence, and certainly no visual or photo verification, that there were any U.S. POWs remaining in the Son Tay camp. There was at least one agent insertion, but upon his return, he could not confirm that there were any POWs in the compound.[44] On the other hand, 24 hours before the mission departed, DIA received information from what it considered a normally reliable source that the Son Tay prison camp was in fact closed.[45] Despite the lack of positive confirmation and the existence of some negative information, SACSA, DIA, the JCS, Secretary of Defense Melvin Laird, and President Nixon all approved the departure of the rescue force.

How and why, then, could the responsible authorities sanction a rescue mission when there appeared little likelihood that any hostages were at the target? That question remains essentially unanswered. Yet this query is not the sole problem posed by the unsuccessful rescue mission. The compartmentalized planning of the mission provoked several other embarrassing intelligence-related problems.

Perhaps the most serious blunder was the lack of coordination among U.S. intelligence agencies. Cloud-seeding operations conducted by the CIA in Laos were intensified between March and November 1970, which was coincidentally timed with the seasonal southwest monsoons.[46] The subsequent flooding that erupted in the region inundated that portion of North Vietnam, which included Son Tay prison camp. In retrospect, it appears that the CIA cloud-seeding program caused the North Vietnamese to move the U.S. POWs from Son Tay to higher ground further east.[47] Despite CIA assistance in the rescue planning, DIA was not apprised of the seeding program nor was Secretary of Defense Laird aware of it until several years later.[48]

No use was made of acoustic or seismic sensors, which might have yielded evidence of traffic in or near the prison camp.[49] The rescue mission commander, Brigadier General Leroy J. Manor, USAF, initially was denied current but classified weather data from SAC's Air Weather Service because he did not possess the correct clearance. Since local SAC authorities were not cleared to know of the rescue, he could not explain why he needed the weather data.[50] A further weakness in coordination was that no use was made of the substantial intelligence resources available in South Vietnam, American and otherwise, for fear the mission could be compromised. While it may not have changed the end result, the Son Tay rescue force was never informed that the prison compound would probably be empty.[51] With their lives at stake, conveying this prospect would seem to have been a moral if not a command imperative.

Ironically, intelligence unrelated to the hostages proved near perfect. North Vietnamese troop disposition, camp layout, surface-to-air missile installations, antiaircraft batteries, and radar locations were all accurately pinpointed to permit near errorless access across 350 miles of rough terrain and hostile territory. So flawless was this tactical intelligence that North Vietnamese prison guards remained unaware of the rescue assault until one minute before U.S. forces touched down.[52]

Nevertheless, the Son Tay mission illustrated a gross lack of on-site intelligence collection, serious intelligence community miscoordination, rigid compartmentalization, and a failure to consult widely for necessary operational information crucial to mission success. These sins of commission and omission relate to the primary purpose of the mission—the rescue of POW hostages.

Of the three rescue missions considered in this chapter, the Mayaguez operation most lacked adequate intelligence. Extensive postseizure appraisals readily document these shortcomings. An in-depth GAO investigation and subsequent congressional hearings and testimony, together with accounts of various military participants, all point to intelligence flaws, omissions, and failures. Because of the decisions of the National Command Authority, most particularly those of President Ford and Secretary of State Kissinger, military units were unprepared and later acted in haste in responding to the seizure.

Lieutenant Colonel Donald Carlile, USA, pointed out two areas of faulty intelligence during the Mayaguez operation, both of which the GAO confirmed earlier in its postcrisis investigation.[53] First, U.S. forces never knew where the Mayaguez crew was located from the time they were commandeered to their voluntary release by local Cambodian military units. Because of the U.S. withdrawal from Cambodia and Vietnam only weeks earlier, only limited intelligence assets were available at the time of the seizure.[54] Following authorization from Washington, it took five hours to launch the first reconnaissance aircraft, a P-3 Orion based at Utapao, Thailand.[55] It arrived over the seizure area after sundown. The ship's location was not confirmed until 18 hours after the boarding of the Mayaguez by hostile Cambodian forces with the flyover of the third reconnaissance flight.[56] When visual observation of some crew members of the Mayaguez occurred, there was no attempt to follow up or confirm the pilot's observation of some 30 or 40 people thought to be Caucasians.[57] Despite the fact that the Mayaguez crew was moved on multiple occasions in broad daylight, reconnaissance missions never could confirm the location of the crew. Throughout the rescue operation, it was assumed the crew was initially on its ship and later transferred to Koh Tang, an offshore island. Neither assumption was accurate.

A second area of faulty intelligence concerned the estimate of Cambodian troop strength on Koh Tang Island, where it was thought the crew was detained. Preassault briefings given to the Marine rescue force indicated that only 20 to 30 Khmer Rouge irregulars were on the island and that they possessed a mixture of only small arms.[58] The more realistic DIA estimate of 150 to 200 regular Khmer troops for some reason never reached the Marine assault force nor the local U.S. command in Thailand, from where the Marines were dispatched.[59] Since Marine service doctrine calls for an initial three-to-one superiority over enemy forces, the failure to communicate accurate force intelligence inevitably pitted the Marine units against high risk. The Marine landing force on Koh Tang also did not possess gridded maps, which severely hampered their small arms fire on the island.[60]

While the GAO later agreed that the use of reconnaisance drones would have been inappropriate because of time limitations and the saturated air environment,[61] the congressional investigative arm concluded that given the ignorance of the crew's location and the conflicting troop estimates on Koh

Tang, the rescue mission was too precipitous a response.[62] The GAO also documented an "apparent lack of a coordinated intelligence appraisal" in the mission.[63] Little effort, for example, was exerted to verify with photography or other available technical means the changing location of the crew.[64] Military reconnaissance aircraft, standardly equipped with photographic or other sensor capabilities, could have pinpointed a 40-man crew and their captors even in darkness. The Department of Defense later acknowledged weaknesses in the initial reconnaissance process that would need improvement.[65]

While intelligence collection and verification, along with air reconnaissance, proved less than adequate, a far more serious question can be raised with respect to the relationship of military planning to hostage extraction, that is, How could intelligence planning not perceive that the assault of Koh Tang Island would not jeopardize the lives of the Mayaguez crew if they were captive there and caught in the midst of U.S.-Cambodian firefights? The GAO could only conclude that "the goal of safely landing the assault force . . . was in direct conflict with the goal of ensuring the safety of possible American prisoners."[66]

From a coordination perspective, the Mayaguez operation presented a far more difficult mission than did either Son Tay or Entebbe. It required a mixed medium (air, sea, and land) intelligence operation. Intelligence collection, coordination, confirmation, and dissemination inevitably posed problems because of different service traditions and threat analyses.[67] An important omission with respect to intelligence collection should here be emphasized. Unlike the two other hostage incidents, no substantive effort was made to learn the intentions for the Cambodian seizure.[68] Such knowledge, at the very least, might have aided rescue mission authorities in assessing the degree of threat and level of risk *before* inserting U.S. air, ground, and naval forces in a hostile environment.

Former CIA Executive Director Lyman Kirkpatrick, in his revealing study of World War II intelligence failures, observes that good intelligence "must assess what the enemy will do under various circumstances" and that "the information available on the enemy [must get] to the men who must fight the battle."[69] Mayaguez intelligence failed this acid test. The Marine rescue force invaded an island thought to be weakly defended to extract hostages who were never there. The inescapable conclusion is that U.S. combat forces in the Mayaguez rescue were committed to battle with inadequate and inaccurate military intelligence.[70]

MISSION FORCE STRUCTURE AND EXECUTION

The unique character of hostage incidents requires a case-by-case response in terms of rescue force structure and execution. Unlike normal battle operations, small operational, support, and contingency forces typify rescue missions. The emphasis is on a quick strike and rapid disengagement. A routine sequence of military action must take place with split-second timing—undetected approach and penetration, silent tactical deployment, close coordination among mission elements, selective fire, unified hostage extraction, and rapid withdrawal. Above all, surprise, boldness, and precise firepower comprise the trinity of hostage rescue in a hostile environment.

Mission force structure is most determined by the complexity of the hostage rescue plan and anticipated hostile force disposition, readiness, and weaponry. Special communications and logistics requirements will be treated later. Table 18.1 displays the basic force structure for the three rescue operations.

While the various details of mission planning offer useful insights into the rescue operations, the chief concern here is with the execution of the missions at the point of hostage extraction. Although several successful hostage rescue missions have taken place more recently, notably in Holland and the Somali Republic, the Son Tay, Mayaguez, and Entebbe missions were then unprecedented. Not since the days of the Barbary pirates, for example, had an operation like Son Tay been attempted.[71] With the exception of some U.S. Civil War parallels, there had never been a successful rescue of U.S. prisoners from a POW camp.[72] More than 60 POW raids were conducted in Southeast Asia during the Vietnam War, but only one POW was extracted; he died later of his wounds.[73] Even the highly lauded search and rescue (SAR) missions in the Vietnam War recovered only 13 percent of downed U.S. airmen in a period of three years.[74] Prior to the Mayaguez mission, the last ship boarding by U.S. Marines took place in 1826.[75] The Entebbe mission was the longest one-way rescue operation in air history—a distance of nearly 2,500 miles.[76] So each of these hostage rescues were "firsts" in modern history.

Brigadier General Manor, commander of the U.S. Air Force Special Operations Force at Eglin Air Force Base, in Florida, served as the Son Tay mission commander. A veteran of 275 combat missions over Southeast Asia and commander of the 37th Tactical Fighter Wing at Phu Cat Air Base in South Vietnam, he was an experienced operations officer. For his deputy and head of the ground rescue force, General Manor chose Colonel Arthur D. Simons, USA, an experienced special operations officer who had commanded joint U.S.-South Vietnamese intelligence teams in North Vietnam.[77]

After three months of rigorous tactical and night training at Eglin Air Force Base, the rescue force left for Thailand, the point of departure for the mission. C-130s transported the primary rescue force of 56 men from Takhli Air Force Base to Udorn Air Force Base in northeast Thailand. The six rescue helicopters left Udorn Air Force Base at 10:56 P.M. local time for the five and one-half hour, 687-mile roundtrip flight to Son Tay. The other mission assets, including C-130s, A-1Es, HC-130s, F-4s, F-105s, EC-121s, and a KC-135, joined the helicopters from other Royal Thai Air Force bases. The command plane, an RC-135, took off from Kadena Air Base in Japan.

TABLE 18.1

Rescue Mission Data: Force Structure, Personnel, and Hostage Group

Item	Son Tay	Mayaguez	Entebbe
Hostages	70–100	40	105
Location	Prison compound (stationary)	Undetermined (changing)	Airport lounge (stationary)
Primary rescue force	56	305	280
Description	U.S. Air Force Special Operations forces U.S. Army Green Berets Various service rescue specialists	U.S. Marines	280 paratroopers, including 150 commandos from 35th Airborne Brigade, Golani Infantry Brigade, counterguerrilla force
Primary rescue platforms	Helicopters: Five HH–53 One HH–3E	Helicopters: Six HH–53 Five CH–53	Cargo transports: Four C–130H
Other Air/naval platforms	UH–1 HC–130P C–130 A–1, F–4, F–105 (for close air support, surface-to-air missiles and AA[a] suppression, and MIG defense) EC–121 (command posts) RC–135 (command plane) KC–135 (tanker)	C–130 HC–130 AC–130 A–7 F–4 OV–10 (FAC)[b] 8-ship flotilla: USS *Holt* (destroyer escort) USS *Wilson* (guided missile destroyer) USS *Coral Sea* (carrier) USS *Gridley* (guided missile frigate) USS *Baussell* (destroyer) USS *Land* (destroyer escort) USS *Mispillion* (fleet oiler) USS *Vega* (stores ship)	Boeing 707 (airborne command) F–4 Phantom escorts Boeing 707 (hospital ship at Nairobi) KC–130 (at Mombasa, Kenya) ELINT (electronic intelligence ship operating off East African coast)

[a]Antiaircraft gun batteries.
[b]Forward air controller.
Source: Compiled by the author.

The rescue force arrived over Son Tay at 2:30 A.M. local time, November 21, 1970, having successfully evaded North Vietnamese radar nets and achieved total surprise in approach. According to plan, the HH-3E crash landed in the center of the camp compound. The rescue force swiftly eliminated the North Vietnamese guards in the corner tower, and the remainder fled. With the other North Vietnamese prison guards asleep, hostile forces were unaware of the U.S. presence until one minute before the ground commander landed.[78] Colonel Simons's command ship, with the largest element of the rescue force (21 men), mistakenly put down 400 meters from the prison compound.[79] To their surprise, they were engaged by 100 to 200 Russian or Chinese troops, who had heard the loud choppers coming in. Simons's rescue group killed most of the surprised foreign troops in a five-minute battle.

During the rapid search of the prison compound, no U.S. POWs were found; from visual observation of the prison cells, they had been empty for some time. After 27 minutes on the ground, the rescue force quickly got airborne again and fled the area amid small arms fire and with 30 surface-to-air missiles fired at the departing force.[80] As soon as the choppers were in the air again for Thailand, General Manor was informed that no Americans were found.

With the exception of the landing error by the command chopper, mission execution proved almost flawless. The A-1s knocked out a nearby bridge to prevent enemy reinforcements by land. The F-105s served as decoys for the surface-to-air missiles, successfully jammed North Vietnamese radar equipment, and assisted in the protection of the F-4s, which flew patrol against anticipated MIG opposition. The rescue attempt resulted in only two minor injuries to the U.S. force. But there were no hostages to bring home.

In many ways, the Mayaguez rescue created more operational problems than did either the Son Tay or Entebbe missions. Overall tactical planning for the rescue originated with the Commander-in-Chief, Pacific Command, Admiral Noel Gayler.[81] Unlike the other rescue efforts, the National Military Command authorities—President Ford, Secretary Kissinger, and the National Security Council—exercised very close control of the mission.[82] Regular units of U.S. armed forces in the Pacific theater, including Air Force, Navy, and Marine personnel, executed the rescue operations.

The Mayaguez rescue effort required a two-pronged approach, since the hostage crew were thought to be separated. Consequently, both recovery of the ship and assault of Koh Tang Island were executed. Three of the 11 helicopters for the mission transported 50 Marines, 60 Navy ordnance disposal technicians, six civilians of the Military Sealift Command, and a U.S. Army captain, who spoke Cambodian to the destroyer escort USS *Holt*. The destroyer escort approached the Mayaguez, lying dead in the water, and found the ship unmanned. The USS *Holt* boarding party took control of the vessel, and the ship was made ready to egress the area.[83]

To conduct the twin-assault strategy, 1,100 Marines from the 3rd Marine Division on Okinawa were ferried to Utapao Royal Thai Air Force Base in Thailand. CH-53 and HH-53 helicopters of the 56th Special Operations Wing at Utapao transported approximately 230 Marines for the ship and island assaults. The heavy choppers flew the first 100 Marines from Utapao to Koh Tang Island and encountered heavy ground fire. Of the eight helicopters engaged, three were shot down or seriously damaged and two withdrew to return to Utapao 400 miles away. Presuming the Mayaguez crew to be on the island, no presoftening of Koh Tang took place. The well-armed and fortified 200 Cambodian regular troops took advantage of the dense foliage on the narrow one-by-three-mile island. Proximity of the enemy to Marine units was as little as 20 meters. Only 400 meters separated the three Marine beachheads. Some of the planned Marine insertions proved impossible, preventing adequate concentration of force. Moreover, enemy mortar and gun enplacements curbed reinforcement of the initial Marine party. Three hours after the first Marines landed on Koh Tang, the USS *Wilson* sighted the entire Mayaguez crew, who had been released by the Cambodians and were under steam away from the Cambodian mainland in a fishing vessel.

With the crew free and the ship recaptured, the JCS ordered the Marines to withdraw from Koh Tang as soon as possible. They were unable to do so. A second wave of 100 Marine reinforcements were able to get to a Koh Tang beachhead to assist an isolated group of 22 Marines pinned under fire. The Marine units were unable to depart until 8:15 P.M. local time, under cover of near darkness, having engaged in a 14-hour battle with the larger Cambodian forces. Anticipating emergency extraction of the last Marine contingents, a C-130 dropped a 15,000-pound conventional bomb to clear a landing zone.[84]

In order to prevent Cambodian reinforcement of the Koh Tang garrison and to prevent counterair attack on the U.S. helicopters, President Ford ordered conventional bombing of selected targets on the Cambodian mainland, including the military airfield at Ream, surrounding hangars, and an unused oil refinery. Twenty-five Navy A-6 Intruders and A-7 Corsairs from the USS *Coral Sea* destroyed 17 Cambodian aircraft, mostly old U.S. T-28s, using TV-directed Walleye smart bombs.[85]

The Mayaguez rescue operation encompassed 78 hours from the initial ship seizure on May 12 until the complete withdrawal of the Marine assault force from Koh Tang on May 15. Final U.S. casualties included 18 Marines killed in action and 50 wounded. In a noncombat but related helicopter accident, 23 Air Force personnel perished en route to a staging area for deployment to Koh Tang.[86] There were no severe injuries suffered by the Mayaguez crew held hostage and later released during the course of U.S. offensive operations.

The casualty count, both killed and wounded, make it clear that the Mayaguez mission, at least in this respect, was no flaming success. While the heavy U.S. air and naval action may have prompted the early release of the ship's crew, U.S. military action did not directly produce the release. The operation lacked adequate intelligence, produced a messy and highly inefficient combat environment on Koh Tang, and overall could not be viewed as a model of military strategy. As one Pentagon general officer reportedly admitted, "We were lucky all of the Marines did not get killed."[87]

In retrospect, a number of problems hampered the rescue operation beyond the intelligence functions. Some of these problems have been confirmed, and others remain speculation. Engine problems prevented two aircraft carriers from ever reaching the rescue area, a mishap that prompted the Navy to hire a private management consultant to appraise naval readiness and to examine maintenance systems.[88] The power system on one of the two participating destroyers broke down, making its sole five-inch gun inoperative.[89] The first U.S. ship to arrive on the scene, the USS *Holt*, did not come on station until two full days after the Cambodian seizure.[90] The post-Mayaguez congressional hearings noted that a chief limitation on successful management of the crisis was the absence of U.S. surface ships and sufficient military forces in the area.[91] Although Command-in-Chief Pacific (CINCPAC) Fleet directed an ·Amphibious Ready Group to proceed to the crisis area and support the Marine assault of Koh Tang, the task force could not arrive in time for the extraction operation.[92] While the GAO investigative report praised the assemblage of military forces, in retrospect, it appears that was done with great handicaps.[93]

The Air Force also had its share of problems in the Mayaguez affair. Air reconnaissance could never determine the precise location of the hostage crew; consequently, air and sea bombardment were limited in the target area. At least one report noted Marine Corps criticism of Air Force chopper crews taking them into Koh Tang, claiming that Air Force pilots were unfamiliar with Marine landing procedures, resulting in poor ground deployment.[94] The GAO also argued that Air Force bombing missions were "not closely coordinated with other military action" and implied that the Navy bombing of the Cambodian mainland was unnecessary.[95] With choppers coming in and departing, high-speed fighter aircraft changing off in forward air control and surveillance duty, and naval aircraft operating from the USS *Coral Sea*, effective coordination of the two-pronged rescue effort proved difficult at best.

The Mayaguez rescue effort cannot be characterized by quick strike or rapid disengagement, nor did it illustrate precise and selective firepower. It proved to be a clumsy, inefficient, and costly operation saved perhaps only by the good fortune of the safe return of the Mayaguez crew and their ship. While there is adequate blame in the affair, it must be shared by both civilian and military authorities responsible for the conduct of the rescue operation.

Operational details of the Entebbe hostage rescue are skimpy in comparison with the U.S. missions, and more reliance on unofficial documentation becomes necessary. Tight Israeli military censorship, along with official reluctance to discuss operational tactics, have permitted only partial information to emerge. Like the Son Tay preparations, though with far greater time constraints, Israeli military utilized a mock-up of the hostage environment and conducted a full "dry run" of the rescue operation prior to launch.

Brigadier General Dan Shomron, commander of the Special Air and Commando Service, had overall authority for the mission and led the Israeli Defense Force to Entebbe. Late in the afternoon on July 3, 1976, four C-130s, two 707s, and an HC-130 tanker, with their Phantom escorts, took off for their seven-hour flight to East Africa.[96] The best guess is that the mission's final departure point was Ophir Air Base, near Sharm el-Sheikh, at the southern tip of the Sinai Peninsula.[97] One account claims the Israeli group flew at very low altitude down the middle of the Red Sea, turning over African territory at Djibouti, across southern Ethiopia and northern Kenya into Nairobi.[98] The tanker went on to Mombasa, Kenya, on the East African coast, and the 707 hospital plane landed at Nairobi. The main assault force proceeded due west to Entebbe. To insure protective cover, the Israeli Phantoms reportedly jammed hostile radar en route, aided by an electronic intelligence missile ship stationed off the East African coast.

In terms of opposition, Israel anticipated approximately 70 to 100 Ugandan troops in or near the air terminal at Entebbe in addition to the ten PFLP terrorists. Approximately 10,000 Ugandan troops were thought to be stationed within a 25-mile radius of Entebbe. One researcher of the Entebbe raid claimed Ugandan defenses included a large number of armored troop carriers; at least 50 combat aircraft, including 30 MIG 17s and MIG 21s at Entebbe; and large but unknown quantities of missiles, howitzers, and mortars.[99] The London *Times* credited Ugandan forces with a complement of Soviet T-54 battle tanks and Sagger antitank missiles.[100]

On approach to Entebbe and at half-mile intervals, the C-130s split into two groups, with the 707 command plane circling over the airport. The first pair of two C-130s quietly approached on the older of the two runways and taxied to within 1500 yards of the old terminal, where the hostages were being held.[101]

The lead plane disgorged a black Mercedes limousine, which was identical to President Amin's personal car, along with two Land Rovers, carrying ten Israeli commandos in camouflage. General Shomron deployed four commando groups. One element stormed the old terminal building, killing seven terrorists and perhaps 20 Ugandan troops. A second group neutralized the other local troops in the immediate terminal area. The third unit moved to the far side of the airfield to destroy the Russian MIGs. A fourth group remained to guard the four Israeli C-130s. The brief fire fight began at 12:03 A.M. local time, July 4, 1976, and lasted about 15 minutes.[102] Most of the terrorists never fired a shot, with the whole skirmish in the terminal over in less than two minutes. Ugandan troops who fled the area were not pursued.

Quickly ushering the hostages to the waiting plane, the first of the four C-130s took off 53 minutes after arrival and proceeded to Jerusalem directly following refueling in Nairobi. The last mopping up, including evacuating the casualties and fingerprinting the dead terrorists, took another 30 minutes at Entebbe.[103] By 2:39 A.M. local time, all four C-130s were in Nairobi.[104]

Ugandan armor and troop reinforcements never arrived. Israeli demolition squads blew up 11 MIGs on the ground before departing. General Amin apparently slept through the entire raid in his headquarters near Entebbe Airport. He remained unaware of the hostage rescue for several hours after the Israeli withdrawal.

While much information about the rescue operation remains unexplained, plaudits that the mission was "tactically brilliant" appear justified.[105] Israeli commandos knew precisely the location of the hostage group and the disposition of the terrorists and allied Ugandan troops. The use of a Mercedes car identical to that of President Amin's apparently provided sufficient margin for the near total surprise of the hostages' captors. General Gur, Israeli Defense Force chief of staff, later commented that the commandos had freed the hostages within 45 seconds after entering the terminal.[106]

Of the 105 total hostages, only four perished. Three civilians were killed in the rescue, and five more were wounded. The Israeli commandos suffered two deaths and four wounded. One hostage, who had been taken to a local hospital in Uganda for emergency treatment, is believed to have been murdered on Amin's orders after the rescue mission left Entebbe. For casualty comparisons among the three operations, see Table 18.2.

In retrospect the Entebbe raid proved to be a superior combat rescue operation. Characterized by quick strike and rapid disengagement, the mission executed approach, penetration, deployment, coordination, selective fire, and hostage extraction with dispatch and near perfection. Importantly, the elements of secrecy, surprise, and boldness typified the whole operation. Without taking any credit from the Israelis, it should be noted as well how significant just plain good fortune abetted their assault. Runway lights and navigational aids remained operational. Ugandan troops, given the hour and their merrymaking, were caught totally off guard. No serious mechanical failures occurred with the four C-130s. All but a few of the civilian hostages had enough presence of mind to head for cover immediately upon hearing gunfire. Above all, the hostage group was kept together by their captors rather than dispersed at the airport or taken even further away.

LOGISTICS

While many requirements for hostage rescue approximate the needs of other military operations (namely, personnel selection and training), two func-

TABLE 18.2

Mission Casualties: Son Tay, Mayaguez, and Entebee

Operation	Hostage Casualties	U.S./Israel Military Casualties	Enemy Casualties
Son Tay	n.a.*	None killed in action; 2 minor injuries, both recovered	Estimated 30 North Vietnamese killed in action; estimated 100 to 200 Soviet or Chinese troops killed in action
Mayaguez	Short-term effects from U.S. tear gas; none killed in action; no severe injuries	18 killed in action; 50 wounded 23 Air Force Security Police, helicopter crew, and ground crewman perished en route, but not in official Department of Defense count	47 killed in action; unknown number missing in action; 55 wounded (estimated)
Entebbe	3 killed in action; 5 wounded, all recovered	2 killed in action; 4 wounded, all recovered	25 to 45 Ugandans killed in action (estimated); 60 to 80 estimated wounded; 6 to 7 PFLP terrorists killed

*Not applicable.
Source: Compiled by the author.

tional requirements stand out as especially critical. C^3 is one, and logistics is the other. In hostage air rescue missions, the key logistics variables are the air platforms, staging areas, overseas bases, refueling capability, and overflight rights.

The selection and performance of aircraft in hostage rescue emerge as key factors in mission accomplishment. Versatility, trouble-free performance, easy maneuvering, and flight control must characterize the operation. Overwhelming firepower and armor plate, for example, pale in importance to the aforementioned characteristics because a premium is placed on surprise and unimpeded approach.

While the Son Tay and Mayaguez missions utilized helicopter assault and extraction and the Entebbe raid relied solely on fixed wing aircraft, the common air carrier for all three operations was the C-130. In the Son Tay mission, the Combat Talon C-130E, specially equipped with Forward Looking Infrared Radar

(FLIR) for precise navigation, led the six assault choppers and the A-1Es into North Vietnam. This extended range version of the C-130B operates with large underwing fuel tanks and has been a mainstay for Military Air Command and Tactical Air Command since 1962.[107]

Because of their unique surveillance capabilities, Spectre AC-130 gunships were employed in the Mayaguez operation to maintain continuous watch over the crisis area in darkness. A cargo version of the C-130 dropped the 15,000-pound "daisy cutter," the largest conventional bomb in the U.S. arsenal. All three rescue missions relied on the 130/135 tanker series for refueling operations.

In the Entebbe strike, four C-130Hs constituted the sole penetration force into Uganda. Both the E and H configurations of the Hercules aircraft had been operative in the Israeli Air Force since 1971; they were the only Israeli transports that could manage both the distance and hostage numbers in the mission.[108] The C-130H, a four-engine, turboprop, air-refuelable craft, can fly in virtually any conditions, from no visibility to all-weather. These Hercules craft were fitted with jet-powered rockets for rapid takeoff and steep climb in the Entebbe strike, but the extra lift proved unnecessary in the mission. While one report claimed the Israeli C-130s landed fully loaded on 600 feet of runway and a 45-degree angle of attack,[109] experienced Hercules pilots seriously doubt this claim. Nevertheless, range, speed, load capacity, and versatility make the various models of the C-130 a highly valuable asset in rescue operations.

The HH-53 "Super Jolly Green Giant" not only served as the primary penetration vehicle of the Son Tay mission but, along with the CH-53 "Knife" chopper, was the primary assault platform in the Mayaguez effort. A mainstay of the U.S. Air Force Aerospace Rescue and Recovery Service (ARRS) since 1966, the HH-53 carries all-weather avionics, adequate armament, and is air refuelable. The CH-53s, used in the Mayaguez insertion, are normally employed to provide battlefield mobility for the Air Force mobile tactical air control system. While the craft can be fitted with external fuel tanks, its inability to refuel in the air operated as a disadvantage in the lengthy Koh Tang tactical insertion. The extended range, armor plating, and 7.62-millimeter miniguns of the HH-53 and CH-53 models enhance their operational survivability, especially in high-threat hostile environments. Unfortunately, in the difficult Koh Tang environment, it was the CH-53s that suffered the most hits and encountered rather extensive loss or damage. These damages, however, appeared to result from the difficult tactical situation rather than due to aircraft malfunction. In rescue situations where large numbers of hostages are captive, either multiple aircraft or few but high-load capacity air vehicles are required. The more aircraft, the more likely unforeseen operational failures become. The Son Tay and Entebbe missions, however, demonstrate that rescue efforts can succeed with either rotary or fixed-wing platforms, assuming other mission requirements are fulfilled.

Logistic requirements, however, hinge on more than aircraft selection. Both the Son Tay and Mayaguez missions depended upon the use of Royal Thai

Air Force bases as staging areas for the launching of the rescue operations. Long-distance rescue penetrations using air-refuelable rotary aircraft are simply not very practical. Their slow speed and high noise emission alone limit their utility. Moreover, if airborne over hostile territory, the rotary craft become easy prey, even for modest air defense forces. Most especially for missions employing rotary aircraft, either staging areas or overseas bases become critical. Since neither the Son Tay nor Koh Tang locales offered landing facilities for fixed-wing air-craft, only choppers could have been employed, making use of friendly base facilities imperative.

Foreign base facilities for the Son Tay mission were no problem, since the Bangkok government permitted the United States use of Takhli, Udorn, Korat, Nakhon Phanom, and Utapao during the Vietnam War. In 1970, the substantial assets of the Pacific Air Force, Tactical Air Command, and the Seventh Fleet also provided a weighty U.S. presence in the area. Without access to Thai instal-lations, one can imagine how much more difficult hostage rescue might have been from bases in the Philippines or Taiwan. Even if the U.S. facility at Diego Garcia in the Indian Ocean becomes operational, it sits 1,000 miles from the Asian mainland.

Although U.S. forces relied on the use of the Thai Air Force base at Utapao for the Mayaguez operation in 1975, times had changed considerably. Publicly at least, the Thai government strenuously objected to the use of their military facilities by the United States in the Mayaguez affair, filed a formal protest with Washington, and accused the United States of a "breach of faith.[110] Bangkok called its ambassador in Washington home for consultations.[111] Even before the Mayaguez seizure, Bangkok had asked the United States to withdraw all of its troops from Thailand.[112] Despite U.S. efforts to reverse or at least delay the move, all U.S. forces departed in mid-1976. In retrospect, the Maya-guez incident may have hastened U.S. withdrawal. By September 1975, Thailand and other Southeast Asia Treaty Organization (SEATO) members had agreed formally to phase out the 20-year alliance. By 1977, the United States no longer had access to any base facilities in mainland Southeast Asia.

In the event a hostage rescue scenario unfolds in the Southeast Asian area, or for that matter in other regions where the United States lacks base facilities, U.S. authorities will have to request the right to use foreign installations on an ad hoc basis. While such permission ought not to be precluded in advance, re-liance on overseas staging areas cannot be assured. On the positive side, however, for clear and compelling humanitarian reasons, it is likely that many nations might comply with a request for one-time discretionary use of their territory for rescue missions. Certainly, Kenyan approval for Israeli refueling in the Entebbe mission is encouraging for such future ventures. The more recent West German strike to rescue Lufthansa hostages in Somalia benefited from that government's cooperation. In summary, recent hostage extraction missions, which were suc-cessful because of foreign state cooperation, appear to diminish the dire need for overseas base networks in rescue operations.

Israel, of course, possessed no overseas bases, nor could it expect Arab or African states to assist the Israeli Defense Force in the Entebbe hostage rescue. While the C-130 strike force could have barely reached Entebbe without refueling, the rescue force would have had to refuel from petrol tanks at Entebbe or from another nearby location. The roundtrip mission mileage was twice the range of the C-130. Cooperation of the Kenyan government proved to be of critical value to the mission's success. There is no disputing the fact of direct, prerescue, Kenyan cooperation, since the 707 hospital plane and HC-130 tanker put down on Kenyan territory prior to the Israeli Defense Force assault of Entebbe. After extracting the Air France hostages from Entebbe Airport, the four C-130s landed at Nairobi, were refueled, and headed directly back to Israel. The Israeli wounded were treated in Nairobi, and one injured hostage was taken to a hospital in the capital city for treatment. Why and how Kenya cooperated with the Israeli raid still remains controversial.

George Githii, editor of the independent but progovernment Kenyan newspaper, *Daily Nation*, had visited Israel within a short time after the hijacking.[113] Githii knew on a first-hand basis the top authorities in the Kenyan government. A number of reports ascribe different reasons for Kenyan support. The London *Times* claimed that the five terrorists held in Kenyan custody, whose release was demanded by the PFLP, had already been killed by Kenyan police.[114] Certainly there was deep enmity between President Jomo Kenyatta's government and that of President Amin. A *Time* magazine account suggested that in return for Kenya's help, the Israelis promised to destroy the Soviet MIGs stationed at Entebbe Airport.[115] The Israeli Defense Force blew up 11 Soviet MIGs before leaving Uganda.[116] William Stevenson, author of *90 Minutes at Entebbe*, reported that Geoffrey Karithii, commander of President Kenyatta's internal security unit, arranged for Kenya's support of the Israeli mission. Stevenson states that Kenya cooperated on the following conditions: that the refueling be conducted as a "routine" operation and that Nairobi authorities isolate the El Al facilities at the Nairobi air terminal.[117] Local ground crew personnel, implied Stevenson, were offered petty cash by Israeli El Al employees so they would neither interfere nor ask any questions about why other than Israeli commercial aircraft were on the ground. All of these claims with regard to why Kenya cooperated remain plausible. It is also clear that Kenyan aid in the Entebbe mission may have been the key ingredient in moving the Israeli Cabinet to approve the Israeli Defense Force hostage rescue mission.

The permission to use foreign ground facilities and access to adequate refueling services can be one and the same requirement, as in the Entebbe scenario, or two different requirements, as evidenced in the U.S. operations. General T. R. Milton USAF (Ret.), for example, argues in a post-Entebbe operational assessment that adequate tanker services may become a paramount consideration in approving future hostage rescue missions.[118] U.S. refueling capabilities evidenced in MAC fixed-wing tanker platforms and its ARRS rotary refuelable craft could offer distinct advantages in future U.S. extraction operations.'Each rescue mission, however, will need to be evaluated for suitable requirements. This assessment will apply to choice of aircraft, bases versus staging areas, and, when applicable, refueling needs.

A final logistical consideration needs mentioning. None of the rescue operations considered here entailed seeking overflight rights for the extraction effort. Permission to fly over friendly or hostile territory was never sought because opposition was neither anticipated nor expected to constitute a threat to the rescue penetration. That situation, however, is not universal. Hostage rescue planners in the future may well need to gain foreign approval for safe passage of a rescue force. Without prior approval, an air rescue force may be fired on en route to its target. The Egyptian experience at Larnaca Airport in Cyprus in 1978 serves as a cautionary reminder.

COMMAND, CONTROL, AND COMMUNICATIONS

If logistics are considered as the "horses" for hostage rescue, then the C^3 function might qualify as the "reins." Rescue missions necessarily engage both civilian and military professionals in the planning, deployment, and often the operations of an assault. C^3 capabilities ensure that the military and civilian actions most benefit the ultimate goal, which is the safe and rapid extraction of hostages. The paramount need for close coordination among mission elements in hostage rescue puts a high premium on C^3 assets.

Despite the superb military execution of the Son Tay penetration and apparently adequate command and control, a number of communications problems developed.[119] Two EC-121 airborne radar platforms encountered mechanical problems that prevented adequate monitoring of frequency modulation (FM), ultrahigh frequency (UHF), and very high frequency (VHF) radio transmissions. One of the craft aborted its mission because of a broken oil line and the loss of an engine in flight. The other EC-121 had malfunctions in its onboard communications console, preventing receipt of messages from Colonel Simons's raiders in the Son Tay prison compound. Overall command contact with the Son Tay air and ground force became impossible. In his command post in Vietnam, General Manor could not receive visual display of the rescue force because a Marine-operated "computer-buffer" failed, and overall communications were spotty because of local interference. Navy jamming of nearby North Vietnamese radar signals may have caused the distortion. A SAC RC-135 radio relay aircraft did not receive its scheduled add-on equipment for monitoring extended frequency range because the pieces failed to arrive. As a result, the RC-135 could only relay ground transmissions from Son Tay when simultaneous FM and UHF contact occurred. Because of the multiple communications problems in the Son Tay mission, it is also doubtful that President Nixon could have re-called the rescue force had it been necessary.

After the Mayaguez operation, the GAO commended the C^3 functions as "expeditious."[120] The communications system provided a direct voice link be-tween the National Command authorities and officers on the scene, including the airborne command post and the Marine task force on Koh Tang.[121] Oddly enough, communications between Washington and the Gulf of Siam, 12,500 miles away, were far better than local communications. The U.S. military com-mand in Thailand, from where the Marines departed, had no direct communica-tions with U.S. forces on Koh Tang. Consequently, the Marine assault group could not request air strikes because they lost their tactical communications equipment when the helicopter carrying it crashed and burned.[122]

Two criticisms of the command and control function emerged as well. The entire Mayaguez operation was run and controlled from the Oval Office. The instantaneous communications encouraged central direction. A number of mili-tary operations people observed that centralized control in Washington hindered the efficient performance and timely distribution of the available military re-sources. The president's decision to withdraw the Marines from Koh Tang in darkness, for example, prevented the search for U.S. personnel missing and wounded. Asked if there was too much control from Washington, one Pentagon general responded, "Let's say there was enough."[123]

Perhaps the most serious criticism of command and control resulted from the bombing of the Cambodian mainland at the same moment the freed Maya-guez crew was sighted. There are claims that a time lag of 20 to 40 minutes existed between the notification to the president of the crew's release and the Cambodian bombing.[124] Evidence of this time interval spurred charges of "in-adequate civilian control," "loose bombing plans," and punitive bombing.[125]

Mayaguez illustrates an operation wherein communications were "taxed to the limit," as reported by the commander of the USS *Holt*.[126] According to one communications officer, 3,000 priority messages were exchanged between Wash-ington and field commanders in a 24-hour period.[127] The complexity and un-certainty of the Mayaguez mission perhaps insured some of the communications problems that unfolded. One appealing suggestion, made by the GAO, is that a "satellite hotline" be created to link all world capitals.[128] This system, to-gether with the updated U.S. Worldwide Military Command and Communica-tions System (WWMCCS), could well provide more dependable communications in crisis situations.

Details on Israeli C^3 in the Entebbe mission remain very sparse. A Boeing 707 command and communications platform over Entebbe Airport maintained voice link contact between the ground assault force, the medical team in Nairo-bi, and political authorities in Tel Aviv.[129] A number of unconfirmed reports suggest that the United States permitted Israeli use of U.S. communications fa-cilities. The Israeli tradition in command and control varies considerably with

U.S. custom and practice. Once political authorities decide on a military operation, the Israeli military commanders decide how to implement the orders. While there are severe penalties for improper execution or deviation from civilian guidelines, including dismissal and criminal indictment, there is a pervasive confidence between the civil and military authorities. Perhaps this attitude stems from the Israeli view that every citizen is a soldier, an unavoidable Israeli reality for its 30 years of nationhood. Israel, unlike the United States, remains a militarized society.

Aside from the obvious military efficiencies provided by adequate C^3 functions, proper command, control, and communications assets have a direct impact on two other areas. Unless there is confidence in C^3 capabilities, civilian leaders will be reluctant to deploy a rescue force. If the operation goes awry, it is the top officials of the government who become most vulnerable to criticism, if not removal from office. This latter prospect appeared likely for Israeli Prime Minister Yitzhak Rabin if the Entebbe rescue had failed or floundered. By their nature, hostage rescue missions easily make chief executives either instant heroes or unmentionable blackguards. The second and related area on which C^3 operations have an impact is that of the domestic and international reactions to conduct of the rescue.

POSTRAID REACTION

Determining the success or failure of hostage rescue missions obviously hinges on more than hostage recovery, though that certainly is a prerequisite. All three of the missions considered here reflect the importance of postraid reactions to the military operation. Needless to say, public reaction is a mix of both objective and subjective assessments of the conduct and value of rescue missions.

The Son Tay rescue attempt prompted ambivalent but generally negative public reactions. While the effort to free imprisoned POWs sparked a temporary surge of hope among a large segment of the U.S. public, by the fall of 1970, the majority of Americans had become weary of the Vietnam War, with its high casualties, attendant inflation, and elusive claims of "peace at hand." The raid prompted a generally unfavorable congressional reaction and gave new fuel to a revival of antiwar sentiment in the Senate.[130] Testimony by Secretary of Defense Laird further ignited opposition on Capitol Hill. He withheld information on military aspects of the rescue mission; when questioned on why he did so, Laird said he had not been asked about certain aspects.[131] Laird also incensed the Senate Foreign Relations Committee when he bluntly asserted that future rescue missions would not require congressional consultation.[132]

National newspapers generally reacted negatively as well. Characterized as a "desperation effort" and an "abortive exercise in military theatrics," newspaper columnists related the mission to the growing problems and deceit of the Nixon administration.[133] Foreign official and press reactions ranged from a studied disinterest to mild support and ringing criticism. While the London *Times*, for example, praised "the superb execution of the assault," it also concluded that Son Tay was "another intelligence disaster typical of the Vietnam war."[134] Perhaps the most positive view of the rescue effort came much later, when it was learned that the mission boosted the morale of U.S. prisoners in North Vietnamese prison camps.[135]

The Mayaguez operation initially spurred a burst of public enthusiasm, perhaps colorfully related by Senator Barry Goldwater's comment that the U.S. action "showed we still got some balls in this country."[136] But as the casualty figures climbed and flaws in the military operation came to light, the mission generated more criticism. "Hawk" and "dove" interpretations became fashionable again. Initially, Congress grumbled more about alleged violations of the 1973 War Powers Act than about the military execution of the mission.[137] As time passed, substantive congressional criticism of the mission went beyond procedural concerns, but it finally trailed off.[138]

Initially rather circumspect in its judgments, the national press progressively found more fault with the operation, suggesting it was no "famous victory,"[139] was perhaps unnecessary,[140] and violated "common sense."[141] With some minor allusions to "gunboat diplomacy," North Atlantic Treaty Organization (NATO) countries and Japan stood behind the U.S. action.[142] Other foreign opinion tended to be unfavorable for the most part.[143] Although criticism of the military handling of the operation appeared, by far the most negative judgments were pointed at President Ford and his advisors for their political decisions.

Reactions to the Entebbe raid perhaps illustrate the old saw that you cannot argue with success. The Son Tay raid brought no POWs home. The Mayaguez operation did not directly force the release of the crewmen. But the Entebbe mission retrieved most of the large hostage group, with a minimum of casualties. Domestic Israeli reactions without exception were ebullient and laudatory. Israeli success seemed to ratify the Biblical prophecy that the Jews were still Jehovah's chosen people. Disturbed by the postraid dramatics, Israeli General Gur warned that such effusiveness stimulated a false sense of national euphoria.[144]

U.S. press statements saw the Entebbe mission as "an effective declaration of independence from international blackmail"[145] and viewed it as an "audacious airborne rescue."[146] Publicly condemnatory, black Africa nevertheless seemed privately to admire the Israeli feat, especially since the target was Idi Amin of Uganda.[147] The OAU predictably condemned the Israeli operation, but a resolution in the UN to censure Israel failed to pass.[148] Public reaction pointed to the emergence of an 11th commandment: "Thou shalt not bow down to terrorism."[149] For the Israeli Entebbe mission, there was the right mix of drama, pathos, and daring to cultivate a very favorable postraid public reaction.

A FINAL ASSESSMENT

This chapter attempted to select and examine those aspects of the Son Tay, Mayaguez, and Entebbe missions that most contributed to the success or failure of the mission. Other important considerations, such as mission cost, hostile casualties, specialized training, military readiness, international law, and so forth, have not been treated. Lessons derived here are certainly not definitive and may only be suggestive of anticipated future performance. Each rescue scenario has been and will be different. What is suggested is that these issues proved decisive in past hostage rescues and therefore need to be examined seriously. The thundering reality of such rescues is that you only go around once and that one effort better succeed.

There is no need at this point to summarize all of the lessons learned from close analysis of these rescue operations. Some of the deficiencies may already have been remedied. Others reflect deep institutional problems that have emerged and will no doubt surface again. Successes and failures evident in hostage rescue, however, do offer some guideposts for the planning of similar future operations. Despite his wonderfully sophisticated technology, man still learns by trial and error. The irony of rescue operations is that there is very little room for error.

While constant change characterizes the global environment, there exist some fluid constants. Among others, these include the existence of transnational terrorism, small group access to sophisticated weapons, the vulnerability of international air passengers, and the rising frustrations of repressed minorities. Most nations possess neither the inclination nor the capabilities to address these problems. A handful of states officially encourage some of these terrorist activities.

No one would argue that a military rescue is the first or preferred solution to hostage seizures. Risks are unattractively high. Above all, preventive measures can obviate the need for hostage rescue in the first place. Proper maritime warning procedures may have prevented the Mayaguez seizure. Even minimum airport security precautions at Athens might have prohibited armed PFLP terrorists from boarding the Air France plane. Government agencies, such as the departments of State and Defense, now regularly train their personnel in hostage prevention techniques. International business corporations increasingly do likewise. These government and private efforts emphasize the minimal cost and basic common sense that thoughtful preventive measures offer.

When preventive measures, diplomacy, political pressure, and other modes of hostage protection and release fail, military rescue missions employing force become the last resort. Immediate or early resort to the use of force as a pattern may predispose future captors to harm their hostages because of anticipated military action. It must be remembered that the purpose of rescue missions is to extract the hostages safely. Hostage rescue in a hostile environment requires the well-honed skills of a professional military team working closely with the political authorities under severe time constraints. Hostage lives depend on how well the politico-military team does its job.

NOTES

1. Neil Scheehan, "U.S. Information on P.O.W.'s Appears Limited," New York Times, November 24, 1970, p. 16.

2. Benjamin F. Schemmer, The Raid (New York: Harper & Row, 1976), p. 67.

3. Walter Laqueur,"The Continuing Failure of Terrorism," Harper's 253 (November 1976): 69; Brian M. Jenkins, International Terrorism: A New Kind of Warfare (Rand Paper, no. P-5261) (Santa Monica, Calif.: Rand, June 1974), p. 4; Brian M. Jenkins, Hostages and Their Captors—Friends and Lovers (Rand Study, no. P-5519) (Santa Monica, Calif.: Rand, October 1975), pp. 1–2; and International and Transnational Terrorism: Diagnosis and Prognosis (Research Study, no. PR 76 10030)(Washington, D.C.: CIA, April 1976), p. 19.

4. William Stevenson, 90 Minutes at Entebbe (New York: Bantam Books, 1976), p. 29.

5. Tom Fenton (narrator), "Rescue at Entebbe: How They Saved the Hostages," CBS News Special Report, September 14, 1976.

6. "A Daring Rescue in Uganda," Newsweek 88 (July 12, 1976): 29.

7. "Condemned by Arab League," New York Times, July 2, 1976, p. 3.

8. U.S., Congress, House, Seizure of the Mayaguez, Hearings before the Subcommittee on International Political and Military Affairs of the Committee on International Relations, 94th Cong., 2d sess., October 4, 1976, pt.IV (Washington, D.C.: Government Printing Office, 1976), p. 74.

9. Ibid., 94th. Cong., 1st sess., May 14–15, 1975, pt. I (Washington, D.C.: Government Printing Office, 1975), p. 13.

10. Ibid., June 19 and 25, 1975, and July 25, 1975, pt. II (Washington, D.C.: Government Printing Office, 1975), pp. 157–58, 174; U.S., Congress, Senate, "The 'Mayaguez' Incident," Congressional Record, 1975, 121, p. S11572; U.S., Congress, House, Seizure of Mayaguez, pt. IV, p. 68; and R. W. Apple, "Timing of Attack Raises Questions," New York Times, May 16, 1975, p. 14.

11. Apple, "Timing of Attack," p. 14; U.S., Congress, House, Seizure of Mayaguez, pt. I, p. 54; U.S., Congress, House, Seizure of Mayaguez, pt. II, pp. 157–58; U.S., Congress, House, Seizure of Mayaguez, pt. IV, p. 60.

12. U.S., Congress, House, Seizure of Mayaguez, pt. II, p. 159.

13. Roy Rowan, The Four Days of Mayaguez (New York: Norton, 1975), p. 174, and "A Chronology of the Mayaguez Episode," New York Times, May 16, 1975, p. 14.

14. U.S., Congress, House, Seizure of Mayaguez, pt. IV, p. 60.

15. Ibid., p. 125, and Apple, "Timing of Attack."

16. U.S., Congress, House, Seizure of Mayaguez, pt. IV, pp. 68–69.

17. Ibid., pt. II, pp. 157–58, 174.

18. Christopher S. Wren, "Soviet Withholds Comment on Raid," New York Times, May 16, 1975, p. 15, and "China Says Retaking of Vessel by U.S. Was an 'Act of Piracy',"New York Times, May 16, 1975, p. 15.

19. Rowan, Four Days, pp. 68, 80.

20. "Thailand Reports Marines Arrival in Ship's Seizure," New York Times, May 14, 1975, pp. 1, 18; James M. Naughton, "Praise for the President: Domestic and Foreign Triumph Is Seen as U.S. Reassesses Its Presence Abroad," New York Times, May 16, 1975, p. 1; James A. Nathan, "The Mayaguez, Presidential War, and Congressional Senescence,"

Intellect 104 (February 1976): 361; Michael Morrow, "Ford: Fastest Gun in the East," *Far Eastern Economic Reivew* 88 (May 30, 1975): 11; Roger Morris, "What to Make of Maya-guez," *The New Republic* 172 (June 14, 1975): 10; and Rowan, *Four Days*, p. 68.

21. "War-Making after Vietnam," *The Economist* 255 (May 24, 1975): 63.

22. Yeshayahu Ben-Porat et al., *Entebbe Rescue* (New York: Dell, 1977), p. 160.

23. Stevenson, *90 Minutes*, p. 76, and Terence Smith, "Israelis Staged Raid Rehersal," New York *Times*, July 9, 1976, p. 2.

24. "Rescue at Entebbe: How the Israelis Did It," *The Reader's Digest* (October 1976): 125; "The Fallout from Entebbe," *Newsweek* 88 (July 19, 1976): 43; and Steven-son, *90 Minutes*, p. 89.

25. "53 Minutes at Entebbe," *Sunday Times Weekly Review* (London), July 18, 1976, p. 25, and Stevenson, *90 Minutes*, pp. 41, 46.

26. "Rescue at Entebbe: How the Israelis Did It," pp. 124-25; "53 Minutes at Entebbe," p. 25; Stevenson, *90 Minutes*, p. 77; and Philip Ross, "The Illustrated Story of the Great Israeli Rescue," *New York* 9 (August 2, 1976): 34.

27. "53 Minutes at Entebbe," p. 26, and Stevenson, *90 Minutes*, p. 33.

28. Stevenson, *90 Minutes*, p. 92, and Ben-Porat et al., *Entebbe Rescue*, p. 255.

29. Stevenson, *90 Minutes*, p. 78.

30. Ross, "Illustrated Story of Israeli Rescue," p. 34, and "53 Minutes at Entebbe," p. 25.

31. Michael T. Kaufman, "Kenyan Officials Deny Role in Raid," New York *Times*, July 5, 1976, p. 4.

32. Ben-Porat et al., *Entebbe Rescue*, pp. 175-76, and "53 Minutes at Entebbe," p. 26.

33. Ben-Porat et al., *Entebbe Rescue*, p. 211.

34. Fenton, "Rescue at Entebbe."

35. "53 Minutes at Entebbe," p. 26.

36. Schemmer, *The Raid*, pp. 28, 30.

37. Heather David, *Operation: Rescue* (New York: Pinnacle Books, 1971), p. 41.

38. Schemmer, *The Raid*, p. 37.

39. "Regular Flights Made Over North," New York *Times*, November 22, 1970, p. 27, and Robert Smith, "Raid on a P.O.W. Camp: Build-Up—and Letdown," New York *Times*, November 27, 1970, p. 1.

40. Capt. Larry Chesley, *Seven Years in Hanoi: A POW Tells His Story* (Salt Lake City: Bookcraft, 1973), p. 111, and Stephen A. Rowan, *They Wouldn't Let Us Die: The Prisoners of War Tell Their Story* (New York: Jonathan David, 1973), p. 167.

41. Schemmer, *The Raid*, p. 93.

42. Ibid., pp. 98-99, and "AFJ Exclusive: First Publication of SR-71 High-Altitude Photos," *Armed Forces Journal International* 113 (July 1976): 22.

43. "AFJ Exclusive," p. 23.

44. Schemmer, *The Raid*, p. 100.

45. Ibid., pp. 172-73, 176.

46. Ibid., p. 95.

47. Ibid., pp. 80, 95.

48. "AFJ Exclusive," p. 22.

49. Schemmer, *The Raid*, p. 101.

50. Ibid., p. 184.

51. Ibid., p. 94; "AFJ Exclusive," p. 23; and Robert Shaplen, *The Road From War: Vietnam 1965-1971* (New York: Harper & Row, 1971), p. 422.

52. Tad Szulc, "Laird Would Seek Bombing If Enemy Breached 'Accord'," New York *Times*, November 25, 1970, p. 8.

53. Lt. Col. Donald E. Carlile, USA, "The Mayaguez Incident—Crisis Management," *Military Review* 61 (October 1976): 12.

54. U.S., Congress, House, *Seizure of Mayaguez*, pt. IV, p. 72.

55. Ibid.

56. Ibid., p. 73.

57. Ibid.

58. Ibid., pp. 90, 104, and "'Mayday' for the Mayaguez," *United States Naval Institute Proceedings* 102 (November 1976): 104.

59. U.S., Congress, House, *Seizure of Mayaguez*, pt. IV, pp. 60, 91.

60. "'Mayday' for the Mayaguez," p. 105.

61. U.S., Congress, House, *Seizure of Mayaguez*, pt. IV, p. 82.

62. Ibid., p. 95.

63. Ibid., p. 92.

64. Ibid., p. 76.

65. Ibid., pp. 59–60.

66. Ibid., p. 95.

67. "'Mayday' for the Mayaguez," p. 93.

68. Morris, "What to Make of Mayaguez," p. 10, and Maj. Burton R. Moore, USAF, *The Light Was the Mayaguez* (Norfolk, Va.: Armed Forces Staff College, December 9, 1975), p. 13.

69. Lyman B. Kirkpatrick, Jr., *Captains Without Eyes: Intelligence Failures in World War II* (New York: Macmillan, 1969), pp. 5–6.

70. Moore, *Light Was the Mayaguez*, p. 13; "The Mayaguez—What Went Right, Wrong," *U.S. News & World Report* 78 (June 2, 1975): 29; and Morris, "What to Make of Mayaguez," p. 10.

71. U.S., Congress, Senate, *Bombing Operations and the Prisoner-of-War Rescue Mission in North Vietnam*, Hearing before Committee on Foreign Relations, 91st Cong., 2d sess. (Washington, D.C.: Government Printing Office, 1971), p. 25.

72. Schemmer, *The Raid*, p. 59.

73. Ibid., p. 229.

74. Ibid., p. 8.

75. "'Mayday' for the Mayaguez," p. 101.

76. "Israel Apparently Had Raid in Mind All Along," New York *Times*, July 5, 1976, p. 3.

77. William Beecher, "U.S. Rescue Force Landed Within 23 Miles of Hanoi, but It Found POWs Gone," New York *Times*, November 24, 1970, p. 1.

78. U.S., Congress, Senate, *Bombing Operations and Prisoner-of-War Rescue Mission*, p. 10.

79. "AFJ Exclusive," p. 20, and Schemmer, *The Raid*, pp. 204, 207.

80. "Text of Pentagon News Conference on U.S. Rescue Mission into North Vietnam," New York *Times*, November 24, 1970, p. 12, and Schemmer, *The Raid*, p. 5.

81. U.S., Congress, House, *Seizure of Mayaguez*, pt. I, p. 39.

82. U.S., Congress, House, *Seizure of Mayaguez*, Hearings before the Subcommittee on International Political and Military Affairs of the Committee on International Relations, 94th Cong., 1st sess., July 31, 1975, and September 12, 1975, pt. III (Washington, D.C.: Government Printing Office, 1976), p. 258.

83. Carlile, "Mayaguez Incident," p. 10.

84. U.S., Congress, House, *Seizure of Mayaguez*, pt III, p. 94.

85. Rowan, *Four Days*, pp. 215–16, and Apple, "Timing of Attack," p. 14.

86. Phillip Shabecoff, "23 Dead in Copter Crash Related to the Mayaguez," New York *Times*, May 22, 1975, p. 1, and Rowan, *Four Days*, p. 90.

87. "Mayaguez—What Went Right, Wrong," p. 29.

88. "Managing the Navy," *Newsweek* 90 (July 18, 1977): 12.

89. "Mayaguez–What Went Right, Wrong," p. 29, and "Managing the Navy."

90. "Chronology of Mayaguez Episode."

91. U.S., Congress, House, *Seizure of Mayaguez*, pt. I, p. 9, and Moore, *Light Was the Mayaguez*, p. 13.

92. U.S., Congress, House, *Seizure of Mayaguez*, pt. IV, p. 87.

93. Ibid., p. 59.

94. "The Mayaguez–What Went Right, Wrong," p. 29.

95. U.S., Congress, House, *Seizure of Mayaguez*, pt. IV, p. 96.

96. Stevenson, *90 Minutes*, p. 99.

97. "Fallout from Entebbe," p. 44, and Ben-Porat et al., p. 289.

98. Stevenson, *90 Minutes*, p. 100.

99. Ibid., p. 76.

100. "53 Minutes at Entebbe," p. 25.

101. Ben-Porat et al., p. 275.

102. Ross, "Illustrated Story of Israeli Rescue," p. 38.

103. Ibid.

104. "53 Minutes at Entebbe," p. 27.

105. "Hijacking in Reverse: Israelis Go 2,500 Miles to Rescue Hostages," New York *Times*, July 11, 1976, sec. 4, p. 1.

106. "Army Chief Tells Story of Raid to Free Hostages in Uganda: 53 Minutes in Entebbe," The Jerusalem *Post* (weekly overseas edition, no. 819), July 13, 1976, p. 3.

107. S. H. H. Young and John W. R. Taylor," Gallery of USAF Weapons," *Air Force Magazine* (annual Air Force Almanac issue) 59 (May 1976): 118.

108. Stevenson, *90 Minutes*, p. 93.

109. Ibid., p. 126.

110. "Thais Report Withdrawal of Marines after Protest," New York *Times*, May 15, 1975, p. 1; "Thais Had Set Deadline," New York *Times*, May 15, 1975, p. 18; and Malcolm W. Browne, "Thais Accuse U.S. of Breach of Faith," New York *Times*, May 16, 1975, p. 15.

111. Eleanor C. McDowell, *Digest of United States Practice in International Law, 1975* (Department of State Publication, no. 8865 (Washington, D.C.: September 1976), p. 15.

112. Malcolm W. Browne, "Thais, Angry with U.S., Call Their Envoy Home," New York *Times*, May 17, 1975, p. 1.

113. Stevenson, *90 Minutes*, pp. 66–67, and "53 Minutes at Entebbe," p. 26.

114. "53 Minutes at Entebbe," p. 26.

115. "The Rescue: We Do the Impossible," *Time* (July 12, 1976): 21–22, and "How the Israelis Pulled It Off," *Newsweek* 88 (July 26, 1976): 45.

116. Ross, "Illustrated Story of Israeli Rescue," p. 38.

117. Stevenson, *90 Minutes*, p. 77.

118. Gen. T. R. Milton, USAF (Ret.), "Tankers, Task Forces, and Terrorism," *Air Force Magazine* 59 (September 1976), p. 108.

119. Schemmer, *The Raid*, p. 211.

120. U.S., Congress, House, *Seizure of Mayaguez*, pt. IV, p. 59.

121. Moore, *Light Was the Mayaguez*, p. 8; U.S., Congress, House, *Seizure of Mayaguez*, pt. II, p. 181; U.S., Congress, House, *Seizure of Mayaguez*, pt. IV, p. 85; "Mayaguez–What Went Right, Wrong."

122. U.S., Congress, House, *Seizure of Mayaguez*, pt. IV, p. 86.

123. "Mayageuz–What Went Right, Wrong."

124. Morris, "What to Make of Mayaguez," p. 10; Morrow, "Ford: Fastest Gun in the East," p. 11; David Binder, "2D Cambodia Raids Disclosed by U.S.," New York *Times*, May 17, 1975, p. 11; and U.S., Congress, House, *Seizure of Mayaguez*, pt. II, p. 181.

125. Morris, "What to Make of Mayaguez," pp. 10–12; Binder, "2D Cambodia Raids Disclosed"; and U.S., Congress, House, *Seizure of Mayaguez*, pt. IV, p. 96.

126. "'Mayday' for the Mayaguez," p. 97.

127. Personal Interview, U.S. Air Force officer, November 29, 1976.

128. U.S., Congress, House, *Seizure of Mayaguez*, pt. IV, p. 61.

129. "53 Minutes at Entebbe," p. 27, and Ben-Porat et al., *Entebbe Rescue*, p. 300.

130. Beecher, "U.S. Rescue Force Landed Within 23 Miles of Hanoi," and Schemmer, *The Raid*, p. 230.

131. U.S., Congress, Senate, *Bombing Operations and Prisoner-of-War Rescue Mission*, pp. 6–7; Hedrick Smith, "U.S. Said to Offer a New Justification for Raids in North," New York *Times*, December 1, 1970, p. 4; "Mr. Laird's Credibility Gap" (editorial), New York *Times*, December 3, 1970, p. 46; "Laird Reveals U.S. Planned to Keep Camp Raid Secret," New York *Times*, November 26, 1970, pp. 1, 18; and Schemmer, *The Raid*, p. 225.

132. Beecher, "How P.O.W. Camp Raid Was Planned," p. 18.

133. Shaplen, *Road From War*, p. 422, and Max Frankel, "Nixon and the Rescue Mission," New York *Times*, November 24, 1970, p. 14.

134. Fred Emery, "Prison Camp Searched, *Times* (London), November 24, 1970, p. 14; "Mr. Laird's Threat of More Bombing," *Times* (London), November 26, 1970, p. 1.

135. Robinson Risner, *The Passing of the Night: My Seven Years as a Prisoner of the North Vietnamese* (New York: Random House, 1973), 207; John G. Hubbell, *P.O.W.* (New York: Reader's Digest Press, 1976), p. 538; and Chesley, *Seven Years in Hanoi*, p. 114.

136. U.S., Congress, House, *Seizure of Mayaguez*, pt. III, p. 282.

137. Phillip Shabecoff, "Ford Is Backed; Senate Unit Endorses His Right to Order Military Action," New York *Times*, May 15, 1975, p. 18.

138. U.S., Congress, Senate, "The 'Mayaguez' Incident," p. S11572, and Shabecoff, "Ford Is Backed."

139. James Reston, "'Twas a Famous Victory'," New York *Times*, May 16, 1975, p. 37.

140. Tom Wicker, "Raising Some Mayaguez Questions," New York *Times*, May 16, 1975, p. 37.

141. Editorial, Washington *Post*, May 14, 1975, p. A10.

142. Alvin Shuster, "U.S. Action Backed in Europe, but Some See 'Gunboat Politics'," New York *Times*, May 16, 1975, p. 15.

143. "War-Making after Vietnam," p. 64, and William Shawcross, "Making the Most of Mayageuz," *Far Eastern Economic Review* 88 (May 30, 1975): 11.

144. "The Unmaking of Entebbe," *Newsweek* 88 (November 8, 1976): 42.

145. "A Legend Is Born," New York *Times*, July 6, 1976, p. 24.

146. "Israel Apparently Had Raid in Mind All Along."

147. "Amin Says Uganda Retains the Right to Reply to Raid," New York *Times*, July 6, 1976, p. 1; Michael T. Kaufman, "An African Reaction: Public Anger, Private Approval," New York *Times*, July 6, 1976, p. 3; and "The Fallout from Entebbe," p. 41.

148. "Amin Loses Another One," *Newsweek* 87 (July 26, 1976): 51.

149. "Rescue at Entebbe: How the Israelis Did It," p. 128.

19

THE GERMAN GOVERNMENT RESPONSE TO TERRORISM

Hans J. Horchem

TERRORIST ORGANIZATIONS IN GERMANY

The Baader-Meinhof Gang, or the
Red Army Faction

German terrorism consists of three centers of activity: the Red Army Faction, the June 2 Movement, and the Revolutionary Cells. The Red Army Faction is the most dangerous of these three. It has the most consequential political aims, the most convincing ideological conception, the greatest criminal potential, and it receives support from groups that up till now have not yet contravened the law. The Red Army Faction is responsible for the serious terrorist attacks of 1977. The movement was responsible for the murder of Attorney General Siegfried Buback and his guards; it was responsible for the killing of the banker Jürgen Ponto; and it attempted to destroy the buildings of the Federal Justice offices with rockets. Its members, who kidnapped Schleyer and killed his guards, finally killed Schleyer, the president of the Employers Federation, on October 18. The Red Army Faction is the oldest German terrorist organization. It was born with the violent release of Andreas Baader from prison on May 14, 1970. Ulrike Meinhof and Horst Mahler took part in this action. Meinhof justified this action in a statement during her trial on September 13, 1974, calling it an exemplary action. She said that the action comprised all the elements of the strategy of the armed anti-imperialist struggle.

The armed anti-imperialist struggle aims at destroying the imperialistic feudal system, politically, economically, and militarily. The anti-imperialist struggle is being conducted in international actions against the defense allies of the United States—in particular, NATO—and the German Federal Armed Forces. In the national area, the struggle is conducted against the armed forces of the state apparatus, which represents the monopoly of power of the ruling class, that is, the police, the Federal frontier police, and the security services. Also mentioned are the power structures of the multinationals, that is, state and nonstate bureaucracies, the parties, trade unions, and the media. These theses of Meinhof can still be found in the latest publications of the various commandos of the Red Army Faction. Wherever such political aims are mentioned, so-called U.S. imperialism is mentioned as well.

The tracts of Mahler and Meinhof are of considerable importance for the political motivation and justification of all the German terrorists—not just for the Red Army Faction. The three main tracts (the concept of the earlier guerrilla armed struggle in Western Europe, urban guerrilla warfare, and the class struggle) appeared between April 1971 and April 1972. The language of Meinhof has affected the linguistic style of the various commandos to this day.

Between May 11 and May 24, 1972, the Red Army Faction commandos carried out six serious bomb attacks in Frankfurt, Munich, Augsburg, Hamburg, Karlsruhe, and Heidelberg. Four persons were killed and 19 injured. This escalation brought about an intensive search. The population were encouraged to pass on information to the security authorities. As a result of information passed on by the public, the following members of the Red Army Faction were arrested between June 1 and June 15, 1972: Baader, Meinhof, Holger Meins, Jan Karl Raspe, Gudrun Ensslin, and Gerhard Muller.

A year later, in the summer of 1975, the Red Army Faction began to build a follow-up group. This group founded other groups in Hamburg, Frankfurt, and Amsterdam. It intended, through the creation of sufficient logistical measures, to prepare for the main target of the Red Army Faction, namely, the release of their prisoners. They raised the necessary money through bank robberies. On February 4, 1974, this group was destroyed by the concerted action of the security authorities in Hamburg, Frankfurt, and Amsterdam. Nine members were arrested and have been condemned to long prison sentences.

A year later, a new follow-up group was formed, which carried out the attack on the German embassy in Stockholm on April 24, 1975, and during which two officials, the military attaché and the commercial attaché, were shot dead. The terrorists were attempting, by way of these murders, to press for the release of the Red Army Faction prisoners. They expected that the Federal government would react in the same way as they did over the kidnapping of the Christian Democratic Union politician, Peter Lorenz, which had been carried out by a different terrorist organization.

In 1976, it became clear that the Red Army Faction had built up a further follow-up group. On November 30, 1976, the lawyers Siegfried Haag and Roland Mayer were arrested during an autobahn check. Papers found on the two arrested persons showed that new actions were being planned. The bank notes they carried had been stolen during bank robberies in Cologne and Hamburg.

Despite the arrest of the group leader, Haag, the group became strong enough to be able to carry out serious violent actions in 1977, for example, the murder of Buback and his guards, the murder of Ponto, and the murder of Schleyer and his guards.

The Red Army Faction was able to carry out its armed struggle even after the arrest of its most important members. They could rely on a circle of supporters who kept up the link between the arrested terrorists and the "operational" ones. Several lawyers had an essential function for these links. They also succeeded in recruiting new, mostly young lawyers for their cause.

The Red Army Faction succeeded, with the help of supporting groups, in developing propaganda actions designed to portray West Germany as a fascist state and to justify the aims of the terrorists.

During this campaign, the supporters of the Red Army Faction alleged that the imprisoned Red Army members were subjected to "isolation torture." In reality, they enjoyed considerable privileges over other prisoners. Their cells were bigger. They had radio, television, and as many as several thousand books in their cells. The campaigns of their supporters often produced understanding for the Red Army cause in Germany, and in neighboring countries, anti-German standpoints were mobilized, especially in Marxist and neo-Marxist circles.

The campaigns were organized by "committees against torture." Out of these committees developed the Red Army supporting groups, which still exist. They are called Anti Fascist Group, Solidarity Committee for Political Prisoners, or Red Help. They exist in various major cities in Germany, for example, Hamburg, Wiesbaden, Berlin, Frankfurt, and Kaiserslautern. The majority of current active Red Army terrorists stem from these supporting groups. They went underground in 1975 and 1976.

The liaison offices for these groups, which were spread all over West Germany, were lawyers' offices. The most important of these communication centers were the offices of the lawyers Groenewold (Hamburg), Becker/Haag (Heidelberg), and Croissant (Stuttgart). These liaison offices have in the meantime been made ineffective and the lawyers arrested or put to trial.

The organization of the Red Army Faction consists today of three streams:

1. The operating terrorists: they organize themselves into commandos of five to 12 activists for operations. There are about 40 of these, more than half of them women.

2. The lawyers: they act as the liaison between the imprisoned terrorists, the active ones, and the supporting groups.

3. The supporting groups: they organize the campaigns to mobilize the sympathizers in Germany and abroad. Their members are the "criminals without crime." They form the reservoir for the up and coming terrorists. There are about 150 of these in the whole of West Germany, about half of them women. The main centers for these are in Hamburg and Baden-Wurttemberg.

The fact that the Red Army Faction is the most dangerous terrorist organization is clear from the following statistics: (1) of the 40 German terrorists on the wanted list, 29 of them belong to the Red Army Faction, and (2) of the 90 terrorists who are imprisoned, 45 belong to the Red Army Faction.

The Movement of June 2

The June 2 movement has never had the same consistency as the Red Army Faction. It never succeeded in formulating political aims or developing supporting campaigns, such as the campaign against torture.

In their practical tactics, the June 2 movement was often ahead of the Red Army Faction. This is borne out by the kidnapping of Lorenz in Berlin on March 27, 1975. The Federal Government was in a difficult position, as they did not know the hiding place of Lorenz. They gave in to the terrorists' demands to release five prisoners, who were flown out to South Yemen. The June 2 movement was based in Berlin. In the autumn of 1975, it was largely destroyed. One year later, on July 7, 1976, four female members of the group escaped from a Berlin prison. On May 27, 1978, a further member was freed from the same prison. This prisoner, Till Meyer, was arrested, together with three further terrorists on June 22, 1978, in Bulgaria and returned to West Germany. The members of the June 2 movement who had escaped and been "freed" have not committed any further attacks in the name of their group.

The Revolutionary Cells

Since November 1973, the revolutionary cells have committed more than 20 incendiary or bomb attacks. Since 1976, their potential danger has increased, demonstrated by their willingness to commit murder, as was shown in two bomb attacks in Frankfurt on June 1 and December 1, 1976. It is probable that this group, unlike the Red Army, does not operate entirely underground. The majority of their members are not known to the security authorities.

INTERNATIONAL CONNECTIONS

Training in the Middle East

Andreas Baader was released on May 14, 1970. On May 15, 1970, a first bank robbery took place in Berlin. In June, members of the hard core of the Red Army Faction went via Damascus to Jordan to be militarily trained in a Fatah camp. At this time, there was a struggle between the armed Fatah Palestinians and the Jordanian troops, who eventually removed the Palestinians from Jordan. The stay by the Germans did not prove to be a success. The group only indulged in discussions.

Horst Mahler, who, after his return in August 1970, only remained free for another two months, concluded in an essay on the armed struggle that "a fighting group can only exist through struggle itself. All attempts to organize and train a group outside real conditions lead to ridiculous results, often with tragic consequences."[1]

Since the Red Army Faction has always operated independently, the hijacking of the Lufthansa plane in Majorca, whose passengers were eventually freed in Mogadishu, was not planned and coordinated in advance with the Palestinians. The latter only wanted to use the situation that existed after the kidnapping of Schleyer to try to secure the release of two members of PFLP, who had been arrested in Turkey, as well as to obtain a ransom.

Common Operations

German terrorists were also involved in the logistical preparations for the attack on the Israeli Olympic team in Munich in 1972, which ended in a massacre. They came from the Revolutionary Cells.

Direct cooperation in operations did not occur until 1975. Ilich Ramirez-Sanchez ("Carlos") recruited German terrorists for the attempt to shoot down an Israeli airplane at the Paris Orly Airport with a rocket. The German terrorists Gabriele Kröcher-Tiedemann and Hans-Joachim Klein were also involved in the commando raid against the OPEC conference in Vienna (led by Carlos). Brigitte Kuhlmann and Wilfried Böse were recruited by Carlos in 1976 and were members of the commando that hijacked an Air France airplane to Entebbe.

All German terrorists who cooperate with international terrorist organizations either come from the revolutionary cells or offer their services to the foreign organizations after they have left their own or after their own groups have been destroyed. The Red Army Faction has, as an organization, not yet worked together with international terrorist units. This is possibly explained by the fact that the Red Army has its own style of operating. The Palestinians do not, for instance, involve their leaders directly in their operations; in the Red Army, every leader must participate in the attacks.

There has only been one attempt at a large-scale international operation. A group of 50 international terrorists from seven countries wanted to kidnap the former Swedish Minister of Labor, Anna-Greta Leijon, in an attempt to secure the release of terrorists in prison in Germany. This operation was led, however, by the Red Army Faction.

The International Brotherhood

The June 2 terrorists who had been released as a result of the Lorenz operation were flown out to South Yemen. After a short recuperation, they received military training in a camp near Aden. Later, other German terrorists joined them. Other German terrorists were active there as teachers, for example, Hans-Joachim Klein, who came from the Revolutionary Cells and had been seriously wounded during the OPEC attack in Vienna.

Other German terrorists were trained in camps in Lebanon. In Algeria, there were two camps where terrorists from Corsica, Brittany, Northern Ireland, and the Basque provinces of Spain received their training. Germans were there as well.

It is possible that a kind of international fraternity of terrorists could arise from this joint training, which could operate in future operations. Germans could provide mercenaries for international operations in the future.

To date, there has been no detectable direct influence on the activities of German terrorist operations by Soviet or East European intelligence services.

TERRORIST ASSAULTS

Logistics

The logistical phase lasted from the release of Baader in May 1970 until May 1972. (Logistics is defined here as the procurement of money, apartments, garages, vehicles, papers, and passes, as well as the tools for, and means of, repainting cars, changing or forging papers, listening to the radios of the security authorities, and producing their own radio communications network. In addition, it includes the procurement of weapons, arms, ammunition, dynamite, and so forth.)

The larger part of the financial resources of the Red Army Faction come from bank robberies. The most spectacular event during the buildup of the Red Army was the occurrence of three bank robberies on the same day—September 29, 1970—when DM 220,000 was stolen. Twelve criminals were involved, as well as six vehicles.

Up to 1972, the Red Army Faction obtained more than DM 1.2 million through bank robberies. It is estimated that the German terrorists have stolen about DM 11 million to date, mostly between 1975 and 1977.

Explosives

In 1972, the Red Army Faction moved from its logistical phase to that of offensive activity. The series of bomb attacks, with 15 bombs exploding in six different places, began on May 11, 1972, with an attack on the headquarters of the Fifth U.S. Corps in Frankfurt/Main. One U.S. officer was killed. On May 15, 38 people were wounded by the detonation of two bombs at the Axel Springer publishing company in Hamburg. On May 24, there was a serious attack on the headquarters of the U.S. forces in Europe (in Heidelberg). Three soldiers were killed.

These actions by the Red Army Faction were specifically aimed at gaining support and solidarity from organizations and groups of the revolutionary new left. The attacks against the police and U.S. units assumed that people would be killed: the calculation was that other groups of the revolutionary movement would show solidarity as a result of these actions.

Individual Terror

One of the attacks of May 1972 was the bomb attack on Federal Judge Buddenberg in Karlsruhe on May 15, 1972. His wife was wounded. This example of individual terror, to be followed by other actions, marked the beginning of a new stage in the planned actions.

A year previously, Mahler, in his essay on the armed struggle in West Europe, had propagated this kind of specific individual terror and justified it by a detailed interpretation of Lenin. Mahler said that the revolutionary forces proclaimed "the personal responsibility for every activity which was directed against the people." Those concerned should be "judged for their crime and punished accordingly." He mentioned teachers, judges, and state lawyers.

"Revolutionary Terror"

A period of quiet and a pause for regeneration for the terrorist organizations occurred after the arrest of the hard core members in 1972; the destruction of a follow-up group in Hamburg, Frankfurt, and Amsterdam in February 1974; and the failure of the attack on the German embassy in Stockholm. The actions that followed were marked by an escalation of violence. The worst year was 1977: on January 5, on the Basel/Lörrach frontier, there was an attempted murder of a Swiss customs official; on April 7, in Karlsruhe, there occurred the murder of Attorney General Buback and his guards; on May 3, in Singen, there was an attempted murder of police officials during the capture of Verena Becker and Günter Sonnenberg; on August 25, in Karlsruhe, there was an attempted rocket attack on the Federal justice offices; on September 5, in Köln, Schleyer was kidnapped, and three of his guards and his driver were murdered; on September 19, at the Hague, there was an attempted murder of a Dutch policeman; on September 22, in Utrecht, a Dutch policeman was murdered during the arrest of

Knut Folkerts; in October (13-18), in Majorca/Mogadishu, a Lufthansa plane was hijacked (with 91 hostages) and the pilot, Jürgen Schumann, was murdered; on October 18, in Mulhouse, Schleyer was murdered; and on November 10, in Amsterdam, there was an attempted murder of a Dutch official during the arrest of Christoph Wackernagel and Gerd Schneider.

Nineteen terrorist culprits are being sought in connection with these crimes, ten of them women. In preparing for these crimes, the terrorists used 20 apartments; at least 23 bought, hired, or stolen vehicles (including a motorcycle and three mini buses); five bicycles; several semiautomatic guns; machine guns, pistols; a dozen typewriters; tape recorders; video recorders; copying machines; and over 30 forged passes for apartments, hotels, or the acquisition of vehicles.

Three terrorists, suspected of being involved in the kidnapping and murder of Schleyer and his guards, rented helicopters several times in July 1978 and flew over the area between Heidelberg, Frankfurt, and Wiesbaden. It is possible they were preparing an attack on an institution of "U.S. imperialism," such as the headquarters of the U.S. forces in Europe.

This escalation shows that the terrorists had, qualitatively speaking, reached a higher level, both in the preparation and the execution of the action: they had become more daring and had proved by their so-called executions that their small level of caution as far as killing was concerned had disappeared completely; they no longer justified the murder of those not involved (for example, the guards); they were even more determined to eliminate brutally any possible resistance by means of the gun; they became more precise in their planning and more skilled in their technical planning, as well in assessing the habits of their victims; they became cleverer in the art of surprise; and they were not weakened by the success of the security authorities—on the contrary, they were, through their logistical and personnel potential, thoroughly capable of undertaking terrorist activities and supporting measures to put pressure on those with responsibility for decisions. After a pause for regeneration (since the last attacks in the autumn of 1977), new actions are currently being prepared.

The Outcome

The outcome of terrorist (violent) crime in Germany between 1970 and June 1978 is as follows: 28 people were killed, including ten policemen, four justice officials, and three diplomats; 107 people narrowly escaped being killed; 95 people were injured through bombs and shootings; 163 people were taken as hostage; there were ten cases of serious damage through arson; there were 25 cases of bomb attacks; and there were 30 cases of bank robberies, with the loss of DM 5.4 million. A further 21 cases, with a loss of DM 1.6 million, were probably perpetrated by terrorists. Attacks on vehicles carrying money, with a loss of DM 4.6 million, may well have been carried out by terrorists.

THE GOVERNMENT RESPONSE

Countermeasures of the Security Forces

The search for German terrorist organizations is extremely difficult. Their members, particularly the Red Army Faction members, are intelligent, work conspiratorially, have the support of ideological sympathizers, can operate openly in an open society, and are determined to resist any official action by the use of lethal weapons.

The success of the security authorities depends to a large extent on support and information from the person in the street. There was a lack of this information during the logistic buildup of the Red Army Faction between 1970 and 1972. When the state showed itself to be determined to counteract terrorism through large-scale searches, information from the population became more forthcoming. After the escalation of violence in 1975, the willingness of the population to help the security authorities decreased. Between 1975 and 1977, the number of "wanted lists" on show in West Germany diminished considerably. The police were only able to put up a quarter of the previous number of posters in small shops. This example proves that a democratic state can be shaken when the population begins to believe that it is more dangerous to do something for the state than against it.

The arrest of about 90 German terrorists has shown that such groups can be sought out and destroyed by democratic means. The general search measures available to the police do not as a rule suffice. The police have to rely on intelligence so that their searches can be conducted on a more selective basis. Intelligence work in terrorist organizations has its limitations, however; there is the danger of agents of intelligence services becoming agent provocateurs or, at least, becoming involved in criminal activity themselves. In addition, these agents are risking death if they are exposed.

The violent actions of the terrorists have led to an increase in the personnel and material strength of the West German security authorities. The number of jobs in the Federal Criminal Office has increased from 933 in 1969 to over 2,500 in 1977. There are about 22,000 members of the Federal Frontier Protection Force, of which the GSG 9 commando, which operated in Mogadishu, forms a part. (There are approximately 150,000 policemen in West Germany.)

The Federal Criminal Office has been extended to act as the central information and communications office for counteracting terrorism. The collection and collation of intelligence is done with the most modern means of electronic data machinery. The Federal Frontier Protection Force has been extended as a strong addition to the police force. The GSG 9 commando unit has been developed into a special unit for supporting the police in combating violent crime. The Länder have similar special police units. In addition, the Federal Frontier Protection Force is required to safeguard airports, government departments, and diplomatic missions abroad.

The Federal Office for the Protection of the Constitution now has the task of studying all aspects of terrorist activity. It uses electronic methods to collect and evaluate information it receives. The considerable amount of personnel and technical aids available to the security authorities obliges them to use and weigh up their resources selectively. On the one hand, they have to discover the terrorist organizations and arrest the violent criminals; on the other hand, the temptation of covering West Germany with a search net reminiscent of George Orwell's *1984* has to be resisted. An overreaction by the state would play straight into the hands of the terrorists.

New Laws to Combat Terrorism

Following a 1971 law, the hijacking of a plane or attacks on a plane carry a penalty of not less than five years imprisonment. Manslaughter in this context carries imprisonment of not less than ten years. In the same year, the law was extended to include kidnapping of adults. A law against taking hostages was also introduced. In 1976, a law was introduced against those supporting and encouraging serious violent crime.

The right of defense was also partly changed. There is now a possibility of excluding a defense lawyer from a trial if he is suspected of being involved in the crime of the defendant. It is now no longer possible for one defense lawyer to defend several accused persons standing trial. The possibility of carrying on the trial in the absence of the accused (for example, during a hunger strike) was extended in 1974.

In 1976, a law was passed with greater penalties for membership in a terrorist organization. The law concerning the arrest of terrorists was strengthened, and a control of written communication between the defending lawyer and his client was made possible.

In 1977, a law was passed preventing contacts between arrested terrorists and their defending lawyers if the chances of thereby freeing a prisoner were increased. A new law was passed in 1978 allowing for the search of all apartments in an apartment building. During a large-scale police search, control points are allowed on roads. Also, defending lawyers can be disbarred if there are indications that the lawyer is planning a crime together with his client. Dividing panels have been authorized for discussions between the accused and his or her lawyer to prevent the handing over of any objects.

Government Response during Terrorist Assaults

The improved personnel and technical resources of the security authorities, even if they have reached optimal conditions, will not prevent terrorists from committing crimes. The new laws help state institutions to combat terrorism, but they are only one of several means that can contribute to the solution of the problem. The guiding principle for the realization of new legal solutions must be the individual assessment of, and response to, each problem. All generalized responses should be viewed with skepticism. They easily become routinized. Terrorists have always been ingenious enough to deal with generalized laws and can adapt to them easily.

Apart from the search apparatus, there are three important factors in combatting terrorist crimes successfully: (1) security for vulnerable persons and institutions, (2) constant attention being paid to terrorist organizations and their arena with intelligence resources, and (3) a decisive attitude on the part of the government toward the terrorists, especially during and after a terrorist attack.

A successful action by terrorists is usually followed by new violent crimes. Nothing is as successful as success. The occupation of the German embassy in Stockholm and the murder of two German diplomats, in an attempt to release terrorists from German prisons, resulted inter alia from the government giving in to the demands of the terrorists in the kidnapping of Lorenz. The resolute attitude by the government during the attack on the Stockholm embassy contributed to the fact that there were no further serious attacks for the next one and one-half years.

A firm attitude by the government is made more difficult by the publicity given to terrorist actions in the mass media, which, to a certain extent, are a part of the terrorist action itself. During the Stockholm embassy attack in 1975, Swedish Television had a camera focused on the embassy for several hours. After the kidnapping of Schleyer in 1977, the first ultimatum of the terrorists contained two demands for the media: at 10 A.M., one of the prisoners was to inform the commando on television of the departure of the prisoners, who were to have been set free; and the announcement was to be broadcast in the main news at 8 P.M. In the third message, the kidnappers demanded that a video tape of Schleyer reading a letter be broadcast. Copies of video tapes and Polaroid photos with ultimatums and announcements were constantly sent to the domestic and foreign press.

The West German press, at the government's request, conducted itself in its treatment of information during the Schleyer case with remarkable restraint. The terrorists thus lost the publicity that they had calculated would be forthcoming.

When a Palestinian commando in an attempt to exploit the situation during the Schleyer kidnapping hijacked a Lufthansa plane, thereby putting pressure on the government, the government reacted offensively. They ordered the GSG 9 special unit to try to release the hostages. This succeeded in Mogadishu after discussions with the government in Somalia. This led to the suicide of Baader, Ensslin, and Raspe in prison in Stuttgart/Stammheim. Schleyer was murdered.

Each single terrorist attack requires a special defense and reaction determined by the situation. Experience to date has shown that reactions must be determined by one rule: the responsible organs of state must *not* during an attack react in the way the terrorists expect them to. Such a reaction would be the success that would breed a repeated attack. The state institutions must always show that they will not give in to blackmail and that violence will not be tolerated. Otherwise a problem, which is essentially a problem of security, could well become a question of the future existence for free societies and states.

NOTE

1. For details on "Concerning the Armed Struggle in Western Europe" see, for example, Jillian Becker, *Hitler's Children* (London: Granado Publishing, 1978), p. 265.

20

THE UNITED NATIONS RESPONSE TO TERRORISM

Seymour M. Finger

During the first two decades of the UN, international terrorism received only tangential attention in the General Assembly and the Security Council. In its Resolution 177 (II) of November 21, 1946, the General Assembly entrusted the International Law Commission (ILC) with the task of preparing a draft code of offenses against the peace and security of mankind. This draft code, prepared in 1954 by the ILC pursuant to that resolution, deals mainly with the principles recognized in the charter of the Nuremberg tribunal and the judgment of the tribunal; however, it has one paragraph concerned with international terrorism. Article 2, paragraph 6, defines as an offense against the peace and security of mankind "the undertaking or encouragement by the authorities of a State of terrorist activities in another State, or the toleration by the authorities of a State of organized activities calculated to carry out terrorist acts in another State."[1]

No action has been taken on the draft code to date; however, from the standpoint of international terrorism, the single paragraph in the code would add nothing to similar provisions in the Declaration on Principles of International Law Concerning Friendly Relations and Cooperation Among States in Accordance with the Charter of the United Nations, which was approved by the General Assembly in Resolution 2625 (XXV) of October 24, 1970. Relevant portions of that resolution are quoted below:

> The General Assembly . . .
> 1. Solemnly proclaims the following Principles:
> Every State has the duty to refrain from organizing, instigating, assisting or participating in acts of civil strife or terrorist acts in another State or acquiescing in organized activities within its territory directed towards the commission of such acts, when the acts referred to in the present paragraph involve a threat or use of force. . . .

No State may use or encourage the use of economic, political or any other type of measures to coerce another State in order to obtain from it the subordination of the exercise of its sovereign rights and to secure from it advantages of any kind. Also, no State shall organize, assist, foment, finance, incite or tolerate subversive, terrorist or armed activities directed toward the violent overthrow of the regime of another State, or interfere in civil strife in another State.

ACTION BY THE INTERNATIONAL CIVIL AVIATION ORGANIZATION

Since the late 1960s, acts endangering international civil aviation have become alarmingly more numerous and widespread. Such acts have been the object of concern by the UN General Assembly in its Resolutions 2551 (XXIV) and 2645 (XXV) and by the Security Council in its Resolution 268 (1970) and its Decision of June 20, 1972. For understandable reasons, the development of conventions in this area has taken place under the auspices of the International Civil Aviation Organization (ICAO), whose members were encouraged by the UN General Assembly resolutions mentioned above.

The Convention of Offences and Certain Other Acts Committed on Board Aircraft, signed at Tokyo on September 14, 1963, imposes upon states certain obligations concerning the return of a hijacked aircraft and its cargo and the release of the passengers and crew. It is not, however, concerned with the suppression of such acts and offenses, as are the two subsequent conventions.

The Convention for the Suppression of Unlawful Seizure of Aircraft, signed at The Hague on December 16, 1970, obliges states to make such offenses punishable by severe penalties (Article 2). Article 7 obliges the state party in the territory of which the alleged offender is found, if it does not extradite him or her, to submit the case "without exception whatsoever" to its competent authorities for the purpose of prosecution. The system of extradition established by the convention is dealt with in Article 8, which states that the unlawful seizure of aircraft is "deemed to be included" in any extradition treaty existing between states and which also obliges states to include the offense as an extraditable offense in every extradition treaty to be concluded between them. Last, the convention contains provisions obliging State parties to afford one another judicial assistance in any criminal proceedings brought in respect of the offense (Article 10) and to report to the Council of the ICAO any relevant information in their possession (Article 11).

The Convention for the Suppression of Unlawful Acts Against the Safety of Civil Aviation, signed at Montreal on September 23, 1971, establishes a system of suppression that in outline is the same as that laid down in the 1970 Hague convention. The difference is that the Hague convention is concerned with the aircraft itself when it is in flight and when the offense is committed by a person on board the aircraft; the Montreal convention covers a series of acts, mostly committed on the ground, which are likely to cause the destruction of the aircraft or otherwise endanger the safety of aircraft in flight. It also includes a special provision (Article 10) requiring that "contracting States shall, in accordance with international and national law, endeavor to take all practicable measures for the purpose of preventing the offenses mentioned."

All three of these ICAO-launched conventions are now in effect. The increasing concern of most governments with hijacking and other threats to civil aviation is indicated by the pace of ratification. In 1970, after seven years, only 32 countries had ratified or acceded to the Tokyo convention; by May 1978, the total was 91. Also, by May 1978, the Hague convention of December 1970 had 93 adherents and the Montreal convention of September 1971, 86.

Unfortunately, hijackers can still find sanctuary in states that have not adhered to the conventions. Less than half the more than 20 Arab states, as of mid-1978, have ratified or acceded to any of the three conventions. The Arab adherents, as of May 1978, are Egypt, Iraq, Jordan, Lebanon, Morocco, Oman, and Saudi Arabia to all three conventions and Libya to the Tokyo and Montreal conventions. Nor is adherence to a convention necessarily a guarantee of faithful implementation. In the Entebbe hijacking, which we shall discuss later, Uganda failed to implement the Hague convention, to which it was a party. Nevertheless, conventions are instruments of international law and, as such, are not to be underestimated. They have a morally persuasive effect, even when honored in the breach. Consequently, further efforts must be made both to develop new conventions and to persuade more countries to accede to and implement existing conventions.

Occasional threats by IFALPA to boycott safe-haven countries have not been made effective, nor have the giant airlines that carry the bulk of passengers come forward with a boycott. It would appear, therefore, that little further progress can be made on this issue unless there is a major shift of policy in safe-haven states. An even more serious threat to civil aviation might, of course, provoke stronger reactions by pilots, airlines, or governments, but such an increased threat is hardly to be desired.

In sum, the ICAO conventions, while affording some measure of security to international civil aviation, leave significant safe havens for hijackers, and there is no convention in force that deals comprehensively with the protection of human lives from international terrorism.

CONSIDERATION OF INTERNATIONAL TERRORISM BY THE UN GENERAL ASSEMBLY, 1972-73

Two weeks before the opening of the 27th session of the UN General Assembly in September 1972, the subject of international terrorism was thrust upon the consciousness of the world community by the murder of 11 Israeli athletes at the Olympic Village in Munich. A host of other terrorist acts had underscored the increasing threat of terrorism. During 1972 alone, acts of terrorism were committed against 30 airlines of 14 countries, killing 140 people and wounding 99. In the preceding few years, 27 diplomats from 11 countries had been kidnapped, and three had been killed. A new form of terrorism—letter-bombs—was just being unleashed. In the last six months of 1973 alone, the casualty toll from terrorism outside the homeland of the terrorist rose to 268 dead and 571 wounded.[2]

Shocked by the Munich massacre, UN Secretary General Kurt Waldheim decided that the UN could not remain a mute spectator to the acts of terrorism plaguing the world. He consulted first with certain middle powers in the hope that they would propose an item for the agenda. That failing, on September 8, he took the unusual and courageous step of proposing the item himself as an "urgent and important" matter. He was well aware of the opposition his proposal would encounter from the Arab states, which have a strategic position in the Afro-Asian bloc, which, in turn, includes a majority of the votes in the Assembly. Yet he felt that given the state of world opinion, it would be better to take the risk of failure than not to try at all.

The item proposed by the secretary general, "measures to prevent terrorism and other forms of violence which endanger or take human lives or jeopardize fundamental freedoms," cleared its first hurdle, the General Committee, without serious change. By a vote of 15 in favor, seven against, and two absentions, the General Committee recommended to the General Assembly that the item be inscribed on the agenda. But the fact that the seven negative votes were all African and Asian, along with the arguments advanced by the opponents, portended trouble in the full Assembly.

The main thrust of the opposition in the General Committee was the argument that the inclusion of this item "would constitute yet another attempt to classify the legitimate struggle of peoples under the yoke of colonialism and alien domination as 'terrorism.'" This position, advocated in the General Committee by Libya, Mauritania, and Syria and supported by Guinea, Mauritius, and the People's Republic of China was a continuation of the clever and effective Arab tactic of linking the Palestinian cause to the struggle of the black African peoples for independence; it undoubtedly had an impact on many African and Asian delegations. It was also argued that "state terrorism" (suppression of colonial peoples by force) was far more noxious and costly in lives than acts by individuals and guerrilla groups. (The fact that the UN had repeatedly taken a stand against colonial repression appeared to have little impact on these opponents.) Further, it was argued that the underlying causes of violence and terrorism were misery, frustration, grievance, and despair; consequently, the only way to deal with terrorism was to deal with these underlying causes.

This last argument took the form of an amendment when the General Assembly considered inscription of the item on the agenda. Proposed by Saudi Arabia, the amendment adopted by the Assembly added the following to the title of the item: "and study of the underlying causes of those forms of terrorism and acts of violence which lie in misery, frustration, grievance and despair and which cause some people to sacrifice human lives, including their own, in an attempt to effect radical changes." Thus amended, the item was adopted by the Assembly and referred to its Sixth (legal) Committee for consideration.

While no one would deny that the international community must be concerned with causes, the amendment raised a real danger that the net result would be a failure to condemn or take action against terrorism. This danger was signaled in the document prepared by the Secretariat for the Sixth Committee:

> The effort to eliminate those causes should be intense and continuous, as mankind, despite its intellectual powers, has not yet succeeded in creating a social order free from misery, frustration, grievance and despair—in short, an order which will not cause or provoke violence. Yet terrorism threatens, endangers or destroys the lives and fundamental freedoms of the innocent, and it would not be just to leave them to wait for protection until the causes have been remedied and the purposes and principles of the Charter have been given full effect. There is a present need for measures of international cooperation to protect their rights as far as possible. At all times in history, mankind has recognized the unavoidable necessity of repressing some forms of violence which otherwise would threaten the very existence of society as well as that of man himself. There are some means of using force, as in every form of human conflict, which must not be used, even when the use of force is legally and morally justified, and regardless of the status of the perpetrator.[3]

Erik Suy, chairman of the Sixth Committee at the 27th session of the General Assembly and later legal counsel of the UN, made the following observation at a colloquium in March 1973:

> But in reality, a simultaneous study of "causes" and "measures" is a condition impossible to sustain. One of the most frequent manifestations of acts of violence is air piracy; yet, measures have been found without studying the causes. Further, the Commission on International Law has prepared a draft convention on the protection of diplomats without having first elucidated the reasons for the acts of violence directed against them. The demand to consider the question en bloc was in reality nothing more than a maneuver designed to reduce terrorism to a simply political question and to prevent concrete measures from being adopted.[4]

In fact, the majority in the Sixth Committee thrust aside all efforts to condemn terrorism or to take any action against it.

The first concrete proposal was a draft resolution and convention submitted by the United States, carefully drafted so as to omit any constraints on wars of national liberation. Secretary of State William Rogers launched the U.S. proposals in his statement to the General Assembly on September 25, 1972, referring to the need for "a new treaty on the export of international terrorism." The draft convention, circulated the same day, dealt only with the most serious criminal threats (unlawful killing, serious bodily harm, and kidnapping) and only under the following conditions:

1. The act must be committed or take effect outside the territory of a state of which the alleged offender is a national.

2. The act must be committed or take effect outside the territory of the state against which the act is directed.

3. The act must not be committed either by or against a member of the armed forces of a state in the course of military hostilities.

Thus, the proposed draft convention would clearly not affect the efforts of African peoples fighting or struggling for independence, nor would it affect Arab attacks in or against Israel.

Nevertheless, the leaders of the Afro-Asian bloc, with the Arab states carrying on an intensive lobbying campaign, opposed the U.S. draft. The African and Asian states have no major world airlines, few pilots, and relatively few air passengers; hence, the problem of hijacking was not a matter of much direct concern to them. By comparison, the Africans, in particular, were actively interested in the fight against colonialism and apartheid. Since they felt that the United States and other Western powers showed little real concern over those issues, many were not disposed to be accommodating in the area of terrorism. Also, the Arabs, with obvious reference to Vietnam, argued that terrorism by bombing was far worse than the acts of terrorism envisaged in the U.S. draft.

A number of other factors hampered the U.S. effort. First, the draft was introduced by the United States alone. Second, it was presented in a complete form only days after the item had been inscribed and months before the Sixth Committee began discussions, a factor that provoked resentment even among the European friends of the United States. Third, U.S. lobbying at the UN and approaches in capitals in the fall of 1972 had as their prime objective the reduction of the assessed U.S. share of the UN budget from 31.5 percent to 25 percent, an effort that succeeded. While congressional pressure for the reduction made this priority virtually inevitable, the choice did somewhat weaken the amount of effort and influence that could be brought to bear on the issue of international terrorism. Fourth, adoption by the Congress of the Byrd amendment in late 1971, authorizing the importation of chrome and other minerals from Rhodesia in violation of UN sanctions, had infuriated the Africans. Finally, the Arab delegations had their own instruments of influence and pressure, which they used—for example, the Cambodian delegation, faced with a threat to the recognition of its credentials, had little real choice on the terrorism issue.

Conscious that its proposal would not succeed, the United States decided not to press it to a vote in the Sixth Committee. Instead, it supported a compromise proposal sponsored by Australia, Austria, Belgium, Canada, Costa Rica, Great Britain, Guatemala, Honduras, Iran, Japan, Luxembourg, New Zealand, and Nicaragua.[5] The sponsor group, while numerous, failed to include any African countries (the Africans have about one-third of the votes) and had only one Asian developing country—Iran. This situation was not an oversight; it reflected the factors described above.

The draft resolution represented a twofold compromise. First, it slowed down the timetable of the U.S. draft, which called for a conference of plenipotentiaries in 1973 to draft a convention. Instead, a three-stage process was proposed: (1) the Assembly would ask the ILC to draft a convention; (2) this draft would be submitted to the Assembly in the fall of 1973; and (3) a special conference would then be convened "as soon as practicable" to adopt a convention. The second compromise feature was a provision for the president of the General Assembly to appoint an ad hoc committee to study the underlying causes of terrorism.

Shortly after the 14-power draft resolution was submitted, another draft was introduced that reflected the interests and concerns of the Arabs and their black African supporters. Incidental critical references to violence were balanced by a strong affirmation of "the inalienable right to self-determination," support of the "legitimacy" of the national liberation "struggle," and condemnation of "repressive and terrorist acts by colonial, racist, and alien regimes." The draft advanced no concrete proposals for international action to combat terrorism; instead, it merely established a 40-member committee (later, in plenary session, changed to a 35-member committee), appointed by the Assembly president, which would study both the underlying causes of terrorism and "proposals" submitted by various countries "for finding an effective solution to the problem." The next session of the General Assembly would be given a report by the ad hoc committee.

The new draft was sponsored by 16 powers—Afghanistan, Algeria, Cameroon, Chad, the Congo, Equatorial Guinea, Guinea, Guyana, India, Kenya, Madagascar, Mali, Mauritania, the Sudan, Yugoslavia, and Zambia. Most were African states. The non-African states were ones traditionally linked with Third World aspirations.

Normally, since it was introduced before the 16-power draft, the 14-power Western draft would have been voted on first. But as the committee is its own parliamentary master, it voted 76 to 43 with seven abstentions to grant priority to the Afro-Asian draft. That draft was then adopted by a vote of 76 to 34 with

16 abstentions. Had the 14-power resolution been voted upon first, it might very well have received the support of the Soviet Union, since its representative endorsed the idea of the ILC's drafting an international treaty combating terrorism. It is even conceivable that the 14-power draft might have won a majority, but the bloc pattern of voting prevented a test by ballot.

The General Assembly, on December 18, 1972, approved the draft resolution by a similarly lopsided vote, and it became General Assembly Resolution 3034 (XXVII). Under paragraph 9 of the resolution, the president of the General Assembly, after appropriate consultation, appointed the following 35 states to the Ad Hoc Committee on International Terrorism: Algeria, Austria, Barbados, Canada, the Congo, Czechoslovakia, Democratic Yemen, France, Great Britain, Greece, Guinea, Haiti, Hungary, India, Iran, Italy, Japan, Mauritania, Nicaragua, Nigeria, Panama, Sweden, Syria, Tunisia, Turkey, the Ukrainian Soviet Socialist Republic, the Soviet Union, Tanzania, the United States, Uruguay, Venezuela, Yemen, Yugoslavia, Zaire, and Zambia. (Thus, of the 35 members, six were Arab states, whose combined population represented less than 3 percent of the world's population.)

Under paragraph 8, the General Assembly requested the secretary general to transmit an analytical study of the observations of states submitted under paragraph 7 of the same resolution. This was submitted to the ad hoc committee in June 1973.[6]

The overwhelming majority of the states that submitted written observations expressed concern over, and opposition to, acts of international terrorism; these encompassed all the major economic powers, including the Soviet Union, which, however, expressed the following reservation: "It is unacceptable to give a broad interpretation to the term international terrorism and to extend it to cover national liberation movements, acts committed in resisting an aggressor in territories occupied by the latter and action by workers to secure their rights against the yoke of exploiters." Interestingly, this reservation would be fully consistent with the provisions of the U.S. draft convention, tending to substantiate other indications that the Soviets might have eventually gone along with something like the U.S. draft had the Afro-Asian group, spearheaded by the Algerians, not blocked a vote on the 14-power proposal in the Sixth Committee.

Of the 34 written replies, only two—those of Syria and Yemen—took positions that would constitute a series obstacle to a workable convention on terrorism. Syria stated that

> official terrorism . . . contains the most drastic form of savagery and barbarism and the greatest dangers threatening the security and safety of peoples. Any consideration that evades coming face to face with terrorism practiced by the State, as the real source of violence, blackmail, domination and illegitimate exploitation, would defeat the very purposes and objectives of the Charter it intends to defend.

While it is true that violent acts by states cause far more suffering and loss of life than terrorism by individuals or groups, the fact is that such state actions against peoples of other states are already dealt with in the Charter, notably in chapter VII, while terrorism by individuals or groups is not. Also, as pointed out by a number of representatives to the ad hoc committee, the Declaration on Friendly Relations amply covered interstate violence, and acts committed by armed forces during military operations were already the subject of extensive treaty law and were being considered in the context of the protection of human rights in armed conflicts.

Discussion in the ad hoc committee, which met from July 23 to August 11, 1973, substantially reflected the same fundamental divisions that had become apparent in the Sixth Committee discussion in the fall of 1972. First, there was the issue of state terrorism, as outlined above. Second, there was the argument that

> since the acts of violence described as acts of terrorism were in fact merely the logical outcome of certain situations, it would be a serious mistake, and one fraught with consequences, to seek to eliminate such acts by means of punitive measures before having clearly identified the causes from which they sprang.

Other representatives, while acknowledging that analysis of the causes should not be sacrificed to the devising of preventive and punitive measures, observed that the study of the political or socioeconomic causes of international terrorism would necessarily take much time and that the adoption of the necessary protective measures could not be postponed pending completion of that study. In this connection, it was noted that in their domestic legislation, states did not wait for the underlying causes of crime to be identified before enacting penal laws.[7]

The committee members were also divided as to what measures should be taken to deal with the problem. Some representatives emphasized the need for each state initially to take action at the national level. Others stressed the desirability of bilateral agreements, in particular, on the subject of extradition.

A number of representatives expressed support for the preparation of multilateral treaty provisions. They stressed the principle that states be obliged either to proceed to extradite the alleged offender or to bring him or her before the competent authorities for the purpose of judicial proceedings (as in the U.S. draft). Some expressed the view, however, that it would be better to draw up several conventions, each dealing with a specific category of acts of terrorism (for example, the taking of hostages or the use of letter-bombs) rather than attempt to draw up a general convention on the subject.

As its meeting on July 31, the ad hoc committee set up three subcommittees, dealing, respectively, with the definition, the underlying causes, and measures for the prevention of international terrorism. In the first subcommittee, it soon became evident that there was substantial disagreement as to whether or not a definition was either necessary or desirable. In the second, there was a rerun of the debate as to whether measures could be undertaken to restrain terrorism parallel with efforts to deal with underlying causes or whether elimination of the causes must precede such measures. Again, no consensus or compromise was reached.

This same conflict was repeated in the third subcommittee. In addition, there were differences as to whether to aim for a general convention on terrorism or a series of conventions, each related to a specific type of act, for example, the taking of hostages for political extortion, the kidnapping of diplomats, or the sending of letter-bombs. There was also a dispute on whether such conventions should cover state terrorism.[8]

With no consensus or compromise emerging from any of the subcommittees, it is not surprising that the committee's report to the General Assembly was little more than a summary of the divergent views. The draft proposals and suggestions submitted to the various subcommittees are reproduced in the annex to the report. In general, they reflect the divergences described above; however, certain individual state proposals warrant special attention.[9]

For example, the following submission of Nigeria shows that at least one major African country—the largest—had a serious concern with international terrorism:

> The Nigerian delegation is of the opinion that acts such as the recent Portuguese massacre, the kidnapping of diplomats attending a cocktail party and their subsequent murder, hijacking of aircrafts or even holding at bay innocent tourists in a hotel lobby with the muzzles of submachine guns pointing at them all constitute some forms of international terrorism. These acts do *not* include the activities, within their own countries, of those peoples struggling to liberate themselves from foreign oppression and exploitation.

Nigeria also expressed a willingness to consider the U.S. and British proposals as a basis for negotiation, offering reasonable suggestions for modification.

Among the Asian delegations on the committee, Iran was noteworthy for its efforts to achieve a compromise, based on a reference to state terrorism, as well as that of individuals and groups. Also, there were indications that Yugoslavia would be interested in constructive action, as it demonstrated at the 28th session, when the Convention on the Prevention and Punishment of Crimes Against Internationally Protected Persons was considered.

In the present world political atmosphere, it is doubtful that any of these three important members of the Third World could or would take the lead in the General Assembly toward additional measures against terrorism. Naturally, this forecast could change radically if a settlement was reached on the Palestinian issue and in Southern Africa, but such developments appear unlikely in the near future.

At its 28th session, in 1973, the General Assembly did not consider the item or the ad hoc committee's report for "lack of time," and it was deferred to the 29th session. Since then, the committee's work has been so discouraging to those who want an effective convention that in December 1978, all Western countries either voted against or abstained on General Assembly Resolution (32/147) continuing its existence.

CONVENTION ON THE PREVENTION AND PUNISHMENT OF CRIMES AGAINST INTERNATIONALLY PROTECTED PERSONS

In contrast with the failure of the General Assembly to deal effectively with the general question of international terrorism at its 27th session, it did succeed at its 28th session in adopting a Convention on the Prevention and Punishment of Crimes Against Internationally Protected Persons Including Diplomatic Agents (Resolution 3166 [XXVIII] of December 14, 1973). Moreover, the adoption in both the Sixth Committee and the Assembly was by consensus.

In view of the numerous similarities between provisions of this convention and the draft convention on terrorism proposed by the United States, it is useful to analyze the reasons why one succeeded and the other failed. This analysis will take the form of examining the history of the 1973 convention, including the steps leading to its preparation and adoption, similarities and differences between that convention and the U.S. proposal, and whether lessons of substance, procedure, and tactics learned from the successful enterprise might usefully be applied to future efforts to negotiate conventions in this area.

The origins of the concern of the ILC with the protection of diplomatic agents is summarized succinctly in two paragraphs of the ILC's 1972 report:

As its twenty-second session, in 1970, the Commission received from the President of the Security Council a letter dated 14 May 1970 transmitting a copy of document S/9789 which reproduced the text of a letter addressed to him by the representative of the Netherlands to the United Nations concerning the need for action to ensure the protection and inviolability of diplomatic agents in view of the increasing number of attacks on them. The Chairman of the Commission replied to the foregoing communication by a letter dated 12 June 1970 which referred to the Commission's past work in this area and stated the Commission would continue to be concerned with the matter.

At the twenty-third session of the Commission, in 1971, in connection with the adoption of the Commission's agenda, the suggestion was made by Mr. Kearney (U.S.) that the Commission should consider whether it would be possible to produce draft articles regarding such crimes as the murder, kidnapping and assaults upon diplomats and other persons entitled to special protection under international law. The Commission recognized both the importance and the urgency of the matter, but deferred its decision in view of the priority that had to be given to the completion of the draft articles on the representation of States in their relations with international organizations. In the course of the session it became apparent that there would not be sufficient time to deal with any additional subject. In considering its programme of work for 1972, however, the Commission reached the decision that, if the General Assembly requested it to do so, it would prepare at its 1972 session a set of draft articles on this important subject with the view to submitting such articles to the twenty-seventh session of the General Assembly.[10]

Omitted from the above summary are the political and shock effects produced by the murder of the Yugoslav ambassador in Stockholm on April 7, 1971, shortly before the ILC met. Thus, the strong interest and motivation of a leading state member of the Third World was added to the earlier Western concern. At its fall session that year, the General Assembly adopted Resolution 2780 (XXVI) of December 3, 1971, requesting

(a) the Secretary General to invite comments from Member States before 1 April 1972 on the question of the protection of diplomats and to transmit them to the International Law Commission at its twenty-fourth session; and

(b) the Commission to study as soon as possible, in the light of the comments of Member States, the question of the protection and inviolability of diplomatic agents and other persons entitled to special protection under international law, with a view to preparing a set of draft articles dealing with offences committed against diplomats and other persons entitled to special protection under international law for submission to the General Assembly at the earliest date which the Commission would consider appropriate.

The comments of 26 member states, including a working paper submitted by Denmark,[11] were provided to the ILC at its 24th session, along with a working paper produced by Uruguay and one by Richard Kearney, U.S. member of the ILC. Some ILC members wanted to extend the concern of the convention beyond "specially protected persons" to provide some means of protection against terrorist acts in general. The majority, however, expressed the view that the question of the scope of draft articles on the subject had been determined by Resolution 2780 (XXVI) of the General Assembly. The ILC functioned accordingly, producing agreed draft articles on the prevention and punishment of crimes against diplomatic agents and other internationally protected persons. (It finished its work two months before the murder of the 11 Israeli athletes at Munich.)

At the 27th session of the General Assembly, the ILC draft was discussed extensively; there were still many delegations that had doubts about the wisdom of negotiating a new convention on the subject. Some stressed that existing instruments, notably the Vienna conventions on diplomatic and consular relations and the convention on special missions, gave substantial coverage; that draft articles on the representation of states in their relations with international organizations were in an advanced state of preparation; and that the ILC was engaged in the elaboration of articles on state responsibility. Some also questioned whether it was wise to protect one group of persons without protecting other victims of international terrorism. Others argued that strict application of existing conventions was the real need rather than a new convention. Finally, there was the same argument that had been raised against the proposal for a convention on international terrorism (considered under another item at the same session), that is, the right answer was to eliminate the causes of such violent acts.

There was also disagreement over whether a new convention should be treated as an urgent matter and whether negotiations should take place at a special conference or in the Sixth Committee.[12]

Despite these differences over desirability, substance, urgency, and procedures, the General Assembly at its twenty-seventh session decided to include in the provisional agenda of its 28th session an item entitled "Draft convention on the prevention and punishment of crimes against diplomatic agents and other internationally protected persons with a view to the final elaboration of such a convention by the General Assembly" (paragraph 3). Meanwhile, states, the specialized agencies, and other interested organizations were invited to submit comments and observations to the secretary general, who would, in turn, circulate them to member states.

At the 28th session, the Sixth Committee, acting as a negotiating conference, succeeded in negotiating a convention that the General Assembly adopted by consensus—a notable achievement, considering the many different views expressed during the 27th session and in marked contrast to its failure to act on international terrorism.

A comparison of the convention on internationally protected persons, adopted in Resolution 3166 (XXVIII), and the proposed U.S. draft on international terrorism shows that they are largely parallel; the obvious difference is that the scope of the former, in terms of the acts covered, is wider. Both cite as crimes murder, kidnapping, or other bodily harm, as well as attempts to commit such acts or serving as accomplices. The convention further covers violent attacks "upon the official premises, the private accommodation or the means of transport of an internationally protected person likely to endanger his person or liberty" and threats or attempts to commit such attacks or serving as an accomplice to them.[13]

Both call upon each state party to make the crimes cited punishable by appropriate penalties.[14] Both call upon each state party to take such measures as may be necessary to establish its jurisdiction.[15]

Both call upon each state on whose territory the act has been committed, if it has reason to believe an alleged offender has fled from its territory, to communicate to other states all pertinent facts regarding the offense committed and all available information regarding the identity of the alleged offender.[16]

Both call upon the state in whose territory the alleged offender is present to take appropriate measures under its internal law to insure his or her presence for prosecution or extradition.[17] Both provide for extradition or, as an alternative, prosecution in accordance with internal law.[18] Thus, both seek to deny safe haven to offenders. Both call for guarantees of "fair treatment at all stages of the proceedings."[19] Both call on State parties to afford one another the greatest measure of assistance in connection with criminal proceedings.[20]

Significant differences between the two instruments, other than the fact that the convention covers a wider range of acts against a narrower range of persons, are as follows:

1. Article 12 of the convention stipulates that its provisions

shall not affect the application of the Treaties on Asylum, in force at the date of the adoption of this Convention, as between the States, which are parties to those Treaties; but a State Party to this Convention may not invoke those Treaties with respect to another State Party to this Convention which is not a party to those Treaties.

This article was introduced as an amendment by Bolivia during the Sixth Committee consideration of the draft convention prepared by the ILC and supported by the Latin Americans in general. (Given the strong tradition on asylum among Latin Americans, a similar amendment would presumably be introduced with respect to any future conventions in this area (there is a provision on asylum in the Organization of American States [OAS] Convention of 1972 against terrorism.)[21]

2. The U.S. draft (Article 16) provides for the establishment of a three-member Conciliation Commission to deal with disputes between state parties over the interpretation of any of its provisions, with decisions or recommendations to be made by a majority vote. The commission may ask "any organ that is authorized by or in accordance with the Charter of the United Nations to

request an advisory opinion from the International Court of Justice to make such a request regarding the interpretation or application of the present articles."

Article 13* of the convention provides that

> 1) any dispute between two or more States Parties concerning the interpretation or application of this Convention which is not settled by negotiation shall, at the request of one of them, be submitted to arbitration. If within six months from the date of the request for arbitration the parties are unable to agree on the organization of the arbitration, any one of those parties may refer the dispute to the International Court of Justice by request in conformity with the Statute of the Court.
>
> 2) Each State Party may at the time of signature or ratification of this Convention or accession thereto declare that it does not consider itself bound by paragraph 1 of this article. The other States Parties shall not be bound by paragraph 1 of this article with respect to any State Party which has made such a reservation.

3. On November 15, 1973, a group of 34 African countries introduced an amendment to add the following article to the convention: "No provision of the present articles shall be applicable to peoples struggling against colonialism, alien domination, foreign occupation, racial discrimination and *apartheid* in the exercise of their legitimate rights to self-determination and independence."[22]

After extensive consultations by the chairman of the Sixth Committee and negotiations in the drafting committee, a compromise proposal was submitted on December 6 by the chairman of the drafting committee on its behalf. With one minor change, it was adopted that same day by the Sixth Committee and on December 14 by the General Assembly.

The compromise provided for the simultaneous adoption by the Sixth Committee of a resolution and the convention. Also, paragraph 6 of the resolution (General Assembly Resolution 3166 [XXVIII]) stipulates that "the present resolution, whose provisions are related to the annexed Convention, shall always be published together with it."

The key paragraph of the resolution, on the basis of which 37 Afro-Asian sponsors agreed not to press their amendment to the convention itself, reads as follows:

---

*The Warsaw Pact countries, which were among the first to sign the convention, have all attached a reservation to Article 13, paragraph 1, indicating their position that a dispute may be submitted to the International Court of Justice for arbitration only with the consent of all states' parties to the dispute (statements submitted by East Germany, Poland, the USSR, Byelorussia, the Ukraine, and Bulgaria on signing the convention in May and June 1974).

[The General Assembly] *recognizes also* that the provisions of the
annexed Convention could not in any way prejudice the exercise of
the legitimate right to self-determination and independence, in
accordance with the purposes and principles of the Charter of the
United Nations and the Declaration on Principles of International
Law concerning Friendly Relations and Co-operation among States
in accordance with the Charter of the United Nations, by peoples
struggling against colonialism, alien domination, foreign occupation,
racial discrimination and *apartheid.*

Obviously, this paragraph could be used by a state party so inclined to
justify exceptions to the provisions of the convention. Yet it is less noxious in
this form than if it were in the convention itself, as proposed in the amendment,
and evidently those who negotiated the compromise considered it essential to
the achievement of consensus. Moreover, if the 37 states and their sympathizers
had been outvoted, this fact might have caused a large number of states not to
ratify the convention. It would appear better to aim for universal ratification
and take the risk of exceptions rather than have a large part of the world not
bound at all.

In addition to this compromise, what other factors contributed to the
successful negotiation of this convention, as contrasted to the failure of the U.S.
draft?

First, the scope was limited to "internationally protected persons"; this
includes a class of people—diplomats—for whose protection states have traditionally assumed special responsibilities, many of which are the subject of numerous
existing conventions.[23]

As the second paragraph of the preamble of the convention states, "crimes
against diplomatic agents and other diplomatically protected persons jeopardiz-
ing the safety of those persons create a serious threat to the maintenance of
normal international relations which are necessary for co-operation among
States." It should also be noted that those negotiating the convention were
members of the class to be protected and were well aware of numerous attacks
on diplomats in the recent past.

Second, there was the shock caused by the murder of the Yugoslav ambas-
sardor to Stockholm on April 7, 1971. Had a South African instead of a Yugoslav ambassador been murdered, there is at least some question as to whether
the draft convention for the protection of diplomats would have received the
same impetus toward completion. Similarly, if the 11 Olympic athletes murdered at Munich in September 1972 had been African or Arab, the reaction of
the Afro-Asian group to a proposed convention on terrorism would certainly
have been less antagonistic.

Third, the subject of the prevention and punishment of crimes against
internationally protected persons is more precise in definition and less politically
and emotionally loaded than the term *international terrorism.* While the latter

makes good copy for the media, it is bound to be a handicap in negotiating a legal instrument with African and Arab countries in the present political climate, where one side's terrorists are the other side's freedom fighters. It would appear prudent, therefore, to concentrate on criminal actions rather than the labels of those who commit them.

In this connection, the Yugoslav letter of May 5, 1972, on the subject of internationally protected persons is of great interest.[24] Paragraph 2 of that letter states: "Grave offenses and serious crimes should not be treated as political criminal acts even in those cases where motivations for committing such acts are of a political nature." Paragraph 8 states: "If the perpetrators of criminal acts belong to an organization which instigates, organizes, assists or participates in the execution of those criminal acts, each State is obliged, in addition to punishing the culprits, to undertake effective measures and to dissolve such an organization." If the concepts expressed in those two sentences could be incorporated into a convention for the protection of all innocent civilians outside an area of conflict, a substantial step could be taken to prevent or punish those actions commonly called *international terrorism*. The convention could thus be conceived in terms of international criminal or humanitarian law.

In summary, those planning future efforts toward conventions designed to curb terrorism might profit by a study of the following factors involved in the negotiation of the successful convention:

1. Early efforts should be made to enlist the support of one or more Third World countries of stature; this might involve compromises on both timing and text, particularly on references to the right to struggle for self-determination and independence. Such efforts must be made before a draft is introduced.

2. It might be better to draft the convention in terms of international criminal and humanitarian law rather than use the emotionally loaded term *terrorism*. As Franck and Lockwood commented: "Terrorism is an historically misleading and politically loaded term which invites conceptual and ideological dissonance.[25]

3. The ILC, which combines professionalism and expertise with broad political representation, should be considered as a vehicle for developing the draft articles.

There should, of course, be no illusion that any combination of tactics will succeed if the international political atmosphere is fundamentally unfavorable. Even when conventions are completed, as in the case of the three ICAO instruments, the failure of a significant number of Arab states to ratify or comply with their provisions makes safe havens readily available. Progress toward solution or alleviation of the Palestinian problem would not only pave the way for additional and more effective international instruments but would, as the Arabs and many Africans argued during consideration of the question, eliminate many acts of terrorism by eliminating the causes.

As for foregoing indicates, dealing with the causes of much terrorism—misery, frustration, and repression—must be a crucial factor in eliminating or substantially reducing such acts. But given the present international situation and the dismal record of human history, what other approaches might be useful?

Here, one is again drawn to the Yugoslav logic: "Grave offenses and serious crimes should not be treated as political acts even in those cases where motivations for committing such acts are of a political nature."* Next efforts, therefore, might be directed to offenses so grave and crimes so heinous that all states, or at least the preponderant majority of states, are prepared to legislate against such acts. Logical candidates for international instruments might be:

1. A convention to prevent the export of violence to countries not parties to a conflict (This might, in substance, be similar to the U.S. draft on terrorism, but a new effort might have a better chance of success by avoiding use of that term; by enlisting Third World sponsorship, with appropriate modifications to accommodate their views; and by working on a less hurried timetable, thus allowing for drafting by the ILC and a certain cooling-off period after the emotions generated in the fall of 1972.)

2. A convention against the dispatch, through the international postal service, of letter-bombs and other explosive devices

3. A convention against the taking of child hostages or other violent acts against children

The foregoing are illustrative and are by no means exhaustive. In any such moves, the politically loaded term *terrorism* should be avoided, leaving it to polemics and the media. Further, as Franck and Lockwood argue, governments and individuals should be equally enjoined from carrying out such actions.[26]

Apparently with such considerations in mind, West Germany proposed to the UN General Assembly at its 31st session the drafting of an international convention against the taking of hostages. The word *terrorism* was not used. Even so, Libya introduced an amendment to the German draft resolution that would have restricted protection to "innocent" hostages. Intensive negotiations

---

*Note also the following paragraph on hijacking, which was worked out at the 1971 session of the Institute of International Law at Zagreb, as quoted in Verzyl, *International Law in Historical Perspective*, vol. 5 (Leydon: Sijthof, 1972), p. 309:

No purpose or objective, whether political or other, can constitute justification for such illegal acts; and . . . every State whose territory the authors of such acts may be found has the right and the obligation, if it does not extradite such persons, to undertake such persons, to undertake criminal prosecution against them.

led to a compromise, which avoided making any distinction among hostages and which was acceptable to all countries. Libya agreed to stop insisting on references to "innocent" hostages, and West Germany dropped the provision expressly calling for the prosecution or extradition for prosecution of those who take hostages; the punishment of hostage takers is left implicit. The compromise formula was adopted by consensus in the General Assembly on December 15, 1976, as Resolution 31/103, which established a 35-member Ad Hoc Committee on the Drafting of an International Convention against the Taking of Hostages.

The ad hoc committee held two sessions, in 1977 and 1978, without agreement on a draft convention. The committee's Working Group II has carried out extensive work on nine draft articles, based on a draft convention submitted by West Germany and related working papers submitted by other delegations.[27] Its report presented tentative formulations, on which there were various stages of agreement concerning the following: (1) obligations of states to take measures to prevent preparations in their respective territories for the taking of hostages; (2) measures to be taken to ease the situation and secure the release of hostages; (3) obligations of states to return "any object" illegally obtained as a result of the taking of hostages; (4) suggestions as to the type of penalties to be imposed; (5) obligations to take offenders into custody; (6) rights of persons taken into custody to communicate with, or be visited by, a representative of the state of which he or she is a national; and (7) matters concerning extradition.

Again, as in the case of the proposed convention against international terrorism, the main obstacle has been disagreement over the status of national liberation movements. Algeria, on behalf of a group of committee members, proposed the inclusion of the following paragraph in the convention:

> For the purposes of this Convention, the term "taking hostages" shall not include any act or acts covered by the rules of international law applicable to armed conflicts in which peoples are fighting against colonial domination and foreign occupation and against apartheid and racist regimes, in the exercise of the right of peoples to self-determination embodied in the Charter of the United Nations and the Declaration on Principles of International Law concerning Friendly Relations and Co-operation among States in accordance with the Charter of the United Nations.[28]

Other members favored a comprehensive approach—to the effect that the scope of the convention should be broad enough to encompass all cases of taking of hostages and that the convention would supplement, if necessary, the Geneva conventions of 1948 and the 1977 additional protocols. In that connection, France proposed that the preamble include the statement that "the taking of hostages is and must be prescribed always, everywhere and in all circumstances."

Despite this clash of views, the committee recommended that the General Assembly again invite it to continue its work in 1979. Its first two sessions have been notably more businesslike and productive than those of the committee on terrorism, discussed above.[29] But further progress will probably depend either on an improvement in the international political situation, notably in the Middle East and Southern Africa, or a compromise, like the one worked out in the adoption of the Convention on the Prevention and Punishment Against Internationally Protected Persons, described earlier.

A concrete case involving hostages came before the Security Council in July 1976, following the dramatic Israeli rescue of hostages from terrorist confinement at the Entebbe, Uganda, airport. An Air France airplane had been hijacked en route from Athens to Paris and taken to Entebbe. The hijackers then released non-Jews and some non-Israeli Jews but continued to hold more than 100 Jewish hostages, mostly Israelis. On July 4, Israel sent a small force to Entebbe, which, after an hour and a half on the ground, rescued the hostages and returned with them to Israel. Three of the hostages, one Israeli soldier, and a number of Ugandan soldiers were killed, and several Ugandan aircraft were destroyed.

At the Security Council session on July 12, William Scranton, the U.S. representative, characterized the Israeli action as the exercise of "a well-established right (under international law) to use limited force for the protection of one's own nation from an imminent threat of injury or death in a situation where the State in whose territory they are located either is unwilling or unable to protect them." Scranton then urged that the Security Council address itself to the cause of incidents like the one at Entebbe, namely, the scourge of hijacking. Two days later, the United States and Great Britain presented a draft resolution under which the Security Council would have condemned hijacking and all other acts that threatened the lives of passengers and crews. The Security Council itself had on September 9, 1970, adopted by consensus Resolution 286 appealing for the immediate release of all passengers and crews held as a result of hijackings and calling on states "to take all possible legal steps to prevent further hijacking or any other interference with international civil air travel." Again, on June 20, 1972, the Security Council had stated its grave concern "at the threat to the lives of passengers and crews arising from the hijacking of aircraft." Moreover, 12 of the 15 states that sat on the Security Council in 1976 had ratified the Convention for the Suppression of Unlawful Seizure of Aircraft by Hijacking, signed at The Hague on December 16, 1970. In effect, then, the British/U.S. draft was a reaffirmation of views already endorsed by the Security Council, not a breaking of new ground. Yet this time, because of political overtones, the British/U.S. draft received only six votes, with Panama and Romania voting in the negative and the other seven members not voting. Since nine votes were required, it was not adopted.

On the other hand, a draft resolution introduced by Benin, Libya, and Tanzania, which would have condemned Israel's "flagrant violation" of Uganda's sovereignty, was not pressed to a vote. Evidently, the sponsors knew that they could not get the required nine votes. In light of the anti-Israel bias of a majority of the Security Council's members, the standoff could be considered an Israeli success.

The next year, in the fall of 1977, a Lufthansa plane was hijacked in an attempt to use the passengers as hostages in bargaining for the release of terrorists in West Germany. German commandos, in the pattern of the Israeli operation at Entebbe, stormed the plane and rescued the passengers. This time, however, the commandos operated in cooperation with the government of the country where the hijacked plane and hostages were being held—Somalia. IFALPA, outraged by the acts of the terrorists, threatened a massive strike unless the UN General Assembly took action. Thereupon, the Assembly, on November 3, unanimously adopted Resolution 32/8, which (1) reaffirmed its condemnation of hijacking or other interference with civil aviation by the threat or use of force and all acts of violence directed at passengers, crew members, or airplanes; (2) called upon all states to take the necessary measures to prevent such acts and to cooperate with the UN and ICAO in order to assure that passengers and crew members "are not used as a means of extorting any advantage whatsoever"; (3) appealed to all states that had not yet ratified the three ICAO conventions to urgently envisage ratification of, or adherence to, them; and (4) urgently called upon ICAO to undertake stronger measures to assure the safety of civil aviation. The forceful language and unanimous adoption of this resolution appeared to be encouraging; however, General Assembly resolutions are recommendations and are not binding on states. Nor, as noted earlier, did the resolution's adoption appear to give any help to those working in the ad hoc committee for the adoption of an international convention against the taking of hostages. It did, however, give an additional argument and a psychological boost to the Western countries in their campaign of bilateral approaches to win additional accessions to the three ICAO treaties.

Let there be no illusions. In the prevailing political atmosphere of a UN dominated by a Third World majority, negotiating any convention against terrorism will be an uphill struggle. As long as the problems of Southern Africa and the Palestinians remain unsolved, there is little likelihood that a convention without major loopholes can be adopted. But certain feasible steps, both bilateral and multilateral, can be taken in the UN and ICAO to supplement outside actions that offer greater promise of dealing effectively with terrorism.

First, efforts should be continued in the UN toward the formulation and adoption of a convention against the taking of hostages. Many other conventions and declarations have taken long years to negotiate, for example, the convention against racial discrimination and the human rights covenants. The UN is not a superstate that can coerce governments—a fact of life for which the West is often grateful. But it is an institution where government attitudes can be changed through persuasion, negotiation, and compromise. Perhaps the compromise adopted in connection with the Convention on the Prevention and Punishment of Crimes Against Internationally Protected Persons, in the form of a separate and concurrent resolution concerning liberation movements (described above), would facilitate agreement on a new convention with widespread support.

Second, new efforts should be directed toward working out conventions against grave offenses and serious crimes that the international community could agree to condemn and punish regardless of political motives, for example, the export of violence to countries not party to the conflict or the dispatch of letter-bombs and other explosive devices through the international postal service.

Third, current Western efforts to persuade more countries to accede to the three ICAO conventions should be intensified and carried out persistently. As adherence to the conventions grows, so will the moral pressure on the holdouts. Moreover, the international climate for punitive measures against offending states will be improved.

Fourth, the secretary general of the UN should be required by states to report to the General Assembly annually on the exact position *as regards ratification and implementation of hijacking conventions*. He should be authorized to seek this information formally from each state. The need to report regularly on one's shortcomings is a morally effective technique. Such reports should be given adequate coverage by the media.

Fifth, the public denunciation of hijacking should be maintained, with airlines and aircrew taking the initiative. Regular conferences and public meetings should keep resolutions flowing to all the relevant international agencies.

Sixth, airlines should combine to blacklist countries that have consistently failed to take action or which have conspired with hijackers. IFALPA should call upon its members to refuse to fly to such countries. In this, they should be supported by the unions and associations of other members of aircrews and ground personnel. Ground personnel could refuse to service aircraft of the blacklisted state.[30]

Now, in 1978, major industrial nations are planning new measures. Meeting at Bonn in early August, the heads of government of Great Britain, Canada, West Germany, France, Italy, Japan, and the United States decided that their countries. which represent almost 70 percent of the non-Communist world's air traffic, would work out an agreement to take "prompt, effective and co-ordinated" action against countries that harbor hijackers. The agreement would stop all air traffic between the seven and such safe-haven countries. If the country that was the final destination of a hijacked plane did not punish the hijacker or extradite him or her to another country for punishment, as well as return the plane, the sanctions would go into effect automatically. This would mean that all air traffic of every airline would be halted between that country and the seven countries that signed the Bonn agreement. The sanctions could be removed only when the country harboring the hijacker extradited or prosecuted him or her and returned the hijacked plane.

Other useful steps might be the following: (1) coordinated intelligence and contingency planning, (2) improved technology of electronic surveillance to detect metals and explosives, (3) more stringent customs procedures, (4) stepped-up security at embassies and airports, (5) development of screening profiles to identify terrorists, (7) improved aircraft construction to partition passengers from pilots, (8) bilateral and multilateral extradition agreements, (9) direct pressure on states that harbor terrorists, and (10) development of clandestine counterterrorist organizations to combat guerrilla groups or to create incentives for other states to support actions against terrorism.[31]

Such action outside the UN and ICAO is highly desirable and is likely to be more effective than what can be accomplished at the UN or ICAO under current conditions. But it is not an either/or proposition. Action inside the UN should be complementary to efforts outside it. Above all, there must be persistence and patience. These are not easy problems. There are no easy answers.

NOTES

1. United Nations, General Assembly, Report of the International Law Commission on the Work of Its Sixth Session (supp. 2 [A/2693]).

2. *The Interdependent* (March 1974); UN Association of the USA, New York, N.Y., United Nations General Assembly, p. 1.

3. *Summary Records* (A/C 6/418), p. 41.

4. *Reflexions sur la Definition et la Repression du Terrorisme* (Brussels: Editions de l'Universite de Bruxelles, 1974), pp. 194-96.

5. United Nations, (Doc. A/C. 6/L. 879).

6. United Nations (Doc. A/AC./60/2) (June 22, 1973).

7. United Nations, General Assembly, *Report of the Ad Hoc Committee on International Terrorism* (supp. 28 [A/9028]), p. 6.

8. Ibid. For a legal analysis of the divergences on key points, see Thomas M. Franck and Bert B. Lockwood, pp. 72-82, and *Relfexions sur la Definition et la Repression du Terrorisme*, pp. 105-97.

9. United Nations, General Assembly, *Report of the Ad Hoc Committee on International Law Commission.*

10. United Nations, General Assembly, *Report of the International Law Commission on the Work of Its 24th Session* (A/8710/Res. 1) (1972), p. 88, pars. 54 and 55.

11. Ibid., pp. 108-24.

12. United Nations, General Assembly, *Report of the Sixth Committee on Agenda Item 85* (A/8892) (November 21, 1972), pp. 41-72.

13. United Nations, Convention Article 2 (1), U.S. draft Article 1.

14. United Nations, Convention Article 2 (2), U.S. draft Article 2.

15. United Nations, Convention Article 3, U.S. draft Article 4.

16. United Nations, Convention Article 5, U.S. draft Article 5.

17. United Nations, Convention Article 6, U.S. draft Article 6.

18. United Nations, Convention Articles 7 and 8, U.S. draft Article 7.

19. United Nations, Convention Cert. 9, U.S. draft Article 8.

20. United Nations, Convention Article 10, U.S. draft Article 2.

21. Organization of American States Official Documents, CP/December 1970, Res. 1, Corr. 1 and GY/Res. 4 (1/70), Res. 1—Convention to Prevent and Punish Acts of Terrorism Taking the Form of Crimes Against Persons and Related Extortion That Are of International Significance.

22. GAOR (Doc.A/9407), p. 50.

23. See list in United Nations, General Assembly, *Report of the International Law Commission on the Work of Its 24th Session*, p. 108.

24. Ibid., p. 124.

25. Franck and Lockwood, p. 89.

26. Ibid., p. 90.

27. United Nations, General Assembly, *Report of the Ad Hoc Committee on the Drafting of an International Convention Against the Taking of Hostages* (General Assembly Official Records, 32d sess., supp. no. 39 [A/32/39]), annex II.

28. Ibid., p. 110.

29. See United Nations, General Assembly, *Report of the Ad Hoc Committee on the Drafting of an International Convention Against the Taking of Hostages* (General Assembly Official Records, 33rd sess., supp. no. 39 [A/33/39]).

30. Security Council Official Records, July 12, 1976.

31. I am indebted, for some of these suggestions, to William Clifford, *How to Combat Hijacking* (Canberra: Australian Institute of Criminology, 1978).

32. These steps are suggested in Rosen and Frank, "Measures Against Instructional Terrorism," in *International Terrorism and World Security*, ed. David Carlton and Carlo Schaerf (New York: Halsted Press, 1975), pp. 60–68.

APPENDIX A
TERRORISM—
AN OVERVIEW, 1970–78

Charles A. Russell

AN UPWARD TREND

Terrorist activities have increased steadily over the past eight years. From a recorded total of 293 acts in 1970, terrorist operations, worldwide, rose gradually to 388 incidents in 1974. (See Figure A.1.) Since then, the upward trend has been dramatic: 572 incidents in 1975, 728 in 1976, 1,256 in 1977, and 867 through October 4, 1978—with a projected 1978 total of 1,155. Of particular concern is the fact that 58.2 percent of all terrorist actions recorded since January 1970 have taken place within the past 33 months—2,851 acts out of an eight-year total of 4,899.

INCREASED SOPHISTICATION

While the past three years have seen the greatest overall growth since 1970 in the number of terrorist acts, they also have witnessed a significant rise in the level of terrorist sophistication, Kidnapping, assassination, and attacks against business, government, and police facilities all require detailed planning, a highly trained cadre, available safe houses, vehicles, automatic weapons, an efficient support structure, a capable intelligence collection network, and a high degree of coordination within the individual terrorist teams. In short, to carry out these complex actions successfully, the individual terrorists must be better trained and equipped than those involved in bombings, which are relatively simple.

Published as *Executive Risk Assessment*, vol. 1, no. 2 (December 1978). Reprinted with permission from Risks International, Inc., Alexandria, Virginia.

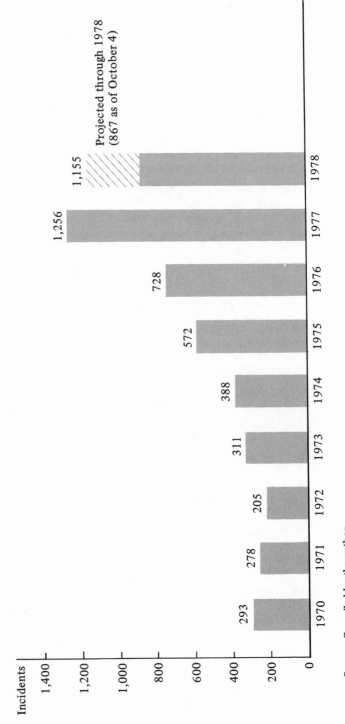

FIGURE A.1

Terrorist Incidents, 1970–78

Projected through 1978
(867 as of October 4)

Source: Compiled by the author.

Accordingly, it is disturbing to note that 49 percent of all kidnappings conducted since 1970 have taken place in the past 33 months, as well as 62.5 percent of all assassinations and 57 percent of all attacks on facilities. Simply said, the terrorists operating today—with their overall success rate of 80 percent—are brighter, better organized, and much more effective than their counterparts of the early 1970s. In addition, they are willing to take greater operational risks.

HIGHER RISKS ACCEPTED

Each of the tactics mentioned above is clearly a high-risk undertaking. Armed guards are assigned in greater numbers to corporate and government figures overseas—the primary kidnap and assassination targets. In Italy alone, executives and firms employ an estimated 85,000 armed private security personnel. Security systems and human protection are standard in many European, Latin American, and Middle Eastern commercial and government offices. Thus, the increasing emphasis on attacking intrinsically dangerous targets would seem to indicate a much greater willingness on the part of terrorists to risk death, injury, or imprisonment to achieve their ends. Generally, this was not the case in the early 1970s. When this willingness to take on high-risk operations is coupled with the trend toward nihilism (destruction for destruction's sake) so evident in many groups today, the modern terrorist becomes a formidable opponent.

BUSINESS: A PRIORITY TARGET

Terrorist targeting (both human and nonhuman) over the past eight years has persistently focused on business. Of the 5,250 individual targets hit in the 4,899 incidents recorded since January 1970, 44.3 percent were business connected. (See Figure A.2.) Of these, 11.1 percent were U.S. corporations and firms. If we look at only the past three years, total business targeting approaches 50 percent. Today, there is little question that business organizations are a priority terrorist target.

The evolution of terrorist targeting to a focus on business is a direct result of pragmatic and ideological considerations. It is not a sudden development but, rather, one that has grown over the past eight years.

The priority targets for terrorist attack have changed substantially since 1970. An analysis of the 4,899 incidents that took place between January 1, 1970, and October 4, 1978, indicates three separate and distinct stages in the process.

During the early 1970s (1970-73), terrorist groups in Europe and Latin America, as well as in most other areas of the world, focused their efforts on

FIGURE A.2

Terrorist Targets, January 1970–78

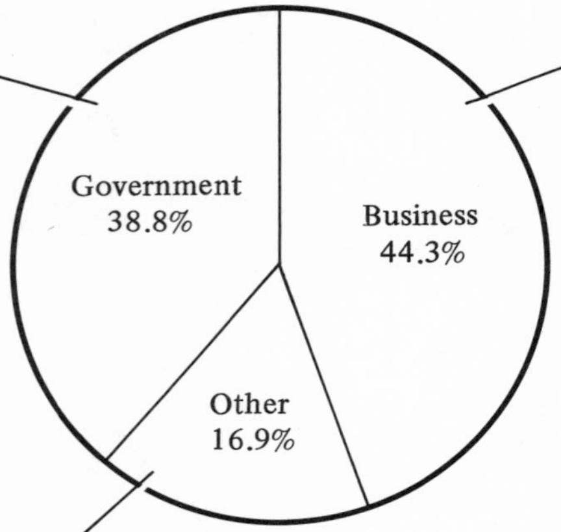

Business 44.3%		
Domestic	17.0%
United States	10.0%
Foreign	6.0%
Transport non-United States	5.0%
Media	3.2%
Utilities non-United States	2.0%
Utilities United States	1.0%
Transport United States	1.0%
	44.3%

Government 38.8%	
Police–Military Domestic	12.0%
Diplomatic non-United States	9.0%
Government Domestic	8.0%
Police–Military United States	6.0%
Diplomatic United States	3.0%
Government, United States	.8%
	38.8%

Other 16.9%	
Other Foreign	8.0%
Political non-United States	6.0%
Other United States	2.0%
Unknown	.9%
	16.9%

Source: Compiled by the author.

attacking police and government facilities and personnel. These groups expected such acts to move governments to meet their demands. The failure of this strategy was quickly evident. Governments did not collapse, and police shot back. By 1973, terrorist targeting had shifted rather definitively to assaults against diplomatic establishments and the abduction of foreign diplomats and ranking government personnel. Again, the terrorist belief was that governments would bow to their demands as a result of the leverage gained through these abductions.

Despite acute embarrassment in many cases, governments did not give in. Instead, they often increased security measures and began active counterterrorist programs. By 1975, therefore, corporate targets became a top terrorist priority. In the succeeding three years, almost 50 percent of all terrorist operations were directed against business facilities and personnel. Unable to lock their doors—as in the case of government offices and diplomatic facilities—corporations and business firms have become primary targets for robbery, assault, or arson. Individual businessmen, as kidnap victims, are invaluable to the modern terrorist. Today, their ransoms are the primary source for operational terrorist funds.

REGIONAL REVIEW

On a regional basis, terrorist activities have accelerated most significantly in Europe and Latin America during the last three years. (See Figure A.3.) In Europe, incidents rose from 421 in 1976 to 734 in 1977 and are estimated to reach 674 for all of 1978 (506 recorded as of October 4, 1978). Throughout this three-year period, Italy was the most active country in the region, followed by Spain, West Germany, and Northern Ireland.

In Italy, bombings, attacks against business facilities, and kidnappings of corporate executives and government personnel were the preferred tactics, while in Spain, assassination and bombing were paramount. Targets of Italian terrorists were primarily industrial and business facilities (including those of U.S. and other foreign corporations), and among these, Italian domestic firms were hit most frequently. Particular attention was focused on Fiat, Breda, Alfa Romeo, Lancia, Italsider, Montedison, and the joint Italian-German firm, Sit-Siemens. U.S. corporate targets included the Chemical Bank, IBM, and Honeywell.

In contrast to Italy, Spanish terrorists emphasized attacks on police, military, and government targets. Significant 1977-78 operations included the assassination of ranking military, police, and judicial officials in Madrid and Barcelona, assaults on police and government facilities throughout Spain, the deliberate execution of police officers (20 since the first of October), and a $5.6 million attack on the nuclear reactor facility at Lemóniz. The contractor for this project, Iberduero, a major Spanish electrical supplier, incurred losses of over $700,000 from some 80 terrorist assaults during 1977-78.

FIGURE A.3

Terrorist Incidents, by Region

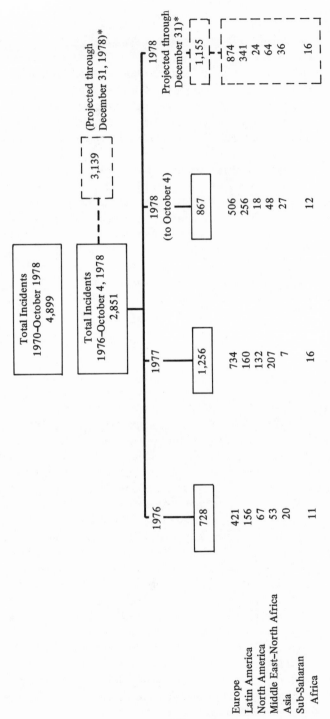

*Projections based on monthly incident rate by area, January 1 to October 4, 1978, continuing throughout the remainder of the year.
Source: Compiled by the author.

As is evident from Figure A.3, 1977 was a peak year for terrorist activity in Europe. A slight decline is projected for 1978—from 734 incidents in 1977 to 674 during 1978. This moderate drop may be attributed to a combination of factors. Significant among these are tough antiterrorist laws adopted in Italy, Spain, and West Germany. These new laws permit the use of wiretap equipment in terrorist surveillances, as well as mail interception. They also include provisions for the rapid legal processing of those involved in terrorist acts. Intra-European police cooperation also has improved, particularly in the exchange of data on terrorist operations, tactics, groups, and personalities. Perhaps even more significant are the losses in trained cadre suffered by West German, Italian, and Spanish groups during late 1977 and early 1978.

As pointed out previously, many of the operations carried out by terrorists in recent years have been essentially high-risk actions. Substantial numbers of experienced cadre have been lost in these activities—killed, wounded, or imprisoned. This was particularly true in Spain and Italy. In Italy, the Red Brigades, Armed Proletarian Nuclei, and First Line, all major terrorist groups, lost most of their leadership elements. Other similar losses were evident in West Germany and Spain. As a result, with the exception of a few high-visibility propaganda operations, such as the kidnap-execution of former Italian Premier Moro, 1978 has been—to a certain extent—a year of retrenchment for many of these groups. The emphasis has been on recruiting new members, improving security, training new personnel, reestablishing damaged support mechanisms, and, in general, preparing for the future. This means that the major terrorist groups in Spain, Italy, and West Germany are far from wiped out, despite significant police successes. They are still intact and to be reckoned with.

The other major area of terrorist activity during the entire 1970–78 time span has been Latin America. Unlike the dramatic rise in incidents that has characterized Europe over the past three years, the overall upward trend in Latin America has been evident since the early 1970s. Initially, the focal points were Argentina and Uruguay. The most active areas today are Colombia, El Salvador, Nicaragua, Mexico, and Guatemala. In addition to bombing, a highly favored terrorist tactic in all these nations, the kidnapping of business and corporate personnel for ransom has attracted terrorist attention. In these operations, both domestic and foreign (including U.S.) corporations have been targeted. To date, the $41 million ransom paid for the release of the Born brothers, executives in the Argentine firm of Bunge and Born, stands as one of the highest ransom payments anywhere for the release of a corporate executive. For U.S. corporations, the 1974 payment of $14.2 million to free Victor Samuelson, an official of Esso Argentina, is the highest publicly recorded ransom for a U.S. executive.

El Salvador, Colombia, and Mexico currently are the leading Latin American nations in regard to the kidnapping of foreign (including U.S.) business personnel. In El Salvador, between November 24 and December 8, 1978, four executives of Dutch, British, and Japanese firms were abducted for ransom by the Marxist oriented Armed Forces of National Resistance (FARN). In the case of Franz Schuitema, a Phillips Corporation executive, payments for ransom, food distribution, and international media publicity for the FARN exceeded $2 million. A ransom of $5 million reportedly was demanded for the release of Japanese executive Takakazu Suzuki, associated with Synthetic Industries of Central America. In May 1978, the Japanese manager of this same firm was kidnapped and killed when group demands for a $4 million ransom were not met. In August, Kjell Bjork of the Swedish firm Telefonica LM Ericson was kidnapped and subsequently released upon publication of a communique, which had been demanded by FARN. The terms for the release of two British executives associated with the Bank of London and South America have not been made public.

In Colombia, kidnapping and attacks against primarily domestic business firms have been popular operations with the Communist-directed Revolutionary Armed Forces of Colombia (FARC). As reported in the November issue of *Executive Risk Assessment*, one of the more significant 1978 abductions was that involving Nicolas Escobar Soto, manager of Texaco operations in Colombia. Other recent victims there include Miguel de German Ribon, an industrialist and former ambassador to France. A $500,000 ransom for his release was demanded. Three other kidnappings in Colombia have involved the children of wealthy industrialists, including one for whom a $270,000 ransom was demanded. In connection with another, the child's driver and bodyguard were wounded.

A slightly different type of target in Colombia involved a rancher held for $100,000 and the proprietor of several rural farms who was held for $27,000. Among foreign business targets was an Italian industrialist, owner of the Bartoplast Plastic Corporation. He was held for $1.4 million ransom. Two Americans, Peter Boutre, manager of Lafayette in Colombia, and Gregory Esteaver, were kidnapped and detained for ransoms of $150,000 and $700,000, respectively. Most of these operations took place in major urban areas, particularly Bogota.

Latin America lacks the trained and equipped police forces and the intelligence-exchange agreements on terrorist operations and groups found in Europe. Moreover, considering the lucrative aspects of kidnapping, terrorist operations in this area are expected to rise. While it is not anticipated that actions in El Salvador, Colombia, or Mexico will reach the state of terrorist activity found in Argentina or Uruguay during the early 1970s, a significant upward movement is anticipated in 1979. In this rise, domestic and foreign business firms will remain priority targets.

KIDNAPPING: THE FAVORED TACTIC

As indicated in the November 1978 *Executive Risk Assessment* ("Executive Kidnapping—A Growing Threat")* and as evident from the preceding para-

---

*The November 1978 *Executive Risk Assessment* is devoted to a detailed analysis of this activity.

graphs, kidnapping is favored by most sophisticated terrorist groups. Like facility attacks and assassination, it is a complex operation, requiring skilled personnel, an outstanding intelligence-collection capability, and a superior support apparatus. Such resources are responsible for a success rate in these operations of over 94 percent. The abduction of corporate executives for ransom has become a major source of funds for terrorist groups. It is, therefore, not surprising that 54 percent of all terrorist kidnappings since 1970 have targeted business personnel.

Over the 1970–78 time span, 62 percent of all terrorist kidnappings took place in Latin America versus 21 percent in Western Europe. If actions in each region are viewed over the last three years, however, the growth patterns are reversed. In Latin America, 41 percent of all kidnappings since 1970 have occurred in the last three years, whereas in Western Europe, the figure is 75 percent. Europe has thus become an important area for kidnapping. The leading nations there are Italy and Spain.

In Latin America, kidnappings during the early and mid-1970s were concentrated in Argentina. Uruguay, Guatemala, and Mexico. Most targets were government officials, police officers, or persons affiliated with domestic business firms. Within the past three years—and particularly the last four months—kidnapping operations have been centered in Colombia, El Salvador, Nicaragua, and Mexico. In these nations, prime targets have been employees of foreign business firms, including those of U.S. corporations. Considering the inclination of some firms to meet ransom demands, terrorist operations against these targets are expected to continue.

U.S. nationals have been targets in 19.7 percent of all kidnappings since 1970. Fifty-five percent of these Americans have been business personnel. Data available for 33 percent of all kidnappings since 1970 indicate ransom demands totaling $290,180,000. Known payments in these cases reached at least $145,209,000.

FACILITY ATTACKS: INCREASED USE

Terrorist assaults against business, police, and government facilities have skyrocketed since the early 1970s. From a total of 29 operations in 1972, the yearly figure jumped to 201 during the first nine months of 1978. In all, 777 such actions took place during the 1970–78 time span. (See Table A.1.) Of these operations, 46.5 percent were directed against business installations. Fifty-seven percent of all facility attacks occurred within the last three years.

Dollar losses in terrorist operations against facilities (to include those resulting from bank robberies and other thefts) have totaled $129,653,000 since January 1970. Eighty-one percent of these losses ($105,050,000) took place in 1976, 1977, and 1978. In addition, 1,349 persons were killed, 902 wounded, and 3,286 taken hostage.

TABLE A.1

Facility Attacks, by Region

Area	January 1970–October 1978	January 1976–October 1978
Total facility attacks:	777	443
Europe	46%	49%
North America	5%	4%
Latin America	35%	32%
Middle East–North Africa	10%	9%
Asia	3%	4%
Sub-Saharan Africa	1%	2%

Source: Compiled by the author.

Geographically, as indicated above, by far the largest number of facility attacks occurred in Europe, followed by Latin America and the Middle East–North Africa region. Within Europe, the upward trend in these operations has been evident since 1972. The 18 significant attacks in that year were followed by 39 in 1975, 81 in 1977, and 89 in 1978 (as of October 4). Primary targets were domestic business firms, police posts, and government offices. Key countries were Italy, Spain, and Northern Ireland.

In addition to using automatic weapons, terrorist teams involved in facility attacks frequently resorted to arson. In Italy, Red Brigades arson activities against the Fiat Mirafiori Plant in Turin cost that corporation $2.7 million between December 1977 and April 1978. Overall, arson attacks by Italian terrorists resulted in industrial and commercial losses of more than $150 million between 1970 and October 1978.

Latin American terrorists have attacked primarily police and government installations. Frequently hit were those in Mexico, Guatemala, Nicaragua, El Salvador, and Colombia. In most countries within the region, calculated long-term terrorist campaigns against specific foreign or domestic business firms (as have developed against Fiat in Italy) are not a problem.

In contrast to Europe, where the trend in facility attacks rose gradually from the mid-1970s to a high point in 1978, similar operations in Latin America accelerated only recently. Prior to 1977, the yearly total was between 25 and 30 serious actions (significant damage or loss of life). In 1978, it jumped to 91 operations. Much of this rise is attributable to expanded terrorist activity in Colombia, El Salvador, and Nicaragua. Foreign and domestic business firms, as well as government and police facilities, have been priority targets.

ASSASSINATION: A LIMITED THREAT TO BUSINESS

Like kidnappings and facility attacks, assassination actions increased rapidly over the last three years. Sixty-two and one-half percent of all such operations took place during the 1976–78 time span. Three hundred and sixty-three of the 581 attempted or successful assassinations recorded since 1970 occurred within this three-year period. The focal point for this activity was Europe. Latin America held second place. In Europe, Spain led all other nations, followed by Italy, Northern Ireland, and West Germany. Within Latin America, the most active nations were Mexico, El Salvador, Nicaragua, and Colombia. During the early 1970s, Argentina and Uruguay also were significant.

Since Europe and Latin America have some of the most sophisticated and skilled terrorist groups active today (outside the various Palestinian organizations and the Japanese Red Army [JRA]), the prominence of assassination in these two regions is not unexpected. As with kidnappings and facility attacks, a successful assassination requires careful advance planning, technical skill on the part of those involved, an excellent support and logistics network, accurate intelligence, and highly dedicated personnel.

TABLE A.2

Assassinations, by Region

Area	January 1970– October 1978	January 1976– October 1978
Total assassinations:	581	363
Europe	45%	48%
North America	8%	3%
Latin America	29%	31%
Middle East–North Africa	12%	14%
Asia	3%	1%
Sub-Saharan Africa	3%	3%

Source: Compiled by the author.

Despite the overall increase in assassination operations during recent years, businessmen are not a significant target. As hostages held for ransom, corporate executives are valuable sources of income for the terrorist. As assassination victims, they no longer are useful for bargaining purposes. Of the 858 terrorist assassination victims recorded since 1970, only 13 percent were business connected. Three percent of these were U.S. corporate personnel, 2 percent foreign businessmen, and 8 percent persons associated with domestic business firms. In contrast, 42 percent of all assassination victims were police officers and 18 percent diplomats and government personnel. Table A.2 depicts the geographic distribution of assassination operations since 1970.

BOMBINGS AS A TERRORIST TOOL

While kidnappings, facility attacks, and assassinations have increased at a proportionately greater rate than other terrorist tactics, bombings still lead quantitatively overall. Of the 4,899 significant terrorist incidents recorded since 1970, 3,043 were bombings.* Of these, 47 percent were directed against business targets (including commercial establishments, business offices and factories, transportation facilities, and utilities). Globally, bombing incidents reached a peak in 1977, with 857 acts (28 percent of all bombings since January 1970). As of October 4, the 1978 count was 448, with a projected total of 597 by the end of the year—a decrease of 260 incidents from 1977.

Fifty-four percent of all bombings since 1970 have taken place in Europe, primarily in Italy, Spain, Northern Ireland, and West Germany. (See Table A.3.) As mentioned previously, the major targets in these countries have been government, police, and business facilities. After Europe, the other five world regions ranked as follows: North America (primarily the United States) with 19 percent; Latin America, 13 percent; Middle East–North Africa, 12 percent; Asia, 2 percent; and Sub-Saharan Africa, less than 1 percent.

In North America, 575 acts, or 86.2 percent of 667 terrorist incidents recorded since January 1970 have been bombings. Police offices, corporations, and utilities were the primary targets. Within Latin America, most bombings over the past eight years occurred in Colombia, El Salvador, Argentina, Nicaragua, Guatemala, and Mexico. Business, government, and police installations were the targets. In the Middle East, Israel, Lebanon, Turkey, and Iran were the most active areas.

Overall, terrorist bombing activities carried out between January 1970 and October 1978 resulted in 745 killed, 2,530 wounded, and reported dollar losses of more than $108 million.

Within the past three years, as is evident from Table A.3, bombing incidents rose rapidly in Europe between 1976 and October 1978. Of the 1,779 major

---

*Bombings recorded in the Risks International data base are only those where (1) material or human loss is significant, (2) the device involved is unique, (3) the target is significant, or (4) the methods used to emplace the device are unusual.

TABLE A.3

Bombing Incidents, by Region

Area	January 1970–October 1978	January 1976–October 1978
Total bombings	3,043	1,779
Europe	54%	63%
North America	19%	11%
Latin America	13%	13%
Middle East–North Africa	12%	12%
Asia	2%	—*
Sub-Saharan Africa	—*	—*

*Less than 1 percent.
Source: Compiled by the author.

bombings recorded for this time span, 1,126 (or 63 percent) took place there. This represents a sharp rise from the overall European figure of 54 percent for the entire 1970-78 time span. Most of this increase is attributable to expanded terrorist bombing campaigns in Italy, Spain, and Northern Ireland. In North America, the drop in reported incidents coincides with the end to the Vietnam conflict and reduced overall activity by U.S. terrorist groups, such as the Weather Underground (WUO) and the New World Liberation Front (NWLF). Dollar losses from bombings during the 1976-78 time period totaled $58,764,000, or 54 percent of all bomb damage since 1970.

OTHER TACTICS

In addition to the primary tactics already discussed, terrorists have exploited numerous other techniques to attack business targets and personnel. Leg shooting (*azzoppare*, "laming"), for example, has long been a favorite in Italy. Since May 1975, 65 of these actions have taken place. Often carried out by two or more terrorists, the tactic involves one person approaching the victim to ask an innocuous question. While the target is temporarily distracted, another terrorist walks up to him, points at his legs, and fires one to 11 rounds at point-blank range. The weapon normally used is a nine-millimeter pistol. However, submachine guns have now come into vogue. As a result, several leg shootings have resulted in fatalities.

Italian executives who have been leg-shooting victims include the manager of the Alfa Romeo plant in Turin, the director of foreign operations at Pirelli Tire in Milan, the Fiat Mirafiori plant manager in Milan, and the manager of the

Chemical Bank in Milan. With the exception of one action of this type in West Germany and another in Spain (December 9, 1978), this tactic has been confined to Italy thus far.

Another tactic used infrequently to date is disruption. Confined essentially to West Germany, operations by the Revolutionary Cells there involved the use of acid to damage fare machines in several urban subway systems. As in the case of leg shooting, this tactic has been confined to a limited geographic area.

Hijacking, a popular terrorist tool during the early 1970s, has declined substantially in recent years. Twenty-four of the 78 terrorist hijackings since 1970 took place during the 1976-78 time span. A number of these cases did not involve aircraft, however, and concerned only buses, trains, and small ships. Over the 1970-78 time period, 29 percent of all hijackings took place in Europe, followed by the Middle East-North Africa (22 percent), Latin America (22 percent), Asia (18 percent), North America (5 percent), and Sub-Saharan Africa (4 percent). Eighty-one percent of these operations involved aircraft, and 19 percent involved other modes of transportation. The high-point years for hijackings were 1970 and 1972, with 22 percent occurring in 1970 and 18 percent in 1972.

OUTLOOK

Although total terrorist incidents declined slightly during 1978 from an all-time high in 1977, the overall trend since 1974 has been sharply up. (See Figure A.4.) The marked rise in complex operations (assassinations, kidnappings, and facility attacks) is significant and indicates an increased capability upon the part of existing terrorist groups. While the total number of individuals involved in terrorism today may be fewer than in 1970-73, those so engaged are more sophisticated at their craft.

In short, the terrorist of 1978 is more professional, more skilled, better organized, and more dedicated than his or her counterpart of the early 1970s. This is doubly significant, since the largest dollar losses to business have come from complex terrorist operations—specifically, facility attacks and kidnappings. Together, these two types of operations account for $254,228,000 of the $362,306,000 known direct dollar losses attributable to terrorism. In addition, such operations have resulted in 1,349 persons killed, 902 wounded, and 3,705 hostages taken (3,286 in facility attacks and 419 in kidnappings).

While it is not anticipated that terrorist operations in 1979 will exceed the 1978 projected total, a continued and steady rise in kidnappings and facility attacks is expected, primarily in Europe and Latin America. Colombia, El Salvador, Nicaragua, Guatemala, and Mexico will remain key nations in Latin America. Italy and Spain will continue as the leading targets in European terrorism.

FIGURE A.4

Terrorist Tactics and Incidents, 1976–78

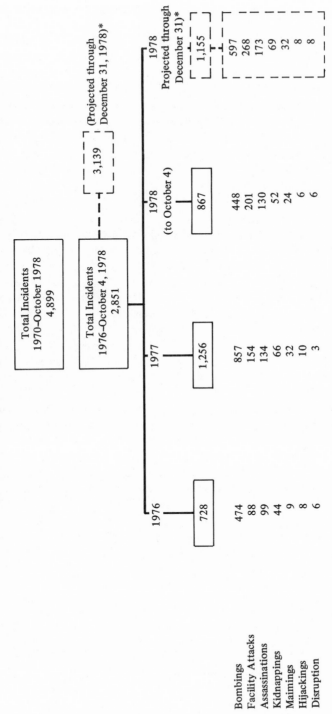

	1976	1977	1978 (to October 4)	1978 Projected through December 31)*
	728	1,256	867	1,155
Bombings	474	857	448	597
Facility Attacks	88	154	201	268
Assassinations	99	134	130	173
Kidnappings	44	66	52	69
Maimings	9	32	24	32
Hijackings	8	10	6	8
Disruption	6	3	6	8

Total Incidents
1970–October 1978
4,899

Total Incidents
1976–October 4, 1978
2,851

3,139 [Projected through
December 31, 1978)*

*Projections based on monthly incident rate by tactic, January 1 to October 4, 1978, continuing throughout the remainder of the year.
Source: Compiled by the author.

TERMINOLOGY AND DATA BASE DESCRIPTION

All statistical information contained in this report was derived from the Risks International data base.

For purposes of the data base, terrorism is defined as the threatened or actual use of force and violence to attain a political goal through fear, coercion, and intimidation. Materials contained in the Risks International data base relate only to significant actions carried out by terrorist groups operating within the United States and overseas, excluding Communist countries. Actions by criminal elements are not recorded in the data base.

The 5,000 plus terrorist operations included in the data base are categorized by type of activity. Categories used are: (1) kidnapping, (2) hijacking, (3) assassination, (4) maiming, (5) attacks against facilities, and (6) bombing. In this latter category, it is impossible to record all terrorist bombings worldwide. Within Italy alone, over 2,000 such actions take place each year. Accordingly, bombings are included in the data base if any of the following pertain: (1) the device involved is unique, (2) the damage done is substantial, (3) the target is significant, or (4) the methods used to emplace the device are unusual. In regard to both bombings and attacks against facilities, data on damages/thefts is based upon government/corporate statements regarding loss, press reporting on the subject, or a reasonable estimate when possible. All foreign loss figures have been converted to dollars based upon the existing exchange rate at the time of the incident.

Information contained in the data base is derived from foreign and U.S. government reports, police reports, and the foreign/English-language press. Data relating to damages, persons killed and wounded, and hostages taken are dependent upon the accuracy of such reporting. In many nations, government policies preclude the publication of such data. Accordingly, the figures cited for these categories can give only a relative approximation of actual human and material losses.

APPENDIX B
CHRONOLOGY OF TRANSNATIONAL
TERRORIST ATTACKS UPON
AMERICAN BUSINESS PEOPLE, 1968–78

Edward F. Mickolus

October 27, 1968, Brazil: Sears Roebuck and Company store bombed.

May 30, 1969, Israel: The Popular Front for the Liberation of Palestine (PFLP) claimed responsibility for blowing up a section of the Trans-Arabian pipeline, owned by Aramco, in the Israel-occupied Golan Heights of Syria.

June 20, 1969, Uruguay: Two Tupamaros dressed in police uniforms entered the Montevideo offices of General Motors (GM) and set fire to it in protest to Nelson Rockefeller's visit. Damage was estimated at $1 million.

June 26, 1969, Argentina: The Fuerzas Armadas Revolucionarias (FAR) bombed 14 Minimax supermarkets in protest to the arrival of Nelson Rockefeller in Argentina. Seven stores were completely destroyed, with the other seven severely damaged. Total losses were estimated at $3 million.

June 27, 1969, Uruguay: 500 million pesos were stolen from the GM plant in Penarol.

October 6, 1969, Argentina: Bombs damaged the offices of Pepsi-Cola, Squibb, Dunlop Tires, and the First National City Bank in Cordoba, as well as International Business Machines (IBM) and General Electric (GE) in San Miguel de Tucuman.

October 8, 1969, Argentina: A branch of the Bank of Boston in Buenos Aires was bombed by unknown individuals, while the Santa Fe office of Remington Rand came under a similar attack.

This chronology is limited to attacks in which U.S. business people were singled out as victims of the operations. Cases in which the victims' selection was indiscriminate, for example, passengers on a skyjacked airliner, are not included.

November 5, 1969, Brazil: A father and son team kidnapped P. Dolan, the son of a U.S. businessman, and demanded $12,500 ransom. The perpetrators were arrested, but the boy was found dead near Sao Paulo.

November 20, 1969, Argentina: The Peronist Armed Forces (FAP) claimed responsibility for bombing the offices of 15 foreign firms, nine of which were U.S. owned.

January 20, 1970, Italy: Unknown individuals bombed the Turin branch of the Bank of America and Italy, causing slight damage.

March, 1970, Ethiopia: Five members of a National Geographic film crew, including a U.S. producer, were taken hostage by members of the Eritrean Liberation Front (ELF). No ransom demands were made, and the hostages were released unharmed after being held for 17 days.

May 8, 1970, West Germany: Two groups of demonstrators attempted to rush barricades erected in front of the Munich Amerika Haus. A small group of 20 to 30 apparently benign protesters congregated on the Consular General lawn but were dispersed without difficulty by police. Additionally, during the citywide demonstrations, various U.S. businesses were attacked, and the Bank of America lost a window and a glass door. American Express Bank lost two windows, and the Armed Forces Network received several paint sacks. In addition, a Molotov cocktail was thrown at the offices of Pan American (Pan Am).

June 18, 1970, Argentina: The Buenos Aires Parke-Davis pharmaceutical plant was severely damaged by an explosion that reportedly killed three employees.

June 27, 1970, Argentina: U.S. firms were among the nine whose facilities were bombed in Buenos Aires, Rosario, and Cordoba.

July 21, 1970, Bolivia: Members of the Ejército de Liberación Nacional (ELN) kidnapped two West German technicians in Teoponte. They burned the offices of the U.S.-owned gold-mining firm South American Placers and stole $5,000. They demanded the release of ten prisoners being held by the Bolivian government within 48 hours. The government yielded the next day, and the two technicians were released unharmed on July 23 after the prisoners were flown to Arica, Chile. The ten freed individuals included those accused of participating in attacks headed by Ché Guevara, and included Loyola Guzman, Enrique Ortega, Gerardo Bermudez, Felix Melgar Antel, Oscar Busch, Victor Cordoba, Roberto Moreira, Rodolfo Saldana, Juan Sanchez, and Benigno Coronado. Reports claimed that they had reached Cuba via Mexico on August 30.

August 7, 1970, Uruguay: Dr. Claude Fly, a Food and Agricultural Organization (FAO) and United States Agency for International Development (USAID) agronomist working as a contractor for International Development Services, was kidnapped by the Tupamaros and held for 208 days, at one point being placed in a six-foot by seven-foot wire cage. The terrorists demanded the release of 150 prisoners and the publication of a manifesto. During his captivity, the 65-year-old Fly suffered a heart attack. A prominent heart specialist was kidnapped to confirm that Fly was in need of treatment. The two were released in front of the Hospital Britannica.

September 11, 1970, Uruguay: Tupamaros robbed the offices of Esso of $1,800.

October 8, 1970, Chile: Unknown individuals bombed the Santiago offices of Ford Motor Company.

December 1, 1970, Uruguay: A Tupamaro-planted bomb exploded in the Montevideo offices of International Telephone & Telegraph (ITT), causing much damage.

January 22, 1971, Philippines: The Manila headquarters of Caltex and Esso were damaged by bombs, with one Filipino employee killed. Police said a note found near the Caltex office read, "This is the anger of the Filipino people against American imperialism. People's Revolutionary Front."

March 13, 1971, Greece: Members of the Greek Militant Resistance bombed the Athens offices of the Esso-Pappas Oil Company.

March 25, 1971, France: Forty members of the Movement of Youthward Brothers in War of the Palestinian People threw stones and three Molotov cocktails at offices of the Bull Computer Company, a subsidiary of GE.

April 2, 1971, Jordan: Fedayeen damaged an extension of the Aramco-owned Trans-Arabian pipeline carrying oil to the Zarka refinery. The sabotage resulted in blocking 440,000 barrels a day of Saudi oil and the loss of transit fees to Lebanon, Syria, and Jordan.

April 22, 1971, Argentina: Members of the Angel Bengochea Command of the People's Revolutionary Army (ERP) stole equipment from the Parke-Davis Laboratory in La Plata.

April 27, 1971, Argentina: Members of the Luis Blanco and Adolfo Bello units of the ERP placed 11 bombs in U.S. business offices in Rosario.

May 12, 1971, Bolivia: The manager of a U.S.-owned gold mine was kidnapped by peasants, who ransomed him for a tractor to be used in road construction.

June 23, 1971, Uruguay: The Organization of the Popular Revolution–33 (OPR-33) kidnapped Alfredo Cambon, a legal adviser to several large Uruguayan companies backed by U.S. capital. He was released after being questioned for two days. Other reports attribute the attack to the Tupamaros.

July 8, 1971, Greece: Nighttime bombs in Athens damaged a railway track and a tank truck of Esso-Pappas.

July 8, 1971, Northern Ireland: The fifth consecutive day of rioting in Londonderry included the firebombing of a U.S.-owned factory, Essex International Brakelining of Fort Wayne, Indiana.

September 9, 1971, Jordan: Fedayeen damaged the Trans-Arabian pipeline in Jordan near the Syrian border. Other attacks occurred on September 15 and October 24. Jordan accused the Syrians of involvement.

October, 1971, Guatemala: The PGT/FAR robbed a Coca-Cola plant of $12,000.

October 14, 1971, Colombia: Members of the United Front for Guerrilla Action
bombed a Sinclair pipeline.

November 3, 1971, Brazil: Fire bombs in Sao Paulo damaged a car belonging to
the U.S. consul general, as well as the homes of officials of Swift and
Company and Chicago Bridge Company.

November 10, 1971, Jordan: Four explosions rocked the Intercontinental Hotel
in Amman, which was managed by Americans and used to have a small
amount of U.S. financing.

November 19, 1971, Mexico: Leftist rural guerrillas commanded by Genaro
Vazquez Rojas kidnapped Dr. Jaime Castrejon Diez, rector of the State
University of Guerrero and millionaire owner of the Coca-Cola bottling
concession. He was released on December 1 after his family paid a $200,000
ransom and nine political prisoners were flown to Cuba.

January, 1972, Guatemala: A U.S. businessman's home was bombed by left-
wing extremists.

January, 1972, Kuwait: Two incidents, one confirmed as sabotage, saw damage
to the facilities of the Kuwait Oil Company, which is partially U.S. owned.

February 22, 1972, West Germany: The Black September Organization (BSO)
damaged an Esso Oil pipeline near Hamburg, accusing the company of
helping the Israelis.

May 12, 1972, Argentina: One Dutch and four U.S. firms were bombed by the
Comite Argentino de Lucha Anti-Imperialista in protest to U.S. escalation
of the Vietnam War.

May 23, 1972, Venezuela: The Caracas offices of ITT were bombed, causing
heavy damage.

May 25, 1972, France: Members of the Committee of Coordination bombed the
U.S. consulate in Paris and offices of the American Legion, Pan Am, and
Trans World Airlines (TWA), in protest to U.S. bombing in North Vietnam.

May 26, 1972, Rhodesia: Two Lebanese hijacked a South African Airways jet.
They attempted to extort money from the Anglo-American Mining Company, but after forcing the plane to Blantyre, Malawi, the hijackers were
overpowered by security forces. They were given 11-year sentences.

June 3, 1972, Italy: Bombs damaged the offices of Honeywell, IBM, and the
Bank of America and Italy in Milan and a Honeywell factory in a Milan
suburb. Leaflets found at the bomb sites referred to the "struggle of the
Vietnamese people against American imperialism" and the victories "of
the revolutionary and Communist army in Vietnam."

June 9, 1972, Argentina: Sixteen bombs exploded in Buenos Aires, Cordoba,
Rosario, and Santa Fe, damaging many business offices, including four
U.S. firms, the offices of the newspaper La Opinion, and a steel plant.
The bombings occurred on the 16th anniversary of an abortive Peronist
military coup.

July 28, 1972, Uruguay: Members of OPR-33 kidnapped Hector Menoni, manager of the Uruguayan branch of United Press International (UPI) and released him unharmed the next day.

August, 1972, Guatemala: A U.S. businessman was kidnapped and freed after the payment of a sizable ransom.

September 16, 1972, Mexico: Independence Day celebrations saw the bombing of 12 firms in four cities, which injured one person and caused considerable damage. Seven of the blasts involved U.S. firms.

October 10, 1972, United States: Two New York women active in U.S. Zionist circles received letter-bombs bearing Malaysian postmarks. Although the recipients opened the envelopes, the bombs did not explode.

October 16, 1972, Argentina: A bomb exploded at the 24-story Sheraton Hotel in Buenos Aires, killing an American woman and seriously injuring two other Americans. An anonymous phone call said the blast was the work of the Marxist Liberation Armed Forces, but hotel employees found pamphlets signed by the Maximo Mean Command, an extremist group of Peron followers. Twelve bombs had exploded earlier in the day in Buenos Aires and other Argentine cities.

November 5, 1972, El Salvador: Unknown bombers caused much damage to the San Salvador main ticket office of Pan Am.

November 9, 1972, Argentina: A powerful bomb damaged the San Miguel de Tucuman offices of IBM.

December 8, 1972, Australia: A U.S. businessman on vacation was killed by a bomb that exploded in an automobile parked outside a Serbian Orthodox church in Brisbane.

December 12, 1972, United States and Canada: The Cuban Secret Government claimed responsibility for bombing a travel agency and three offices handling packages for Cuba in Miami, New York, and Montreal.

December 27, 1972, Argentina: Vicento Russo, director general of operations for Standard Electric of Argentina, a subsidiary of ITT, was kidnapped by the Descamisados Peronistas Montoneros and released unharmed on December 29. Reports conflict on the size of the ransom paid, with amounts ranging from $100,000 to $1 million. ITT has refused to comment.

January 1, 1973, Jordan: A Syrian and a Palestinian who had been sent into Jordan from Syria by Al Fatah to sabotage the Trans-Arabian pipeline were captured by a Jordanian Army patrol.

January 17, 1973, Lebanon: A small bomb wrecked a basement restroom in the American University of Beirut.

January 24, 1973, Iran: A bomb exploded at the Tehran offices of Pan Am.

February 3, 1973, Argentina: Norman Lee, an Argentine executive of a Coca-Cola bottling company in Buenos Aires, was kidnapped and released after the payment of $1 million to the Argentine Liberation Front (FAL). In the face of the continuing threat of kidnapping and extortion, several foreign companies, including Coca-Cola, ITT, John Deere, Otis Elevator, and IBM moved company executives and their families out of the country.

March 28, 1973, Argentina: Unidentified guerrillas kidnapped Gerardo Scalmazzi, Rosario branch manager of the First National Bank of Boston. He was released on April 4 after the reported payment of between $500,000 and $1 million.

April 2, 1973, Argentina: The FAL kidnapped Anthony R. DaCruz, a naturalized U.S. citizen serving as technical operations manager for Eastman Kodak Company, as he was on his way to work. He was released unharmed on April 7 after Kodak paid a $1.5 million ransom. Although U.S. firms had previously been the targets of ransom demands, this was the first case of an American being taken prisoner by kidnappers in Argentina.

April 8, 1973, Argentina: British citizen Francis Victor Brimicombe, president of the British-American Tobacco Company's subsidiary Nobleza Tabacos was kidnapped outside of his Buenos Aires home. He was freed unharmed on April 13, after his company paid a reported $1.5 million ransom.

April 14, 1973, Lebanon: Masked raiders, apparently members of the Lebanese Revolutionary Guard, destroyed a U.S.-owned oil storage tank, badly damaged two others, and slightly damaged a fourth in the Sidon area, in protect to U.S. support to Israel. An Army demolitions team took charges from 16 other tanks.

April 14, 1973, Saudi Arabia: Members of the Saudi National Guard discovered an explosive device wired to the Trans-Arabian pipeline near Rafha.

April 16, 1973, Lebanon: Two members of the PFLP and PFLP-GC (General Command) attempted to blow up the Trans-Arabian pipeline to Zahrani, but only dented it, not affecting the flow of oil. On February 27, 1974, a military court sentenced the two to seven years imprisonment. The attack was in retaliation for an Israeli raid into Beirut on April 10, 1973.

April 29, 1973, El Salvador: Extensive damage was caused by a bomb that exploded in the IBM offices in San Salvador.

April 30, 1973, Argentina: Serious damage was caused by an ERP bomb that exploded in a building owned by Goodyear Rubber in Cordoba. No injuries were reported.

May 1, 1973, Argentina: The ERP bombed the Cordoba offices of Goodyear.

May 2, 1973, Spain: Two fire bombs caused considerable smoke damage and broke all of the windows of the Pan Am offices in Barcelona.

May 7, 1973, Greece: Pipe bombs damaged cars belonging to a U.S. citizen employed at Athens Airport and a U.S. European Exchange System vendor.

May 13, 1973, Greece: Pipe bombs damaged cars belonging to two U.S. military men and to a Greek-American movie producer in Athens.

May 21, 1973, Argentina: The president of the Coca-Cola bottling plant in Cordoba, Oscar Castells, was kidnapped. He was released on June 4 after payment of $100,000.

May 21, 1973, Argentina: Luis V. Giovanelli, Ford Motor Company executive, and a woman employee in a second car were machine gunned by the ERP when plant guards attempted to intervene in a kidnapping attempt. Giovanelli later died of his wounds. The ERP's communique said the victims were shot because they resisted and demanded that Ford provide 154 ambulances to eight provinces, give $200,000 to the children's hospital and $200,000 for a children's home, as well as give $200,000 worth of powdered milk for children in Buenos Aires's squatter slums. The group warned that if the demands were not met, it would invade the Ford plant and take retribution against company officials.

May 23, 1973, Argentina: A bomb was defused at a Buenos Aires Ford Motor Company plant. Ford officials agree to comply with ERP demands for $1 million, paying $200,000 in medicine for the Buenos Aires children's hospital; $200,000 in instruments for the Catamarca children's hospital; 22 ambulances equipped for emergencies, one for each province; $180,000 for food for poor areas of Buenos Aires; and $300,000 in school supplies for needy schools in the Buenos Aires area.

May 31, 1973, Argentina: The ERP threatened to attack and kidnap officials of Otis Elevator Company and their families if the company did not make $500,000 in charitable contributions similar to those made by Ford and double the wages of 1,300 Otis employees in Argentina. Otis refused and ordered the families of 13 executives flown to Sao Paulo, Brazil. In a June 9 press conference, the ERP denied responsibility for the threats. The group may have been members of ERP–August 22, a splinter group of the ERP.

June 18, 1973, Guatemala: The FAR kidnapped Roberto Galvez Federico Timeus, manager of the U.S. company Corn Products. He was released after $50,000 ransom was paid.

June 18, 1973, Argentina: The ERP kidnapped John R. Thompson, the president of Firestone Tire and Rubber Company's Argentine subsidiary, and demanded $3 million in ransom. He was released on July 6 after the ransom was paid. Some reports claim that bargaining for his release had taken place openly at the Presidents Hotel in Buenos Aires. An undisguised ERP negotiator was said to have haggled over the price with Firestone officials. The ransom, in 500-peso note bundles, was reported to have filled an armored car provided by the group.

July, 1973, Guatemala: Left-wing extremists killed the son of a resident U.S. businessman.

July 2, 1973, Argentina: Raul Bornancini, Argentine assistant manager of the Buenos Aires branch of the First National City Bank of New York, was kidnapped. He was released unharmed on July 13 after the payment of a $1 million ransom.

July 4, 1973, Argentina: Norman Lee, an executive of the Coca-Cola bottling company in Buenos Aires, was kidnapped for a second time by a group of armed men. He was released unharmed after convincing his abductors that his firm would not pay for him twice, but the group took his car and $100 from his wallet.

September 21, 1973, Argentina: David George Heywood, an accountant for Nobleza Tabacos, a subsidiary of the British-American Tobacco Company, was kidnapped in Buenos Aires. He was released on October 20 after his relatives paid $300,000. Police stormed the site where he was being held and seized four of the seven kidnappers and more than $280,000 of the ransom.

September 24, 1973, Lebanon: Bombers attempted to damage the oil pipeline of the Tapline Company in the An-Nabitiyah district. The explosion made a hole in the ground without damaging the pipeline.

September 28, 1973, Italy: Unidentified people poured gasoline on the main doors of the office of ITT Standard S.A. in Rome and ignited it, but the fire was quickly put out and damage was slight.

October 1, 1973, Argentina: Pan Am and Braniff International received notes from a group claiming to be a faction of the ERP, demanding that each company pay $1 million to the group.

October 4, 1973, Colombia: Willis Leon Dotsun and Rene Francis Kast, U.S. employees of the Frontino Gold Mines, were kidnapped by the ELN. The group demanded a ransom of $168,990 (4 million pesos). The board of directors of International Mining in New York decided to pay the ransom. However, Colombian authorities seized the money when corporate representatives tried to pay off the kidnappers. The Colombian Army rescued the two men on March 7, 1974.

October 8, 1973, Argentina: The anniversary of Ché Guevara's death was celebrated by unknown attackers who fired 12 rockets at the Buenos Aires Sheraton Hotel. Only two of the rockets hit the building, causing little damage. Meanwhile, considerable damage was caused by fire bombs, thrown at the office of the Bank of America.

October 9, 1973, Argentina: Bombs exploded at the offices of Coca-Cola, Firestone, and Mercedes-Benz in Cordoba, causing some damage but no injuries.

October 18, 1973, Lebanon: Five members of the Lebanese Socialist Revolutionary Organization shot their way into the Bank of America in Beirut and held about 50 employees and customers as hostages. They demanded the payment of $10 million to finance the Arab war effort against Israel, the release of Palestinian guerrillas being held in Lebanese jails, and safe passage to Algeria or South Yemen. All parties refused their demands. After 25 hours, security forces stormed the bank. John Crawford Maxwell, a U.S. employee of Douglas Aircraft Company, had been executed by the terrorists. In the battle, one policeman was killed and six were wounded; five bank employees and five passersby were also injured. Two terrorists were killed in the attack, one was critically wounded, a fourth surrendered unharmed, and a fifth was captured later. The surviving members of the attack squad were sentenced by a Beirut court on March 9 of the following year, with Adel Najin Abu-Asi sentenced to death for the murder of Maxwell.

October 23, 1973, Argentina: David B. Wilkie, Jr., president of Amoco Argentina, a subsidiary of Standard Oil Company of Indiana, was kidnapped in suburban Buenos Aires. He was released on November 11 after the payment of an undisclosed ransom, which reports have claimed ranged from $1 million to $3.5 million.

November 17, 1973, West Germany: Bombs exploded in Nuremburg and West Berlin, damaging local offices of ITT.

November 22, 1973, Argentina: John Albert Swint, U.S. citizen and general manager of the Ford subsidiary Transax, and three of his bodyguards were assassinated in an ambush by 15 individuals in Cordoba. Swint was on his way to work when he found his motorcade blocked by two trucks from the front and by small cars from the rear. Swint was killed instantly, and his guards were mortally wounded in the terrorists' initial fusillade. Police said a tall, blond gunman completed the job with a machine-gun burst before the terrorists fled. Conflicting reports credited the ERP and FAP with the attack. Twenty-two Ford executives and their families departed from Argentina soon after this attack.

December 3, 1973, Greece: In Piraeus, a bomb damaged a building housing a branch of the Bank of America. No injuries were reported. A new antigovernment group called Greek People claimed credit for the explosion, as well as for the bombing of a branch of the Commercial Bank of Greece in Athens.

December 6, 1973, Argentina: Victor E. Samuelson, an Esso executive, was kidnapped from a company lunchroom by the ERP, who demanded $10 million ransom in food, clothing, and construction materials to be distributed in poor neighborhoods across Argentina, publication of a terrorist communique in several major newspapers, and $4.2 million for flood victims. Certain unspecified problems made the distribution of goods by Esso impossible, and the company gave the group $14.2 million in cash on March 11, 1974. Samuelson was finally released on April 29, 1974, and returned to the United States. On June 12, the ERP announced that it had distributed $5 million of the ransom to members of the Revolutionary Coordinating Junta, whose members included Argentinian, Bolivian, Uruguayan, and Chilean terrorist groups.

December 21, 1973, Great Britain: Two Irish Republican Army (IRA) bombs exploded outside the London Hilton Hotel bar, causing minimal damage and no injuries.

December 21, 1973, Argentina: Charles Robert Hayes, construction superin-
tendent of the U.S. engineering firm McKee-Tesca and Company, a joint
venture between an Argentine company and Arthur G. McKee and Company, an engineering and construction firm headquartered in Cleveland,
Ohio, was kidnapped in La Plata on his way to work. He was released on
January 31, when a reported $1 million ransom was paid.

December 31, 1973, Italy: In Rome, explosions caused heavy damage to three
buildings housing offices of ITT subsidiaries. Leaflets found in the area
said, "ITT organized the coup in Chile and it is made up of Fascist and reactionary elements."

January 3, 1974, Argentina: Douglas Gordon Roberts, the administrative director of Pepsi-Cola S.A., was abducted outside his home in the Buenos
Aires suburb of Martinez. He was released on February 2, apparently after
the payment of a ransom of undisclosed size. Some of the kidnappers were
arrested by the police, who had followed them after they picked up the
ransom.

February 1, 1974, Mexico: Bombs damaged Pepsi-Cola and Union Carbide
plants in Guadalajara, as well as a Coca-Cola bottling plant, a bakery, and
federal offices in Oaxaca. Total damage was more than $400,000. No
casualties or arrests were reported.

February 11, 1974, Israel: Fire bombs damaged three Christian establishments in
Jerusalem—the offices of Baptist House (operated by the U.S. Southern
Baptist Convention), the U.S.-owned Zion House Bible Shop, and the
chapel of the Swedish Theological Institute. The Jewish Defense League
(JDL) and extremist yeshiva students were responsible for similar bomb-
ings in February 1973.

February 23, 1974, Greece: Two Greek demolition experts were killed while
attempting to defuse a bomb found in the Dow Chemical plant at Lavrion.

March 1, 1974, France: The Sonolar factory, owned by a French ITT subsidiary,
was destroyed by fire. We Must Do Something claimed responsibility,
saying it was a welcome for the Chilean ambassador to France.

March 14, 1974, Venezuela: Arsonists damaged a supermarket partly owned by
the Rockefeller family. The Red Flag, the National Liberation Armed
Forces, and several other guerrilla groups vied with each other in claiming
credit for the fire.

March 26, 1974, Ethiopia: The ELF seized the pilot and passengers of a Tenneco
helicopter. The passengers included two Tenneco employees, a Texaco
employee, and a UN worker. The ELF demanded that Tenneco assist them
in gaining the release of 75 political prisoners, employ a journalist to pub-
lish the ELF story, suspend further exploration, and not return the hostages to Ethiopia once they were released. A second helicopter was sent to
the area when the ELF agreed to release two of the hostages, but the pilot
was taken hostage. He was released unharmed on June 23; the first pilot

was released unharmed on June 26, and the other hostages were released on September 10. It was not disclosed whether the company had paid the $1 million ransom that was also demanded. (During the incident, on May 27, ELF members attacked the American Evangelical Mission in Ghinda, Eritrea, and kidnapped one American and one Dutch nurse, killing the latter. The American woman was released on June 23 with the pilot, after negotiations with the missionary group and the ELF regarding medical care for inhabitants of the area.)

May 27, 1974, Argentina: Members of the ERP robbed a U.S. citizen of $52,000 in currency and valuables in Buenos Aires.

June 19, 1974, Argentina: Eight bombs detonated during the evening, damaging several firms in Buenos Aires, including the Bank of London, the Bank of America, and the Coca-Cola Bottling Company.

September 11, 1974, Argentina: A series of bombs exploded at U.S. and other foreign companies in Buenos Aires and other cities, marking the anniversary of the overthrow of Allende in Chile.

September 16, 1974, Argentina: Approximately 40 bombs were directed against ceremonies celebrating the military revolt that ended Peron's first period of rule. Montoneros slogans and banners were left at many of the sites. Victims included the following: three Ford showrooms, Peugeot and IKA-Renault showrooms, Goodyear and Firestone tire distributors, Riker and Eli Lilly pharmaceutical laboratories, Union Carbide Battery Company, Bank of Boston and Chase Manhattan Bank branches, Xerox Corporation, and Coca-Cola and Pepsi-Cola bottling companies.

October 6, 1974, Italy: Four terrorists invaded the Milan warehouse of Face-Standard, an ITT communications subsidiary, and set fire to it, resulting in about $9 million damage. Meanwhile, the Avis Milan offices were bombed, with damage estimated to be $15,000. A note claimed that the warehouse arson was revenge for ITT's role in Chile.

October 10, 1974, Syria: The Arab Communist Organization claimed responsibility for the bombing of the Damascus office of the National Cash Register Company, resulting in the death of an office boy and the wounding of a cleaning woman.

October 11, 1974, Lebanon: The Arab Communist Organization claimed credit for the bombing of the First National Bank of Chicago in Beirut. A statement found in the bank's entrance demanded the release of Adel Abn Asi, a Lebanese who was sentenced to death for the attack on the Beirut branch of the Bank of America on October 18, 1973.

November 5, 1974, Italy: Three Molotov cocktails were thrown into the Milan Trade Center, which was under the jurisdiction of the U.S. Department of Commerce, causing minor fire damage. Police assumed that the attack was made by the same group of leftists who fire bombed other U.S. facilities in Rome during Secretary of State Henry Kissinger's visit.

November 14, 1974, Mexico: In Cuernavaca, a U.S. real-estate dealer's wife, Sara M. Davis, was kidnapped. Her captors demanded a ransom of $1 million in food and land for the poor. Two communiques found in a Mexico City subway station were signed by the United Popular Liberation Army of America.

November 18, 1974, Mexico: A wave of bombings hit a number of Mexico City commercial establishments, including Sears Roebuck and a U.S.-owned restaurant and drug store. The 23rd of September Communist League appeared responsible.

November 25, 1974, Argentina: Explosions, presumably set by leftists, rocked a branch of the First National City Bank of New York and two GM showrooms in Buenos Aires.

December 15, 1974, France: The right-wing Youth Action Group claimed responsibility for the bombings of TWA and Coca-Cola offices in Paris, as well as the December 16 bombing of Minnesota Mining and Manufacturing. The group said that the blasts were a protest against the meeting in Martinique of the presidents of the United States and France.

February 11, 1975, Lebanon: Members of the Arab Communist Organization bombed a U.S. firm's offices.

May 31, 1975, Lebanon: The Beirut office of ITT was bombed. No injuries were reported.

June 19, 1975, Sweden: A McDonald's hamburger restaurant in Stockholm was bombed.

June 23, 1975, Israel: A small bomb damaged a car belonging to a TWA employee. No injuries were reported. The car was parked 50 meters from the U.S. Embassy.

July 14, 1975, Ethiopia: Steve Campbell and Jim Harrell, assigned by the Collins International Service Company to a U.S. military communications facility at Asmara, were kidnapped by individuals claiming to be members of the ELF-Revolutionary Council. The six, including four Ethiopians, were abducted about 10:45 A.M. and were driven off in a company truck that security forces later found abandoned 17 miles west of Asmara. The two were released on May 3, 1976, with V. H. Burwood-Taylor, honorary British consul, who had been seized in October. State Department officials said that the government had paid no ransom but would not rule out the possibility that a private transaction had been worked out between the company and the kidnappers.

August 2, 1975, Lebanon: Constance Stransky, a U.S. citizen, was held hostage by an unidentified Palestinian group for 11 days.

August 2, 1975, Syria: Four Palestinians and a Syrian, members of the Arab Communist Organization, accused of the recent bombing of offices of the American Life Insurance Company in Kuwait, were sentenced to death in Damascus.

August 5, 1975, Colombia: Five gunmen and a woman kidnapped Donald E. Cooper, vice president for merchandising for the Sears Roebuck chain of department stores in Colombia, from his home during the evening. Police sources said the kidnappers, wearing masks and armed with pistols and submachine guns, fired one shot that barely missed the ear of Cooper's chauffeur and pushed and struck his maid. After lengthy negotiations with his company, the group released him unharmed on November 2, 1975.

August 19, 1975, Sweden: An explosion rocked a McDonald's restaurant in Stockholm for the second time, smashing windows and much of the interior but causing no casualties.

August 23, 1975, Ethiopia: Two Americans were killed when a land mine exploded while they were driving on a road near Asmara. The men worked for Collins International Service Company, under contract with the Navy at a naval communications unit in Asmara. They were identified as William D. Trower and Aldworth R. Brown, Jr.

August 30, 1975, Philippines: Two U.S. employees of Boise-Cascade were abducted from a timber concession near Zamboanga, apparently by Moslem dissidents. They were released less than 24 hours later.

September 24, 1975, Argentina: A bomb explosion ripped through the Cordoba offices of Xerox Argentina, smashing windows but causing no injuries.

October 9, 1975, Angola: John S. Robinson, an American missing in Luanda since October 9, was turned over to civilian police by the MPLA on October 27.

October 29, 1975, Lebanon: Herman Huddleston, a U.S. pilot for Trans-Mediterranean Airlines, was kidnapped by four men who seized him at his home as he was watching television with his wife. They were suspicious of his radio equipment and accused him of being a spy, but released him unharmed three days later.

November 12, 1975, Lebanon: David Doge, a long-time U.S. resident of Beirut, was picked up by gunmen during the evening and robbed of his car and about $50 dollars before being released unharmed.

November 21, 1975, Angola: Don Webster of CBS and photographer Bill Mutschmann were detained by the MPLA and questioned about being Central Intelligence Agency (CIA) agents. On their December 11 release, the two complained of poor treatment, inedible food, unsanitary conditions, and much harassment by their captors. They reported that at least one prisoner was horribly beaten every night but that the two of them were not beaten.

December 22, 1975, Ethiopia: U.S. citizen Ronald B. Michalke, an employee of Collins International Service Company, was kidnapped from his home in Asmara by five armed men, members of the ELF. One week later, Osman Saleh Sabbi, secretary general of the ELF, claimed to have persuaded the military commanders holding Michalke to drop their demand for a $5 million ransom. Michalke was released on June 3, 1976.

January 10, 1976, Lebanon: Two groups of armed men entered the American University of Beirut campus and its hospital, fired guns to scare off the guards, and stole two station wagons.

January 29, 1976, Argentina: Fifteen terrorists, including two women, burst into the Buenos Aires offices of the local subsidiary of the Bendix Corporation of New York and shot and killed two Argentine executives.

February 17, 1976, Lebanon: A Palestinian student was arrested and charged with shooting two professors at the American University of Beirut. It is believed he was acting out of revenge, having been expelled in 1974 for radical activity.

February 27, 1976, Greece: Bombs exploded in front of two U.S. banks in Athens, causing slight damage.

February 27, 1976, Venezuela: William E. Niehous, vice president and manager of the Owens-Illinois Glass Company in Venezuela, was kidnapped from his Caracas home by seven gunmen. In a seven-page communique signed by the Revolutionary Commandos, Operation Argimiro Gabaldon, the kidnappers stated that Niehous was to be put on trial for crimes against the Venezuelan people. His wife said that two of the kidnappers who had tied up her and the couple's three teen-age sons were youths she had hired earlier to cut her lawn. The kidnappers overpowered Niehous as he was watching television and injected him with a sedative. His wife at first laughed at the uniformed men, thinking they were carnival pranksters. The company agreed to pay a $116 bonus to each of its 1,600 employees in Venezuela and paid for publication of a leftist political document in the New York *Times*, London *Times*, and *Le Monde*. It has been reported that the group also demanded a $2.3 million ransom. The government of Venezuela announced that it would confiscate Owens's $25 million investment in Venezuela in retribution for paying off the kidnappers. As of June 1979 Niehous remains a captive.

March 13, 1976, El Salvador: The Farabundo Marti Liberation Labor Forces took credit for two fire bombings on the second floor of the Siman store in San Salvador and inside a Sears store. The Sears fire bomb did not set the building on fire due to action by the night watchmen.

March 26, 1976, Argentina: Two security guards of a Ford Motor Company executive were killed by machine-gun fire from a speeding car.

March 31, 1976, Turkey: A bomb damaged the offices of Pan Am and Philips Electronic in Ankara.

April 2, 1976, Colombia: A bomb exploded at the entrance of a branch of the First National City Bank near the U.S. embassy in Bogota. No injuries resulted from the explosion, but damage was extensive. No one claimed responsibility.

April 3, 1976, Greece: An incendiary bomb exploded in the Athens offices of the American Express Company, causing minor damage.

April 7, 1976, Argentina: Left-wing guerrillas attacked the home of Hugo Carlos Sardan, an Argentine executive of the U.S. Pfizer Drug firm, killing one guard and wounding another.

April 13, 1976, Argentina: Two men and two women firing from a moving car sprayed the suburban home of Argentine executive Antonio Claudio Trigo, administrative manager of the local subsidiary of Goodyear, with machine-gun bullets, killing a father and son bodyguard team.

April 14, 1976, Argentina: Gunmen shot a navy captain, an Argentine Chrysler Corporation executive, and three policemen to death in Buenos Aires.

April 20, 1976, Lebanon: Los Angeles *Times* correspondent Joe Alex Morris was kidnapped during the evening in Beirut by two armed men as he drove home after work. He was taken to a deserted area, where his kidnappers forced him from the car, took his identity papers, and released him, forcing him to go on foot.

April 22, 1976, Greece: A bomb exploded at an Athens branch of the First National City Bank.

May 23, 1976, Mexico: Gayle Moony, the eight-year-old daughter of a U.S. businessman, was released in Acapulco by her kidnappers 23 days after her abduction. The Armed Vanguard of the Proletariat had demanded $400,000.

May 31, 1976, Brazil: Forrest E. Fitzpatrick of Detroit, the manager of a Ford tractor plant in Sao Paulo, was found dead in his apartment there.

June, 1976, Ethiopia: Spokesmen for the ELF claimed to have kidnapped four individuals, three identified as Ian Machesney, Brian Hazlehurst, and Bruce Thompson. Two are said to be British and one American. The fourth prisoner might have been an Ethiopian citizen of Polish origin.

July 3, 1976, Brazil: John W. Davis, a U.S. rancher, and his two sons were shot on their Amazon ranch in an ambush set up by Brazilian peasant squatters. The Davises had paid for their ranch and held legal title to it, but the squatters simply moved onto the land, put up mud-and-straw shacks, and began growing crops to eat and sell. The Davises tried several methods to force the 1,000 squatters off their property—blocking access roads to the shacks and forcing the squatters off a lake they had been using. Accusations were made that the Davises had also hit the peasants and set fire to their huts. Sixty farmers participated in the ambush. Twenty-three suspects were taken into custody.

August 13, 1976, Israel: An estimated $13,000 worth of equipment being used by a U.S. company in the occupied West Bank of the Jordan was damaged by unknown individuals during the night. The U.S. company had been conducting seismic tests for oil near the town of Jenin.

August 28, 1976, Iran: The Mujahidden E. Khalq was believed responsible for the assassination of three U.S. employees of Rockwell International: William C. Cottrell, Robert R. Krongard, and Donald G. Smith. They were assassinated at about 7 A.M. as they were being driven to work at an Iranian Air Force installation in a crowded industrial and residential district of southeastern Tehran. The Americans' car, a Dodge, was cut off by a Volkswagen, another car cut off the Dodge from the rear, and four terrorists appeared, firing into the Dodge with submachine guns. The terrorists were understood to have ordered the chauffeur to lie down and then to have started firing into the car, killing all three Americans on the spot. Reports indicate that they had taken the same route to the Doshen Tappeh Iranian Air Force Base each morning. The three were experts on aircraft missiles and had been installing a secret electronic intelligence-gathering system code—named Project IBEX, estimated to cost up to $500 million. Cottrell had joined Rockwell in 1975 to be overseas manager for the project, and another of the victims was the engineering manager, Hassan Ellaj-Pour, the driver of the Volkswagon, was killed in a shoot-out with police on September 2.

September 15, 1976, Argentina: Guerrillas fired submachine guns and threw hand grenades against the home of an Argentine executive of Ford Motor Company. No casualties were reported.

September 22, 1976, Italy: A bomb damaged the Rome regional office of Westinghouse. No injuries were reported, and no group claimed responsibility for the attack.

September 25, 1976, Italy: A huge rally of students protesting the Syrian intervention in Lebanon was followed by more than a dozen bombings and fire bombings against American, Jewish, and Lebanese Christian installations in Rome. The Ghassan Kanafani Commandos claimed credit for bombs that exploded outside three branches of the Bank of America and Italy, inside a suburban office of Avis, in the Rome office of the United Hias Service, outside a synagogue, and outside a Lebanese Maronite monastery.

September 28, 1976, Colombia: Gustave George Curtis, 55, manager of GranColombia Industries, a subsidiary of Chicago-based Beatrice Foods, was kidnapped in Bogota. A vehicle carrying four men and a woman forced his car to the side of the road in the western part of the city. His chauffeur was tied up and abandoned. Near the university campus was a note instructing his family to pay 3 million pesos (approximately $100,000) in ransom.

October 13, 1976, Portugal: Two luxury hotels were bombed around midnight in Lisbon, causing little damage and no injuries. One bomb exploded near an office block close to the entrance of the Sheraton, the other on a Ritz porch.

November 3, 1976, Argentina: Carlos Souto, Argentine executive of the Chrysler Corporation, was shot by two leftist gunmen as he left his Buenos Aires home for work.

November 30, 1976, Mexico: The 23rd of September Communist League was believed responsible for four bombs which exploded in Mexico City on the eve of the inauguration of President-elect Jose Lopez Portillo. A number of commercial buildings were damaged, including the Johnson and Johnson laboratory. The Poor People's Army claimed credit, however.

December 8, 1976, Mexico: The Mexican plant manager of the U.S.-owned Sylvania Electronics plant in Ciudad Juarez was killed by five members of the 23rd of September Communist League as the terrorists were leaving the plant after distributing communist propaganda to arriving workers. Two or three suspects were identified, but press reports conflicted on whether any of them had been arrested.

December 13, 1976, Italy: Emanuela Trapani, 17, daughter of the Milan representative of the U.S. firm Helene Curtis, was kidnapped as she was being driven to school. The Italian girl was released unharmed on January 27, 1977, and found in a telephone booth. (Kidnapping is a common crime in Italy, and this may be a criminal case, rather than one with political overtones.)

December 13, 1976, Mexico: A Mexican employee at the Mexico City Chrysler plant was shot by members of the 23rd of September Communist League when he attempted to prevent them from distributing pamphlets to plant workers.

December 16, 1976, Colombia: A bomb went off in the pocket of a boy walking through the Chapinero store of a U.S. firm. Seventeen additional bombs were found after the store was searched.

January 20, 1977, Mexico: Mitchell Andreski, the American president of Duraflex Corporation, and his Mexican associate, Guillermo Flores France, 30, were shot and killed by members of the 23rd of September Communist League when they tried to prevent the group from passing out propaganda leaflets. Two other persons were wounded. The duo was inspecting a construction site in the northeastern section of Mexico City.

January 25, 1977, Argentina: Montoneros fired machine guns and threw a pipe bomb at the vacant suburban Buenos Aires home of a Goodyear executive. Leaflets were left at the home, the tire plant, and the surrounding area supporting laborers in recent strife.

February 2, 1977, Northern Ireland: Jeffrey S. Adgate, 58, British-born managing director of the DuPont International plant in Londonderry, was gunned down as he stepped from his car outside his home on the city's outskirts. The IRA was believed responsible.

March 27, 1977, Argentina: Six bombs exploded during the night in Buenos Aires, including one at the Sheraton Hilton which injured nine people.

March 31, 1977, Colombia: The ELN exploded three bombs at the Bogota Sears store, causing minor damage, to commemorate the death of Alexis Umana, a university student, during a 1976 confrontation with police.

April 11, 1977, Costa Rica: The Revolutionary Commandos of Solidarity claimed credit for bombs which exploded at the offices of Pan Am and

Henderson and Company, as well as at a San Jose government building housing the U.S. military mission. Heavy damage but no injuries were reported. It was believed that the attack was in reprisal for the recent death in Nicaragua of FSLN leader Carlos Aguerero Echeverria, who was a Costa Rican.

April 11, 1977, Argentina: Leftist terrorists shot and killed an Argentine executive of a local firm operating under license from General Motors. The Montoneros claimed credit for the early morning attack in Buenos Aires.

May 16, 1977, Portugal: FLEC said in Lisbon that it would blow up Gulf Oil's offshore drilling complex in Cabinda. The group criticized Gulf for paying the Angolan government $2 million per day in oil royalties.

June 19, 1977, Guatemala: Roberto Rischer Sandhoff, 17, died on June 21 from a bullet wound he received when four men attempted to kidnap him in Guatemala City. He was the son of Roberto Fischer Saravia, a Ford dealer and director of the El Dorado-Americana Hotel. One of his kidnappers also died.

July 14, 1977, Greece: American Express in Athens was bombed, shattering windows and damaging the main door. No injuries were reported.

August 6, 1977, Turkey: Automatic weapons fire was directed at the Istanbul Intercontinental Hotel, which is owned by Pan Am. Several windows were broken, but no one was injured. Later in the month, 23 members of the Acilciler faction of the Turkish Peoples Liberation Party/Front were arrested for this incident as well as numerous bombings and bank robberies.

August 6, 1977, Rhodesia: A bomb exploded in Woolworth's in Salisbury, killing 11 and injuring 76, mostly blacks. The dead—8 blacks and 3 whites—included a black child under the age of 10. The second floor of the store was wrecked by the blast, which knocked out a 30 x 15 foot section of the 8-inch thick outer wall. Police said the bomb was composed of 75 pounds of TNT, and had been placed at a parcel check-in site. Authorities blamed Rhodesian guerrillas for the blast, although no group claimed credit. A suspect was arrested on October 28, 1977.

August 9, 1977, Mexico: US business executive William A. Weinkamper was dragged at gunpoint from his car while he was on his way home from his Mexico City office. He was released three days later after the payment of what some sources reported as a $2,250,000 ransom. Weinkamper is manager of Clevite de Mexico, an automobile parts manufacturing subsidiary of Gould, Inc., of Cleveland. On August 19, police arrested 2 youths and recovered $100,000 of the ransom.

August 28, 1977, West Germany: Molotov cocktails were thrown into an IBM office building in Hamburg, causing slight damage and no injuries.

September 6, 1977, El Salvador: Elena Lima de Chiorato, wife of U.S. constrution industrialist Louis Chiorato, was kidnapped in El Salvador in front of her husband's company offices as she was about to get into her family's car by individuals armed with machine guns who engaged in a shootout with her bodyguards.

September 6, 1977, Colombia: A bomb exploded in a Sears store in Cali, injuring three persons.

September 13, 1977, Mexico: Dozens of bombs planted by the Popular Armed Revolutionary Front exploded in three towns, causing considerable damage and five casualties. A bomber was seriously injured by an explosion at the Woolworth store in Guadalajara. Some reports indicated that the group responsible was the Union del Pueblo.

September 14, 1977, Mexico: Bombs went off in a Sears Roebuck store and the Mexican-American Cultural Institute. Unexploded bombs were found outside a General Motors assembly plant and the headquarters of the Colgate-Palmolive subsidiary.

October 13, 1977, Argentina: A bomb exploded at the home of an Argentine executive of the Chrysler subsidiary. The explosion, which went off inside a car parked in front of the residence, killed a man and a woman and injured two other women. It was believed to have been placed by two individuals who were seen near the car that morning shortly before the blast.

October 17, 1977, Argentina: San Justo police killed two leftists in front of a Chrysler plant after the duo was discovered awaiting workers who were to enter the factory. Setting down their pamphlets, the two opened fire on the police before being killed.

November 29, 1977, Indonesia: Gunmen, claiming membership in the Front for the Liberation of Aceh, Sumatra, attacked the Arun airstrip in the town of Lhok Sukon, where employees of Bechtel, a U.S. firm, were laying pipeline for a liquified natural gas plant. According to the Indonesian Defense Ministry, the "wild robbers" were armed with old rifles and machetes, and fired random shots at the workers. One American, George Pernicone, 53, assistant superintendant of Bechtel, was killed, and Donald Stayer, 22, was wounded and flown to Singapore for an emergency operation. The group then seized a company van and ordered its driver to take them to the jungle. The group was reportedly headed by an Indonesian who had lived for 20 years in the United States.

December 2, 1977, Argentina: Gunmen in two vehicles machine gunned a car of a Chrysler executive's bodyguards in a southern suburb of Buenos Aires, killing two and seriously wounding a third.

December 21, 1977, Colombia: *El Tiempo* reported that a U.S. woman with the surname of Speyton was kidnapped. She was identified as the daughter of a principal Coca-Cola stockholder.

January 14, 1978, Philippines: Four security guards at a B.F. Goodrich rubber plantation were killed when Moslem rebels set off a landmine under their truck on Basilan Island. Eight other civilians, mostly Goodrich workers travelling in a guarded convoy, were wounded when the rebels attacked them after the explosion.

January 19, 1978, France: A bomb exploded near the U.S.-owned Discount Bank in central Paris, injuring no one. At a fire in a nearby Paris school, police found pamphlets calling for revenge for the death of Andreas Baader in a West German prison in previous October.

January 18, 1978, Philippines: Ten armed Moslem guerrillas kidnapped Pak Hwa Choon, a South Korean employee of the U.S.-owned Fisher Engineering and Maintenance Company, in central Mindanao province while he was supervising a highway construction project financed by the Asian Development Bank. Pak was released on February 2 after the payment of a ransom. The group initially demanded a $200,000 ransom, although press reports indicated that the rebels settled for $133,000. FEMCO refused to verify these reports.

January 21, 1978, Greece: Powerful time bombs heavily damaged the Thessaloniki offices of USIA and the American Express Bank and travel agency. No injuries were reported. The explosions occurred hours before U.S. Secretary of State Cyrus Vance arrived in Athens. No group claimed responsibility for the pre-dawn blasts, but officials announced a close surveillance of members of EOKA-B and of Palestinian residents.

March 17, 1978, Nicaragua: Three members of the FSLN stole 120,000 cordobas from a Bank of America branch. They escaped in a stolen vehicle.

April 7, 1978, Philippines: Unidentified men ambushed a B.F. Goodrich truck, killing four people on their way to vote in parliamentary elections in Zamboanga. Ten others were wounded.

May 11, 1978, Italy: A masked man and woman fired four shots into the legs of Marzio Astarita, 37, the Italian manager of the Chemical Bank of New York, on a Milan street. The attackers escaped in a stolen car. An anonymous man called ANSA to claim credit for the Front Line and Fighting Communist Formations, two ultra-leftist organizations. The shooting was the 20th kneecapping in 1978 in Italy, and the third in Milan in four days.

May 13, 1978, Italy: Five guerrillas overpowered a night watchman and two cleaning men, spread gasoline around, and lit it, causing $1 million damage to a repair and warehouse facility of the Honeywell computer company in Milan. The Front Line and Fighting Communist Formations claimed responsibility.

May 29, 1978, Colombia: Nicolas Escobar Soto, general manager of the Texas Petroleum Company in Colombia and president of the Bank of Colombia's board of directors, was kidnapped in an elegant residential district in northern Bogota by six men and two women. Soto died at the hands of his captors in January, 1979, as police rushed their hideout. Several terrorists also died in the shootout.

August 8, 1978, Argentina: A bomb exploded in front of the Buenos Aires home of the president of General Motors in Argentina, destroying the front gate but causing no injuries.

September 14, 1978, Iran: The Northrop motor pool in Isfahan was the target of nine Molotov cocktails and two bombs which destroyed one car but injured no one.

October 11, 1978, Iran: Two individuals on a motorcycle threw two pipe bombs into a bus ferrying ten American employees of Bell Helicopter International in Isfahan. One of the bombs exploded, slightly injuring three of the workers.

October 18, 1978, Nicaragua: Four armed men who arrived in a taxi at 9:30 A.M. robbed the Ciudad Jardin branch of the Bank of America of $100,000. They were assumed to be members of the Sandinist National Liberation Front, which in five years was reported to have stolen $800,000.

October 20, 1978, Turkey: A group of students bombed the Istanbul Pan American Airlines offices.

October 27, 1978, Nicaragua: Young guerrillas raided a Managua branch of the Bank of America during the afternoon, stealing 1.5 million cordobas (approximately $220,000). The thieves, armed with revolvers, attacked a delivery car, wounding the driver.

October 30, 1978, Nicaragua: Four young members of the FSLN armed with revolvers raided the Bank of America branch in Santo Tomas during the morning, stealing an undisclosed amount of cash.

November 1978, Ethiopia: Members of the Tigre Peoples Liberation Front kidnapped an American pilot and three Ethiopians working on a locust control project. The pilot was released unharmed in January, 1979.

November 9, 1978, Colombia: M-19 guerrillas attacked a Bogota installation of the Chrysler Colmotores Company, stealing radiocommunications equipment and weapons. Pamphlets left by M-19 attacked the Colombian government.

November 13, 1978, Iran: At 9 P.M. a car transporting the U.S. deputy director of the Oil Services Company in Ahvaz was attacked by three Iranian men who threw a Molotov cocktail. The car burned and exploded, but no injuries occurred.

November 14, 1978, Iran: Two bombs exploded under a minibus used by Beech Aerospace Services employees in Semnan. The bus sustained minor damages. No Americans were injured.

November 17, 1978, El Salvador: A bomb exploded at 4 A.M. in a McDonald's restaurant in San Salvador. In a communique, the Farabundo Marti Popular Liberation Forces took responsibility.

November 18, 1978, Greece: The Revolutionary People's Strugglers set off two bombs at a Coca-Cola plant outside Thessaloniki, damaging the building and two trucks. A third bomb failed to explode.

November 30, 1978, Italy: The Proletarian Squad exploded a powerful bomb outside a Bologna warehouse of IBM, smashing windows and a wall but causing no casualties.

December 5, 1978, Iran: The homes of three Americans were firebombed in Tehran.

December 8, 1978, Iran: Demonstrators burned down the Isfahan headquarters of Grumman Corporation, a U.S. defense contractor. No injuries were reported.

December 20, 1978, Iran: The car of a Telemedia Corporation employee was firebombed in front of his Isfahan home. The vehicle was destroyed. The next evening, the car of a Bell Helicopter employee parked on the same street was slightly damaged by a firebomb. The car of a second BHI employee was firebombed in Isfahan the night of December 22.

December 21, 1978, Iran: During the night, a Molotov cocktail was thrown into the Tehran home of an American employee of General Telephone and Electronics, damaging the house and slightly burning the American resident.

December 23, 1978, Iran: Paul Grimm, 56, acting general manager in Ahvaz for the Oil Services Company, was assassinated by three gunmen as he drove to work at 7 A.M. An Iranian production supervisor for the firm, Malek Boroujerdi, was killed in a simultaneous attack.

SELECTED BIBLIOGRAPHY

Adelson, Alan. *SDS: A Profile*. New York: Charles Scribner's Sons, 1972.

Alexander, Robert J. *The Bolivian National Revolution*. New Brunswick, N.J.: Rutgers University Press, 1958.

Alexander, Yonah. *The Role of Communications in the Middle East Conflict: Ideological and Religious Aspects*. New York: Praeger Publishers, 1973.

——. ed. *International Terrorism: National, Regional, and Global Perspectives*. New York: Praeger Publishers, 1976.

Alexander, Yonah, and Friedlander, Robert A., eds. *Self-Determination: National Regional and Global Perspectives*. Boulder, Colo.: Westview Press, 1979.

Alexander, Yonah, and Kittrie, Nicholas. *Crescent and Star: Arab-Israeli Perspectives on the Middle East Conflict*. New York: AMS Press, 1972.

Alexander, Yonah, and Finger, Seymour M., eds. *Terrorism: Interdisciplinary Perspectives*. New York: John Jay Press, 1977/Maidenhead: McGraw-Hill, 1977.

Alexander, Yonah; Carlton, David; and Wilkinson, Paul, eds. *Terrorism: Theory and Practice*. Boulder, Colo.: Westview Press, 1979.

Ali, Tariq, ed. *The New Revolutionaries: A Handbook of the International Radical Left*. New York: William Morrow, 1969.

Andreski, Stanislav. *Parasitism and Subversion: The Case of Latin America*. New York: Pantheon, 1967.

Arey, James A. *The Sky Pirates*. New York: Charles Scribner's Sons, 1972.

Ariel, Dan. *Explosion!* Tel Aviv: Olive Books, 1972.

Avineri, Shlomo, ed. *Israel and the Palestinians: Reflections on the Clash of the Two National Movements*. New York: St. Martin's Press. 1971.

Avner (pseud.) *Memoirs of an Assassin*. New York: Yoseloff, 1959.

Avrich, Paul. *The Russian Anarchists*. Princeton, N.J.: Princeton University Press, 1967.

Baudovin, Jean. *Terrorisme et Justice*. Montreal: Editions du Jour, 1970.

Baumann, Carol Edler. *The Diplomatic Kidnappings: A Revolutionary Tactic of Urban Terrorism*. The Hague: Marinus Nijhoff, 1973.

Bayo, Alberto. *150 Questions to a Guerrilla*. Translated by R. I. Madigan and Angel de Lumus Medina. Montgomery: Air University, n.d.

Bell, J. Bowyer. *The Myth of the Guerrilla: Revolutionary Theory and Malpractice*. New York: Knopf, 1971.

——. *The Secret Army: The IRA 1916–1974*. Cambridge, Mass.: MIT Press, 1974.

——. *Transnational Terror*. Washington, D.C.: American Enterprise Institute, 1975.

——. *On Revolt*. Cambridge, Mass.: Harvard University Press, 1976.

Berkman, Alexander. *Now and After: The ABC of Communist Anarchism*. New York: Vanguard Press, 1929.

——. *Prison Memoirs of an Anarchist*. New York: Schocken Books, 1970.

Black, Cyril E., and Thornton, Thomas P. *Communism and Revolution*. Princeton, N.J.: Princeton University Press, 1964.

Bloomfield, Louis M, and Fitzgerald, Gerald F. *Crimes Against Internationally Protected Persons: Prevention and Punishment (An Analysis of the U.N. Convention)*. New York: Praeger Publishers, 1975.

Bocca, Geoffrey. *The Secret Army*. Englewood Cliffs, N.J.: Prentice-Hall, 1968.

Borisov, J. *Palestine Underground: The Story of Jewish Resistance*. New York: Judea, 1947.

Boston, Guy D.; Marcus, Marvin; and Wheaton, Robert J. *Terrorism: A Selected Bibliography*. Washington, D.C.: National Criminal Justice Reference Service, March 1976.

Brinton, Crane. *The Anatomy of a Revolution*. Englewood Cliffs, N.J.: Prentice-Hall, 1965.

Broehl, Wayne G. *The Molly Maguires*. Cambridge, Mass.: Harvard University Press, 1964.

Brown, Richard M. *Strain of Violence: Historical Studies of American Violence and Vigilantism*. London: Oxford University Press, 1975.

Carlton, David, and Schaerf, Carlo, eds. *International Terrorism and World Security*. London: Croom Helm, 1975.

Carr, E. H. *Studies in Revolution*. New York: Grosset & Dunlap, 1964.

Chailand, Gerald. *The Palestinian Resistance*. Baltimore: Penguin Books, 1972.

Chase, L. J., ed. *Bomb Threats, Bombings and Civil Disturbances: A Guide for Facility Protection*. Corvallis, Oreg.: Continuing Education Publications, 1971.

Clark, Michael K. *Algeria in Turmoil*. New York: Praeger Publishers, 1959.

Clutterbuck, Richard. *Living with Terrorism*. London: Faber and Faber, 1975.

——. *Kidnap and Ransom: The Response*. London and Boston: Faber and Faber, 1978.

Clyne, P. *Anatomy of Skyjacking*. London: Abelard-Shumann, 1973.

Coogan, Tim Patrick. *The IRA*. New York: Praeger Publishers, 1970.

Crelinsten, Ronald S.; Laberge-Altmeja, Danielle; and Szabo, Denis, eds. *Terrorism and Criminal Justice*. Lexington, Mass.: Lexington Books, 1978.

Crooty, William J. *Assassination and the Political Order*. New York: Harper & Row, 1971.

Crozier, Brian. *South-East Asia in Turmoil*. Baltimore: Penguin Books, 1965.

——. *Ulster: Politics and Terrorism*. London: Institute for the Study of Conflict, 1973.

——, ed. *Annual of Power and Conflict, 1973-1974: A Survey of Political Violence and International Influence*. London: Institute for the Study of Conflict, 1974.

——, ed. *Annual of Power and Conflict, 1974-1975: A Survey of Political Violence and International Influence*. London: Institute for the Study of Conflict, 1975.

——, ed. *Annual of Power and Conflict, 1975-1976: A Survey of Political Violence and International Influence*. London: Institute for the Study of Conflict, 1976.

——, ed. *Annual of Power and Conflict, 1976-1977: A Survey of Political Violence and International Influence*. London: Institute for the Study of Conflict, 1977.

Curtis, Michael, et al., eds. *The Palestinians: People, History, Politics*. Edison, N.J.: Transaction Books, 1975.

Dallin, Alexander, and Breslauer, George W. *Political Terror in Communist Systems*. Stanford, Calif.: Stanford University Press, 1970.

Davies, Jack. *Political Violence in Latin America*. London: International Institute for Strategic Studies, 1972.

Davies, James C., ed. *When Men Revolt and Why*. New York: The Free Press, 1971.

Debray, R. *Revolution on the Revolution*. New York: Monthly Review Press, 1967.

DeGrazia, Sebastian, and Stecchini Livio C., *The Coup d'Etat: Past Significance and Modern Technique*. China Lake: U.S. Ordinance Test Station, 1965.

Dillon, Martin, and LeHane, Denis. *Political Murder in Northern Ireland*. Baltimore: Penguin Books, 1974.

Dobson, Christopher. *Black September: Its Short, Violent History*. New York: MacMillan, 1974.

Dortzbach, Karl, and Dortzbach, Debbie. *Kidnapped*. New York: Harper & Row, 1975.

Draper, Theodore. *Castro's Revolution: Myths and Realities*. New York: Praeger Publishers, 1962.

Duncun, Patrick. *South Africa's Rule of Violence*. London: Methuen, 1964.

Eckstein, Harry., ed. *Internal War*. New York: The Free Press, 1964.

Elliot, John D., and Gibson, Leslie K., eds. *Contemporary Terrorism: Selected Readings*. Gaithersburg, Md.: International Association of Chiefs of Police, 1978.

Ellis, Albert, and Gullo, John. *Murder and Assassination*. New York: Stuart Lyle, 1971.

Evans, Alona E., and Murphy, John F., eds. *Legal Aspects of International Terrorism*. Lexington, Ky.: Lexington Books, 1978.

Fairbairn, G. *Revolutionary Guerrilla Warfare–The Countryside Version*. Middlesex: Penguin Books, 1974.

Fanon, Franz. *Towards the African Revolution: Political Essays*. Translated by Haakon Chevalier. New York: Grove Press, 1967.

——. *The Wretched of the Earth*. New York: Grove Press, 1968.

Ferguson, J. Halcro. *The Revolution of Latin America*. London: Thames and Hudson, 1963.

Fitzgerald, Charles P. *Revolution in China*. New York: Praeger Publishers, 1952.

Frank, Gerald. *The Deed*. New York: Simon & Schuster, 1963.

Fromm, Erich. *The Anatomy of Human Destructiveness*. New York: Holt, Rinehart & Winston, 1973.

Gablonski, Edward. *Terror from the Sky: Airwar*. Garden City, N.Y.: Doubleday, 1971.

Galula, Davis. *Counterinsurgency Warfare: Theory and Practice*. New York: Praeger Publishers, 1964.

Gaucher, Roland. *The Terrorists: From Tzarist Russia to the O.A.S.* Translated by P. Spurlin. London: Secker and Warburg, 1968.

Gellner, J. *Bayonets in the Streets: Urban Guerrilla at Home and Abroad*. Ontario: Collier-MacMillan Canada, 1974.

Giap, Vo-nguyen. *People's War, People's Army: The Viet Cong Insurrection Manual for Underdeveloped Countries*. New York: Praeger Publishers, 1962.

Gillo, M. E. *The Tupamaro Guerrillas*. New York: Ballatine, 1970.

——. *The Tupamaro Guerrillas*. Introduction by Robert Alexander. Translated by Anna Edmondston. New York: Saturday Review Press, 1972.

Gott, Richard. *Guerrilla Movements in Latin America*. London: Thomas Nelson, 1970.

Graham, Hugh D., and Gurr, Ted R., eds. *Violence in America: Historical and Comparative Perspectives*. Washington, D.C.: National Commission of the Causes and Prevention of Violence, 1969.

Greene, T. N., ed. *The Guerrilla: And How to Fight Him*. New York: Praeger Publishers, 1962.

Grimshaw, Allen. *Racial Violence in the United States*. Chicago: Aldine, 1970.

Grundy, Kenneth W. *Guerrilla Struggle in Africa: An Analysis and Preview*. New York: Grossman, 1971.

Guevara, Ché. *Reminiscences of the Cuban Revolutionary War*. Translated by V. Ortiz. New York: Monthly Review Press, 1968.

Guevara, Ernesto. *Ché Guevara on Guerrilla Warfare*. Translated by Harries-Clichy Peterson. New York: Praeger Publishers, 1961.

——. *Obra Revolucionaria*. 4th ed. Mexico: Ediciones Era, 1971.

Guillen, Abraham. *The Philosophy of the Urban Guerrilla: The Revolutionary Writings of Abraham Guillen*. Translated by Donald Hodges. New York: Morrow, 1973.

Gurr, Ted Robert. *Why Men Rebel*. Princeton, N.J.: Princeton University Press, 1970.

Hackey, Thomas. *Voices of Revolution: Rebels and Rhetoric*. Hinsdale, Ill.: Dryden Press, 1973.

——, ed. *The Problem of Partition: Peril to World Peace*. New York: Rand McNally, 1972.

Halperin, Ernst. *Terrorism in Latin America*. Beverly Hills, Calif.: Sage Publications, 1975.

Harkabi, Y. *The Arab's Position in Their Conflict with Israel*. Jerusalem: Israeli Universities Press, n.d.

Heilbrunn, Otto. *Partisan Warfare*. New York: Praeger Publishers, 1962.

Hodges, Donald Clark. *National Liberation Fronts: 1960–1970*. New York: Morrow, 1972.

——. *Philosophy of the Urban Guerrilla*. New York: Morrow, 1973.

Hofstadter, Richard, and Wallace, Michael, eds. *American Violence: A Documentary History*. New York: Knopf, 1970.

Horn, Stanley. *Invisible Empire: The Story of the Ku Klux Klan, 1866–1871*. Boston: Houghton Mifflin, 1939.

Horowitz, Irving Louis, ed. *The Anarchists*. New York: Dell Publishers, 1964.

——. *The Struggle Is the Message: The Organization and Ideology of the Anti-war Movement*. Berkeley, Calif.: Glendessary Press, 1970.

Horrell, Muriel. *Terrorism in South Africa*. Johannesburg: South African Institute of Race Relations, 1968.

Hosmer, Stephen T. *Viet Cong Repression and Its Implications for the Future*. Lexington, Mass.: Heath Lexington Books, 1970.

Huberman, Leo, and Sweezy, Paul M. *Cuba: Anatomy of a Revolution*. 2d ed. New York: Monthly Review Press, 1960.

Hyams, Edward. *Terrorists and Terrorism*. New York: St. Martin's Press, 1974.

Hyde, Douglas Arnold. *The Roots of Guerrilla Warfare*. Chester Springs, Pa.: Dufour Editions, 1968.

Jackson, Sir Geoffrey. *Surviving the Long Nights: An Autobiographical Account of a Political Kidnapping*. New York: Vanguard, 1974.

Jenkins, Brian Michael. *The Five Stages of Urban Guerrilla Warfare*. Santa Monica, Calif.: Rand, 1971.

——. *Soldiers versus Gunmen: The Challenge of Urban Guerrilla Warfare*. Santa Monica, Calif.: Rand, 1974.

——. *Terrorism Works—Sometimes*. Santa Monica, Calif.: Rand, 1974.

Johnson, Chalmers A. *Revolutionary Change*. Boston: Little, Brown, 1966.

Johnson, John J. *The Military and Society in Latin America*. Stanford, Calif.: Stanford University Press, 1964.

Joll, James. *The Anarchists*. New York: Grossett & Dunlap, 1964.

Joyner, Nancy D. *Aerial Hijacking as an International Crime*. Dobbs Ferry, N.Y.: Oceana, 1974.

Kaplan, Morton A., ed. *The Revolution in World Politics*. New York: Wiley, 1962.

Karagueuzian, Dikran. *Blow It Up!* Boston: Gambit Press, 1971.

Kautsky, Karl. *Terrorism and Communism: A Contribution to the Natural History of Revolution*. Translated by W. H. Kerridge. London: George Allen and Unwin, 1920.

Kirkham, J. F., and Levy, S. *Assassination and Political Violence*. National Commission on the Causes and Prevention of Violence. Washington, D.C.: Government Printing Office, 1969.

Kitson, Frank. *Low Intensity Operations: Subversion, Insurgency, Peace-Keeping*. Hamden, Conn: Archon Books, 1974.

Kobetz, Richard W., and H. H. Cooper. *Target Terrorism*. Gaithersburg, Md.: International Association of Chiefs of Police, 1978.

Kohl, J., and Litt, J. *Urban Guerrilla Warfare in Latin America*. Cambridge, Mass.: MIT Press, 1974.

Kupperman, Robert H., and Trent, D. *Terrorism: Threat, Reality, Response*. Stanford, Calif.: Hoover Institution Press, 1979.

Laffin, John. *Fedayeen*. New York: MacMillan, 1973.

Lambrick, H. T. *The Terrorist*. London: Rowman, 1972.

Laqueur, Walter. *Guerrilla: A Historical and Critical Study*. Boston: Little, Brown, 1976.

———. *Terrorism*. Boston: Little, Brown, 1977.

———. *The Terrorism Reader: A Historical Anthology*. Philadelphia: Temple University, 1978.

Lasswell, Harold, and Lerner, Daniel, eds. *World Revolutionary Elites: Studies in Coercive Ideological Movements*. Cambridge, Mass.: MIT Press, 1965.

Leiden, Carl, and Schmitt, Karl M., eds. *The Politics of Violence*. Englewood Cliffs, N.J.: Prentice-Hall, 1968.

Leites, Nathan, and Wolf, Charles, Jr. *Rebellion and Authority: An Analytical Essay on Insurgent Conflicts*. Chicago: Markham, Lieuwen, Edwin, 1970.

Lens, Sidney. *Radicalism in America*. New York: Thomas Y. Cromwell, 1966.

Lesch, Moseley. *The Politics of Palestinian Nationalism*. Los Angeles: University of California Press, 1973.

LiBonachea, Ramon. *The Cuban Insurrection*. Brunswick, N.J.: Marta San Martin, 1964.

Livingston, Maurius, ed. *International Terrorism in the Contemporary World*. Westport, Conn.: Greenwood Press, 1978.

Lorch, Netanel. *The Edge of the Sword: Israel's War of Independence, 1947–1949*. New York: Putnam, 1961.

Lun, Dyer. *A Concise History of the Great Trial of the Chicago Anarchists*. Chicago: Socialistic, 1887.

MacStiofan, Sean. *Revolutionary in Ireland*. London: G. Cremonesi, 1975.

McKnight, G. *Mind of the Terrorist*. London: Michael Joseph, 1974.

McWhinney, E. W., ed. *Aerial Piracy and International Law*. Leiden: A. W. Sijthoff, 1971.

Mallin, Jay. *Terror in Viet Nam*. Princeton, N.J.: D. Van Nostrand, 1966.

——, ed. *Terror and Urban Guerrillas: A Study of the Tactics and Documents*. Coral Gables, Fla.: University of Miami Press, 1971.

Malloy, James M. *Bolivia: The Uncompleted Revolution*.Pittsburgh: Pittsburgh University Press, 1970.

Mao Tse-tung. *On Guerrilla Warfare*. New York: Praeger Publishers, 1961.

——. *Basic Tactics*. New York: Praeger Publishers, 1966.

Mardor, Munya. *Strictly Illegal*. London: Robert Hale, 1964.

——. *Haganah*. New York: New American Library, 1966.

Marighella, Carlos. *For the Liberation of Brazil*. Harmondsworth: Penguin Books, 1972.

——. *Minimanual of the Urban Guerrilla*. Havana: Tricontinental, January–February, 1970.

Masotti, Louis H., and Bowen, Don R., eds. *Riots and Rebellion: Civil Violence in the Urban Community*. Beverly Hills, Calif.: Sage Publications, 1968.

Mathur, L. P. *Indian Revolutionary Movement in the United States of America*. Delhi: S. Chand, 1970.

Max, Alphonse. *Guerrillas in Latin America*. The Hague: International Documents and Information Center, 1971.

Mercader, A., and de Vera, J. *Tupamaros: Estratagia y Accion*. Montevideo: Editorial Alfa, 1969.

Merleau-Ponty, Maurice. *Humanism and Terror: An Essay on the Communist Problem*. Boston: Beacon Press, 1969.

Miller, Michael J., and Gilmore, Susan. *Revolution at Berkeley*. New York: Dial Press, 1965.

Momboisse, R. M. *Blueprint of Evolution: The Rebel, the Party, the Techniques of Revolt*. Springfield, Ill.: Charles C. Thomas, 1970.

Morris, Michael. *Terrorism*. Cape Town: Howard Timmins, 1971.

Morton, Marian J. *Terrors of Ideological Politics*. Cleveland: Case Western Reserve, 1972.

Moss, Robert. *Urban Guerrillas*. London: Temple Smith, 1972.

——. *The War for the Cities*. New York: Coward, 1972.

Naipaul, V. S. *Guerrillas*. New York: Knopf, 1975.

Nasution, Abdul Haris. *Funadmentals of Guerrilla Warfare*. New York: Praeger Publishers, 1965.

Neiburg, H. L. *Political Violence: The Behavioral Process*. New York: St. Martin's Press, 1969.

Nkrumah, Kwame. *Handbook of Revolutionary Warfare*. New York: International Publishers, 1972.

Nolin, Thierry. *La Haganah: L'Armee Secrete d'Israel*. Paris: Ballard, 1971.

Nomad, Max. *Aspects of Revolt: A Study in Revolutionary Theories and Techniques*. New York: Noonday Press, 1959.

O'Farrell, Patrick. *Ireland's English Question*. London: Batsford, 1971.

O'Flaherty, Liam. *The Terrorist*. London: E. Archer, 1926.

Oppenheimer, Martin. *The Urban Guerrilla*. Chicago: Quadrangle Books, 1969.

Osanka, Franklin Mark. *Modern Guerrilla Warfare: Fighting Communist Guerrilla Movements 1941-1961*. New York: The Free Press, 1962.

Paret, Peter, and Shy, John W. *Guerrillas in the 1960's*. Rev. ed. New York: Praeger Publishers, 1962.

Payne, Pierre S. R. *Zero, the Story of Terrorism*. New York: Day, 1950.

——. *The Terrorists: The Story of the Forerunners of Stalin*. New York: Funk & Wagnalls, 1967.

Peres, Shimon. *David's Sling*. New York: Random House, 1970.

Pomeroy, William J. *Guerrilla Warfare and Marxism*. New York: International Publishers, 1968.

Porzicanski, A. C. *Uraguay's Tupamaros: The Urban Guerrilla*. New York: Praeger Publishers, 1968.

Possony, Stefan T., and Bouchey, L. Francis. *International Terrorism—The Communist Connection*. Washington, D.C.: American Council for Freedom, 1978.

Pryce-Jones, David. *The Face of Defeat: Palestinian Refugees and Guerrillas*. London: Weiderfeld and Nicholson, 1972.

Pye, Lucien. *Guerrilla Communism in Malaya:. Its Social and Political Meaning*. Princeton, N.J.: Princeton University Press, 1956.

Rapoport, David C. *Assassination and Terrorism*. Toronto: Canadian Broadcasting System, 1971.

Reed, David. *111 Days in Stanleyville*. New York: Harper & Row, 1965.

Regush, Nicholas M. *Pierre Vallieres: The Revolutionary Process in Quebec*. New York: Dial Press, 1973.

Rotberg, R. J., and Mazrui, Ali A., eds. *Protest and Power in Black Africa*. New York: Oxford University Press, 1970.

Russell, D. E. H. *Rebellion, Revolution and Armed Force*. New York: Academic Press/Harcourt, Brace, Jovanovich, 1974.

Sale, Kirkpatrick. *SDS*. New York: Random House, 1973.

Schiff, Zeev, and Rothstein, Raphael. *Fedayeen: Guerrillas Against Israel*. New York: David McKay, 1972.

Silvert, Kalman H. *Reaction and Revolution in Latin America*. New Orleans: Hauser Press, 1961.

Sinclair, Andrew. *Guevara*. London: William Collins and Sons, 1970.

Skobnick, Jerome, ed. *The Politics of Protest*. New York: Ballantine Books, 1969.

Sobel, Lester A. *Political Terrorism*. New York: Facts on File, 1975.

——. *Political Terrorism, 1974–78*. Vol. 2. New York: Facts on File, 1975.

——, ed. *Palestinian Impasse: Arab Guerrillas and International Terror*. New York: Facts on File, 1977.

Sorel, George. *Reflections on Violence*. New York: Collier Books, 1961.

Stewart, Anthony Terence Quincey. *The Ulster Crisis*. London: Faber and Faber, 1967.

Suchlicki, Jaime. *University Students and Revolution in Cuba, 1920–1968*. Coral Gables, Fla.: University of Miami Press, 1969.

Taber, Robert. *The War of the Flea*. New York: Lyle Stuart, 1965.

Tanham, George Kilpatrick. *Communist Revolutionary Warfare*. New York: Praeger Publishers, 1961.

Teixeira, Bernardo. *The Fabric of Terror: Three Days in Angola*. New York: Devin-Adair, 1965.

Trelease, Allen W. *White Terror: The Ku Klux Klan Conspiracy and Southern Reconstruction*. New York: Harper & Row, 1971.

Turi, Robert T., et. al. *Descriptive Study of Aircraft Hijacking*. Huntsville, Tex.: Institute of Contemporary Corrections the the Behavioral Sciences, 1972.

Van den Haag, Ernest. *Political Violence and Civil Disobedience*. New York: Harper & Row, 1972.

Waddis, Jack. *New Theories of Revolution*. New York: International Publishers, 1972.

Walter, Eugene Victor. *Terror and Resistance: A Study of Political Violence*. New York: Oxford University Press, 1969.

Walzer, Michael. *The Revolution of the Saints: A Study in the Origins of Radical Politics*. Cambridge, Mass.: Harvard University Press, 1965.

Whelton, Charles. *Skyjack!* New York: Tower Publications, 1970.

Wilkinson, Paul. *Political Terrorism*. London: MacMillan Press, 1974.

——. *Political Terrorism and the Liberal State*. New York: Wiley, 1977.

Woodstock, George. *Anarchism*. New York: World Publishing, 1971.

Yaari, Ehud. *Strike Terror*. New York: Sabra Books, 1970.

Zwiebach, Burton. *Civility and Disobedience*. New York: Cambridge University Press, 1975.

INDEX

Abalone, 18
abduction, 69
Abdul Khaalis, Khalifa Hammas, 27
Aberrant Behavior Center, 111, 112, 141
Aden, 51, 250
aerosol dispersal, 10
Afghanistan, 263
Africa, 29, 38, 218
African states, 234
Afro-Asian bloc, 260, 262, 263, 264, 271, 272
AGREXCO, 48
Agrippa, 112
Air Force, 161, 214, 226, 227, 228, 232
Air France, 47, 48, 51, 104, 214, 218, 234, 239, 249, 276
Air Line Pilots Association (ALPA), 132, 134, 135, 137, 138
Air Transportation Security Act of 1974, 162
Air War College Associate Program, 212
Alaska, 17, 18
Alaska Pipeline, 17
Alfa Romeo Plant, 74, 83
Algeria, 29, 40, 42, 44, 47, 250, 264, 275
Algiers, 28
Allende, Salvador (Gossens), 13, 42, 48, 86
Aman, 259
American Civil Liberties Union, 20
Amin, Idi, 186, 216, 218, 219, 229, 230, 234, 238
Amsterdam, 246, 251, 252
Angola, 48
Anglo-Saxon Protestants, 115
ANTHRAX, 7
Anti-Castro Cubans, 13, 16, 26–27, 37
Anti-Fascist Group, 247
Antihijacking Act of 1974, 161
April 17th Movement, 37
Arab-Israeli Conflict, 47
Arab League, 41, 216
Arab Liberation Front, 38, 51
Arabs, 35, 262, 263
Arab states, 234, 259, 260
Arab Summit Conference, 46

Arafat, Yassar, 45, 216
Arctic, 17–18
Argentina, 42, 72, 80, 85, 93, 94, 153, 156
Argentinian People's Revolutionary Army (ERP), 36, 72, 94
Arguello, Patrick Joseph, 50
Arhus Middle East Group, 40
Armadillo, 18
Armed Commandos of Liberation (CAL), 29
Armed Revolutionary Independence Movement (MIRA), 29
Arms Control and Disarmament Agency, 124
Arms Export Control Act, 164
Army, 162, 205
Army Mathematics Research Center, 5
Asia, 38, 58, 80
Athens, 51, 104, 276
Athens Airport, 49
atomic reactor, 142
attacks by proxy, 47–48
Attorney General, 162
Australia, 263
Austria, 157, 263, 264
automatic weapons, 5

Baader, Andreas, 48, 83, 245, 246, 248–49, 250, 256
Baader-Meinhof Gang, 38, 43, 45, 47, 49, 51, 136, 143, 245
Bacillus anthracis, 10
bacterial cultures, 103
Baghdad, 43
Bakke Case, 27
Bakunin, 56
Bangkok, 232, 233
Bank of America, 48
Bank of Columbia, 73
Banker's Trust, 15
banks, 140, 141, 144, 146, 147, 149
Barbados, 264
Barbary Pirates, 224
Bar-Lev, Baruch, 216
Barrow, 17
Barrow Conference, 17–18
Bay Area Research Collective (BARC), 15, 24

ABOUT THE EDITORS AND CONTRIBUTORS

YONAH ALEXANDER (co-editor) is Professor of International Studies and Director of the Institute for Studies in International Terrorism, State University of New York and, concurrently, Research Associate, The Center for Strategic and International Studies at Georgetown University. He is editor-in-chief of *Terrorism: An International Journal*, editor of *Terrorism: National, Regional, and Global Perspectives*, and co-editor of *Terrorism: Theory and Practice, Control of Terrorism: International Documents*, and *Self-Determination: National Regional and Global Dimensions*.

DR. ROBERT A. KILMARX (co-editor) has written many books on security and economic issues. He served many years as an intelligence specialist with the Department of Defense, a professional lecturer on economic and business topics. He is Director of Business and Defense Studies at the Center for Strategic and International Studies and Director of BKW Associates, Inc., a management consulting firm.

THOMAS M. ASHWOOD of TWA is Secretary of the Airline Pilots Association (ALPA) since 1970. Captain Ashwood headed every flight security committee of the Association. He is currently Chairman of ALPA International Flight Security Committee and Chairman of the International Federation of the Airline Pilots Association's Flight Security Study Group.

LOUIS G. FIELDS, JR. is Assistant Legal Advisor for Special Functional Problems, Department of State and a graduate of the University of Florida and the University of Virginia Law School. Mr. Fields had served in various official capacities with the U.S. Government.

SEYMOUR M. FINGER is Professor of Political Science at the College of Staten Island and the Graduate School of the City University of New York. He also serves as Director of the Ralph Bunche Institute on the United Nations at CUNY. Previously, he was Ambassador and Senior Advisor to the Permanent U.S. Representatives to the United Nations. Professor Finger is coeditor of *Terrorism: Interdisciplinary Perspectives*.

DAVID GODFREY is the Director of Security for the Bank of Montreal, and responsible for coordinating all security related matters affecting the Bank, both nationally and internationally. He previously was employed in various overseas territories as an Intelligence Officer. Prior to assuming his present position, he was involved in providing security consultancy on behalf of the Government of Canada to the aviation industry.

C. ALLEN GRAVES is an Assistant Professor of Criminal Justice at the University of Alabama at Birmingham. He received his doctorate from Claremont Graduate School, Masters in Criminology from California Long Beach State, and Bachelor in Public Administration from the University of Southern California. Dr. Graves coordinated a seminar on terrorism at the University of Alabama at Birmingham.

HANS JOSEF HORCHEM studies law, history, and political science at the Universities of Mainz and Cologne. Dr. Horchem served as a Judge in the Rheinland (1955-57) and then worked with the Federal Office for the Protection of the Constitution in Cologne. Since 1969, he is the head of the Office for the Protection of the Constitution in Hamburg. His research includes works on terrorism and political extremism.

DAVID G. HUBBARD has done pioneer research in directly applying the findings from psychiatric and psychological studies of terrorists to the disrupted social events they produce. He is creator of widely recognized pragmatic industrial programs and Director of the Aberrant Behavior Center and psychological consultant to major corporations. He is author of the *SKYJACKER*.

ROBERT H. KUPPERMAN is Chief Scientist of the U.S. Arms Control and Disarmament Agency. He received his B.A. and Ph.D. degrees from New York University in Applied Mathematics. Dr. Kupperman held executive positions in both government and industry. He directed several interagency study efforts to combat terrorism and co-authored *Terrorism: Threat, Reality, Response*.

BROOKS McCLURE is Director of Operations for the International Management and Resources Corporation, Washington, D.C. A veteran of U.S. Foreign Service, he served with the Commerce Department's Working Group on Terrorism. A graduate of the University of Maryland and the Naval War College, Mr. McClure is the author of *The Dynamics of Terrorism* and a contributor to *International Terrorism in the Contemporary World* and *Contemporary Terrorism*.

EDWARD F. MICKOLUS is a political analyst with the U.S. Central Intelligence Agency's International Issues Division of the Office of Regional and Political Research. He is completing a doctoral dissertation in political science at Yale University. He has written extensively on political violence, international law and organization, regional politics, simulation and gaming, political psychology, and teaching political science.

ABRAHAM H. MILLER is Professor of Political Science at the University of Cincinnati. He was a visiting faculty fellow with the U.S. Department of

Justice, Law Enforcement Assistance Administration from 1976 to 1977. He has contributed numerous articles to academic journals and is co-editor of *Black Power and Student Rebellion.*

BOWMAN H. MILLER spent nine years with the United States Air Force where he specialized in counterintelligence and terrorism analysis. His lectures and previous publications have centered on the sociological profile of terrorists and on terrorist tactics, their variety and application. He is presently in charge of threat analysis in the Department of State's Office of Security.

FRANK OCHBERG is Director of the Michigan Department of Mental Health, Consultant—F.B.I., Advisor U.S. Secret Service, and Member, National Security Council Committee to Combat Terrorism. A graduate of Harvard (B.A.), Johns Hopkins (M.D.), and Stanford (Psychiatry), Dr. Ochberg is co-editor of *Victims of Terrorism.*

ROBERT L. RABE is Assistant Chief of Police, Inspectional Services Officer, Inspectional Services Bureau, Metropolitan Police Department, Washington, D.C. He is a graduate of the School of Justice, American University. Mr. Rabe attended numerous specialized criminal justice courses in many educational and governmental institutions.

JULIAN G.Y. RADCLIFFE, a graduate of New College Oxford University, is Managing Director of Investment Insurance International (Managers) Limited. He is also Director, Control Risks Limited.

CHARLES A. RUSSELL, formerly with the Counterintelligence Directorate of the U.S. Air Force Office of Special Investigations, is affiliated with Risks International, Inc., a firm engaged in computer analysis of terrorist incidents. Dr. Russell, also an attorney, received his graduate degree from American University. He has contributed many articles on terrorism to various publications and lectures extensively in this field in the United States and abroad.

MARTIN ELLIOT SILVERSTEIN, M.D., F.A.C.S., is Associate Professor of Surgery, College of Medicine, The University of Arizona and Chief, Section on the Surgery of Trauma, Arizona Health Sciences Center, Tucson, Arizona. A graduate of Columbia College and New York Medical College, Dr. Silverstein is Advisory Director, Emergency Medical Services, Arizona Department of Public Safety.

JAMES E. WINKATES is the educational Advisor to the Air Force War College, Maxwell Airbase, Alabama. A graduate of Beloit College, Dr. Winkates received his graduate degrees in International Affairs from the University of Virginia. His research interests are in the fields of national security affairs, economic development, and Africa.

JOHN B. WOLF is Professor and Chairman of the Department of Criminal Justice at Union College. He has written extensively on the subject of antiterrorism for various foreign and domestic publications including those sponsored by the United States Information Agency and the International Association of Chiefs of Police. He also lectures on the application of intelligence methods to control terrorism in programs sponsored by various American State Police Organizations, other law enforcement groups and the United States Air Force's Special Operation School. He is the author of *The Police Intelligence System* and a specialist in the management of the intelligence process.